the Alaska Almanac®
Facts About Alaska

24th Edition

Alaska Northwest Books™

First edition published 1976
Twenty-fourth edition 2000
Previously published as FACTS ABOUT ALASKA: The ALASKA ALMANAC®

ISBN 0-88240-531-4
ISSN 0270-5370
Key title: The Alaska Almanac

✴

Cover and interior design: Michelle Taverniti
Cover illustration: Mindy Dwyer
Editor: Rosanne Pagano
Compiler: Nancy Gates
Yearly Highlights: Rosanne Pagano
Page composition/editorial assistance: Fay L. Bartels
Maps: Gray Mouse Graphics
Permissions/credits for illustrations and photographs are on page 10.

Alaska Northwest Books™
An imprint of Graphic Arts Center Publishing Company
P.O. Box 10306, Portland, OR 97210
(503) 226-2402
www.gacpc.com

Printed in the United States of America

To Our Readers

Alaska Northwest Books once again welcomes the wisdom, wit and wackiness of Mr. Whitekeys to this, our 24th edition of The Alaska Almanac®. Thousands of visitors and Alaskans alike enjoy his Alaska-based comedy, songs and dance showcased at Anchorage's Fly By Night Club. Originator of the infamous "Whale Fat Follies," Mr. Whitekeys brings his distinctive insights on Northland life— from moose nuggets to politics—to the pages of The Alaska Almanac®.

Alaskans rank No. 1 in the nation in attainment of high-school degrees, No. 1 in ownership of Harley Davidson motorcycles, No. 1 in consumption of ice cream, and Alaskans are the second-highest per capita consumers of SPAM® in the nation. To top it off, the makers of Itch-X anti-itch gel, named Wasilla "The 17th Itchiest City in the United States." Life has been good to Alaska for another year.

Contents

Acknowledgments

This 24th edition of The Alaska Almanac® *has been compiled and updated from information supplied by many helpful state and federal offices, publications, consultants, organizations, experts and individuals. The editors gratefully acknowledge:*

Bill Aberle
Alaska Agricultural Statistics Service, Palmer
Alaska Newspapers Inc.
Alaska Public Lands Information Centers
Alaska Wilderness Recreation and Tourism Assoc.
Anchorage Convention and Visitors Bureau
Anchorage Daily News
Anchorage International Airport
Bob Armstrong
Barbara Beedle, Cordova Iceworm Festival
John Boucher, Alaska Department of Labor
Ed Bovy, Bureau of Land Management
Virginia Breeze, Alaska Division of Elections
George Bryson
Cindy Caserta, Fairbanks Convention and Visitors Bureau
R.N. DeArmond
Lana Decker
Fairbanks Convention and Visitors Bureau
Fairbanks Daily News-Miner
Michael Fastabend, IPM Forestry Program
Fly By Night Club
Donna and Lew Freedman
Neal Fried, Alaska Department of Labor
Mary Furness, National Marine Fisheries Service
Norma Goodman, Northern Television
Faith Guthert, Alaska Division of Tourism
Jane Haigh
Jim Haines, Alaska Department of Natural Resources
Jim Hanson, Alaska Oil and Gas Conservation Commission
Anne Haydon, Alaska Department of Health and Social Services
George Herben
Ed Holsten, U.S. Forest Service
Integrated Pest Management (IPM) Newsletter
Nick Jans
Journal of Alaska Business and Commerce
Sara Juday
Kristi Kantola, U.S. Forest Service
Jim Kelly, Alaska Permanent Fund Corp.

Gunnar Knapp, University of Alaska Anchorage
JoLynda Leal, *The Book of Lists*
Logistics Inc.
Cam McIntosh, U.S. Bureau of the Census
Stephen McMains, Alaska Oil and Gas Conservation Commission
Bert Mead, U.S. Department of Agriculture
Glenn Mitchell, Alaska Division of Tourism
Mushing Magazine
Peninsula Clarion
John Quinley, National Park Service
Rose Ragsdale
Dean Rasmussen, Alaska Department of Labor
Diane Regan, Alaska Department of Fish and Game
Julie Riley, Cooperative Extension Service, University of Alaska Anchorage
Herman Savikko, Alaska Department of Fish and Game
Brian Schneider, Alaska Sea Grant College Program
Jill Shepherd
Bill Sherwonit
Skagway Convention & Visitors Bureau
Southeast Alaska Visitors Center
Joette Storm, Federal Aviation Administration
Jerry Stroebele, U.S. Fish and Wildlife Service
Kent Sturgis, Epicenter Press
Jennifer Summers, KNIK-FM
Evan Swensen
Donna Rae Thompson, *Alaska* magazine
Tom Walker
Pat R. Wendt, Hostelling International-Anchorage
Ellen Wheat

Mr. Whitekeys would like to thank the following twisted sources of fabulous facts: Mary Pae of KTVA News, The Cool J, *Valdez Vanguard, Cordova Times, Seward Phoenix Log, Anchorage Daily News,* Douglas Veltre, Ken Bell, Ralph Ashley, Terry—The Concierge King at The Regal Alaskan Hotel, Ron Eagley, and Gwennie's Old Alaska Restaurant, Michael Wiedmer and the fish number crunchers at the Alaska Department of Fish and Game, Karen Laing, Heather Brock, Dermot Cole and the *Fairbanks Daily News-Miner,* and Randy Brandon for his phabulous photograph. The facts are true—and we who are about to lie salute you!

Miscellaneous Facts About Alaska

Motto: *"North to the Future"*

Nickname: *"The Last Frontier"*

State capital: *Juneau*

Purchased from Russia: *1867*

Organized as a territory: *1912*

Entered the Union: *Jan. 3, 1959, as 49th state*

Governor: *Tony Knowles*

Land area: *570,373.6 square miles, or about 365,000,000 acres, according to revised figures from the U.S. Bureau of the Census in 1996. The largest state in the country, Alaska is one-fifth the size of the combined Lower 48 states.*

State population: *622,000, according to July 1999 figures from the Alaska Dept. of Labor*

Largest city in population: *Anchorage, home to 259,391 people*

Largest city in area: *Sitka, with 4,710 square miles, 1,816 square miles of which is water. Juneau is second, with an area of 3,108 square miles.*

Typical Alaskan: *According to recent figures from the U.S. Bureau of the Census, the median age for Alaskans is 30.9 years, the second-youngest state population in the country.*

Per capita personal income: *$25,675 in 1998, 20th in the nation*

Area per person: *About 0.92 square mile for each person in Alaska. New York State has 0.003 square mile per person.*

Highest/lowest temperatures: *Highest 100°F at Fort Yukon, 1915. Lowest −80°F at Prospect Creek Camp, 1971.*

Heaviest annual snowfall: *974.5 inches at Thompson Pass near Valdez, during the winter of 1952–53*

Tallest mountain in North America: *Mount McKinley, 20,320 feet*

Tourism: *In 1999, German-speaking Europe provided the largest number of international visitors to Alaska, according to the Anchorage Convention and Visitors Bureau.*

Farthest-north city in the United States: *Barrow, 350 miles north of the Arctic Circle*

World's largest and busiest seaplane base: *Anchorage's Lake Hood accommodates more than 800 takeoffs and landings on a peak summer day.*

Largest contiguous state park in the nation: *Wood-Tikchik State Park, with 1.6 million acres of wilderness*

State's largest newspaper: *Anchorage Daily News with a paid circulation of 94,843 on Sundays*

America's biggest earthquake: *Occurred March 27, 1964, Good Friday. Measured 8.6 on the Richter scale (has since been revised upward to 9.2—the strongest ever recorded in North America) and devastated much of southcentral Alaska.*

Second-greatest tide range in North America: *38.9 feet near Anchorage in Upper Cook Inlet*

World's largest producer of zinc: *Red Dog Mine in the Northwest Arctic Borough of Alaska*

Greatest concentration of glaciers in the nation: *About 29,000 square miles—5 percent of the state—is covered by glaciers.*

Most popular park: *The National Park Service reports that 693,883 people visited Klondike Gold Rush National Historical Park in Skagway in 1999.* ✻

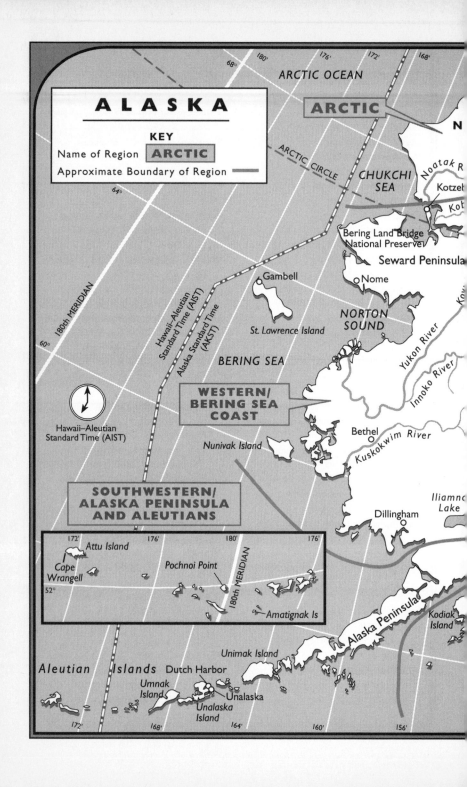

ALASKA

KEY

Name of Region ARCTIC

Approximate Boundary of Region

ARCTIC OCEAN

ARCTIC

N

ARCTIC CIRCLE

CHUKCHI SEA

Noatak R

Kotzebue

Kot

Bering Land Bridge National Preserve

Seward Peninsula

Nome

68°

180°

176°

172°

168°

64°

Gambell

St. Lawrence Island

NORTON SOUND

Kow

Yukon River

Innoko River

Hawaii–Aleutian Standard Time (AIST)

Alaska Standard Time (AKST)

180th MERIDIAN

60°

BERING SEA

WESTERN/ BERING SEA COAST

Bethel

Kuskokwim River

Hawaii–Aleutian Standard Time (AIST)

Nunivak Island

Dillingham

Iliamna Lake

SOUTHWESTERN/ ALASKA PENINSULA AND ALEUTIANS

172° Attu Island 176° 180° 176°

Cape Wrangell

52°

Pochnoi Point

180th MERIDIAN

Amatignak Is

Alaska Peninsula

Kodiak Island

Unimak Island

Aleutian Islands Dutch Harbor

Umnak Island

Unalaska

Unalaska Island

172° 168° 164° 160° 156°

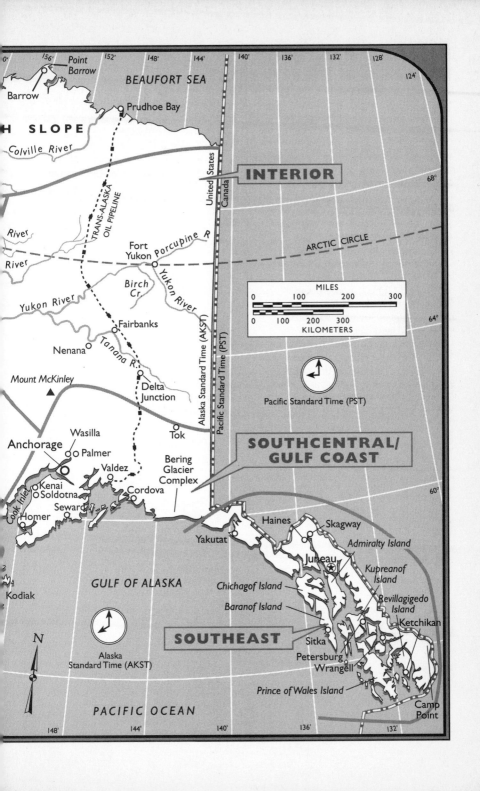

Permissions/Credits for Photos and Illustrations

Selected illustrations are by Val Paul Taylor and David Berger. Other credits are as follows:

Page 3, Mr. Whitekeys' photo by Randy Brandon. 14, courtesy of Carmen Jefford Fisher. 21, J. E. Thwaites, courtesy of the Anchorage Museum of History and Art. 24, Barbara Paxson. 30, Roy Corral. 34, Bill Sherwonit. 40, Bill Sherwonit. 43, Picture Alaska Art Gallery, #199. 50, Robert Williamson. 58, Special Collections Division, University of Washington Libraries, #14501. 67, Roy Corral. 68, Alaska Division of Tourism. 71, Joe Upton, 75. Ann Chandonnet. 78, Marybeth Holleman. 81, U.S. National Archives. 93, Special Collections Division, University of Washington Libraries, Nowell photo #14507. 94, Alaska Historical Library, Mary Nan Gamble Collection, PCA 270-224. 95, *Indian Art and Culture of the Northwest Coast*, Della Kew and P. E. Goddard, Vancouver, B.C.: Hancock House, 1974.

99, Tom Walker. 102, Alaska Division of Tourism. 110, Anchorage Museum of History and Art, B70.28.190. 113, Nick Jans. 114, Tom Walker. 123, courtesy of Randy Acord. 127, Karen Jettmar. 130, Bill Sherwonit. 140, Tom Walker. 144, George Herben. 148, Bill Sherwonit. 149, Alissa Crandall. 154, Bill Sherwonit. 161, Roy Corral. 164, Yukon Archives, Whitehorse. 178, Special Collections Division, University of Washington Libraries, #14505. 195, Whatcom Museum of History and Art, J. W. Sandison Collection, #710. 198, Karen Jettmar. 213, Karen Jettmar. 218, Alaska Division of Tourism.

See Suggested Reading for sources of photos, illustrations and text excerpts. Every attempt has been made to locate the owners of art and photos to obtain permission to reproduce them.

Agriculture

Agriculture in Alaska ranges from backyard gardens to 3,000-acre farms. Extremes of weather and a short growing season challenge cultivation in the state, but certain crops—notably potatoes and carrots—thrive in the cool soil temperatures. Overall, climate is not the greatest impediments to Alaska farming. More significant hurdles are high production costs and competition from the Lower 48.

Alaska's traditional farming is concentrated in two regions: the Matanuska Valley, northeast of Anchorage, which in 1998 contributed 55 percent of the state's farm production value, and the Tanana Valley, which was responsible for 34 percent.

Total Acreage of Alaska Cropland by Region

Region	Percent
Tanana Valley	58.8
Matanuska Valley	33.4
Kenai Peninsula	7.5
Southeast & Southwestern Alaska	0.3

An estimated 15 million to 18 million acres in Alaska are believed to be arable, but only 910,000 acres—less than one-half of 1 percent of the state—are currently considered land in farms. In 1999, crops covered 31,000 acres; the balance was in pasture and uncleared land.

Total market value of Alaska's agricultural products in 1998 was $47 million. Feed crops accounted for $3 million of total market receipts, and vegetables (including potatoes) were $3.43 million of the total.

Aquaculture now accounts for the largest portion of the Alaska market basket, at $19.2 million. Shellfish farming and finfish ranching make up these market receipts.

Greenhouse and nursery industries—a substantial portion of the state's agricultural picture—amounted to $13.5 million, or 29 percent of total cash receipts for 1998.

More than 98 percent of the barley grown in 1998 was harvested in the Tanana Valley. Total production netted 154,800 bushels, yielding 33.7 bushels an acre. Production value for the 1999 barley crop was roughly $581,000, up from the 1998 crop of $442,000. Harvest of oats yielded 41.4 bushels an acre for a total of 62,100 bushels at an estimated value of $152,000. This reflects a decrease from 45,000 bushels valued at $117,000 in 1998.

Another Alaska agricultural enterprise is the raising of reindeer. Officials estimate there are about 23 herds throughout Alaska, or a total of approximately 24,000 head. Most of the reindeer are located on the Seward Peninsula and Nunivak Island, where they contribute significantly to the local economies. Among the by-products of reindeer is the powder made from clipped antlers, most of which is exported to the Far East. Sales related to reindeer were valued at $562,000 in 1998, down $587,000 in 1997.

The annual milk production in 1999 totaled 13.6 million pounds, a decrease of 700,000 pounds from 1998. Dairy products brought in $2.55 million in 1999. Economic stresses continue to reduce the number of farmers involved in this capital-intensive industry. In 1988, 2,100 cows produced nearly 3.57 million gallons of milk. By 1999, the number of cows had decreased to 900. Only 10 dairies were operating in the state on Jan. 1, 1999.

The small vegetable gardens of the Russian fur traders are believed to constitute the first Alaska

> **When flying into the village of Ruby on the Yukon River, the pilot pointed out the now-closed University of Alaska agricultural research farm. He explained that the state had spent several million dollars on the project, but closed it after several years of farming experimentation had proven that the best they could do in that area was grow potatoes at $29 per pound!**

Crops—Volume in Thousands	Acres Harvested	1999 Value
Hay (23.2 tons)	20,300	$4,524,000
Potatoes (218 cwt.)	850	3,922,000
Barley, for grain (154.8 bushels)	4,600	581,000
Oats, for grain (62.1 bushels)	1,500	152,000
Source: Alaska Agricultural Statistics Service		

agriculture. Gold rush days saw growing interest in local farming possibilities, but it wasn't until 1935 that there was a concerted effort to introduce commercial growing. President Franklin Roosevelt's New Deal resettlement plan transplanted 200 farm families from the Midwest to the Matanuska Valley, where they were to create a food source for the territory. Although most produce comes from Outside, local farmers still supply the Anchorage area with some fresh produce and dairy products. The growing season averages 115 days; there are some days with more than 19 hours of sunlight in the summer (which help produce giant-sized vegetables).

The Tanana Valley growing season is shorter than that of the Matanuska Valley, with about 95 frost-free days. Because growing-season temperatures are warmer in the Tanana Valley, many experts consider the area to have greater agricultural potential. Barley and oats are raised for grain and hay. Most Alaska-grown grain is used for domestic livestock feed. All are spring varieties since few winter types survive the cold.

Beef, pork, hay, eggs and fresh produce are produced throughout the Railbelt region and are easily transported to major markets. (The Railbelt is the region linked by the Alaska Railroad, from Seward north to Fairbanks.) Umnak and Unalaska Islands provide grazing area for nearly 1,400 sheep, down considerably from 27,000 in 1970.

Across Alaska, the pressure of urban development is reducing the number of acres available for farming. At the same time, the state is attempting to increase the number of farms through sales of agriculture tracts. Many Alaskans rely on farming to supplement other income. In 1999, there were 570 farms with annual sales of $1,000 or more.

Since 1978, state land sales have placed more than 165,000 acres of potential agricultural land into private ownership. Most of this acreage is in the Delta Junction area, where tracts of up to 3,200 acres were sold by lottery for grain farming. The Nenana area is among those under consideration for future agricultural development.

Additional information is available from the Alaska Agricultural Statistics Service, P.O. Box 799, Palmer 99645; (907) 745-4272.

Blue-Ribbon Veggies

At the Palmer State Fair every August, gardeners from the Matanuska Valley vie for record vegetables. The grower of the largest cabbage receives a prize of $2,000. Current record-holders are:

Radish	9.5 pounds	1985
Mushroom	2.5 pounds	1993
Rutabaga	53 pounds	1994
Cabbage	98 pounds	1990

Air Travel

Alaska is the "flyingest" state in the Union; the only practical way to reach many areas of rural Alaska is by airplane. According to the Federal Aviation Administration, Alaska Region, in May 1999 there were 10,605 registered pilots and 8,053 registered aircraft. Alaska has approximately six times as many pilots per capita and 14 times as many airplanes per capita as the rest of the United States. From its inception in

1946 through 1999, the federal airport improvement program provided $1.103 billion for airport development throughout the state. These federal funds provided for 1,044 projects. Forty-seven projects totaling $79 million were undertaken in 1999.

According to the FAA, Alaska has 325 airports, plus 1,000 recorded landing areas and 103 seaplane bases. That puts Alaska sixth, behind Texas, Illinois, California, Pennsylvania and Florida, in the number of airports in any state. Of the seaplane bases, Lake Hood in Anchorage is the largest and busiest in the world. On a yearly basis, an average of 234 takeoffs and landings occur daily, and more than 800 on a peak summer day. Merrill Field in Anchorage recorded 207,418 flight operations during 1999 and 1,247 on a peak day in July. Anchorage International Airport saw more than 5 million passengers pass through in 1999. Anchorage International is the No. 1 airport in the United States for cargo traffic, based on all-cargo aircraft landed weights. In fiscal 1999, 3.6 billion pounds of cargo moved through the airport. Operating revenue for fiscal 1999 was more than $50 million.

Anchorage has become a hub for air cargo carriers, with more than a dozen companies, both domestic and international, zeroing in during the early months of 1998. In fiscal 1999, AIA counted 33,932 revenue landings of cargo aircraft, up from 26,674 in 1996.

Pilots who wish to fly their own planes to Alaska should have the latest federal government flight information publication, *Alaska Supplement.* Travel and safety information is available from the Federal Aviation Administration, 222 W. Seventh Ave., No. 14, Anchorage 99513-7587 or www.alaska.faa.gov.

Air taxi operators are found in most Alaska communities, and aircraft can be chartered to fly you to a wilderness spot and pick you up later at a prearranged time and location. Most charter operators charge an hourly rate, either per plane load or per passenger (sometimes with a minimum passenger requirement); others may charge

on a per-mile basis. Flightseeing trips to area attractions are often available at a fixed price per passenger. Charter fares range from $140 to $175 per person (four-person and up minimum) for a short flightseeing trip, to $350 an hour for an eight-passenger Cessna 404.

A wide range of aircraft is used for charter and scheduled passenger service in Alaska. The larger interstate airlines—Alaska, America West, Continental, Delta, Northwest, Reno Air, TWA and United—use jets (Douglas DC-8, DC-10, Boeing 727, 737, 757, 767); Reeve Aleutian flies Electra, Boeing 727 and YS-11. Prop jets and single- or twin-engine prop planes on wheels, skis and floats are used for most intrastate travel. A few of these types of aircraft flown in Alaska are: 19-passenger de Havilland Twin Otter, 10-passenger Britten-Norman Islander, 7-passenger Grumman Goose (amphibious), DC-3, 4-passenger Cessna 185, 9-passenger twin-engine Piper Navajo Chieftain, 5- to 8-passenger de Havilland Beaver, 3- to 4-passenger Cessna 180, 5- to 6-passenger Cessna 206 and single-passenger Piper Super Cub.

International Service

Several international carriers provide cargo or passenger service in Alaska through the Anchorage gateway. The list includes Air China, Alaska Airlines (to Russia and Mexico), Asiana, Cathay, China Airlines, ERA Aviation, Federal Express, Korean Air, Nippon Cargo Airlines, Northwest Airlines, Singapore Airlines, United Airlines and United Parcel Service.

Interstate Service

U.S. carriers providing interstate passenger service: Alaska Airlines, America West, Continental Airlines, Delta Air Lines, ERA Aviation, Northwest Airlines, Peninsula Airways, Reeve Aleutian Airways, Reno Air, Southcentral Air, TWA and United Airlines. These carriers also provide freight service between Anchorage and Seattle. For

By the 1930s, the airplane had replaced the dog team as carrier of U.S. mail to many Alaska villages. From *Winging It!* by Jack Jefford.

commercial passenger information, consult city phone directories, chambers of commerce or your travel agent.

Alaska-Canada Boundary

In 1825, Russia, in possession of Alaska, and Great Britain, in possession of Canada, established the original boundary between Alaska and Canada. The demarcation was to begin at 54°40' north latitude, just north of the mouth of Portland Canal, follow the canal to 56° north latitude, then traverse the mountain summits parallel to the coast as far as 141° west longitude. From there it would conform with that meridian north to the Arctic Ocean. The boundary line along the mountain summits in southeastern Alaska was never to be farther inland than 10 leagues—about 30 miles.

After purchasing Alaska in 1867, the United States found that the wording about the boundary line was interpreted differently by the Canadians. They felt the measurements should be made inland from the mouths of bays, while Americans argued the measurements should be made from the heads of the bays. In 1903, however, an international tribunal upheld the American interpretation of the treaty, providing Alaska the 1,538-mile-long border it has with Canada today. The southeastern Alaska border is 891 miles long, and 181 miles of that border is over water. If the Canadians had won their argument they would have had access to the sea, and Haines, Dyea and Skagway now would be in Canada.

The 20-foot-wide vista—a swath of land 10 feet on each side of the boundary between southeastern Alaska, British

Alaska's Largest Air Cargo Carriers
(Ranked by 1998 Revenue Cargo Ton-Miles in Alaska)

Current Ranking	Company Name, Location	1998 Revenue Cargo Ton-Miles	Employees in Alaska	Year Estab.
1.	Northern Air Cargo Inc., Anchorage	18,260,218	230	1956
2.	HEI/Danzas, Anchorage	9,000,000	10	1972
3.	Alaska Air Forwarding, Anchorage	6,000,000	6	1975
4.	Reeve Aleutian Airways, Anchorage	5,726,449	344	1948
5.	ERA Aviation, Anchorage	5,563,353	600	1948

Source: *The Book of Lists,* 2000

Columbia and Yukon Territory—was surveyed and cleared between 1904 and 1914. Portions of the 710-mile-long boundary were again cleared in 1925, 1948, 1978 and 1982 by the International Boundary Commission. Monument and vista maintenance in 1978 and 1982 was conducted by the Canadian section of the commission and by the U.S. section in 1983, 1984 and 1985.

The Alaska-Canada border along the 141st meridian was surveyed and cleared between 1904 and 1920. Astronomical observations were made to find the meridian's intersection with the Yukon River; then, under the direction of the International Boundary Commission, engineers and surveyors of the U.S. Coast and Geodetic Survey and the Canadian Department of the Interior worked together north and south from the Yukon. The vista extends from Demarcation Point on the Arctic Ocean south to Mount St. Elias in the Wrangell Mountains (from there the border cuts east to encompass southeastern Alaska). This part of the border stretches for 647 miles in one of the world's longest straight lines, as well as the world's longest unguarded border.

Monuments are the actual markers of the boundary and are located so they tie in with survey networks of both the United States and Canada. Along the Alaska boundary most monuments are 2 1/2-foot-high cones of aluminum-bronze set in concrete bases or occasionally cemented into rock. A large pair of concrete monuments with a pebbled finish marks major boundary road crossings. Because the boundary is not just a line but in fact a vertical plane dividing land and sky between the two nations, bronze plates mark tunnel and bridge crossings. Along the meridian, 191 monuments are

placed, beginning 200 feet from the Arctic Ocean and ending at the south side of Logan Glacier.

Alaska Highway (SEE ALSO HIGHWAYS)

The Alaska Highway runs 1,488 miles through Canada and Alaska from Milepost 0 at Dawson Creek, British Columbia, through Yukon Territory to Fairbanks, Alaska. Until this overland link between Alaska and the Lower 48 was built in 1942, travel to and from Alaska was primarily by water.

History. The highway was built to relieve Alaska from the hazards of shipping by water and to supply a land route for equipment during World War II.

By agreement between the governments of Canada and the United States, the highway was built in eight months by the U.S. Army Corps of Engineers and was dedicated in November 1942. Crews worked south from Delta Junction, Alaska, north and south from Whitehorse, Yukon, and north from Dawson Creek, British Columbia.

The building of the highway was recognized as one of the greatest engineering feats of the 20th century. Two major sections of the highway were connected on Sept. 23, 1942, at Contact Creek, Milepost 588.1, where the 35th Engineer Combat Regiment working west from Fort Nelson met the 340th Engineer General Service Regiment working east from Whitehorse. The last link in the highway was completed Nov. 20, 1942, when the 97th Engineer General Service Regiment, heading east from Tanacross, met the 18th Engineer Combat Regiment, coming northwest from Kluane Lake, at Milepost 1200.9. A ceremony commemorating the event was held at Soldiers Summit on Kluane Lake, and the first truck to negotiate the entire

Looking Back

November 1942

The Alaska-Canada Military Highway, dubbed the "Alcan," opened for military traffic in November 1942. Built in just over eight months, the highway spanned 1,400 miles of wilderness.

From *Along the Alaska Highway* by Gloria J. Maschmeyer (text) and Alissa Crandall (photographs).

highway left that day from Soldiers Summit and arrived in Fairbanks the next day.

After World War II, the Alaska Highway was turned over to civilian contractors for widening and graveling, replacing log bridges with steel and rerouting at many points. Road improvements continue on the Alaska Highway today.

Preparation for Driving the Alaska Highway. Make sure your vehicle and tires are in good condition before starting out. A widely available item to include is clear plastic headlight covers to protect your headlights from flying rocks and gravel.

You might also consider a wire-mesh screen across the front of your vehicle to protect paint, grille and radiator from flying rocks.

For those hauling trailers, a piece of 1/4-inch plywood fitted over the front of your trailer offers protection from rocks and gravel.

You'll find well-stocked auto shops in the North, but may wish to carry your own emergency items: flares; first-aid kit; mosquito repellent; trailer bearings; good bumper jack with lug wrench; a simple set of tools, such as hammer, screwdrivers, pliers, wire, crescent wrenches, socket and/or open-end wrenches, pry bar; electrician's tape; small assortment of nuts and bolts; fan belt; one or two spare tires (two spares for traveling any remote road);

and any parts for your vehicle that might not be available along the way.

Include an extra few gallons of gas and water, especially for remote roads. You may wish to carry a can of brake, power steering and automatic transmission fluids.

Along the Alaska Highway, dust is at its worst during dry spells, following heavy rain (which disturbs the road surface) and in construction areas. If you encounter much dust, check your air filter frequently. To help keep dust out of your vehicle, try to keep air pressure in the car by closing all windows and turning on the fan. Filtered heating and air-conditioning ducts in a vehicle bring in much less dust than open windows or vents. Mosquito netting placed over the heater/fresh-air intake and flow-through ventilation will help eliminate dust.

Alcoholic Beverages
The legal age for possession, purchase and consumption of alcoholic beverages is 21 in Alaska. As of 1995, under-age drinkers may lose their driver's licenses for 90 days.

Any business that serves or distributes alcoholic beverages must be licensed by the state. The number of different types of licenses issued is limited by the population in a geographic area. Generally one license of each type may be issued for each 3,000 persons or fraction thereof. Licensed premises include bars, some restaurants and clubs. Packaged liquor, beer and wine are sold by licensed package stores. Licenses are renewed biennially.

Recreational site licenses, caterer's permits and special events permits allow the holder of a permit or license to sell at special events, and allow nonprofit fraternal, civic or patriotic organizations to serve beer and wine at certain activities.

State law allows liquor outlets to operate from 8 A.M. to 5 A.M., but provides that local governments may impose tighter restrictions.

Dozens of communities have banned possession and/or sale and importation of alcoholic beverages (knowingly bringing, sending or transporting alcoholic beverages into the community). Others have banned the sale of all alcoholic beverages. Contact the ABC Board at (907) 277-8638 for a current list. Or check www.revenue.state. ak.us/abc/abc.htm.

Alyeska (SEE ALSO SKIING)

Pronounced Al-YES-ka, this Aleut word means "the great land" and was one of the original names of Alaska. Mount Alyeska, a 3,939-foot peak in the Chugach Mountains south of Anchorage, is the site of the state's largest ski resort.

Amphibians In Alaska,

there are three species of salamander, two species of frog and one species of toad. In the salamander order, there are the rough-skinned newt, long-toed salamander and north-western salamander. In the frog and toad order, there are the boreal toad, wood frog and spotted frog. The northern limit of each species may be the latitude at which the larvae fail to complete their development in one summer. While some species of salamander can overwinter as larvae in temperate southeastern Alaska, the shallow ponds of central Alaska freeze solid during the winter. All but the wood frog, *Rana sylvatica,* which with its shortened larval period is found widespread throughout the state and north of the Brooks Range, are found primarily in southeastern Alaska.

Anchorage (SEE ALSO REGIONS

OF ALASKA) Anchorage is located on a broad peninsula in Cook Inlet, defined by Knik Arm and Turnagain Arm, and bordered to the east by the Chugach Mountains. Anchorage and the Kenai Peninsula comprise the region Alaskans call "South-central," a region milder in climate than the Interior, with average temperatures of 15°F in January and 58°F in July, and an average snowfall of about 70 inches a year.

Anchorage's daylight has a daily maximum of 19 hours, 21 minutes in summer and reaches a minimum of 5 hours, 28 minutes in winter.

Anchorage's population was 1,856 in 1920, and remained at a few thousand until after World War II.

In 1994, Anchorage, Alaska's most populous city, broke the quarter million mark for the first time ever; in 2000 it is home to 259,391 people (about 41 percent of the state's population).

Anchorage suffered millions of dollars in damage in a devastating earthquake on March 27, 1964, originally measured at 8.6 on the Richter scale, but later upgraded to 9.2—the strongest ever recorded in North America. (*See also* Earthquakes)

Sometimes called the "Air Crossroads of the World," Anchorage is a gateway for international travelers. Surrounded by dense spruce, birch and aspen forests, it is just a step away from wilderness and multiple recreational opportunities. Anchorage also serves as a jump-off point for tourists—heading 200 miles north to visit Denali National Park and Mount McKinley, North America's highest mountain; or south 52 miles to view Portage Glacier, one of the state's most-visited sights; or even to one of Alaska's Bush locations for hunting, fishing, skiing, hiking, nature photography or sightseeing.

Although bear and moose may occasionally wander the city's highways and byways, Anchorage offers many of the attractions of any large metropolis, such as art galleries, museums, libraries, cultural diversity, music—including a symphony orchestra, opera and dance—and theaters big enough to stage productions by national

---

Name Game

Congress authorized a railroad to be built from the ocean port of Seward to Fairbanks in the Interior in 1914, and the anchorage at the mouth of Ship Creek was chosen as the construction camp and headquarters for the Alaskan Engineering Commission. The name Anchorage was confirmed by the federal government with the establishment of a postal office in 1915; it had been variously called "Knik Anchorage," "Ship Creek" and "Woodrow." ✷

touring companies. Anchorage has more than 200 churches and approximately 80 schools, including the University of Alaska Anchorage and Alaska Pacific University. Restaurants offer everything from fine dining and ethnic cuisine to fast food. Accommodations are offered at more than 70 hotels, motels and approximately 100 bed-and-breakfasts. Anchorage has more than 6,000 hotel/motel rooms.

Contact the Anchorage Convention and Visitors Bureau for a free visitor's guide, maps and additional information, 524 W. Fourth Ave., Anchorage 99501; phone (800) 478-1255; e-mail info@anchorage.net; home page www.anchorage.net.

Antiquities Laws

(SEE ALSO NATIONAL HISTORIC PLACES) State and federal laws prohibit excavation or removal of historic and prehistoric cultural materials without a permit. Nearly all 50 states have historic preservation laws; Alaska's extends even to tidal lands, making it illegal to pick up artifacts on the beach while beachcombing.

It sometimes is difficult to distinguish between historic sites and abandoned property. Old gold-mining towns and cabins, as well as areas such as the Chilkoot and Iditarod Trails, should always be considered historic sites or private property.

A federal government–sponsored archaeological dig on the North Slope during the summer of 1999 produced a total of four bone beads, but the leader of the expedition dropped one in the tundra and it was never found again. The expedition therefore lost 25 percent of its entire summer's discovery!

Also, cabins that appear to be abandoned may be seasonally used trapping cabins; the structure and possessions are vital to the owner.

Alaska law prohibits the disturbance of fossils, including prehistoric animals such as mammoths.

Archaeology (SEE ALSO

BERING LAND BRIDGE) Alaska has a long and rich archaeological history. The first human migrants to North and South America some 40,000 to 15,000 years ago came first to Alaska, crossing over the now-submerged Bering Land Bridge that connected Siberia to Alaska in the Ice Age.

Some of the oldest archaeological materials that demonstrate human occupation of Alaska come from Trail Creeks Cave north of Nome, where a 15,000-year-old cracked bison leg bone and bone point were found. Better evidence can be found for human occupation from 11,000 years ago. Small hunting tools have been found throughout Alaska, probably belonging to nomadic hunting and gathering peoples. The archaeological record becomes more complicated about 4,000 years ago, when it reveals cultural patterns characteristic of Alaska Native groups still extant at the time of contact with Europeans.

In 1993, the presence of what may be the oldest documented site of human habitation in North America was discovered. Called the Mesa Site, it is located about 150 miles north of the Arctic Circle in the foothills of the Brooks Range. The 11,700-year-old hunting site is perched atop a 200-foot mesa overlooking the surrounding plain. It probably was used for 2,000 years as a hunters' lookout for prey such as caribou.

There is still much to discover about Alaska's prehistory. Many archaeological sites are small, representing the camps of wandering hunters and gatherers; some sites, especially along the coast where rich natural resources allowed people to become more sedentary and established, are large and deep. Where permafrost occurs, preservation of even the most perishable organic materials offers a wealth of information on life in the past. There are several thousand known archaeological sites in the state. One of the most famous is the 500-year-old Utkeaviq Site at Barrow, where a "frozen family" was unearthed from Mound 44 in the Birnirk archaeological site during 1982–83.

Archaeological excavations, or digs, are

almost always confined to the summer months. The University of Alaska in both Fairbanks and Anchorage frequently sponsors digs, as do several state and federal agencies. Recent excavations have taken place near Unalaska, Tok, Kodiak, Fairbanks, Prince William Sound, Point Franklin, Sitka and on the Kenai Peninsula.

Participants, who will be required to pay a fee, are invited to take part in a dig on Afognak. Inquire with the Afognak Native Corp., P.O. Box 1277, Kodiak 99615. (800) 770-6014; e-mail dig@afognak.com.

Tourists are invited to dig for free at a 10,000-year-old site near Unalaska. For information call Rick Knecht or Belinda Sunderland, (907) 581-5150, or e-mail aleutian@arctic.net; Web site: www. aleutians.org.

Arctic Circle (SEE ALSO DAYLIGHT HOURS)

The Arctic Circle (*see* map, pages 8–9) is the latitude at which the sun does not set for one day at summer solstice and does not rise for one day at winter solstice. The latitude, which varies slightly from year to year, is approximately 66°34' north from the equator and circumscribes the northern frigid zone.

A solstice occurs when the sun is at its greatest distance from the celestial equator. On the day of summer solstice, June 20 or 21, the sun does not set at the Arctic Circle, and because of refraction of sunlight, it appears not to set for four days. Farther north, at Barrow (the northernmost community in the United States), the sun does not set from May 10 to August 2.

At winter solstice, December 21 or 22, the sun does not rise for one day at the Arctic Circle. At Barrow, it does not rise for 67 days.

Arctic Winter Games

The Arctic Winter Games are held every two years in mid-March for northern athletes from Alaska, northern Alberta, Greenland, Northwest Territories, Yukon and Russia. The first games were held in 1970 in Yellowknife, Northwest

Territories, and have since been held in Fairbanks and Whitehorse, Yukon. Greenland and Nunavut will host the next games in March 2002.

In 2000, 316 athletes, coaches and

And the Winners Are...

The Arctic Winter Games, March 5–11, 2000, were held at Whitehorse, Yukon Territory. Among the Alaskan winners:

One-foot High Kick: Junior women, Bronze: Amy Allen. Junion men, Silver: Andrew Constantine. Senior women, Silver: Noel Gould. Senior women, Bronze: Nicole Johnston. Senior men, Gold: Bradley Weyiouanna. Senior men, Silver: Phil Blanchett (tied with Elias Irwin, NWT). Senior men, Bronze: George Melton
Triple Jump: Junior men, Gold: Andrew Constantine. Junior men, Bronze: William Brown. Senior women, Silver: Nicole Johnston
Arm Pull: Junior men, Gold: Andrew Constantine. Senior women, Gold: Nicole Johnston
Kneel Jump: Junior women, Bronze: Jenna Ring. Senior women, Gold: Nicole Johnston. Senior women, Silver: Noel Gould
One-Hand Reach: Senior men, Silver: Gary Hull. Senior men, Bronze: Bradley Weyiouanna (tied with Jimmy Merkosat)
All-Around: Junior women, Silver: Jenna Ring. Junior men, Gold: Andrew Constantine
Dene Games: Snow Snake, Silver: Maxim Dolchok. Stick Pull, Silver: Daniel Amidon. Hand Games, Bronze: Alaska
Alaska High Kick: Junior women, Silver: Jenna Ring. Senior women, Gold: Nicole Johnston. Senior men, Gold: George Melton. Senior men, Bronze: Bradley Weyiouanna
Russian Sledge Jump: Senior women, Gold: Emily Frantz
Airplane: Senior men, Bronze: Bradley Weyiouanna
Two-Foot High Kick: Junior women, Silver: Jenna Ring. Junior men, Gold: Andrew Constantine. Senior men, Silver: Phil Blanchett ✹

Source: Anchorage Daily News

support staff from Alaska participated in the games. Competition includes: alpine skiing, arctic sports (traditional Inuit and Dene games), badminton, basketball, curling, cross-country skiing, dog mushing, figure skating, gymnastics, hockey, short track speed skating, ski biathlon, snowboarding, snowshoeing, indoor soccer, volleyball and wrestling. Cultural events and performances encourage participation by people of all ages. Consult their web site at www.awg.ca.

Aurora Borealis

The Phenomenon. The aurora borealis (northern lights) is produced by charged electrons and protons striking gas particles in the earth's upper atmosphere. The electrons and protons are released through sunspot activity on the sun and emanate into space. A few drift the one- to two-day course to Earth, where they are pulled to the most northern and southern latitudes by the planet's magnetic forces.

The color of the aurora borealis varies, depending on how hard the gas particles are being struck. Auroras can range from simple arcs to draperylike forms in green, red, blue and purple. The lights occur in a pattern rather than as a solid glow because electric current sheets flowing through gases create V-shaped potential double layers. Electrons near the center of the current sheet move faster, hit the atmosphere harder and cause the different intensities of light observed in the aurora.

Displays take place as low as 40 miles above the Earth's surface, but usually begin about 68 miles above and extend hundreds of miles into space. They concentrate in two bands roughly centered above the Arctic Circle and Antarctic Circle (the latter known as aurora australis) that are about 2,500 miles in diameter. In northern latitudes the greatest occurrence of auroral displays is in the spring and fall months, because of the tilt of the planet in relationship to the sun's plane. Displays may occur on dark nights throughout the winter.

If sunspot activity is particularly intense and the denser-than-usual solar wind heads to Earth, the resulting auroras can be so great that they cover all but the tropical latitudes.

Some observers claim that the northern lights make a sound similar to the rustle of taffeta, but scientists say the displays cannot be heard in the audible frequency range.

Residents of Fairbanks, located on the 65th parallel, see the aurora borealis an average of 240 nights a year. The University of Alaska Fairbanks issues weekly aurora forecasts in winter.

Photographing the Aurora Borealis. To capture the northern lights on film, you will need a 35mm camera that has adjustable f-stop and shutter speed, a sturdy tripod, a locking-type cable release (some 35mm cameras have both *time* and *bulb* settings, but most have *bulb only,* which calls for use of the locking-type cable release) and an f3.5 lens (or faster).

f-stop	ASA 200	ASA 400
f1.2	3 sec.	2 sec.
f1.4	5	3
f1.8	7	4
f2	20	10
f2.8	40	20
f3.5	60	30

It is best to photograph the lights on a night when they are not moving too rapidly. And, as a general rule, photos improve if you manage to include recognizable subjects in the foreground—trees and lighted cabins are favorites of many photographers. Set up your camera at least 75 feet back from the foreground objects to make sure that both the foreground and aurora are in sharp focus.

Normal and wide-angle lenses are best. Try to keep your exposures under a minute—a 10- to 30-second exposure is generally best. The lens openings and exposure times are only a starting point, since the amount of light generated by the aurora is inconsistent. (For best results, bracket widely.)

Ektachrome 200 and 400 color film can be push-processed in the home darkroom or by most custom-color labs, allowing use of higher ASA ratings (800, 1200 or even 1600 on the 400 ASA film, for example). Kodak will push-process film if you include an ESP-1 envelope with your standard film-processing mailer. (Consult your local camera store for details.)

A few notes of caution: Protect the camera from low temperatures until you are ready to make your exposures. Some newer cameras have electrically controlled shutters that will not function properly at low temperatures.

Wind the film slowly to reduce the possibility of static electricity, which can lead to streaks on the film. Grounding the camera when rewinding can help prevent the static-electricity problem. (To ground the camera, hold it against a water pipe, drain pipe, metal fence post or other grounded object.) Follow the basic rules and experiment with exposures.

The first photographs to show the aurora borealis in its entirety were published in early 1982. These historic photographs were taken from satellite-mounted cameras specially adapted to filter unwanted light from the sunlit portion of the earth, which is a million times brighter than the aurora. From space, the aurora has the appearance of a nearly perfect circle.

Baidarka
The *baidarka* (also spelled bidarka or bidarkee), or Aleut kayak, is a portable decked boat made of skins (usually seal) stretched over wood frames. The *baidarka* (a Russian term for the skin boats) was widely used by Aleuts and Alaska coastal Natives for transportation and hunting in areas associated with Russian influence. *Baidarkas* were the only form of kayak commonly built with three hatch-ways, and generally had a forked bow.

Baleen
(*SEE ALSO* BASKETS *AND* WHALES *AND* WHALING) Baleen (often mistakenly called whale "bone") hangs from the upper jaw of baleen whales in long, fringed, bonelike strips. Baleen whales, such as humpback, bowhead, minke and gray, feed by taking in seawater and filtering small fish, plankton and the

Three-hatch baidarka, *ca. 1909. From* Baidarka *by George Dyson.*

tiny, shrimplike creatures called krill through the baleen. Baleen is made of keratin, a substance found in human fingernails. The outer edge of baleen is hard; the inside edges of the baleen plates form a fringe of coarse bristles that resembles matted goat hair.

The number of plates along an adult humpback's jaw, the largest of the baleen whales, varies from 600 to 800 (300 to 400 a side); the roof of the mouth is empty of plates. The bowhead whale has 600 plates, some of which reach 14 feet or more in length. Baleen varies in thickness and texture. Baleen from humpback whales is coarse; sei whales have finely textured baleen.

Baleen was once used for corset stays, Venetian blinds, hairbrushes and buggy whips. It is no longer of significant commercial use, although Alaska Natives use brownish black bowhead baleen to craft fine baskets and model ships to sell.

Barabara
Pronounced buh-RAH-buh-ruh, this traditional Aleut or Eskimo dwelling is built of sod supported by driftwood or whale ribs.

Baranov, Alexander

(*SEE ALSO* SITKA) Alexander Andreyevich Baranov (1747–1819), sometimes called "Lord of Alaska," was manager of the Russian American fur-trading company and the first governor of Russian Alaska.

A failed Siberian fur businessman, Baranov seemed an unlikely choice for overseeing the expansion of the Russian American empire when he arrived at Kodiak in 1790. But his aggressiveness and tough political skills proved indispensable. Within seven years, he had eliminated all competitors and secured the entire south Alaska coast, from the Aleutian Islands to Yakutat, for the Russian-American Company.

Learning to handle a *baidarka* and navigate a seagoing sloop, he established Fort St. Michael at remote Sitka Bay in 1799 and in 1804 reestablished the post following its destruction by Tlingit warriors.

Baranov was a pragmatic ruler. He encouraged marriage between European men and Native women. The settlement's need for clerks and artisans led him to require basic schooling for all children. Lacking military support to exclude British and American ships from Alaska waters, he cultivated cordial relations with foreign captains. By the time he retired in 1818, Russian influence in the North Pacific stretched from Siberia to Fort Ross in northern California.

Baranov died of fever aboard ship en route to St. Petersburg in 1819.

Barrow

(*SEE ALSO* MUSEUMS; NATIVE PEOPLES; *AND* REGIONS) Situated 350 miles north of the Arctic Circle, Barrow is the northernmost city in the United States and the largest Inupiat Eskimo community in the world.

Barrow was called Utqiagvik by its Inupiat founders. Because of its key location at the junction of the Chukchi and Beaufort Seas, Barrow became an important whaling site. The town remains a center of subsistence whaling and harvesting of other land and water species.

More than 4,400 people live in this polar environment, unconnected to any other community by road. Within the 21-square-mile city limits however there are 28 miles of roadway covering three distinct areas of settlement: the traditional Inupiat community of Barrow, the former Naval Arctic Research Laboratory, and portions of the Distant Early Warning (DEW) Line station.

Barrow is the seat of government of the North Slope Borough, and serves as a regional center for the 89,000-square-mile borough. It is also the corporate headquarters for the Arctic Slope Regional Corp. and the Ukpeagvik Inupiat Corp., which were established under the Native Claims Settlement Act.

Barrow has a strong and growing tourist industry. Visitors are attracted by everything from traditional whaling celebrations to polar bear watching, northern lights and the midnight sun. A monument across from the airport is dedicated to Will Rogers and Wiley Post, commemorating the deadly 1935 airplane crash 15 miles south of Barrow.

Baseball

Six teams play baseball in Alaska, making up the Alaska Baseball League: Fairbanks Goldpanners, Anchorage Bucs, Hawaiian Island Movers, Anchorage Glacier Pilots, Kenai Peninsula Oilers and the Mat–Su Miners.

Baseball season opens in June and runs through the end of July. Each team plays a round-robin schedule with the other Alaska teams in addition to scheduling games with visiting Lower 48 teams.

The Anchorage Bucs began playing during the 1981 season. They defeated Team USA in 1991, defeated the Moscow Red Devils in 1992 and won the Alaska League championship several times. In 1993, the Bucs were recognized as America's No. 1 summer collegiate team.

The Anchorage Glacier Pilots are entering their 30th year. This semi-pro team drafts collegiate athletes from all over the United States. More than 80 former players have gone on to play in the major leagues. The Pilots consistently finish in the top seven at the annual NBC Championships in Wichita, Kansas.

The caliber of play in Alaska is some of the best nationwide at the amateur level. Major league scouts rate Alaska baseball at A to AA, visiting each season to check out talent for possible recruitment.

The list of major league players who were once on Alaska teams is impressive, and includes stars Tom Seaver, Mark McGwire, Chris Chambliss and Dave Winfield. Some 20 former Bucs now playing in the majors include Wally Joyner, Mike McFarlane, Bobby Jones and Jeff Kent.

Baskets (SEE ALSO BALEEN AND NATIVE ARTS AND CRAFTS)

Native basketry varies greatly according to materials locally available. Athabascan Indians of the Interior, for example, weave baskets from willow root gathered in late spring. The roots are steamed and heated over a fire to loosen the outer bark. Weavers then separate the material into fine strips by pulling the roots through their teeth.

Eskimo grass baskets are made in river delta areas of southwestern Alaska from Bristol Bay north to Norton Sound and from Nunivak Island east to interior Eskimo river villages. Weavers use very fine grass harvested in fall. A coil basketry technique is followed, using coils from 1/8 to 3/4 inch wide. Seal gut, traditionally dyed with berries (today with commercial dyes), is often interwoven into the baskets.

Baleen, a glossy, hard material that extends in slats from the upper jaw of some types of whales, is also used for baskets. Baleen basketry originated about 1905 when Charles D. Brower, trader for a whaling company at Point Barrow, suggested, after the decline of the whale-bone (baleen) industry for women's corsets, that local Eskimo men make the baskets as a source of income. The baskets were not produced in any number until 1916. The weave and shape of the baskets were copied from the split-willow Athabascan baskets acquired in trade. A decorative "knob" of ivory is often added.

Later, baleen baskets were also made in Point Hope and Wainwright.

Most birch-bark baskets are made by Athabascan Indians, although a few Eskimos also produce them. Baskets are shaped as simple cylinders, or canoe shapes, held together with spruce root lashings. Sometimes the birch bark is cut into thin strips and woven into diamond or checkerboard patterns. Birch bark is usually collected in spring and early summer; large pieces free of knots are preferred. Birch-bark baskets traditionally were used as cooking vessels. Food was placed in them and hot stones added. Birch-bark baby carriers also are still made, chiefly for collectors.

Among the finest of Alaska baskets are the tiny, intricately woven Aleut baskets made of rye grass, which in the Aleutians is abundant, pliable and very tough. The three main styles of Aleut baskets—Attu, Atka and Unalaska—are named after the islands where the styles originated. Although the small baskets are the best known, Aleuts also traditionally made large, coarsely woven baskets for utilitarian purposes.

Tlingit, Haida and Tsimshian Indians make baskets of spruce roots and cedar bark. South of Frederick Sound, basket material usually consists of strands split from the inner bark of red cedar. To the north of the sound, spruce roots are used. Maidenhair ferns are sometimes interwoven into spruce root baskets to form patterns resembling embroidery. A large spruce root basket may take months to complete.

Examples of Alaska Native

From the February 17 police blotter of the *Seward Phoenix Log*: "8:43 P.M. Caller from Eagle [grocery store] advised of a 3-year-old boy lost in store. Parents paged. No response. Located parents on Dora Way. Boy was left behind when they left the store with his other six siblings."

Tlingit spruce-root basket. From Indian Baskets of the Pacific Northwest and Alaska by Allen Lobb, Art Wolfe and Barbara Paxson.

basketry may be viewed in many museums, including the University of Alaska Museum, Fairbanks; the Anchorage Museum of History and Art, Anchorage; the Sheldon Jackson Museum, Sitka; and the Alaska State Museum, Juneau.

Prices for Native baskets vary greatly. A fine-weave, coiled beach grass basket may cost from $100 to $500; birch bark baskets may range from $35 to $125; willow root trays may cost $800; finely woven Aleut baskets may cost $200 to $800; cedar bark baskets may range from $30 to $80; and baleen baskets range in price from $600 to more than $2,200 for medium-sized baskets. These prices are approximate and are based on the weave, material used, size and decoration added, such as beads, embroidery or ivory.

Beadwork (SEE ALSO NATIVE ARTS AND CRAFTS AND PARKA) Eskimo
and Indian women create a variety of handsomely beaded items. Before contact with Europeans, Indian women sometimes carved beads of willow wood or made them from seeds of certain shrubs and trees. Glass seed beads became available to Alaska's Athabascan Indians in the mid-19th century, although some types of larger trade beads were in use earlier. Beads quickly became a coveted trade item. The *Cornaline d'aleppo,* an opaque red bead with a white center, and the faceted Russian blue beads were among the most popular types.

The introduction of small glass beads sparked changes in beadwork style and design. More colors were available and the smaller, more easily maneuvered beads made it possible to work out delicate floral patterns impossible with larger trade beads.

Historically, beads were sewn directly onto leather garments or other items with the overlay stitch. Contemporary beadwork is often done on a separate piece of felt that is not visible once the beads are stitched in place.

Alaska's Athabascan beadworkers sometimes use paper patterns, often combining several motifs and tracing their outline on the surface to be worked. The most common designs include flowers, leaves and berries, some in very stylized form. Many patterns are drawn simply from the sewer's environment. Since the gold rush, magazines, graphic art, advertising and patriotic motifs have inspired Athabascan beadworkers, although stylized floral designs are still the most popular.

Designs vary regionally as do the ways in which they are applied to garments or footgear. Skilled practitioners execute beadwork so distinctive it can be recognized at a glance.

Bears (SEE ALSO MAMMALS AND MCNEIL RIVER STATE GAME SANCTUARY)
Three species of bear inhabit Alaska: the black, the brown/grizzly and the polar bear. Most of Alaska can be considered bear country, and for those wishing to spend time in Alaska's great outdoors, bear country becomes "beware" country. Sows are extremely aggressive if their young are around, and bears will guard a moose kill against all passersby. Bear behavior should always be considered unpredictable. Bear scat or a large concentration of flies in one area are signs for hikers to watch for and retreat from. The Alaska Department of Fish and Game publishes *The Bears and You,* recommended reading for hikers and campers.

Black Bears. Black bears are usually jet black or brown with a brown-yellow muzzle, and weigh from 100 to 200 pounds as adults. The brown color phase can sometimes be confused with grizzlies but

Future of the Brown Bear

The settlers and developers of the United States nearly wiped out the brown bear in the Lower 48, killing the animal whenever possible and destroying its habitat. In Alaska, the great bear has been luckier. Large expanses have been set aside in parks, preserves, refuges, and forests, giving it the space and solitude it needs. Because of the brown bear's demands for space and food, it is sometimes considered an indicator species, one whose well-being serves as a measure of an ecosystem's health.

—Bill Sherwonit, *Alaska's Bears*

black bears are generally smaller and lack the grizzly's distinct shoulder hump. Black bear habitat covers three-fourths of Alaska, with high concentrations found in Southeast, Prince William Sound and the coastal mountains and lowlands of southcentral Alaska. Low to moderate densities are found in interior and western Alaska. Their range is semi-open forests, and though omnivorous, their diet consists mainly of vegetation due to the difficulty of getting meat or fish. Black bears often spend their lives within 5 miles of their birthplace and will frequently return to their home range if transplanted. They easily climb trees; both cubs and adults use trees as a place of escape. Cubs are generally born in late January or February weighing 8 to 10 ounces. Average litter size is two cubs, but three or four cubs in a litter is not unusual. Black bears den in winter for up to six months but are not true hibernators. Their body temperature remains high and they awaken easily—even in midwinter.

Brown/Grizzly Bears. Fur colors of brown/grizzly bears vary from blond to black with shades of brown and gray in between. As adults, they can weigh over 1,000 pounds, but are usually smaller; size depends on sex, age, time of year and geographic location. Coastal bears, referred to as "browns" or "brownies," are the largest living omnivorous land mammals in the world and grow larger than Interior "grizzlies." Browns or grizzlies are found in most of Alaska except for islands in the extreme southeastern part of the state. The lowest populations are found in the northern Interior and the Arctic. Their range is wherever food is abundant, but

the bears prefer open tundra and grasslands. Diet consists of a wide variety of plants and animals, including their own kind, and humans under some circumstances. In their realm, grizzlies are king and fear no other animal except humans with a firearm. While attacks on people are the exception, the results can be tragic. These bears are also tremendously strong and have been seen carrying—off the ground—an 800-pound moose. One to two hairless cubs are usually born in late January or February weighing 8 to 10 ounces, and sows have been known to adopt orphaned cubs. Time of year and duration of denning varies with the location and physical condition of the bear, and can be up to six months of the year. Dens are frequently on hillsides or on mountain slopes.

Polar Bears. The only areas on a polar bear not covered with heavy, white fur are its eyes and large, black nose. The bear, seemingly aware that his nose gives him away to prey, will hold a paw up to hide it when hunting. An adult polar bear weighs 1,500 pounds or more and has a long neck with a proportionately small head. Their habitat is the Canadian–eastern Alaska Arctic and the western Alaska Arctic–eastern Russia, the latter being home to the world's largest polar bears. Their range is the arctic ice cap, and they are more numerous toward the southern edge of the ice pack. Occasionally polar bears will come ashore, but generally stay near the coast. While ashore they eat some vegetation, but their diet consists primarily of ringed seals, walrus, stranded whales, birds and fish. Cannibalism of cubs and young

25

coast, on offshore islands, on shorefast ice and on drifting sea ice.

Bering, Vitus

Vitus Jonassen Bering (1681–1741) is credited as the first European to discover Alaska. A Danish captain serving Russia under the crown of Peter the Great, Bering was in command of an expedition to find out if the continents of Asia and America were connected and to claim new lands for Russia.

He piloted his first expedition in 1728 through the strait that now bears his name, concluding that Asia and America were not joined. On that voyage however he never saw the fog-shrouded Alaska mainland. The expedition was considered a failure.

In June 1741, Bering set sail again as captain of the ill-fated *St. Peter*. Also on board was the German naturalist Georg Steller; biologists still refer to the Steller sea lion and Steller's jay stemming from his field work on the journey. A second ship piloted by Aleksei Chirikov accompanied the *St. Peter*.

During the voyage, Bering and Chirikov lost contact in foul weather, never to meet again. In July both ships sighted southern Alaska. On July 16, Steller led a landing party on what is now Kayak Island at Cape St. Elias, just east of Prince William Sound.

Short of food and weakened with scurvy, Bering was anxious to set sail for Kamchatka before winter. Against the advice of Steller, the explorer sailed for home. In heavy seas the *St. Peter* ran aground on a rocky island off the Siberian coast, since known as Bering Island. Twenty sailors, including Bering, died of scurvy. The remaining sailors survived by eating fish and seals, eventually built a boat from the wreckage of the *St. Peter*, and returned to Russia.

Bering's voyage not only laid the basis for Russian claims to Alaska but also opened the fur trade. His crews brought back many pelts, among them 800 sea otter skins. By the late 1700s, the Russian fur trade had

Brown/grizzly bears range throughout much of Alaska. From *Alaska's Bears* by Bill Sherwonit (text) and Tom Walker (photographs).

bears by older males is not unusual. Polar bears are strong swimmers; reports exist of swimming bears found 50 miles from the nearest land or ice. When swimming, they use their front paws for propulsion and trail their rear paws. Mother bears have been seen with a cub hanging onto their tail, towing it through the water. Cubs are born in December with two being the common litter size. They weigh about a pound at birth and remain with their mother for about 28 months. Usually only pregnant sows den up, for an average of six months in the winter. Polar bears need stable, cold areas for denning, and dens in Alaska have been found 30 miles inland, along the

It was recently reported that a person is statistically more likely to be killed by a bear in Alaska than run over by a taxi in New York City.

become the richest fur enterprise in the world, setting the stage for the extinction of Steller's sea cow by 1768 and the near-extinction of the sea otter in the 1820s.

Bering Land Bridge

The Bering Land Bridge was formed when the glaciers of the Wisconsinan period flowed across the northern cap of the earth. A great deal of the earth's water was absorbed, somewhat like a sponge, causing the ocean levels to lower and exposing previously submerged land. Close to the Arctic Circle, a 1,000-mile-wide stretch of grasslands gradually appeared, connecting North America with Asia. Now known as the Bering Land Bridge, it enabled the slow migration of ancient peoples and animals between 40,000 and 15,000 years ago.

When the glaciers retreated, the water returned to the sea, which resubmerged the bridge and created the Bering Strait between Alaska and Siberia. Today a national preserve protects this prehistoric bridge to the Americas from Asia. Recognizing the need to preserve the area's unique archaeological record, both discovered and undiscovered, the U.S. Congress created in 1980 the Bering Land Bridge National Preserve, managed by the National Park Service. The preserve occupies 2.7 million acres of the Seward Peninsula in northwest Alaska.

Visitors will find extensive lava flows and maar lakes formed by ash and steam explosions, unique beaches, tundra and Serpentine Hot Springs, which is considered one of the preserve's highlights. Located in a valley of granite spires called tors, the hot springs attracts those who come to bathe, hike, relax and observe wildlife.

More than 400 species of plants have been listed in the preserve. The Bering Land Bridge also has a rich and diversified bird life. Animals found here include musk-oxen, bears, moose, wolves, wolverine, reindeer, caribou, foxes and other smaller species.

Depending on the season, access is possible only by air taxi, boat, dogsled, foot, skis or snowmobile. Recreational options include camping, hiking, back-packing, photography and coastal boating. In winter, visitors come to snowmobile, mush dogs and cross-country ski.

Road access ends 400 miles from Bering Land Bridge National Preserve, but the information superhighway now leads right to it. The BLBNP's home page (www.nps.gov/bela) gives a detailed look at the region.

Berries
Wild berries abound in Alaska, with the circumboreal lingonberry/lowbush cranberry (*Vaccinium vitisidaea*) being the most widespread. Blueberries of one species or another grow in most of the state. Some 50 other species of wild fruit are found in Alaska including strawberries, raspberries, cloudberries, salmonberries, crowberries, nagoonberries and crab apples. Highbush cranberries (which are not really cranberries) can be found on bushes even in the dead of winter; the frozen berries provide a refreshing treat to the hiker.

The fruit of the wild rose, or rose hip, is not strictly a berry but is an ideal source of vitamin C for Bush dweller and city resident alike. A few hips will provide as much of the vitamin as a medium-sized orange. The farther north the hips are found, the richer they are in vitamin C.

Alaska does have one poisonous berry, the baneberry. Sometimes called doll's eyes or chinaberries, baneberries may be white or scarlet in color. As few as six berries can induce violent symptoms of poisoning in an adult.

Lingonberry/ Lowbush Cranberry (Vaccinium vitisidae). From *Alaska Wild Berry Guide and Cookbook.*

Billiken
This smiling ivory figure with a pointed head, though long a popular Northland souvenir, is not an Eskimo invention. The billiken was patented in 1908 by Florence Pretz of Kansas City.

A small, seated, Buddha-like figure, the original billiken was manufactured by the Billiken Co. of Chicago and sold as a good luck charm. Thousands of these figurines were sold during the 1909 Alaska-Yukon-Pacific Exposition in Seattle.

Billikens vanished soon afterward from most Lower 48 shops; however, someone had brought them to Nome, and the Eskimos of King Island, Little Diomede and Wales began carving replicas of the billikens from walrus ivory and walrus teeth.

A popular notion contends that rubbing a billiken's tummy brings good fortune.

Birds
Authorities at the Alaska State Office of the National Audubon Society acknowledge 456 naturally occuring bird species in Alaska. If unsubstantiated sightings are included, the species total increases.

Thousands of ducks, geese and swans wing north to breeding grounds each spring. Millions of seabirds congregate in nesting colonies on exposed cliffs along Alaska's coastline, particularly on the Aleutian Islands and on islands in the Bering Sea.

Migratory birds reach Alaska from many corners of the world. Arctic terns travel up to 22,000 miles on their round trip each year from Antarctica. Others come from South America, Hawaii, the South Pacific islands and Asia.

Each May one of the world's largest concentrations of shorebirds funnels through the Copper River Delta near Cordova. Waterfowl such as trumpeter swans and the world's entire population of dusky Canada geese breed here.

More than 100 species of birds can be spotted in the Seward area.

Other key waterfowl habitats include the Yukon–Kuskokwim Delta, Yukon Flats, Innoko Flats and Minto Lakes. During migration, huge flocks gather at Egegik, Port Heiden, Port Moller, Izembek Bay, Chickaloon Flats, Susitna Flats and Stikine Flats.

Raptors, led by the bald eagle, range throughout the state. The largest gathering of eagles in the world takes place in Alaska every winter between October and February. In 1982, the Alaska Chilkat Bald Eagle Preserve was set aside to protect the 3,000-plus eagles that assemble at the site along the Chilkat River near Haines.

Alaska has three subspecies of peregrine falcon: arctic, American and Peale's. Arctic and American peregrine falcons join the

Eskimo curlew, the spectacled eider and short-tailed albatross on the endangered or threatened species list for the state. The Steller's eider and the spectacled eider have been added to the threatened species list by the U.S. Fish and Wildlife Service; the Aleutian Canada goose was removed in 1999.

Following is a list of some geographically restricted birds whose origins are in Siberia or Asia, as well as a few of the state's more well-known species:

Aleutian Tern. Breeds in coastal areas, marshes, islands, lagoons, rivers and inshore marine waters. Nests in Alaska on the ground in matted, dry grass. Casual sightings in southeastern Alaska in spring and summer, and in northern Alaska in summer.

Arctic Tern. Breeds in tidal flats, beaches, glacial moraines, rivers, lakes and marshes. Nests in colonies or scattered pairs on sand, gravel, moss or in rocks. The arctic tern winters in Antarctica, bypassing the Lower 48 in its 20,000-mile round-trip migration. Common sightings in southeastern, southcoastal and western Alaska in spring, summer and fall, and in southwestern Alaska in spring and fall.

Arctic Warbler. Nests on the ground in grass or moss in willow thickets. Common sightings in the Alaska Range, the Seward Peninsula and the Brooks Range in spring, summer and fall.

Bald Eagle. Found in coniferous forests, deciduous woodlands, rivers and streams, beaches and tidal flats, rocky shores and reefs. Nests in old-growth timber along the coast and larger mainland rivers. In treeless areas, nests on cliffs or on the ground. There are more bald eagles in Alaska than in all the other states combined, and sightings commonly occur in southeastern, southcoastal and southwestern Alaska year-round.

Bluethroat. Nests on the ground in shrub thickets in the uplands and the foothills of western and northern Alaska. Casual sightings in southwestern Alaska in spring and fall.

Emperor Goose. Nests near water in grassy marsh habitat on islands or banks or

Arctic tern near the Mendenhall Glacier, Juneau. From Alaska's Birds *by Robert H. Armstrong.*

in large tussocks. The bulk of the world's population nests in the Yukon–Kuskokwim Delta, with a few others nesting farther north to Kotzebue Sound and a few more in eastern Siberia. Rarely is an emperor goose seen east or south of Kodiak. Common sightings in southwestern Alaska in spring, fall and winter, and in western Alaska in spring, summer and fall.

Horned Puffin. Nests on sea islands in rock crevices or in burrows among boulders, on sea cliffs and on grassy slopes. Breeds inshore, in marine waters and on islands. Common sightings in southwestern and western Alaska in spring, summer and fall.

Pacific Loon. Breeds on lakes in coniferous forests or on tundra lakes, and nests on projecting points or small islands. Folklore credits the loon with magical powers and several legends abound. Common sightings in southeastern and southcentral Alaska in spring, fall and winter, and in southwestern, central, western and northern Alaska in spring, summer and fall.

Red-faced Cormorant. Habitat includes inshore marine waters. Nests in colonies on ledges of sea cliffs, small piles of rocks and shelves on volcanic cinder cones. In North

Bald eagle in flight. From *A Child's Glacier Bay* by Kimberly Corral with Hannah Corral (text) and Roy Corral (photographs).

America this bird appears only in Alaska. Common sightings in southcoastal and southwestern Alaska year-round.

Red-legged Kittiwake. Breeds in the Pribilof Islands, and on Buldir and Bogoslof Islands in the Aleutians. Nests on cliff ledges and cliff points. Common sightings near breeding areas in southwestern Alaska in summer.

Whiskered Auklet. A small gray diving seabird with white whiskers. It nests only in the Aleutians, particularly at the eastern end of Unalaska Island and on nearby Baby Islands.

White Wagtail. Found in open areas with short vegetation usually along the Seward Peninsula coast. Nests near or on the ground in crevices or niches in old buildings. Casual sightings in central Alaska in spring, and in southwestern Alaska in spring and summer.

About 10 million swans, geese and ducks also nest in Alaska each year, making the state critical habitat for many of the continent's waterfowl. In North America some species and subspecies use Alaska as exclusive nesting grounds, while more than half the North American population of other species nests in the state.

Five chapters of the National Audubon Society are based in Alaska: the Anchorage Audubon Society, Inc. (P.O. Box 101161, Anchorage 99510), the Juneau Audubon Society (P.O. Box 021725, Juneau 99802), the Arctic Audubon Society (P.O. Box 82098, Fairbanks 99708), the Kodiak Audubon Society (P.O. Box 1756, Kodiak 99615) and the Prince William Sound Audubon Society (P.O. Box 2725, Cordova 99574). Except for Fairbanks the local chapters coordinate more than 20 annual Christmas bird counts around the state. The Fairbanks Bird Club (P.O. Box 81791, Fairbanks 99708) conducts the annual Christmas count for that area. The Alaska State Office of the National Audubon Society is located at 308 G St., Suite 217, Anchorage 99501.

Bird-watchers gather during the first week of May for the Copper River Delta Shorebird Festival in Cordova and the Kachemak Bay Shorebird Festival in Homer. Ketchikan holds an annual rufous hummingbird festival. The Bald Eagle Festival is held in Haines each November.

Blanket Toss
As effective as a trampoline, the blanket toss (or *nalukataq*) features a walrus-hide blanket grasped by a number of people in a circle. They  toss a person on the blanket as high as possible for as long as that person can remain upright. Every true Eskimo festival and many non-Native occasions include the blanket toss, which originally was used to allow Eskimo hunters to spot game such as walrus and seal in the distance. Depending on the skill of the person being tossed and the number of tossers, a medium-weight person might typically go 20 feet in the air.

Boating
(*SEE ALSO* BAIDARKA; CRUISES; *AND* FERRIES) Travel by boat is an important means of transportation in Alaska where highways serve only about one-third of the state. Until the advent of the airplane, boats often were the only way

to reach many parts of Alaska. Most of Alaska's supplies still arrive by water and in Southeast—where precipitous terrain and numerous islands make road building impossible—water travel is essential.

According to the U.S. Coast Guard, there are approximately 40,300 vessels registered in Alaska. Of these, 20,376 are between 16 and 26 feet, and 3,859 are between 26 and 40 feet.

Moorage. To accommodate the needs of this fleet, there are approximately 8,000 rental slips and 2,000 transient slips available at public small-boat harbors in Alaska. State officials say actual service capacity is somewhat greater because of the transient nature of many boats and certain management practices allowing "double parking." There are also harbors at various remote locations; no services other than moorage are provided at these harbors.

Local governments have the major responsibility for operating public floats, grids, docks, launching ramps and associated small-boat harbor facilities throughout the coastal areas of the state. Moorage facilities constructed by the state are intended for boats up to a maximum of 100 feet, with a limited number of facilities for larger vessels where large boats are common. With the exception of Ketchikan, Sitka and Juneau, there are no private marine facilities.

Recreational Boating. Alaska ranks 16th nationally in per capita ownership of recreational boats. Recreational boating opportunities in Alaska are too numerous and varied to list here; Alaska has thousands of miles of lakes, rivers and sheltered seaways. For information about boating within national forests, parks, monuments, preserves and wildlife refuges, contact the appropriate federal agency. For travel by boat in southeastern Alaska's Inside Passage and the sheltered seaways of southcentral Alaska's Prince William Sound—or elsewhere in Alaska's coastal waters—NOAA nautical charts, pilot guides and tidal current tables are available. (*See* Information Sources)

Sea kayakers from around the world are drawn to Alaska to paddle its sheltered waterways and challenge its open coast. Kayakers in Alaska may visit tidewater glaciers and natural hot springs, meeting whales and sea otters along the way.

Inland boaters will find hundreds of river and lake systems suitable for traveling by boat, raft, kayak or canoe. Canoe routes have been established on the Kenai Peninsula (contact Kenai National Wildlife Refuge, P.O. Box 2139, Soldotna 99669; (907) 262-7021); in Nancy Lake State Recreation Area (contact Superintendent, Mat–Su District, HC32, Box 6706, Wasilla 99687; (907) 745-3975); and on rivers in the Fairbanks and Anchorage areas (contact Bureau of Land Management, 1150 University Ave., Fairbanks 99709; (907) 474-2200, and 222 W. Seventh Ave., No. 13, Anchorage 99513; (907) 271-5960).

Travel by water in Alaska requires extra caution. Weather changes rapidly and is often unpredictable; it's important to be prepared for the worst. Even in midsummer, Alaska waters are cold. A person falling overboard may become immobilized by the cold water in only a few minutes. And since many of Alaska's water routes are far from civilization, help may be a long way off.

Persons inexperienced in traveling Alaska's waterways might consider hiring a

> **Only in Alaska** would a judge from the Ship Creek Silver Salmon Derby report that within one week, anglers first only begrudgingly moved from their favorite fishing spots to allow police access to recover a drowning victim, and later were unhappy because police asked for space to investigate a shooting at a nearby hotel.

charter boat operator or outfitter. Guides offer local knowledge and provide all necessary equipment. The Division of Tourism (P.O. Box 110801, Juneau 99811) maintains current lists of such services. Recreation information on both state and federal lands is available at the four Alaska Public Lands Information Centers: 605 W. Fourth Ave., Suite 105, Anchorage 99501, (907) 271-2737; 250 Cushman St., Suite 1A, Fairbanks 99701, (907) 456-0527; P.O. Box 359, Tok 99780, (907) 883-5667; and 3031 Tongass Ave., Ketchikan 99901, (907) 228-6220. Web site: www.nps.gov/aplic.

Bore Tide (SEE ALSO TIDES)

A "bore" is an abrupt rise of tidal water moving rapidly inland from the mouth of an estuary into a constricted inlet; the term derives from the Middle English word for "wave."

There are only a handful of bore tides in the world, among them the Bay of Fundy and England's Severn Bore.

Cook Inlet has one of the largest fluctuating tides in the world. Maximum tidal range here approaches 40 feet, incoming tides are further compressed in the narrowing of Knik and Turnagain Arms and tidal bores are commonly seen. One- to 2-foot bores are common but spring tides in Turnagain Arm in particular can produce spectacular bores up to 6 feet high, running at speeds of up to 10 knots. Good spots to view Turnagain's bore tides are along the Seward Highway, between 26 and 37 miles south of Anchorage. They arrive there about 2 hours and 15 minutes later than the tide book prediction for low tide at Anchorage.

Breakup (SEE ALSO NENANA

ICE CLASSIC) Breakup occurs when melting snows raise the level of ice-covered streams and rivers sufficiently to cause the ice to break apart and float downstream.

Breakup is one of two factors determining the open-water season for river navigation,

the second being the depth of the river. Peak water conditions occur just after breakup.

The navigable season for the Kusko-kwim and Yukon rivers is June 1 through September 30; the Nushagak River, June 1 through August 31; and the Noatak River, late May through mid-September.

Breakup is a spectacular sight-and-sound show. Massive pieces of ice crunch and pound against one another as they push their way downriver racing for the sea, creating noises not unlike many huge engines straining and grating. The spine-tingling sound can be heard for miles. It marks the finale of winter and the arrival of spring in Alaska.

Sometimes great ice jams occur, causing the water to back up and flood inhabited areas. Flooding occurred at Fort Yukon in spring 1982, at McGrath in 1990 and at Allakaket in 1993.

Bunny Boots Bunny boots,

also called vapor barrier boots, are large, insulated rubber boots that protect feet from frostbite. Black bunny boots are generally rated to –20°F, while the more common white bunny boots are even warmer and have been used in the most extreme conditions, including the heights of Mount McKinley, even though they're cumbersome for climbing. They are no longer made but are still in demand. Used bunny boots could fetch $50 to $150 a pair.

Bush Originally used to describe

large expanses of wilderness beyond the fringes of civilization inhabited only by trappers and prospectors, "Bush" has come to stand for any part of Alaska not accessible by road. A community accessible only by air, water, sled or snowmachine is considered a Bush village and anyone living there is someone from the Bush.

The Bush is home to most of Alaska's Native people and to many individuals who live on homesteads, operate mines or work as guides, pilots, teachers, trappers or fishermen.

The term "Bush" is also applied to

the small planes and their pilots who service areas lacking roads. Bush planes are commonly equipped with floats and skis to match terrain and season. For their oftentimes courageous air service, Alaska Bush pilots have become modern frontier heroes.

Bus Lines
Scheduled bus service is available in summer to and within Alaska, although buses  don't run as frequently as in the Lower 48. (Local transit service is also available in some major communities.) Service may be infrequent; consult current schedules.

Alaska Direct Buslines, 125 Oklahoma St., Anchorage 99504; (907) 277-6652. Provides service between Anchorage, Fairbanks, Tok, Skagway and Whitehorse.

Alaska Sightseeing/Cruise West, 349 Wrangell St., Anchorage 99501; (907) 276-1305. Provides service between Anchorage, Denali National Park and Preserve, Columbia Glacier, Fairbanks, Prince William Sound and Valdez.

Eagle Custom Tours, P.O. Box 212529, Anchorage 99521; (907) 277-6228. Provides group transportation and tours throughout Alaska and the Yukon.

Gray Line of Alaska/Westours, 745 W. Fourth Ave., Anchorage 99501; (907) 277-5581. Provides local city sightseeing tours, travel between Anchorage, Denali National Park, Fairbanks, Kenai Peninsula, Dawson, Prudhoe Bay, Skagway, Valdez, Ketchikan, Juneau and Whitehorse.

Park Connection, P.O. Box 22-1011, Anchorage 99522; (907) 245-0200 or (800) 208-0200. Provides service between Anchorage, Seward, Denali National Park and Talkeetna.

Princess Tours, 6441 Interstate Circle, Anchorage 99518; (800) 426-0500. Provides sightseeing excursions and tours throughout Alaska; operates several hotels.

Seward Bus Lines, P.O. Box 1338, Seward 99664; (907) 563-0800. Provides daily service between Anchorage and Seward.

Cabin Fever
Cabin fever is a state of mind blamed on cold, dark, winter weather when people are often housebound. It is characterized by depression, preoccupation, discontent and occasionally violence, and has been described as "a 12-foot stare in a 10-foot room." Today these symptoms are known as seasonal affective disorder, or SAD.

Cabin fever is commonly thought to afflict miners and trappers spending a lonely winter in the wilderness but, in truth, these people are active and outdoors enough to remain content. It is more likely to strike the snowbound, city dwellers who do not ski or mush dogs, or the disabled. The arrival of spring or a change of scene usually relieves the symptoms.

Cabins (SEE ALSO CAMPING; NATIONAL FORESTS; AND STATE PARK SYSTEM)
Rustic cabins in remote Alaska places can be rented from the Forest Service, the Bureau of Land Management (BLM), the Alaska State Parks and the U.S. Fish and Wildlife Service. The modest price ($15 to $65 a night per cabin) makes this one of the best vacation bargains in Alaska. Visitors should prepare for rigorous backcountry travel and be ready to seek emergency shelter should they be unable to reach their cabin.

Almost 200 Forest Service cabins are scattered through the Tongass and Chugach National Forests in southeastern and southcentral Alaska. Some are located on salt water, others on freshwater rivers, streams or lakes. Some of the cabins can be reached by boat or trail but because of the remote locations, visitors frequently arrive by chartered aircraft.

The average cabin is 12 feet by 14 feet and is usually equipped with a table, an oil or wood stove and wooden bunks without mattresses. Most will accommodate a group of four to six. There is no electricity. Outhouses are within walking distance. Visitors need to bring food, bedding, cooking utensils and stove fuel. It's advisable to have a gas or propane stove for cooking, a lantern and insect repellent. Splitting mauls are provided on site for

Mulcahy View Cabin in Shuyak Island State Park. From Alaska's Accessible Wilderness by Bill Sherwonit.

cutting firewood. Since firewood is scarce and often wet, visitors should carry a supply of dry wood. Reservations may be made in person or by mail. Payment must accompany the reservation. Permits for use are issued on a first-come, first-served basis, up to 180 days in advance. Length of stay for some cabins is limited.

General information on all public-use cabins is available from the Alaska Public Lands Information Centers: 605 W. Fourth Ave., Anchorage 99501, (907) 271-2737; P.O. Box 359, Tok 99780, (907) 883-5677; 250 Cushman, Suite 1A, Fairbanks 99701, (907) 451-7352; 50 Main St., Ketchikan 99901, (907) 228-6220. Web site: www.nps.gov/aplic/center.

For information on National Forest cabins in Alaska, contact: USDA Forest Service Information Center, 101 Egan Drive, Juneau 99801, (907) 586-8751 or Southeast Alaska Visitor Center, 50 Main St., Ketchikan 99901, (907) 228-6220.

The **Forest Service** recommends that visitors contact the Information Center and request Forest Service cabin information. It's a good idea to do this at least six months ahead. A booklet contains the applications for cabin use and tips on planning a stay.

The **Bureau of Land Management** has about a dozen public-use cabins in the White Mountains National Recreation Area east of Fairbanks, used primarily by winter recreationists. Only three cabins are accessible during summer months. Cabins must be reserved prior to use and a fee is required. Contact the BLM Support Center, 1150 University Ave., Fairbanks 99709-3844, (907) 474-2350.

The **U.S. Fish and Wildlife Service** maintains public-use cabins within Kodiak National Wildlife Refuge. Contact the Refuge Manager, 1390 Buskin River Road, Kodiak 99615.

Alaska State Parks maintains 46 public-use cabins throughout the state. For reservations and information contact the Department of Natural Resources Public Information Center, 3601 C St., Suite 200, Anchorage 99503-5929, (907) 269-8400. TDD (907) 269-8411. Fax (907) 269-8901. Open 11 A.M. to 5 P.M. weekdays.

Internet access is now available for cabin information. For national forest cabins: www.nrrc.com. For state park cabins: www. dnr.state.ak.us/parks/parks.htm. This site includes photos, descriptions of the cabins and an availability calendar.

Cache

Pronounced "cash," this small storage unit is built to be inaccessible to marauding animals. A cache tradionally is a miniature log cabin mounted on stilts. It is reached by a ladder that bears, dogs, foxes and other hungry or curious animals can't climb. Extra precautions include wrapping tin around the poles to prevent climbing by clawed animals and extending the floor a few feet in all directions from the top of the poles to discourage those clever enough to get that high.

Squirrels are the most notorious of Alaska's cache-crashing critters. To be truly animal-proof, a cache should be built in a clearing well beyond the

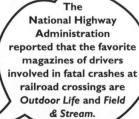

The **National Highway Administration** reported that the favorite magazines of drivers involved in fatal crashes at railroad crossings are *Outdoor Life* and *Field & Stream.*

30-foot leaping distance a squirrel can manage from a treetop.

Bush residents use the cache as a primitive food freezer for game and fish in winter. A cache may also store furs from a trapline, extra fuel and bedding. Size is determined by need. Sometimes a cache will be built between three or four straight trees growing close together.

Like "mush" *(marché)*, the word "cache" is borrowed from French-Canadian voyageurs.

Camping (SEE ALSO BOATING; CABINS; CHILKOOT TRAIL; HIKING; NATIONAL FORESTS; NATIONAL PARKS, PRESERVES AND MONUMENTS; NATIONAL WILDLIFE REFUGES; AND STATE PARK SYSTEM)

Numerous public and privately operated campgrounds are found along Alaska's highways. Electrical hookups and dump stations are scarce. The dump station at Russian River campground is available for Chugach National Forest visitors. Alaska's backcountry offers virtually limitless possibilities for wilderness camping. Get permission before camping on private land. If the

(Continued on page 39)

Calendar of Annual Events 2001

January
Anchorage—Anchorage Folk Festival; Great Alaska Beer Festival.
Big Lake—Klondike 300 Sled Dog Derby; Snowmachine racing.
Chistochina—Copper Basin 300.
Girdwood—Nastar Ski Races, Alyeska; Gallery Walk.
Glennallen—Copper Basin 300 Sled Dog Race.
Haines—Alcan 200 Road Rally.
Juneau—Alascom Ski Challenge; Rainier Downhill Challenge Cup; State Legislature convenes.
Kenai—Tustumena 200 Sled Dog Race.
Ketchikan—Winter Festival.
Kodiak—Russian Christmas and Starring; Russian New Year and Masquerade Ball.
Nome—Iditaswim.
Seward—Polar Bear Jump Festival.
Sitka—Alaska Airlines Basketball Tournament; American Legion Basketball Tournament; Northwest Coast Arts Symposium; Russian Christmas and Starring.
Soldotna—KPHA New Year's Tournament; Tustumena 200 Sled Dog Race; Ty-Clark Memorial Races (sled dog); Winter Games.
Unalaska—Qawalangin Tribe Annual Masquerade Ball; Russian Orthodox Christmas Eve and Starring; Russian New Year's Eve.
Valdez—Quest for Gold Sled Dog Race.
Willow—Winter Carnival.

February
Anchorage—Fur Rendezvous; World Championship Sled Dog Races.
Anchor Point—Snow Rondi Fest.
Big Lake—Iditasport.
Chistochina—Fun Days.
Cordova—Iceworm Festival.
Dillingham—Nushagak Classic Sled Dog Race.
Fairbanks—Iron Dog Gold Rush Classic; Yukon Quest International Sled Dog Race.
Homer—Winter Carnival.
Juneau—Gold Medal Basketball Tournament.
Kenai—Peninsula Winter Games; Quilt Artist Show.
Ketchikan—Festival of the North; Taste of Ketchikan; Valentine Card Show.
Nenana—Tour de Minto Sled Dog Race.
Nome—Iron Dog Gold Rush Classic Snow Machine Race.
Seldovia—Winter Carnival. *(Continued)*

More Calendar of Annual Events

February (continued)

Skagway—Trail of 98 Sled Dog Race.

Soldotna—Hockey Championships; Peninsula Winter Games; Ski Joring; Sled Dog Races; Village Fair.

Tok—Trek Over the Top.

Valdez—Alaskan Local Snowboarding Championship.

Wasilla—Iditarod Days; Iditarod Races; Iron Dog Gold Rush Classic.

Wrangell—Tent City Festival.

March

Anchorage—Iditarod Trail Sled Dog Race; International Ice Carving Competition; Tour of Anchorage Cross-Country Ski Race.

Big Lake—Iditarod Trail Sled Dog Race.

Chatanika—Chatanika Days.

Dillingham—Beaver Round Up; Western Alaska Sled Dog Classic.

Fairbanks—Festival of Native Arts; North American Sled Dog Championships; Winter Carnival; World Ice Art Championship.

Girdwood—Alaska Extreme Skiing Snowboard Trials.

Homer—Kachemak Bay Marathon Ski; Snomads' Poker Run; Winter King Salmon Tournament.

Juneau—Gold Medal Men's Basketball Tournament; Rainier Downhill Challenge Cup; Sourdough Pro/Am Ski Race; Southeast Championships.

Kenai—Alaska Native Art Show; Central Peninsula Writers' Night.

Kodiak—Comfish Alaska; Pillar Mountain Golf Classic.

Nenana—Nenana Ice Classic Tripod Weekend.

Nome—Bering Sea Ice Golf Classic; Businessmen's Dog Team Race; Dart Tournament; Iditarod Awards Banquet; Iditarod Basketball Tournament; Iditarod Sled Dog Race; Miners and Mushers Ball; Nome-Council Sled Dog Race; Nome-Golovin Snowmachine Race.

North Pole—Winter Carnival.

Palmer—Lions Club Gun Show.

Skagway—Buckwheat Ski Classic; Windfest.

Soldotna—Hockey Tournament; Lions Club Fish Fry and Auction; St. Patrick's Day Celebration.

Tok—Race of Champions.

Trapper Creek—Cabin Fever Reliever.

Unalaska—Soup-Off; Tanner Round Up Community Festival.

Valdez—Eureka to Valdez Snow Machine Run; Frosty Fever WinterFest; Mayor's Cup Snowmachine Race; Mountain Man Snowmachine Hill Climb; Snowman Festival; Snow Sculpting Event; Trek Over the Top.

Wasilla—Iditarod Trail Sled Dog Race.

April

Anchorage—Native Youth Olympics.

Barrow—Spring Festival.

Bethel—Camai Dance Festival.

Fairbanks—Arctic Man Ski and Snow-Go Classic.

Girdwood—Alyeska Spring Carnival.

Juneau—Alaska Folk Festival; Eaglecrest Spring Carnival; Earth Day Games.

Kenai—Alaska Native Art Show.

Kodiak—Whale Fest; Old Harbor Whaling Festival.

Nome—Cannonball Run.

Seward—Gray Whale Watch Weekends.

Sitka—Blessing of the Fleet; Gathering of the People.

Skagway—Mini-folk Festival; White Pass Rotary Plow Event.

Soldotna—Hockey Championships.

Tok—Tok Trot.

Unalaska—Archaeology Week.

Valdez—King and Queen of the Hill Snowboard Competition; World Extreme Ski Championships.

Wrangell—Garnet Festival.

May

Anchorage—Irish Music Festival; Saturday Market begins.   *(Continued)*

More Calendar of Annual Events

Cold Bay—Silver Salmon Derby.
Cordova—Copper River Delta Shorebird Festival; First Fish Festival.
Delta Junction—Buffalo Wallow Square Dance Festival.
Haines—Great Alaska Craftbeer and Homebrew Festival; Koot to Kat Skat Biathlon; King Salmon Derby.
Homer—Crafts Fair; Halibut Derby begins; Kachemak Bay Wooden Boat Festival; Shorebird Festival.
Juneau—Bike Races; Blessing of the Fleet; Foot Races; Jazz and Classics Festival; May Day Mud Run.
Ketchikan—Celebration of the Sea; King Salmon Derby.
Kodiak—Chad Ogden Ultramarathon; Crab Festival; Great Alaska Rubber Duck Race; International Migratory Bird Day; Old Harbor Whaling Festival.
Nome—Polar Bear Memorial Day Swim in the Bering Sea; Stroke and Croak Triathlon.
Palmer—Operation Clean Sweep.
Petersburg—Little Norway Festival; Salmon Derby.
Seward—Exit Glacier 5K and 10K Runs.
Sitka—Julie Hughes Triathlon; Salmon Derby.
Soldotna—Lions Club Gun Show; State Parks Annual Kenai River Clean Up.
Talkeetna—Miners' Day Festival.
Unalaska—Clean Up Week; Ironman Triathlon; Preservation Week/Memorial.
Valdez—Halibut Derby.
Wrangell—King Salmon Derby.

June

Anchorage—AWAIC Summer Solstice Festival; Juneteenth; Mayor's Midnight Sun Marathon; Semi-Pro Baseball; Ship Creek Salmon Derby; The Taste of Anchorage; Three Barons Fair.
Anchor Point—All-American Kids Fishing Derby.
Barrow—Nalukataq Whaling Festival.
Big Lake—Regatta Water Festival.

Cordova—Alaska Salmon Runs; Salmon and Seafood Festival.
Dillingham—Nushagak King Derby.
Eagle River—Highland Games.
Fairbanks—Midnight Sun Run; Midnight Sun Baseball Game; Summer Fine Arts Camp; Summer Solstice Celebration; Yukon 800 Boat Race.
Girdwood—Challenge Alaska Glacier Dash.
Haines—Bike Relay; King Salmon Derby; Summer Solstice Celebration.
Homer—Aalska Run for Women; Halibut Derby; 10K Spit Run.
Hyder/Stewart—International Rodeo.
Juneau—Bike, Foot, and Skating Races; Gold Rush Days.
Kenai—Kenai River Festival.
Ketchikan—King Salmon Derby.
Kodiak—All American Soap Box Derby; Fil-Am Heritage Week.
Moose Pass—Summer Solstice Festival.
Nenana—Beaver Sports Bike Race; Ride for Sobriety; River Daze.
Nikiski—Family Fun in the Midnight Sun.
Nome—Midnight Sun Festival; River Raft Race.
North Pole—Farmers' Market; Christmas in June Parade.
Palmer—Colony Days.
Sitka—Salmon Derby; Summer Music Festival; Writers' Symposium.
Skagway—International Softball Tournament.
Soldotna—Chip Away 9-Hole Tourney; Pop Drop; Quilting on the Kenai.
Unalaska—Archaeological Dig program begins; Dutch Harbor Remembrance Day; Halibut Derby.
Valdez—Halibut Derby; Pink Salmon Derby; Prince William Sound Theatre Conference.

July

(Fourth of July celebrations take place in most towns and villages.)
Delta Junction—Buffalo *(Continued)*

More Calendar of Annual Events

July (continued)

Barbeque; Deltana Fair.

Dillingham—Nushagak King Derby.

Eagle River—Bear Paw Festival.

Fairbanks—Golden Days; Summer Arts Festival; Summer Fine Arts Camp; World Eskimo-Indian Olympics.

Girdwood—Forest Faire.

Glennallen—Brown Bear Arts Festival; Ahtna Arts and Crafts Fair.

Haines—Chilkoot Chum Run.

Homer—American Legion Carnival; Concert on the Lawn; Halibut Derby; Summer Street Fair.

Kenai—Photographers' Guild Summer Exhibition; Run for Women.

Kodiak—Bear Country Music Festival; Bear-foot in the Park Quintathlon.

Naknek—Fishtival.

Nome—Anvil Mountain Run.

Palmer—Palmer Pride Picnic.

Petersburg—Canned Salmon Classic.

Seldovia—Salmon Shuffle.

Seward—Halibut Tournament; Mount Marathon Race; Softball Tournaments.

Skagway—Ducky Derby; Soapy Smith's Wake; International Softball Tournament.

Soldotna—Dog Show; Funny River Festival; Golf Tournament; Progress Days.

Sterling—Moose River Raft Race.

Sutton—Old Timers' Picnic.

Talkeetna—Moose Dropping Festival.

Unalaska—Mount Ballyhoo Run.

Valdez—Halibut Derby; Silver Salmon Derby (July to September).

Wasilla—Water Festival.

Willow—Volleyball Challenge.

August

Anchor Point—Salmon Derby.

Dillingham—No-See-Ums Festival.

Fairbanks—Tanana Valley State Fair.

Haines—Bald Eagle Music Festival; Southeast Alaska State Fair; Sam Donajkowski Memorial Triathlon.

Homer—Silver Salmon Derby.

Houston—Founders' Day.

Juneau—Golden North Salmon Derby.

Kenai—Photographers' Guild Summer Exhibition; Women's Resource and Crisis Centers' Run for Women.

Ketchikan—Blueberry Arts Festival; Salmon Derby.

Kodiak—Pilgrimage to St. Herman's Monk's Lagoon; Pink Salmon Jamboree.

Ninilchik—Kenai Peninsula State Fair.

Palmer—Alaska State Fair.

Seward—Silver Salmon Derby.

Skagway—Flower and Garden Show.

Soldotna—Silver Salmon Derby; State Fair; 10K Run for Women.

Talkeetna—Bluegrass Festival.

Tok—Mainstreet Alaska Sourdough Potlatch.

Unalaska—Labor Day Carnival; Tundra Golf Classic; Summer Bay Classic Bike/Run; Unangan Culture Camp.

Valdez—Sourdocees Silver Salmon Shindig; Gold Rush Days.

September

Anchorage—Make It Alaskan Festival.

Eagle River—Outrageous Dinner and Auction.

Fairbanks—Equinox Marathon.

Homer—End of Halibut Derby; Halibut Derby Banquet.

Kenai—Lion's Rubber Ducky Race; Silver Salmon Derby.

Ketchikan—Great Alaskan Sportfishing Championship; Salmon Derby.

Kodiak—Silver Salmon Derby; State Fair and Rodeo.

Nome—Great Bathtub Race; Rubber Duck Race.

Seward—Fall Classic 5K and 10K Run.

Sitka—Running of the Boots; Mudball Classic Softball Tournament.

Skagway—Klondike Trail of '98 Relay.

Soldotna—Golf Tournaments.

Unalaska—Blueberry Bash; Island Half Marathon; World *(Continued)*

More Calendar of Annual Events

September (continued)
Record Halibut Derby ends.
Valdez—Silver Salmon Derby; Oktoberfest.

October
Anchorage—Quyana Alaska.
Homer—Octoberfest; Taste of Homer.
Kenai—Chamber of Commerce Wine Tasting.
Kodiak—Oktoberfest.
Petersburg—October ArtsFest Celebration.
Sitka—Alaska Day Festival.
Soldotna—Pie Auction.

November
Anchorage—Great Alaska Shootout Basketball Tournament (includes men's and women's teams); Tree Lighting Ceremony.
Fairbanks—Athabascan Old-Time Fiddling Festival; Top of the World Classic (basketball); beginning of Winter Solstice Celebration.
Haines—Bald Eagle Festival.
Juneau—Public Market Arts and Crafts.
Kenai—Christmas Comes to Kenai and City of Lights Parade; Potters' Guild Exhibit.
Ketchikan—Festival of Lights; Singing in the Rain Festival; Winter Arts Faire.
Petersburg—Festival of Lights.
Sitka—Whale Fest.

Soldotna—Craft Bazaars; Tech Fair.
Unalaska—Arts and Crafts Fair; Chamber of Commerce Christmas Raffle.

December
Anchorage—Swedish Christmas Celebration.
Barrow—Christmas Festival.
Cordova—Community Christmas Tree Lighting Ceremony; Bidarki Christmas Bazaar.
Dillingham—Christmas Bazaar.
Eagle River—Community Tree Lighting; Merry Merchants Munch.
Fairbanks—Candle Lighting Service; Winter Solstice Celebration.
Homer—"The Nutcracker."
Juneau—Gallery Walk.
Ketchikan—Festival of Lights Holiday Ball; Winter Art Walk.
Kodiak—Harbor Stars Boat Parade.
Nome—Firemen's Carnival.
North Pole—Candle Lighting Ceremony.
Palmer—Colony Christmas.
Petersburg—Julebukking.
Sitka—Christmas Boat Parade.
Soldotna—Tree Lighting Ceremony.
Talkeetna—Bachelor Society Ball and Wilderness Women Contest; Christmas Lighting.
Wrangell—Festival of Lights and Christmas Tree Lighting. ✻

(Continued from page 35)
land is publicly owned, it's worthwhile to contact the managing agency for regulations and hiking/camping conditions.

The U.S. Forest Service maintains 26 campgrounds in the Tongass and Chugach National Forests, most with tent and trailer sites and minimum facilities. Most campgrounds are available on a first-come, first-served basis. Stays are limited to 14 days except in Russian River camp-ground where the limit is three days during the salmon run. Campground fees are $8 to $16 per night depending upon facilities which can include firegrates, pit toilets, garbage pickup, picnic tables and water. Most campgrounds are open from Memorial Day through Labor Day, weather permitting.

For further information about camping in the Chugach National Forest, contact the Forest Service Information Center, 101 Egan Drive, Juneau 99801; (907) 586-8751.

The state's Division of Forestry requires permits for open burning in most areas of interior and southcentral Alaska. Permits

Wood-Tikchik State Park's vast wilderness attracts kayakers, backpackers and anglers. From Alaska's *Accessible Wilderness* by Bill Sherwonit.

are not required if fires are in approved burn barrels or are used for signaling.

The National Park Service at Denali National Park and Preserve offers one walk-in campground, three campgrounds accessible by private vehicles and three campgrounds accessible only by shuttle bus.

Denali National Park has a reservation system for three campgrounds and all shuttle bus transportation services in the park. Reservations for 75 percent of the shuttle bus seats and all campsites in Riley Creek, Savage River and Teklanika River Campgrounds can be made by calling (907) 272-7275 or (800) 622-7275. The hours of operation for the reservation system are 8 A.M.–6 P.M. Monday through Friday, and 9 A.M.–5 P.M. Saturday and Sunday (Alaska time). The remaining bus seats and campsites for Sanctuary and Igloo Creek can be reserved in person up to two weeks in advance at the

Denali Visitor Center. Reservation requests can also be faxed until Sept. 1 to (907) 264-4684 or mailed to: Denali Park Resorts, Visitor Transportation System, 241 W. Ship Creek Ave., Anchorage 99501. Phone reservations can be made every day up to the day before travel. Faxes must be received two days before the date of travel. Reservations that are mailed in must be received 30 days prior to departure.

The shuttle bus fee ranges from $12.50 (to Toklat) to $31 (to Kantishna). Payment can be made by MasterCard, VISA or American Express, and up to eight tickets may be reserved at a time.

Reservations for most shuttle bus seats and campsites in all campgrounds are available in advance by phone. The remaining bus seats and campsites will be available for reservation in person, up to two days in advance.

Situated near the park entrance and open year-round are Riley Creek, for tents and trailers, and Morino, for walk-in tent

A Denali Park ranger reported leading a hike to the top of a small mountain in an area where there were no trails. An apprehensive tourist asked, "If there are no trails, how will we know when we get to the top?"

campers. The other campgrounds are open between May and September, depending on weather. Brochures may be obtained from Denali National Park and Preserve, P.O. Box 9, Denali Park 99755. Reservations should be made well in advance by contacting Denali National Park at (907) 683-2215. The toll-free out-of-state number for bus and campground reservations is (800) 622-7275.

Glacier Bay and Katmai National Parks each offer one campground for walk-in campers; Katmai requires reservations, which may be obtained in advance by calling (800) 365-2267. Backcountry camping is permitted in Denali, Glacier Bay, Katmai and Klondike Gold Rush National Parks, as well as other national parks and monuments.

Alaska State Parks (3601 C St., Suite 200, Anchorage 99503) maintains the most extensive system of roadside campgrounds and waysides in Alaska. All are available on a first-come, first-served basis. Fees are charged and a yearly pass is offered. Call (907) 269-8400, 11 A.M.–5 P.M. Monday through Friday, or visit the Web site at www.dnr.state.ak.us/parks.

U.S. Fish and Wildlife Service (State Office, 1011 E. Tudor, Anchorage 99503) has several wildlife refuges open to campers, although most are not accessible by highway. The Kenai National Wildlife Refuge (P.O. Box 2139, Soldotna 99669) has several campgrounds accessible from the Sterling Highway linking Homer and Anchorage.

The Bureau of Land Management (222 W. Seventh Ave., No. 13, Anchorage 99513) maintains 11 campgrounds in interior Alaska. In 1994, BLM opened its first fully developed campground on the Dalton Highway at Mile 180 (5 miles north of Coldfoot). Fees vary by location. Brochures describing BLM campgrounds are available.

Looking Back

1941

Only 75,000 residents lived in all of the Alaska Territory, while 100 airfields— all unpaved—served about 200 airplanes.

The **Alaska Public Lands Information Centers** provide information on all state and federal campgrounds in Alaska, along with state and national park passes and details on wilderness camping. Visit or contact one of the following centers: 605 W. Fourth Ave., Anchorage 99501, (907) 271-2737; P.O. Box 359, Tok 99780, (907) 883-5677; 250 Cushman, Suite 1A, Fairbanks 99701, (907) 451-7352; 50 Main St., Ketchikan 99501, (907) 228-6220.

For a recording of state parks area conditions, call (907) 762-2278. Web site: www.nps.gov/aplic.

Since the late 1950s, the Forest Service has charged fees for using campgrounds. Some campgrounds are now "fee demo projects," and at least 80 percent of the money collected is returned to the administering unit for maintenance and improvements at the site. Pack Creek Bear Viewing Area charges fees from early June through mid-September. Begich–Boggs Visitors Center charges no admission, but will charge for viewing the movie *Voices from the Ice*.

Private Campgrounds. For information, contact the Alaska Campground Owners Association, P.O. Box 84884, Fairbanks 99708; (907) 883-5877.

Chambers of Commerce (SEE ALSO CONVENTION AND VISITORS BUREAUS AND INFORMATION CENTERS)

Alaska State Chamber, 217 Second St., Suite 201, Juneau 99801; (907) 586-2323, Fax (907) 463-5515. P.O. Box 91896, Anchorage 99501; (907) 278-2722, Fax (907) 278-6643. asccjuno@ptialaska.net or www.alaskachamber.com

Anchor Point Chamber, P.O. Box 610, Anchor Point 99556; (907) 235-2600.

Anchorage Chamber, 441 W. Fifth Ave., Suite 300, Anchorage 99501-2309;

(907) 272-2401, Fax (907) 272-4117. info@anchoragechamber.org or www.anchoragechamber.org

Barrow, City of, P.O. Box 629, Barrow 99723; (907) 852-5211.

Bethel Chamber, P.O. Box 329, Bethel 99559; (907) 543-2911. home.gci.net/~chamber1/bethel

Big Lake Chamber, P.O. Box 520067, Big Lake 99652; (907) 892-6109.

Chugiak–Eagle River Chamber, P.O. Box 770-353, Eagle River 99577; (907) 694-4702, Fax (907) 696-0084. info@cer.org or www.cer.org

Copper Valley (Greater) Chamber, P.O. Box 469, Glennallen 99588; (907) 822-5555, Fax (907) 822-3010.

Cordova Chamber, P.O. Box 99, Cordova 99574; (907) 424-7260, Fax (907) 424-7259. cchamber@ptialaska.net or www.ptialaska.net/~cchamber.

Delta Junction Chamber, P.O. Box 987, Delta Junction 99737; (907) 895-5068, Fax (907) 895-5141. deltacc@wildak.net

Dillingham Chamber, P.O. Box 348, Dillingham 99576; (907) 842-5115. dlgchmbr@nushtel.com or www.nushtel.com/~dlgchmber

Fairbanks (Greater) Chamber, 250 Cushman, Suite 20, Fairbanks 99701; (907) 452-1105.

Haines Chamber, P.O. Box 1449, Haines 99827; (907) 766-2202, Fax (907) 766-2271. chamber@seaknet.alaska.edu or www.haineschamber.org

Healy Chamber, P.O. Box 437, Healy 99743-0437; (907) 683-4636.

Homer Chamber, P.O. Box 541, Homer 99603; (907) 235-7740 or (907) 235-5300, Fax (907) 235-6557. homer@xyz.net or www.homeralaska.org

Juneau Chamber, 3100 Channel Drive, Suite 300, Juneau 99801; (907)463-3488, Fax (907) 463-3489.

Kenai Chamber, 402 Overland, Kenai 99611; (907) 283-7989, Fax (907) 283-7183. kencc@ptialaska.net or www.kenaichamber.org

Ketchikan Chamber, P.O. Box 5759, Ketchikan 99901; (907) 225-3184, Fax (907) 225-3187. kchamber@ktn.net or www.ketchikanchamber.com

Kodiak Area Chamber, P.O. Box 1485, Kodiak 99615; (907) 486-5557, Fax (907) 486-7605. chamber@kodiak.org or www.kodiak.org

Kotzebue, City of, P.O. Box 46, Kotzebue 99752; (907) 442-3401.

Nenana, City of, P.O. Box 70, Nenana 99760; (907) 832-5441.

Ninilchik Chamber, P.O. Box 39164, Ninilchik 99639; (907) 567-3571, Fax (907) 567-1041.

Nome Chamber, P.O. Box 240, Nome 99762; (907) 443-3879, Fax (907) 443-2742.

North Peninsula Chamber, P.O. Box 8053, Nikiski 99635; (907) 776-8369.

North Pole Community Chamber, P.O. Box 55071, North Pole 99705; (907) 488-2242.

Palmer Chamber, P.O. Box 45, Palmer 99645; (907) 745-2880. palmerchambr@akcache.com or www.palmerchamber.org

Petersburg Chamber, P.O. Box 649, Petersburg 99833; (907) 772-3646.

Prince of Wales Chamber, P.O. Box 497, Craig 99921; (907) 826-3870, Fax (907) 826-5467. powcc@ptialaska.net or www.princeofwalescoc.org

Seldovia Chamber, Drawer F-A, Seldovia 99663; (907) 234-7612.

Seward Chamber, P.O. Box 749, Seward 99664; (907) 224-8051 or (907) 224-5353. chamber@seward.net or www.seward.net/chamber

Sitka Chamber, P.O. Box 638, Sitka 99835; (907) 747-8604.

Skagway Chamber, P.O. Box 194, Skagway 99840; (907) 983-1898.

Soldotna Chamber, 44790 Sterling Highway, Soldotna 99669; (907) 262-9814, Fax (907) 262-3566. info@soldotnachamber.com

Talkeetna Chamber, P.O. Box 334, Talkeetna 99676; (907) 733-2330.

Tok Chamber, P.O. Box 389, Tok 99780; (907) 883-5887, Fax (907) 883-3682.

Unalaska/Port of Dutch Harbor Chamber, P.O. Box 920833, Dutch Harbor 99692; (907) 581-4242. veda@arctic.net

Valdez Chamber, P.O. Box 512, Valdez 99686; (907) 835-2330.

Wasilla Chamber, 1801 Parks Highway, Wasilla 99687; (907) 376-1299, Fax (907) 376-1299. City Hall Fax (907) 373-0788. chamber@wasilla.net

Willow Chamber, P.O. Box 0183, Willow 99688-0183; (907) 495-5858. info@willowchamber.org or www.willowchamber.org

Wrangell Chamber, P.O. Box 49, Wrangell 99929; (907) 874-3901. chamber@seatac.net or www.wrangell.com

Cheechako
Pronounced chee-CHA-ko, or chee-CHA-ker by some old-time Alaskans, the word means tenderfoot or greenhorn. According to *The Chinook Jargon,* a 1909 dictionary of the old trading language used by traders from the Hudson's Bay Company in the early 1800s, the word "cheechako" comes from combining the Chinook Indian word *chee,* meaning "new, fresh or just now," with the Nootka Indian word *chako,* which means "to come, to approach or to become."

Chilkat Blanket
Dramatic, bilaterally symmetrical patterns, usually in black, white, yellow and blue, adorn these heavily fringed ceremonial blankets.

The origin of the Chilkat dancing blanket is Tsimshian. Knowledge of the weaving techniques apparently diffused north to the Tlingit, where blanket-making reached its highest form among the Chilkat group. Visiting traders coined the blanket's name during the late 19th century.

Time, technical skill and inherited privileges were required to weave Chilkat blankets and other ceremonial garments. High-ranking men and women wore the blankets as cloaks. Portions of worn blankets, or smaller weavings, were made into dance aprons and tunics.

Yarn for Chilkat dancing blankets was spun primarily from the wool of the mountain goat. Designs woven into Chilkat blankets are geometric totemic shapes that can be reproduced by the method known as twining. (Early blankets are unadorned or display geometric patterns lacking

Woman in Chilkat blanket, ca. 1900. From *The Alaska Heritage Seafood Cookbook* by Ann Chandonnet.

curvilinear elements.) Often totemic crests on painted house posts and the designs woven into garments were quite similar. Female weavers reused pattern boards of wood painted with a design by men.

A few weavers are producing Chilkat blankets and the related Raven's Tail robes today.

Chilkoot Trail
(SEE ALSO GOLD *AND* SKAGWAY) The Chilkoot Trail, which spans 33 miles from Dyea, just north of Skagway, over Chilkoot Pass to Lake Bennett, British Columbia, was one of the established routes taken by prospectors to Yukon District goldfields during the Klondike gold rush of 1897–98. Thousands of stampeders climbed the tortuous trail over Chilkoot Pass that winter. Those who reached Lake Bennett built boats to float down the Yukon River to Dawson City.

Today the steep and rocky Chilkoot Trail is part of Klondike Gold Rush National Historical Park and is climbed each year by approximately 3,000 backpackers. The Chilkoot Trail begins about 9 miles from Skagway on Dyea Road. There are a dozen campgrounds along the trail and ranger stations on both the Alaska and British Columbia portions of the trail. The trail crosses the international border at 3,739-foot Chilkoot Pass, 16.5 miles from the trailhead. Highlights of the area include Slide Cemetery near the remains of the town of Dyea; the Golden Stairs, a 45-degree climb to the summit; and numerous relics left by prospectors still visible along the trail. The trail ends at Bennett, 8 miles from the nearest roadway. For more information, contact Klondike Gold Rush National Historical Park, P.O. Box 517, Skagway 99840.

Chill Factor (SEE ALSO HYPOTHERMIA)

The wind's chill factor can lower the effective temperature by many degrees. While Alaska's regions of lowest temperatures also generally have little wind, activities such as riding a snowmobile or even walking can produce the same effect on exposed skin.

The wind's chill factor, when severe, can lead to frostnip (the body's early-warning signal of potential damage from cold—a "nipping" feeling in the extremities), frostbite (formation of small ice crystals in the body tissues) or hypothermia (dangerous lowering of the body's core temperature). Other factors that combine with wind chill and bring on these potentially damaging or fatal effects are exposure to wetness, exhaustion and lack of adequate clothing.

Calculating Wind Chill

Temperature (Fahrenheit)	Wind Speed (mph)			
	10	20	30	45
40	28	18	13	10
30	16	4	−2	−6
20	4	−10	−18	−22
10	−9	−25	−33	−38
0	−21	−39	−48	−54
−10	−33	−53	−63	−70
−20	−46	−67	−79	−85
−30	−58	−82	−94	−102
−40	−70	−96	−109	−117

Chitons

Chitons are oval-shaped marine mollusks with shells made up of eight overlapping plates. The gumboot and the Chinese slipper chiton are favorite Alaska edible delicacies. The gumboot, named for the tough, leathery, reddish brown covering that hides its plates, is the largest chiton in the world. It is prized as traditional food by southeastern Alaska Natives.

Climate (SEE ALSO REGIONS OF ALASKA AND WINDS)

Alaska's climate zones are maritime, transition, continental and arctic. With the exception of the transition zone along western Alaska, the zones are divided by mountain ranges that form barriers to shallow air masses and modify those deep enough to cross the ranges. The Brooks Range inhibits southward movement of air from the Arctic Ocean, thus separating the arctic climate zone from the Interior. The Chugach, Wrangell, Aleutian and Alaska mountain ranges often limit northward air movement and dry the air before it reaches the Interior's continental zone.

Other meteorologic and oceanographic factors affecting Alaska's climate zones are air temperature, water temperature, cloud coverage, and wind and air pressure. The amount of moisture that air can hold in a gaseous state is highly dependent on its temperature. Warm air can contain more water vapor than cold air. Therefore precipitation as rain or snow or in other forms is likely to be heavier from warm than from cold air. Water temperatures change more slowly and much less than land temperatures. Coastal area temperatures vary less than those farther inland.

Climate Zones. The maritime climate zone includes Southeast, the Northern Gulf Coast and the Aleutian Chain. Temperatures are mild—relatively warm in the winter and cool in summer. Precipitation ranges from 50 to 200 inches annually along the coast and up to 400 inches on mountain slopes. Storms are frequently from the west and southwest, resulting in strong winds along the Aleutian Islands and the Alaska Peninsula. Amchitka Island's weather station has recorded some of the windiest weather in the state, followed by Cold Bay. Frequent storms with accompanying high winds account for rough seas and occasional waves to 50 feet in the Gulf of Alaska, particularly in fall and winter.

The transition zone may be thought of as two separate zones. One is the area between the coastal mountains and the Alaska Range, which includes Anchorage and the Matanuska Valley. Summer temperatures are higher than those of the maritime climate zone, with colder winter temperatures and less precipitation. Temperatures however are not as extreme as in the continental zone.

Another transition zone includes the west coast from Bristol Bay to Point Hope. This area has cool summer temperatures that are somewhat colder than those of the maritime zone, and cold winter temperatures similar to the continental zone. Cold winter temperatures are partly due to the sea ice in the Chukchi and Bering Seas.

The continental climate zone covers the majority of Alaska except the coastal fringes and the Arctic Slope. It has extreme temperatures and low precipitation. There are fewer clouds in the continental zone than elsewhere, so there is more warming by the sun during the long days of summer and more cooling during the long nights of winter. Precipitation is light because air masses affecting the area lose most of their moisture crossing the mountains to the south.

The Arctic north of the Brooks Range has cold winters, cool summers and desertlike precipitation. Prevailing winds are from the northeast off the arctic ice pack, which never moves far offshore. Summers are generally cloudy and winters are clear and cold. The cold air allows little precipitation and inhibits evaporation.

Because continuous permafrost prevents the percolation of water into the soil, the area is generally marshy with numerous lakes. (*See also* Permafrost)

The chart on pages 46–47 shows normal average monthly temperatures and precipitation for 14 communities in Alaska. Included are annual temperatures, precipitation and mean seasonal snowfall. The chart is based on data from NOAA and the Alaska state climatologist. You may also refer to the Web site of the National Weather Service Forcast Office in Anchorage: alaska.net/~nwsfoanc.

Climate Records. Highest temperature: 100°F, at Fort Yukon, June 27, 1915.

Lowest temperature: −80°F, at Prospect Creek Camp, Jan. 23, 1971.

Most precipitation in one year: 332.29 inches, at MacLeod Harbor (Montague Island), 1976.

Most monthly precipitation: 70.99 inches at MacLeod Harbor, November 1976.

Most precipitation in 24 hours: 15.2 inches, in Angoon, Oct. 12, 1982.

Least precipitation in a year: 1.61 inches, at Barrow, 1935.

Most snowfall in a season: 974.5 inches, at Thompson Pass, 1952–53.

Most monthly snowfall: 297.9 inches, at Thompson Pass, February 1953.

Most snowfall in 24 hours: 62 inches, at Thompson Pass, December 1955.

Least snowfall in a season: 3 inches, at Barrow, 1935–36.

Highest recorded snow pack (also highest ever recorded in North America): 356 inches on Wolverine Glacier, Kenai Peninsula, after the winter of 1976–77.

Highest recorded wind speed: 139 mph, at Shemya Island, December 1959.

During an extreme winter cold snap, the Seward fire chief announced, "The fire department would like to just take appointments for fire calls in cold weather."

Average Temperatures (Fahrenheit) and Precipitation (Inches)

	ANCHORAGE	BARROW	BETHEL	COLD BAY	FAIRBANKS	HOMER	JUNEAU
January							
Temperature	14.9	−13.4	6.7	28.6	−10.1	22.7	24.2
Precipitation	0.80	0.20	0.81	2.71	0.55	2.23	3.98
February							
Temperature	18.7	−17.8	6.0	27.4	−3.6	24.7	28.4
Precipitation	0.86	0.18	0.71	2.30	0.41	1.78	3.66
March							
Temperature	25.7	−15.1	13.3	29.9	11.0	28.0	32.7
Precipitation	0.65	0.15	0.80	2.19	0.37	1.57	3.24
April							
Temperature	35.8	−2.2	23.6	33.3	30.7	35.4	39.7
Precipitation	0.63	0.20	0.65	1.90	0.28	1.27	2.83
May							
Temperature	46.6	19.3	39.9	39.6	48.6	42.8	47.0
Precipitation	0.63	0.16	0.83	2.40	0.57	1.07	3.46
June							
Temperature	54.4	34.0	50.5	45.7	59.8	49.3	53.0
Precipitation	1.02	0.36	1.29	2.13	1.29	1.00	3.02
July							
Temperature	58.4	39.3	55.0	50.5	62.5	53.4	56.0
Precipitation	1.96	0.87	2.18	2.50	1.84	1.63	4.09
August							
Temperature	56.3	37.9	52.9	51.5	56.8	53.3	55.0
Precipitation	2.31	0.97	3.65	3.71	1.82	2.56	5.10
September							
Temperature	48.4	30.5	45.2	47.7	46.5	47.6	49.4
Precipitation	2.51	0.64	2.58	4.06	1.02	2.96	6.25
October							
Temperature	36.6	13.5	29.4	39.6	25.1	37.5	42.2
Precipitation	1.86	0.51	1.48	4.45	0.81	3.41	7.64
November							
Temperature	21.2	−1.7	16.8	34.4	2.7	28.6	33.0
Precipitation	1.08	0.27	0.98	4.33	0.67	2.74	5.13
December							
Temperature	16.3	−11.2	8.5	31.0	−6.5	24.3	27.1
Precipitation	1.06	0.17	0.95	3.16	0.73	2.71	4.48
Annual							
Temperature	35.9	9.4	29.0	38.3	26.9	37.4	40.6
Precipitation	15.37	4.67	16.90	35.84	10.37	24.93	52.86
Mean Seasonal Snowfall (inches)	69.0	28.0	47.0	62.0	68.0	58.0	100.0

KETCHIKAN	KING SALMON	KODIAK	MCGRATH	NOME	PETERSBURG	VALDEZ	
							January
33.9	14.9	29.9	−8.7	7.0	27.6	20.5	Temperature
14.01	1.11	9.52	0.81	0.88	9.31	5.63	Precipitation
							February
38.9	14.8	30.5	−2.6	3.9	31.1	24.1	Temperature
12.36	0.82	5.67	0.74	0.56	7.85	5.08	Precipitation
							March
38.9	22.4	32.9	10.2	8.6	34.7	29.2	Temperature
12.22	1.06	5.16	0.75	0.63	7.19	4.06	Precipitation
							April
42.8	30.2	37.5	26.5	17.6	40.4	37.1	Temperature
11.93	1.07	4.47	0.73	0.67	6.94	2.89	Precipitation
							May
48.6	42.4	43.5	44.5	35.6	47.2	45.2	Temperature
9.06	1.25	6.65	0.84	0.58	5.92	2.74	Precipitation
							June
54.0	50.0	49.6	55.3	45.9	53.0	51.8	Temperature
7.36	1.54	5.72	1.56	1.14	5.00	2.64	Precipitation
							July
58.0	54.7	54.4	58.7	51.5	55.8	54.9	Temperature
7.80	2.10	3.80	2.16	2.18	5.36	3.77	Precipitation
							August
58.4	53.9	55.2	54.3	50.2	55.0	53.5	Temperature
10.60	2.96	4.03	2.87	3.20	7.57	5.73	Precipitation
							September
53.6	47.2	50.0	44.2	42.5	50.3	47.2	Temperature
13.61	2.75	7.18	2.19	2.59	11.15	7.99	Precipitation
							October
46.3	32.4	40.7	24.7	28.0	43.5	38.1	Temperature
22.55	1.98	7.85	1.24	1.38	16.83	8.23	Precipitation
							November
39.0	22.0	34.4	4.4	15.9	35.6	27.4	Temperature
17.90	1.45	6.89	1.18	1.02	11.99	6.09	Precipitation
							December
35.4	15.9	30.8	−6.0	7.3	30.5	22.9	Temperature
15.82	1.19	7.39	1.12	0.82	10.66	6.65	Precipitation
							Annual
45.5	33.5	40.8	25.5	26.2	42.1	37.7	Temperature
155.22	19.28	74.33	16.18	15.64	105.77	61.50	Precipitation
							Mean Seasonal Snowfall (inches)
37.0	46.0	80.0	93.0	56.0	102.0	320.0	

Coal

Coal (*See also* Minerals and Mining) About half of the coal resource of the United States is believed to lie in Alaska. The demonstrated coal reserve base of the state is over 6 billion short tons, identified coal resources are about 160 billion short tons, and hypothetical and speculative resource estimates range upward to 6 trillion short tons. The regions containing the most coal are northwestern Alaska, Cook Inlet–Susitna Lowland and the Nenana Trend. Geologists estimate that perhaps 80 percent of Alaska's coal underlies the 23-million-acre National Petroleum Reserve on the North Slope. Although the majority of the coals are of bituminous and subbituminous ranks, anthracite coal does occur in the Bering River and Matanuska fields In addition to the vast resource base and wide distribution, the important selling points for Alaska coal are its extremely low sulfur content and access to the coast for shipping.

Exploration, technology and economics will ultimately determine the marketability of Alaska's coal. Large-scale exploration programs have been conducted in most of Alaska's coalfields by private industry and state and federal governments. In December 1997, Usibelli Coal Mine Inc. purchased the Wishbone Hill Mine near Palmer. Usibelli will put Wishbone into operation depending on market demand. The company continues to produce from the Nenana coalfield. The Arctic Slope Regional Corp. is working to develop its coal reserves in northwestern Alaska.

Alaska's production of coal in 1999 was 1.1 million short tons and came exclusively from the Usibelli Coal Mine near Healy. Of that amount, one-half was burned in interior Alaska power plants and the remainder was shipped to Korea.

Conk

Conk Alaskans apply this term to a type of bracket fungus. The platelike conks grow on dead trees. When dry and hard, conks are snapped off and  painted by artists or burned as mosquito repellent.

Constitution of Alaska

Constitution of Alaska One of the most remarkable achievements in the long battle for Alaska statehood was the creation of the state's constitution in the mid-1950s. Statehood supporters believed that a constitution would demonstrate Alaska's maturity and readiness for statehood, so in 1955 the territorial legislature appropriated $300,000 to convene a Constitutional Convention in Fairbanks.

For 73 days in 1955–56, a total of 55 elected delegates from all across the territory met in the new Student Union Building (now called Constitution Hall) on the University of Alaska campus. William A. Egan, a territorial legislator and former mayor of Valdez, who later became the first governor of the state of Alaska, was president of the convention. Under his leadership, the disparate group of Alaskans hammered out a document that is considered a model state constitution.

The National Municipal League calls the brief 14,000-word document drafted by the convention delegates "one of the best, if not the best, state constitutions ever written." By an overwhelming margin Alaskans approved the new constitution at the polls in 1956, paving the way for the creation of the 49th state in 1959.

A copy of the constitution is available on the Internet through the lieutenant governor's office at www.gov.state.ak.us/ltgov/akcon/table.html.

Continental Divide

Continental Divide (*See also* Mountains) The Continental Divide extends into Alaska. Unlike its portions in the Lower 48, which divide the country into east–west watersheds, the Continental Divide in Alaska trends through the Brooks Range, separating watersheds that drain north into the Arctic Ocean and west and south into the Bering Sea.

Alaska Science Nuggets says that geologists once regarded the Brooks Range as a structural extension of the Rocky Mountains. Recent thinking however assumes the range to be 35 million to 200 million years older than the Rockies. The Alaska Range is comparatively young—only about 5 million years old.

Convention and Visitors Bureaus and Information Centers

Anchorage Convention and Visitors Bureau, 524 W. Fourth Ave., Anchorage 99501-2122; (907) 276-4118, Fax (907) 278-5559. acvb@alaska.net or www.anchorage.net

Barrow, City of, P.O. Box 624, Barrow 99723; (907) 852-5211.

Begich-Boggs Visitors Center, P.O. Box 129, Girdwood 99587; (907) 783-2326.

Copper Valley (Greater) Visitor Information Center, P.O. Box 469, Glennallen 99588; (907) 822-5555.

Delta Junction Visitor Information Center, P.O. Box 987, Delta Junction 99737; (907) 895-5069.

Fairbanks Convention and Visitors Bureau, 550 First Ave., Fairbanks 99701; (800) 327-5774, Fax (907) 452-4190.

Gustavus Visitors Association, P.O. Box 167, Gustavus 99826; (907) 697-2285.

Haines Visitor Bureau, P.O. Box 530, Haines 99827; (907) 766-2234, Fax (907) 766-3155. hainesak@wwa.com or www.haines.ak.us.

Hyder Community Association, P.O. Box 149, Hyder 99923; (250) 636-2708, Fax (250) 636-2518.

Juneau Convention and Visitors Bureau, 369 S. Franklin St., Juneau 99801; (907) 586-1737, Fax (907) 586-1449. jcvb@ptialaska.net or www.travel juneau.com.

Kenai Visitors and Convention Bureau, 11471 Kenai Spur Highway, Kenai 99611; (907) 283-1991, Fax (907) 283-2230. kvcb@alaska.net

Ketchikan Visitors

Bureau, 131 Front St., Ketchikan 99901; (907) 225-6166, Fax (907) 225-4250. kvb@ktn.net or www.visit-ketchikan.com.

Kodiak Island Convention and Visitors Bureau, 100 Marine Way, Kodiak 99615; (907) 486-4782, Fax (907) 486-6545. kicvb@ptialaska.net or www.kodiak.org.

Kotzebue, City of, P.O. Box 46, Kotzebue 99752; (907) 442-3401.

Matanuska-Susitna Convention and Visitors Bureau, HC0-1, P.O. Box 6166 J21, Palmer 99645; (907) 746-5000, Fax (907) 746-2688. info@alaskavisit.com or www.alaskavisit.com

Nenana, City of, P.O. Box 70, Nenana 99760; (907) 832-5441.

Nome Convention and Visitors Bureau, P.O. Box 240, Nome 99762; (907) 443-6624, Fax (907) 443-5832. tourinfo@ci.nome.ak.us or www.nome alaska.org/.

Palmer Visitor Information Center, 723 S. Valley Road, Palmer 99654; (907) 745-2880.

Petersburg Visitor Information, P.O. Box 649, Petersburg 99833; (907) 772-4636, Fax (907) 772-3646. pcoc@alaska.net or www.petersburg.org.

Seward Visitor Information Cache, P.O. Box 749, Seward 99664; (907) 224-8051.

Sitka Convention and Visitors Bureau, P.O. Box 1226, Sitka 99835; (907) 747-5940, Fax (907) 747-3739. scvb@ptialaska. net or www.sitka.org.

Skagway Convention and Visitors Bureau, P.O. Box 1025, Skagway 99840; (907) 983-2854, Fax (907) 983-3854. infoskag@ptialaska.net or www. skagway.org.

Tok Main Street Visitor Center, P.O. Box 389, Tok 99685; (907) 883-5775. www.tokalaskainfo.com

Unalaska/Port of Dutch Harbor Convention and

Snowmobilers breaking trail for the Iditarod Trail Sled Dog Race discovered that if they wired a can of SPAM® on their exhaust manifold, they had a perfect hot meal in 50 miles!

Visitors Bureau, P.O. Box 545, Unalaska 99685; (907) 581-2612, Fax (907) 581-2613. updhcvb@arctic.net or www.arctic.net/~updhcvb

Valdez Convention and Visitors Bureau, P.O. Box 1603, Valdez 99686; (907) 835-4636 or (800) 770-5954, Fax (907) 835-4845. valdezak@alaska.net or www.valdezalaska.org

Whittier (City of) Visitors Center, P.O. Box 608, Whittier 99693; (907) 472-2327, Fax (907) 472-2404. cowadmin@ pobox.alaska.net

Cook, Captain James

James Cook (1728–79) went to sea as an apprenticed seaman, entering the British Royal Navy at the age of 27. He rose in rank by merit and was sent on two scientific expeditions—the first to the South Pacific (1768–71) and the second to Antarctica (1772–75).

In July 1776, the British Admiralty instructed Cook to proceed to the northwest coast of North America and attempt to find the Northwest Passage, a hoped-for sea link from the Pacific to the Atlantic.

The *Resolution* and *Discovery* sailed from Plymouth via Cape of Good Hope, New Zealand, Tahiti and the Hawaiian Islands, arriving at Nootka Sound on Vancouver Island on March 30, 1778. From then until Oct. 3, Cook cruised north and west to the Arctic Ocean, sketching the chief features of the coast, practically unknown to Europeans before Cook's historic voyage. He named many features of the coast, including Turnagain Arm, where land blocked his ships and they were forced to "turn again."

Failing to find the Northwest Passage, Cook left Unalaska in the Aleutians on Oct. 27. Cook returned to Hawaii, the Big Island, where he was killed by local residents on Feb. 14, 1779. His accounts of the voyage were published in 1784–85 in three volumes and a large atlas.

This pioneering navigator and explorer is commemorated in Alaska by Cook Inlet (named by Vancouver for his predecessor) and Mount Cook. A statue of Cook stands

Coppers, symbols of Native wealth and rank, were shield-shaped copper plaques weighing up to 40 pounds. From The Great Alaska Nature Factbook *by Susan Ewing*

in Anchorage, facing the Knik Arm of Cook Inlet.

Coppers (SEE ALSO POTLATCH)

Coppers *(tinnehs)* are beaten copper plaques that were important symbols of wealth among the Pacific Northwest Coast Natives.

Coppers are shaped something like a keyhole or a shield, are usually 2 feet to 3 feet long and weigh approximately 40 pounds. Coppers varied in value from tribe to tribe.

Early coppers were made of ore from the Copper River area, although western traders quickly made sheet copper available. Some scholars believe that Tlingit craftsmen shaped placer copper into the desired form themselves, while others maintain that coppers were forged by Athabascans. The impressive plaques were engraved or carved in relief with totemic crests.

The value of coppers increased as they were traded or sold, and their transfer implied that a potlatch would be given by the new owner. Coppers were given names, such as "Cloud," "Point of Island" or "Killer Whale," and were spoken of in respectful terms. They were thought of as powerful and their histories were as well known as those of the noblest families.

Coppers were often broken and destroyed during public displays and distribution of wealth. Some parts of the coppers were valued nearly as much as the whole.

To this day, certain coppers that were part of museum collections for years are still valued highly by some tribes, and are displayed as symbols of wealth and prestige during marriage ceremonies and potlatches.

Cost of Living

Determining how expensive it is to live in Alaska not only depends on whom you ask, but how. Labor economists hired by the state to track cost-of-living data rely on several indexes, each with its own methods, focus and results.

For a comparison among cities, the American Chamber of Commerce Researchers Association (ACCRA) offers valuable data as does Runzheimer International, a private research group under contract to the state. To learn how prices have changed in a particular place over time, thte Consumer Price Index (CPI) is a useful gauge of inflation.

One way to unlock cost-of-living data in Alaska is to look at a map of the state's roads; where there are fewer roads and fewer people, costs are generally higher. That's contrary to other places where cost of living tends to be higher in cities. But because transportation to and within Alaska figures into the price of everything from a can of corn to roofing material, costs tend to be far lower in urban centers like Anchorage and Fairbanks, where highways and economies of scale are factors.

The state has limited agriculture and manufacturing so that most goods and foods must be shipped in at added cost. Highest food costs are found in isolated communities dependent on airfreight.

Some studies overlook distinctive elements of Alaska life that play a role in cost of living. For instance, Alaska is among the few places without a state income tax. A recent Runzheimer study showed the portion of income that goes to taxes in Alaska is about 10 percent to 13 percent below the average. A uniquely Alaska factor is pre-tax income distributed annually through the permanent fund dividend program. In 1999 the dividend paid to every qualified resident was $1,769.84.

The ACCRA data places Alaska cities among the most expensive in the nation. The study, which attempts to duplicate spending of a mid-management executive's household, included four Alaska cities— Anchorage, Fairbanks, Juneau and Kodiak—in the fourth quarter of 1999. Anchorage ranked lowest, followed closely by Fairbanks. Cost of living in the two cities was between 20 percent and 25 percent higher than the all-cities' average, the ACCRA said. Juneau and Kodiak were between 30 precent and 35 percent higher.

An ACCRA study for the second half of 1999 showed Anchorage's inflation rate was up by 0.9 percent from the previous year, just a fraction of the 2.5 percent gain for the average U.S. city in the same period. Economists noted that housing costs, typically a consumer's largest monthly expense, continued to hold down inflation in Anchorage. However costs of medical care rose, continuing a nearly 20-year trend in the state's largest city.

Food. Despite its limitations, econimists have long relied on the Cost of Food at Home study prepared by the University of Alaska Cooperative Extension Service, the U.S. Department of Agriculture and Sea Grant. The study offers a comparative measure for Alaska communities that no other survey covers, but it measures limited food items and utility costs. The two costs alone do not fully reflect cost-of-living differences.

In December 1999, Fairbanks at $97.37 led the state with cheapest costs to feed a family of four at home for a week. The price in Anchorage was $99.17, followed by

Juneau at $101.85. (Prices iclude any local sales tax.) The most expensive city at $170.38 a week was Dillingham, off the road system in southwest Alaska.

Housing. The state Labor Department monitors housing costs by studying rental markets in 10 communities statewide. Costs vary widely depending on the local economy, vacancy rates, and demographic and income trends.

In spring 1999, the median adjusted monthly rent was highest in Juneau and Kodiak, where cost of a two-bedroom apartment was $967 in each city, followed by Valdez at $888. Wrangell at $600 was cheapest in this category.

The spring 1999 rental market for three-bedroom homes showed Juneau, Anchorage and Kodiak were the state's most expensive. Median adjusted monthly rents were $1,437; $1,312; and $1,239 respectively.

Taxes. Sample city and borough taxes (compiled in 1998) were: Juneau, 5 percent sales; Anchorage, none; Fairbanks, none; Nome, 4 percent sales; Dillingham, 5 percent sales; Wrangell, 7 percent sales. There is no state income tax in Alaska.

Larger communities such as Anchorage, Cordova and Haines may impose property taxes. Special taxes are issued in some communities, for example: 10 percent tobacco and 8 percent hotel/motel taxes in Anchorage; 2 percent tax on raw fish in the Aleutians East Borough; 7 percent accommodations tax and 6 percent tobacco tax in Juneau; and 1 percent salmon tax in Yakutat.

Personal income. Preliminary figures for 1999 compiled by the federal Bureau of Economic Analysis showed that annual per capita personal income for Alaska was $28,523, positioning the state 17th among the states. The nation's per capita income in 1999 was $28,518. For comparison, Alaska per capita income in 1998 was $27,835.

The permanent fund dividend paid annually to every qualified Alaska resident has been at $1,000 or more since 1996. The dividend program, begun in 1982 to give Alaskans a share in the state's oil wealth, has made an increasing contribution over the years to personal income. In 1997, in the Wade Hampton census district, the dividend accounted for more than 11 percent of per capita income.

A study by the Alaska Permanent Fund Corp. showed that 45 percent of people who planned to spend all or some of their dividend will put the money toward bills or day-to-day expenses. One-third of the respondents said they planned to spend their entire dividend.

For more cost-of-living information, write the Alaska Department of Labor, Research and Analysis section, P.O. Box 21149, Juneau 99802-1149. The department's cost-of-living data can be found at www.labor.state.ak.us by going to "Economic/Occupation" and clicking on "Wages" and "Cost of living."

Courts
The Alaska court system operates at four levels: the supreme court, court of appeals, superior court and district court. The Alaska judiciary is funded by the state and administered by the supreme court.

The five-member supreme court, established by the Alaska Constitution in 1959, has final appellate jurisdiction of all actions and proceedings in lower courts. It sits monthly in Anchorage and Fairbanks, quarterly in Juneau and occasionally in other court locations.

The three-member court of appeals was established in 1980 to

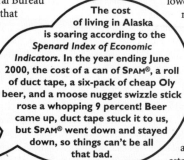

The cost of living in Alaska is soaring according to the *Spenard Index of Economic Indicators*. In the year ending June 2000, the cost of a can of SPAM®, a roll of duct tape, a six-pack of cheap Oly beer, and a moose nugget swizzle stick rose a whopping 9 percent! Beer came up, duct tape stuck it to us, but SPAM® went down and stayed down, so things can't be all that bad.

relieve the supreme court of some of its ever-increasing caseload.

The supreme court retained its ultimate authority in all cases, but concentrated its attention on civil appellate matters, giving authority in criminal and quasi-criminal matters to the court of appeals. The court of appeals has appellate jurisdiction in certain superior court proceedings and jurisdiction to review district court decisions. It meets regularly in Anchorage and travels occasionally to other locations.

The superior court is the trial court with original jurisdiction in all civil and criminal matters and appellate jurisdiction over all matters appealed from the district court. The superior court has exclusive jurisdiction in probate and in cases concerning minors. There are 32 superior court judges.

The district court has jurisdiction over misdemeanor violations and violations of ordinances of political subdivisions. In civil matters, the district court may hear cases for recovery of money, damages or specific personal property if the amount does not exceed $50,000. The district court may also inquire into the cause and manner of death, as well as issue summonses, writs of habeas corpus, and search and arrest warrants. District court criminal decisions may be appealed directly to the court of appeals or the superior court. There are 17 district court judges.

Administration of the superior and district courts is divided by region into four judicial districts: First Judicial District, Southeast; Second Judicial District, Nome–Barrow–Kotzebue; Third Judicial District, Anchorage–Kodiak–Kenai; and Fourth Judicial District, Fairbanks.

District magistrates serve rural areas and help ease the workload of district courts in metropolitan areas. In criminal matters, magistrates may enter judgment of conviction upon a plea of guilty to any state misdemeanor and may try state misdemeanor cases if defendants waives their right to a district court judge. Magistrates may also hear municipal ordinance violations and state traffic infractions without the consent of the accused. In civil matters, magistrates may hear cases for recovery of money, damages or specific personal property if the amount does not exceed $7,500.

Selection of Justices, Judges and Magistrates.

Supreme court justices and judges of the court of appeals, superior court and district court are appointed by the governor from candidates submitted by the Alaska Judicial Council. All justices and judges must be citizens of the United States and residents of Alaska for at least five years. A justice must be licensed to practice law in Alaska at the time of appointment and have engaged in active law practice for eight years.

A court of appeals judge must be a state resident for five years immediately preceding appointment, have been engaged in the active practice of law not less than eight years immediately preceding appointment and be licensed to practice l aw in Alaska. Qualifications of a superior court judge are the same as for supreme court justices, except that only five years of active practice are necessary. A district court judge must be 21 years of age, a resident for at least five years, and (1) be licensed to practice law in Alaska and have engaged in active practice of law for not less than three years immediately preceding appointment, or (2) have served for at least seven years as a magistrate in the state and have graduated from an accredited law school.

The chief justice of the supreme court, selected by majority vote of the justices, serves a three-year term and may not serve consecutive terms.

Each supreme court justice and each judge of the court of appeals is subject to approval or rejection by a majority of the voters of the state on a nonpartisan ballot at the first general election held more than three years after appointment. Thereafter, each justice must participate in a retention election every 10 years. A court of appeals judge must participate every eight years.

Superior court judges are subject to

approval or rejection by voters of their judicial district at the first general election held more than three years after appointment. Thereafter, it is every sixth year. District court judges must run for retention in their judicial districts in the first general election held more than two years after appointment and every fourth year thereafter.

District magistrates are appointed for an indefinite period by the presiding superior court judge of the judicial district in which they will serve.

For additional information about the court system visit the Web site at www.alaska.net/~akctib/ctinfo.htm.

Alaska State Supreme Court, 1960–2000: Justices and Tenure.

Harry O. Arend, 1960–65
George F. Boney, 1968–72
  Chief Justice, 1970–72
Robert Boochever, 1972–80
  Chief Justice, 1975–78
Alexander O. Bryner, 1997–
Edmond W. Burke, 1975–96
  Chief Justice, 1981–84
Walter L. Carpeneti, 1998–
Allen T. Compton, 1980–98
  Chief Justice, 1996–97
Roger G. Connor, 1968–83
John H. Dimond, 1959–71
Robert L. Eastaugh, 1994–
Robert C. Erwin, 1970–77
Dana Fabe, 1996–
James M. Fitzgerald, 1972–75
Walter H. Hodge, 1959–60
Warren W. Matthews, 1977–
  Chief Justice, 1987–90; 1997–
Daniel A. Moore, Jr., 1983–96
  Chief Justice, 1992–96
Buell A. Nesbett, 1959–70
  Chief Justice, 1959–70
Jay A. Rabinowitz, 1965–77
  Chief Justice, 1972–75; 1978–81; 1984–87; 1990–92

Alaska State Court of Appeals, 1980–2000: Judges and Tenure.

Alexander O. Bryner,
  1980–97
  Chief Judge, 1980–97

Pioneering Tourism

The first cruise ships to carry sight-seeing passengers as well as cargo along the [Inside Passage] were lavishly fitted Pacific Coast Steamship vessels. The Idaho took the initial batch of tourists to view Glacier Bay in 1883, and other paddle wheelers like the S.S. Ancon followed in her wake; within a year, there were 1,650 people cruising up here.—Paul and Audrey Grescoe, *Alaska: The Cruise-Lover's Guide* ✴

Robert G. Coats, 1980–
  Chief Judge, 1997–
David Mannheimer, 1990–
James K. Singleton, Jr., 1980–90
David C. Stewart, 1997–

Cruises (*SEE ALSO* BOATING AND

FERRIES) There are many opportunities for cruising Alaska waters aboard charter boats, scheduled boat excursions or luxury cruise ships.

Charter boats are readily available in southeastern and southcentral Alaska. Charter boat trips range from daylong fishing and sightseeing trips to overnight and longer customized trips or package tours. There is a wide range of charter boats, from simple fishing boats to sailboats, yachts and mini-class cruise ships.

In summer, scheduled boat excursions— from day trips to overnight cruises— are available: Ketchikan (Misty Fiords); Sitka (harbor and area tours); Bartlett Cove and Gustavus (Glacier Bay); Juneau (Lynn Canal); Valdez and Whittier (Columbia Glacier, Prince William Sound); Seward (Resurrection Bay, Kenai Fjords); Homer (Kachemak Bay); and Fairbanks (Chena and Tanana Rivers).

For details and additional information on charter boat operators and scheduled boat excursions, contact the Alaska Division of Tourism, P.O. Box 110800, Juneau 99811.

From May through September, 16 cruise lines carry visitors to Alaska via the Inside Passage. Cruise lines include Carnival, Princess, Holland America,

Crystal Cruises, Alaska Sightseeing/Cruise West, Norwegian Cruise Line, World Explorer, Royal Caribbean, Seabourn, Lind Blad Expedition, Glacier Bay Tours and Cruises, Celebrity, Clipper and Cunard. For the phone numbers of the companies, contact Cruise Lines International, (212) 921-0066 Both round-trip and one-way cruises are available, or a cruise may be sold as part of a package tour that includes air, rail and/or motorcoach transportation. (*See* Bus Lines)

Prices vary. A 7- to 11-day Inside Passage cruise costs range from $1,800 to $4,200. Booking by February 14 can yield substantial savings.

The cruise industry in Alaska waters continues to thrive, posting a 2 percent increase in capacity during 1999.

Because of the wide variety of cruise trip options, it is wise to work with a travel agent.

Dalton Highway

(*See also* Highways) The 414-mile-long Dalton Highway begins at Milepost 73.1 on the Elliott Highway.

This all-weather gravel road bridges the Yukon River, crosses the Arctic Circle at Mile 115.3, and climbs the Brooks Range. At Atigun Pass (Mile 246.8) it crosses a continental divide, the highest highway pass in Alaska. Then the road passes through tundra plains before reaching the Prudhoe Bay oil fields at Deadhorse on the coast of the Arctic Ocean. Public travel for the final 8 miles may be restricted. In 1998–99, portions of the Dalton were paved.

The highway was named for James Dalton, a post–World War II explorer who played a large role in the development of North Slope oil and gas industries. It was built as a haul road for supplies and to provide access to the northern half of the 800-mile trans- Alaska oil pipeline during construction. Originally called the North Slope Haul Road, it is still often referred to as the "Haul Road."

The Dalton Highway is open to all

vehicles and is maintained. Services are limited to Yukon Ventures (Mile 56) and Coldfoot Services (Mile 175). As of winter 1997–98, no fuel, food, lodging or automotive services were available from Fox to Coldfoot from October through March. Travelers should call (907) 273-6037 or (800) 478-7675 for current road and weather conditions.

Daylight Hours (*See also* Arctic Circle)

Maximum (at Summer Solstice, June 20 or 21)

	Sunrise	Sunset	Hours of Daylight
Adak	6:27 A.M.	11:10 P.M.	16:43 hrs
Anchorage	3:21 A.M.	10:42 P.M.	19:21 hrs
Barrow	May 10	Aug. 2	84 days continuous
Fairbanks	1:59 A.M.	11:48 P.M.	21:49 hrs
Juneau	3:51 A.M.	10:09 P.M.	18:18 hrs
Ketchikan	4:04 A.M.	9:33 P.M.	17:29 hrs

Minimum (at Winter Solstice, Dec. 21 or 22)

	Sunrise	Sunset	Hours of Daylight
Adak	10:52 A.M.	6:38 P.M.	7:46 hrs
Anchorage	10:14 A.M.	3:42 P.M.	5:28 hrs
Barrow	*	*	0:00 hrs
Fairbanks	10:59 A.M.	2:41 P.M.	3:42 hrs
Juneau	9:46 A.M.	4:07 P.M.	6:21 hrs
Ketchikan	9:12 A.M.	4:18 P.M.	7:06 hrs

*From Nov. 18 through Jan. 24—a period of 67 days—there is no daylight in Barrow.

Diamond Willow Fungi,

particularly *Valsa sordida Nitschke,* are generally thought to be the cause of diamond-shaped patterns in the wood grain of some willow trees. There are 33 varieties of willow in Alaska, at least five of which can develop diamonds. They are found throughout the state but are most plentiful in river valleys. Diamond willow, stripped of bark, is used to make lamps, walking sticks and novelty items.

Dog Mushing (SEE ALSO IDITAROD TRAIL SLED DOG RACE AND YUKON QUEST INTERNATIONAL SLED DOG RACE)

In many areas of the state where snowmachines had nearly replaced the working dog team, the sled dog has returned, due in part to a rekindled appreciation of the reliability of non-mechanical transportation. In addition to working and racing dog teams, many people keep two to 20 sled dogs for recreational mushing.

Sled dog racing is Alaska's official state sport. Races ranging from local club meets to world championships are held throughout the winter.

Championship speed races are usually run over two or three days, with the cumulative time for the heats deciding the winner. Distances for the heats vary from about 5 to 30 miles. The size of dog teams also varies, with mushers using anywhere from four to 20 dogs in their teams. Since racers are not allowed to replace dogs in the team, most finish with fewer than they started with. Attrition may be caused by anything from tender feet to sore muscles.

Sprint mushing is divided into limited and open classes. Limited class ranges from three to 10 dogs and from 3 to 12 miles a day. Open class racing has no limit on the number of dogs and ranges from 10 to 30 miles a day.

Long-distance racing (the Yukon Quest, the Iditarod) pits racers not only against one another but also against the elements. Sheer survival can quickly take precedence over winning when a winter storm catches a dog team in an exposed area. Stories abound of racers giving up their chance to finish "in the money" to help out another musher who has gotten into trouble. Besides the weather, long-distance racers also have to contend with moose attacks on the dogs, sudden illness, straying off the trail and sheer exhaustion. With these and other challenges to overcome, those who finish have truly persevered against the odds.

Purses range from trophies only to a prize of $38,000 for the largest sprint purse at the Open World Championship Sled Dog Race. A purse is split among the finishers. The richest purse in sled-dog racing is the Iditarod, which paid a record $564,862 in 2000.

For information about dog mushing, call the Alaska Dog Mushers Association in Fairbanks, (907) 457-6874 or e-mail *Mushing Magazine* at info@mushing.com.

See charts following for statistics on two of the biggest championship races. Other major races around the state follow.

Open World Championship Sled Dog Race, Anchorage

Scheduled during Fur Rendezvous in February. Best elapsed time in three heats over three days, 25 miles each day. Purse is split among the top 15 finishers. Winners of the previous 11 years:

Winners	Elapsed Time (minutes:seconds)				
	Day 1	Day 2	Day 3	Total	Purse
1990 Charlie Champaine	89:00	96:13	94:01	279:14	$50,000
1991 Charlie Champaine	89:10	94:49	95:43	279:42	70,000
1992 Roxy Wright-Champaine	87:30	89:35	92:22	269:42	70,000
1993 Roxy Wright-Champaine	87:44	90:45	93:21	271:50	75,000
1994 Ross Saunderson	86:26	90:24	*	176:50	50,000
1995 Ross Saunderson	84:19	88:57	85:07	258:23	45,000
1996 Cancelled due to lack of snow					
1997 Axel Gasser	95:47	99:09	102:03	296:59	45,000
1998 Ross Sanderson	96:12	99:20	101:28	291:00	50,000
1999 Egil Ellis	84:02	90:28	88:33	263:03	20,000
2000 Egil Ellis	84:42	90:26	90:59	266:07	38,400

*Trail conditions shortened race to two heats.
Source: Alaska Sled Dog and Racing Association

Open North American Sled Dog Race Championship, Fairbanks

Held in March. Best elapsed time in three heats over three days; 20 miles on Days 1 and 2; 30 miles on Day 3. (Times have been rounded off.) In 1998, the Day 3 heat was shortened to 20 miles. Purse is split among the top 15 finishers. Winners of the previous 11 years:

| Winners | Elapsed Time (minutes:seconds) | | | | |
	Day 1	Day 2	Day 3	Total	Purse
1990 Charlie Champaine	62:47	67:38	95:40	226:05	$45,000
1991 Ross Saunderson	60:12	63:53	97:44	221:50	46,000
1992 Roxy Wright-Champaine	66:17	65:59	94:29	226:46	52,000
1993 Roxy Wright-Champaine	64:48	64:06	95:36	224:31	58,000
1994 Ross Saunderson	*	63:16	91:12	154:28	49,000
1995 Amy Streeper	61:42	65:29	94:48	221:59	46,940
1996 Amy Streeper	68:58	63:17	90:29	222:45	32,500
1997 Neil Johnson	64:06	64:53	94:25	223:24	22,500
1998 Michi Konno	70:05	69:41	67:00	206:47	40,000
1999 Egil Ellis	**	63:07	91:46	154:52	46,300
2000 Egil Ellis	59:58	61:08	90:40	211:46	40,000

*Time not counted because locked gate delayed the first three mushers.
**No first-day time as trail was blocked.

Clark Memorial Sled Dog Race, Soldotna to Hope, 100 miles. Held in January.

Copper River 300, Glennallen. Held in January, covering 300 miles over two to three days.

Iditarod Trail Sled Dog Race. (*See* Iditarod Trail Sled Dog Race)

Junior North American Championships, Fairbanks. For children under 18. Held in March. Three heats, one- to eight-dog classes.

Junior World Championship Race, Anchorage. Three heats in three days. Held in February.

Kusko 300, Bethel to Aniak. Held in January.

Limited North American Championships, Fairbanks. Three heats over three days; one- and two-dog skijoring. Held in March.

Tok Race of Champions, Tok. Two heats in two days, 20.5 miles a day. Held in March.

Willow Winter Carnival Race, Willow. Two heats in two days, 18 miles each day. Held in January.

Women's World Championship Race, Anchorage. Three heats in three days, 12 miles each day. Held in February.

Yukon Quest International Sled Dog Race. (*See* Yukon Quest International Sled Dog Race)

Earthquakes (*See also* Waves)

Between 1899 and mid-1996, 10 Alaska earthquakes occurred that equaled or exceeded a magnitude of 8 on the Richter scale. During the same period, more than 75 earthquakes took place that were of magnitude 7 or greater.

Alaska averages 1,000 earthquakes a year that measure 3.5 or more on the Richter scale. In May 1995 alone, the Alaska Earthquake Information Center detected and located 540 earthquakes in Alaska. The largest of these measured 5.5 and was located 16 miles southwest of Anchorage.

The West Coast/Alaska Tsunami Warning Center is responsible for warning

Earthquake damage in downtown Anchorage, 1964. From Alaska's History by Harry Ritter.

coastal residents of Alaska, Washington, Oregon, California and British Columbia about any earthquake that could generate a tsunami, a seismic sea wave. According to the Center, Alaska's earthquake activity typically follows the same pattern from month to month, interspersed with sporadic swarms, or groups of small earthquakes, and punctuated every decade or so by a great earthquake and its after-shocks. Alaska is the most seismic of all the 50 states, and the most seismically active part of the state is the Aleutian Islands arc system. Seismicity related to this system extends into the Gulf of Alaska and northward into interior Alaska to a point near Mount McKinley. These earthquakes are largely the result of underthrusting of the North Pacific plate. Many earthquakes resulting from this underthrusting occur in Cook Inlet—particularly near Mount Iliamna and Mount Redoubt—and near Mount McKinley. North of the Alaska Range, in the central Interior, most earthquakes are of shallow origin.

The earthquake that created the highest seiche, or splash wave, ever recorded occurred on the evening of July 9, 1958, when a quake with a magnitude of 7.9 on the Richter scale rocked the Yakutat area. A landslide containing approximately 40 million cubic yards of rock plunged into Gilbert Inlet at the head of Lituya Bay. The gigantic splash resulting from the slide sent a wave 1,740 feet up the opposite mountain side, denuding it of trees and soil down to bedrock. It then fell back and swept through the length of the bay and out to sea. One fishing boat anchored in Lituya Bay at the time was lost with its crew of two; another was carried over a spit of land by the wave and soon after foundered, but its crew was saved. A third boat anchored in the bay miraculously survived intact.

The most destructive earthquake to strike Alaska occurred at 5:36 P.M. on Good Friday, March 27, 1964. Registering between 8.4 and 8.6 on the Richter scale in use at the time, its equivalent moment magnitude has since been revised upward to 9.2, making it the strongest earthquake ever recorded in North America. With its primary epicenter deep beneath Miners Lake in northern Prince William Sound, the earthquake spread shock waves that were felt 700 miles away. The earthquake and seismic waves that followed killed 131 people, including 115 Alaskans. Of the 131 deaths, 119 were caused by the tsunami generated by the earthquake.

The 1964 earthquake released 10 million times more energy than the atomic bomb that devastated Hiroshima in World War II, and 80 times the energy of the San Francisco earthquake of 1906. It also moved more earth farther, both horizontally and vertically, than any other earthquake ever recorded except the 1960 Chilean earthquake. In the 69-day period after the main quake, there were 12,000 jolts of 3.5 magnitude or greater.

The highest sea wave caused by the 1964 earthquake occurred when an undersea slide near Shoup Glacier in Port Valdez triggered a wave that toppled trees 100 feet above tidewater and deposited silt and sand 220 feet above salt water.

During June 1996, the Alaska Earthquake Information Center located 567 earthquakes in or near Alaska. The largest of these was a major earthquake on June 9 with a magnitude of 7.9, the largest earthquake to have occurred in North America in more than 10 years. The earthquake was felt sharply at Adak and Atka; minor damage was reported at Adak. This quake generated minor tsunamis in Alaska and other locales in the Pacific Basin.

Through the end of June 1996, 118 aftershocks of magnitude 4 or larger were recorded and many hundreds of smaller aftershocks were observed on seismic records. The seismic energy radiated by the June 9 earthquake was about 30 times that generated by the January 1995 Northridge earthquake in California or the January 1994 Kobe,

Japan, quake, both of which had magnitudes around 7.2. For comparison, the 1964 Good Friday earthquake released about 1,000 times the energy of the Northridge and Kobe quakes.

To learn more about earthquakes, visit the University of Alaska Fairbanks Web site at www.aeic.alaska.edu/seis/.

Economy (*See also* Cost of Living *and* Employment)

While it's tempting to say Alaska's resource-dependent economy is characterized by boom and bust cycles, overall growth has been positive since statehood in 1959. Setbacks such as the recession that hit the state in 1986 often are linked to markets for raw goods; even temporary movement in these global markets can be felt strongly in Alaska where oil, fishing, timber and mining have been key employers. One result of the 1986 recession has been a more diversified Alaska economy.

Alaska's economy expands when it's able to export goods and services, but long distances to market and expensive transportation costs are obstacles as the state works to capitalize on its vast natural resources. Peaks and troughs are cyclical, especially when it comes to oil and mineral prices linked to national or world events well beyond Alaska's control.

Oil and gas industries retained a key role as Alaska entered the 21st century; no industry is more important than oil in generating state revenues. The state Department of Revenue reported in fiscal 2000 that $1.6 billion, or 78 percent, of general purpose revenue was generated by taxes and royalties on North Slope crude oil.

When oil prices are high, so are state revenues: For every $1 a barrel increase in the price of oil, Alaska collects $65 million in

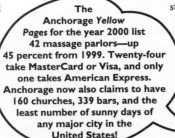

The Anchorage *Yellow Pages* for the year 2000 list 42 massage parlors—up 45 percent from 1999. Twenty-four take MasterCard or Visa, and only one takes American Express. Anchorage now also claims to have 160 churches, 339 bars, and the least number of sunny days of any major city in the United States!

royalty and severance taxes. The link between oil, state revenues and Alaska's economy becomes clear when one considers that more than 20 percent of all jobs in Alaska are linked to state government spending.

Alaska absorbed a blow in 1986 when oil prices sunk and a rippling recession spared few sectors. By 1989, recovery was under way as oil prices began to improve. The *Exxon Valdez* oil spill cleanup effort, also begun in 1989, added about $2 billion to the state's economy over 18 months.

But as any oil-producing nation knows, banking on petroleum is risky business. Alaska, which until recent years accounted for nearly one-fourth of domestically produced oil, has seen its oil-related revenues whipsawed by global volatility. In fiscal 1999, Alaska North Slope crude prices hovered at $12.70 a barrel, contributing $900 million in revenues. In fiscal 2000, with the per-barrel price nearly double, oil revenues hit $1.6 billion.

Alaska's economy expanded for the 12th straight year in 2000, propelled by continued growth in the services sector, which in turn is led by health care. Second-largest source of private-sector job gains in 1999 was retail employment. Eating and drinking establishments added 400 new jobs for the sixth straight year of growth. New retailers in Anchorage, Kodiak and in the Matanuska-Susitna valley contributed another 400 jobs in 1999.

Also contributing to economic growth were construction, air cargo handling, and the visitor industry. Oil producers continued to reduce workforces and Alaska's manufacturing sector also lost jobs.

In all, the economy rebounded from slow growth in 1999 and posted a growth rate of nearly 1 percent, the Department of Labor said. Unemployment was below 8 percent for the sixth consecutive year and inflation was just 1 percent, lowest in a decade. More than 8,000 new jobs were forecast in Alaska over the next two years, labor economists said.

Uncertainty in the state's oil and gas industries defined that sector for much of the year pending federal scrutiny of a $30 billion buyout of Atlantic Richfield Co. by BP Amoco. Satisfied that anti-trust issues were resolved, the Federal Trade Commission approved the deal in April 2000, but labor economists predicted continuation of a long-term trend among oil producers to reduce jobs.

A State Revenue Department forecast said oil prices would remain at about $23 a barrel over the next two years, a dramatic improvement from the year-ago price and among the highest prices since 1990. If reality matches prediction, Alaska's oil field services sector (contractors who provide goods and services to oil producers) should perform better than the production sector, which historically offers high-end jobs.

Economists monitor Alaska's oil field services employment as a rough measure of the oil industry's overall health. Oil field services counted 5,350 workers in 1999, among the roughest years in memory. Unprecedented consolidation in oil field services marked 1999 and some 1,300 jobs were lost in oil and gas. Spurred in part by improved oil prices in 2000, the oil field services sector added 150 jobs and the outlook had turned around, labor economists said. Higher oil prices, coupled with resolution of the BP Amoco-ARCO buyout, should spur renewed interest in Alaska oil exploration and development.

More information about Alaska's revenue sources, including the state's oil price forecasts, is available at Web site www.revenue.state.ak.us/tax.

State government with a payroll approaching $800 million is Alaska's second-largest employer behind the federal government. There were nearly 22,000 state employees in 2000 including the University of Alaska and state-owned corporations such as the Alaska Housing Finance Corp. and the Alaska Railroad. Forecasts call for a slight gain in state government employment in health and social services.

A move to place more public employee jobs into the private sector was expected to continue, the state Labor Department said.

Ongoing privatization at the Alaska Native Medical Center in Anchorage alone will cancel any slight growth in federal employment over the next few years, analysts said. As many as 500 federal jobs were projected to move to the private sector by 2001. (Temporary hiring for the federal census could offset losses to privatization in 2000.)

Alaska's wood products industry notched a slight gain in 1999, based in part on a reporting change involving Ketchikan Pulp Co. administrative employees, but economists said the industry faced dim prospects. The shutdown in 2000 of the Annette Island sawmill coupled with a weak market for round logs were setbacks despite overall indicators that the Southeast economy is resilient. Strong growth in 1999 in services and local government overcame job losses in mining, food stores and the federal government.

Another Alaska-based manufacturer, seafood processors, also confronted an uncertain outlook: Unusual ice conditions in the Bering Sea forced postponement of the opilio crab harvest in January, a severe setback for processing employment. Labor economists said winter seafood processing employment was at its lowest level since 1991. Even though 1999's sockeye salmon run was among the best on record, production capacity was not increased.

Processors also were hit with labor shortages in 1999, a potential significant hurdle to growth, and national and state labor markets remained tight as the 2000 season approached. The Alaska Seafood International plant opened in Anchorage in 1999 and added 100 manufacturing jobs. Peak employment at this unit is estimated at 450.

Alaska's finance, insurance and real estate sector held steady as the industry absorbed news of the takeover of National Bank of Alaska, the state's largest, by Wells Fargo. Observers anticipated consolidation of banking employment, particularly in administration. Bank of America withdrew from Alaska and sold most of its branches to Northrim Bank.

Consolidation also is on the horizon for several gold properties near the Fort Knox mine in Fairbanks—a move that could add jobs. Among Alaska's large-scale units, Fort Knox and Southeast's Greens Creek mine each reported a solid year despite low prices; expansion at Red Dog lead and zinc mine near Kotzebue increased capacity in 1999 and added some jobs.

Several small- to mid-size mines ceased operations in 1999 because of historic low gold prices. And two sites that appeared poised to add jobs, the Pogo project near Delta Junction and the Kensington project north of Juneau, do not anticipate growth soon.

New retail space and hotel construction contributed to a solid year for the state's construction industry, which added 400 jobs in 1999. Higher interest rates combined with oil industry uncertainty have dampened residential construction but several public projects are planned: $300 million in federal funds for highway and street construction; military construction including a replacement hospital at Fort Wainwright; and $280 million in fiscal 2000 construction through the Army Corps of Engineers.

Education (SEE ALSO SCHOOL DISTRICTS AND UNIVERSITIES AND COLLEGES)

According to the 1999–2000 *Alaska Education Directory,* Alaska has 503 public schools. The Bureau of Indian Affairs operated rural schools in Alaska until 1985.

The state Board of Education has seven members appointed by the governor. (In addition, two nonvoting members are appointed by the board to represent the military and public school students.) The board is responsible for setting policy for education in Alaska schools and appoints a commissioner of education to carry out its decisions. The public schools are controlled by 53 school districts, and each school district elects its own school board. There are 19 Regional Education Attendance Areas that oversee education in rural areas outside the 34 city and borough school districts.

Any student in grades kindergarten

through 12 may choose to study at home through the state-operated correspondence school, the Alyeska Central School, which also serves traveling students, GED students, migrant students and students living in remote areas. Home study has been an option for Alaska students since 1939.

Several school districts also operate distance learning correspondence programs available to Alaska school-aged children.

The state Department of Education also operates the Alaska Vocational Technical Center at Seward and a number of other education programs ranging from adult basic education to literacy skills.

Alaskans between 7 and 16 years old are required to attend school. According to state regulations, a student must earn a minimum of 21 high school credits to receive a high school diploma. The state Board of Education has stipulated that four credits must be earned in language arts, three in social studies, two each in math and science, and one in physical education or health. Local school boards set the remainder of the required credits.

Since 1976, the state has provided secondary school programs to any community in which an elementary school is operated and one or more children of high school age wish to attend high school. This mandate was the result of a class action suit initiated on behalf of Molly Hootch, a high school-age student. Prior to the Molly Hootch Decree, high school-age students in villages without a secondary school attended high school outside their village. Of the 127 villages originally eligible for high school programs under the Molly Hootch Decree, only a few remain without one.

There were approximately 7,500 teachers and administrators in the public schools and 133,047 students enrolled in K–12 in public schools in 1999–2000. The size of schools in Alaska varies greatly, from a 1,900-student high school in Anchorage to one- or two-teacher, one-room schools in remote rural areas.

Sixty-six percent of the school district's operating fund is provided by the state, 23 percent by local governments and 11 percent by the federal government. Alaska's average salary for teachers is among the highest in the nation.

The Alaska Legislature passed a law in 1997 that directed the Department of Education to develop the Alaska High School Qualifying Examination. Beginning with the class of 2002, students must pass the exam to receive a high school diploma. Those students who do not pass will receive a certificate of attendance.

Employment (*See also* Economy)

A quick look back as Alaska enters a new century shows key employment mainstays have been around since statehood: Fishing, timber, mining and, in Cook Inlet, the beginnings of an oil and gas sector, all were in place by the 1960s. Fledgling state and local government added jobs while cruise ship visits, combined with air travel, were popular with tourists.

On the horizon were rebuilding after the 1964 Good Friday earthquake, which drew a $400 million federal aid package; construction of the trans-Alaska oil pipeline, a $9 billion project began in 1974; and a $2 billion cleanup following the *Exxon Valdez* oil tanker wreck in Prince William Sound in 1989. These projects helped mold Alaska's infrastructure and revealed key employment sources.

Consolidation was a theme in 1999. California-based Safeway completed purchase of Alaska's Carrs grocery chain, a move that combined two prominent Alaska retailers. Also stalling job growth in 1999 were contractions within the oil and gas industry. In all, the state saw job growth of just under 1 percent, the second-slowest growth rate of the decade. Annual average wage and salary employment in 1999 increased to 277,600.

As in 1999, the biggest contributor to Alaska's job growth in 2000 was the services sector which added 2,700 jobs in 2000 and employed 73,200 people. Pacesetters include hotels and lodging, health care, amusement and recreation services and

Average Annual Employment 1986-99

Employees (in thousands)

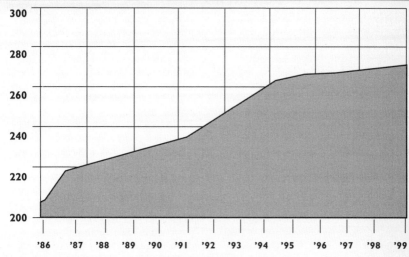

Source: Alaska Department of Labor, Research and Analysis Section, April 2000

Alaska Employment by Month 1995-99

Employees (in thousands)

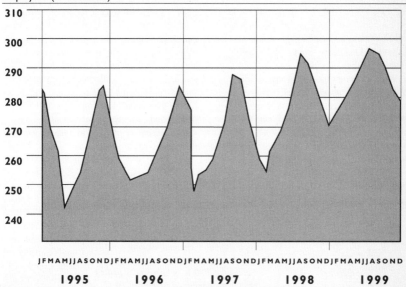

Source: Alaska Department of Labor, Research and Analysis Section, April 2000

business services. A glance at the state's top 10 largest private employers tells the story: Four of the largest are retailers and two are in health care.

Privatization of social services formerly the domain of state government, such as halfway houses and services for those with developmental disabilities, has been another growth area for Alaska.

Barring major recession in the strong national economy, the number of Alaska visitors should continue to climb—a trend hotel chains apparently saw coming. Several new hotels built by 1999 will contribute to the economy by operating for a full year. The sector's single biggest boost in 2000 came when a full-service Marriott hotel opened in downtown Anchorage.

Continued healthy outlooks were projected as well for the construction industry, which employed 13,800 in 1999 and added 450 jobs in 2000. The state's biggest construction project was ongoing capital improvement at Anchorage International Airport. Air transportation, especially air cargo, continued to show growth statewide.

Mining shed 150 jobs in 2000 as gold hit a 20-year low. Alaska's timber products industry, centered largely in Southeast, lost 100 jobs and was projected to continue a decline. Manufacturing employed an average of 13,600 and dropped 300 jobs in 2000.

Federal government employment in Alaska stood at an average of 16,800, unchanged over 1999, but was forecast to drop 600 jobs in part as Indian Health Service jobs are transferred to the private sector. State government added 200 jobs for an average of 22,000 workers in 2000.

On an annual basis, Alaska's economy was projected to gain 2,600 jobs in 2000, compared to most of the 1990s when about 5,000 jobs

were added annually. At 2 percent annual employment growth in 1999, Anchorage led the state, followed by Fairbanks with an annual employment growth of 1.4 percent. However job growth in Fairbanks was projected to keep pace with Anchorage as the $21 million Alaska State Court building heads for completion in 2001. Also in Fairbanks, the University of Alaska has budgeted $10 million to upgrade buildings and hopes to begin a $25 million museum expansion.

Statewide seasonally adjusted jobless-ness rose 0.2 of 1 percent in 2000 to 6 percent, compared to the national rate of about 4 percent. Pockets of high unemployment in Alaska included the Yukon-Koyukuk region, Prince of Wales-Outer Ketchikan and southwest Alaska's Wade Hampton region. Winter unem-ployment in each region approached double digits in 2000. The northern region, including Nome, the North Slope Borough and Northwest Arctic Borough, also saw high unemployment based in part on oil industry declines.

A negative net migration has helped keep Alaska's unemployment rate relatively low, prompting employers to rely increas-ingly on resident workforce to fill new jobs.

Like much about Alaska, where seasonal extremes help explain everything from moodiness (better in summer) to small airplane crashes (worse during hunting season), the state's unemployment rate fluctuates with the time of year. Added jobs linked to tourism and commercial fishing drive down unemployment in summer, while decreased business activity in winter prompts rates to rise again.

Joblessness also varies widely depending on region; high unem-ployment is found in some rural areas where paying jobs are scarce and there is greater reliance on sub-sistence hunting and fishing.

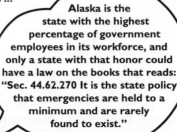

Alaska is the state with the highest percentage of government employees in its workforce, and only a state with that honor could have a law on the books that reads: "Sec. 44.62.270 It is the state policy that emergencies are held to a minimum and are rarely found to exist."

Readers hoping to find work in Alaska are strongly advised to make a visit and gauge possibilities for themselves. Consolidation in petroleum has increasingly turned the state's fabled big-money oil jobs into just that—big dreams. In the populous Railbelt region between Seward and Fairbanks, job seekers will find housing, taxes and food costs more in line with prices in the West, a departure from just a few decades ago when Alaska prices were far higher.

Employment offices are found in most large communities. State government information is available at www.jobs. state.ak.us or by writing the Alaska Department of Labor, Alaska State Employment Service, P.O. Box 3-7000, Juneau 99802. A Labor Department publication, *Alaska Economic Trends,* is an excellent monthly compilation of state

Unemployment Figures for January 1999

Area	Percent
Statewide	7.4
Anchorage	4.9
Fairbanks North Star Borough	7.0
Juneau Borough	5.5
Kodiak Island Borough	7.2
Nome	10.9
Ketchikan Gateway Borough	11.1
Bristol Bay Borough	11.3

Source: Alaska Department of Labor, Research and Analysis Section, April 2000; Preliminary data

Alaska Wage and Salary Employment by Industry 1999

Industry	Percent
Government (federal, state, local)	26.5
Services and Miscellaneous	25.4
Trade	20.6
Transportation/Communications	9.4
Manufacturing	5.0
Construction	5.0
Finance/Insurance/Real Estate	4.6
Mining (includes oil and gas)	3.4

Source: Alaska Department of Labor, Research and Analysis Section, April 2000

workforce issues. Look for it at www.labor. state.ak.us/research/research.htm.

Energy and Power

When it comes to power use, Alaska can be divided into three major regions, each having similar energy patterns, problems and resources: the Extended Railbelt region, the Southeast region and the Bush region. The Extended Railbelt consists of major urban areas linked by the Alaska Railroad (Seward, Anchorage and Fairbanks). The southcentral area of this region uses relatively inexpensive natural gas from Cook Inlet and hydroelectrical power plants for electrical production and heating. The Fairbanks–Tanana Valley area uses primarily coal and oil to meet its electrical needs. Future electrical demand for the Extended Railbelt region will be met by a combination of hydropower and coal- and gas-fired generators.

The Southeast region relies on hydropower for much of its electrical generation. (Most of the existing hydroelectric power projects in Alaska are located in the Southeast region.) In the smaller communities, diesel generators are used.

The Bush region includes all communities that are remote from the major urban areas of the Extended Railbelt and Southeast regions. Electricity in Bush communities is typically provided by small diesel generators. Where wind projects are feasible, such as at Lolo Bay and Unalakleet, wind power can be a viable, fuel-saving alternative to diesel-powered generators. Bush residents rely heavily on heating oil. Wood and kerosene heaters are used to a limited extent. Natural gas is available in Barrow.

Eskimo Ice Cream

Also called *akutak* (the Yupik Eskimo word for Eskimo ice cream), this classic Native delicacy, popular throughout Alaska, is traditionally made of whipped

Soapberry. From Alaska Wild Berry Guide and Cookbook.

berries, seal oil and freshly fallen snow. Sometimes shortening, raisins and sugar are added. Ingredients vary by region. One recipe uses the soopalallie berry, *Shepherdia canadensis* (also called soapberry), a bitter species that forms a frothy mass like soap-suds when beaten.

Exports (SEE ALSO ECONOMY)

Led by fish and seafood, Alaska's exports were valued at $2.6 billion in 1999, a 30 percent increase over 1998 when aftermaths of the Asian economic crisis were felt strongly in Alaska. Asia accounts for 80 percent of Alaska exports, and Japan and Korea are the state's top two markets.

Alaska's top four exports generally returned to pre-crisis levels, while Alaska exports to Korea set a record high of $487 million in 1999.

Fish and seafood posted a 42 percent gain, for an export value of $990 million in 1999. The sector remained Alaska's top export and was lifted by one of the largest commercial fishing harvests on record.

Other top Alaska exports in rank order were oil (much of it Alaska North Slope crude sent to Asia) valued at $722 million, a gain of 13 percent; and wood exported mainly as round logs, valued at $222 million in 1999, a gain of 30 percent. Improvement in wood exports followed very poor performance in 1998 when total values of $172 million were barely half the 1997 figure.

Fairbanks Nicknamed "The Golden Heart City," Fairbanks is located in Alaska's Interior, 200 miles south of the Arctic Circle and 120 miles north of Denali National Park and Preserve.

Long before European explorers and trappers came to the area, Athabascan Indians lived, fished and hunted in the Tanana Valley, site of the present-day city.

Fairbanks was founded through the misadventure of Ohio trader E. T. Barnette, who never intended to establish a town on the Chena River. Barnette and his $20,000 worth of trading goods had set out from St. Michael in late August 1901, bound to establish a trading post at the village of Tanacross, where the Valdez Trail crossed the Tanana Valley. After Barnette's own stern-wheeler was wrecked, he hired Charles Adams, part-owner of the *Lavelle Young*, to take him to Tanacross. Once again Barnette ran into trouble when the 150-foot *Lavelle Young* could not ascend the Tanana past the sandy shallows called the Bates Rapids, a few miles above the mouth of the Chena River. In hopes that the Chena would meet up with the Tanana, Barnette persuaded Adams to carry him up the Chena until the boat ran into shallow water. Adams left Barnette, his party and his goods on the banks of the Chena River near what is now First Avenue and Cushman Street in Fairbanks.

Things were looking bleak for Barnette until Felix Pedro struck gold about 16 miles away on July 22, 1902. Barnette took this opportunity to expand his trading goods business and immediately dispatched Jujiro Wada, a Japanese employee, to Dawson City to spread the good news of a gold strike in the Tanana Valley. Soon the community became the new hub of the Alaska gold rush. A friend of Barnette's, Judge James Wickersham, suggested Fairbanks as the name for the new town, in honor of Indiana Senator Charles Fairbanks. In exchange, Wickersham agreed to move the seat of the District Court from Eagle to Fairbanks, thus ensuring that the town would further flourish.

By 1908, Fairbanks was the largest, busiest city in the territory, boasting electric lights, city sewer, fire and police protection, a courthouse and jail, a hospital, school, library and three newspapers.

Today Fairbanks is Alaska's second-largest city, home to 31,697 residents, and the service and supply center for Interior and Arctic industries. About 84,000 people live in the Fairbanks North Star Borough. Government, oil, mining, construction and tourism are important elements in the Fairbanks economy, as are Fort Wainwright, the first Army airfield in Alaska, and Eielson Air Force Base. The University of Alaska Fairbanks campus overlooks the city.

The "Unknown First Family" is a Fairbanks landmark. From *Fairbanks, Alaska's Heart of Gold* by Tricia Brown (text) and Roy Corral (photographs).

Summer temperatures average 59.5°F, often ranging into the 70s and 80s, with nearly 24 hours of daylight at the solstice, when a Midnight Sun Baseball Game is played after 10:30 P.M. with no artificial lighting. Winter temperatures range from 7.6°F to −19.2°F with the lowest-ever temperature recorded at −62°F in December 1961. The winter snowfall averages 68.9 inches.

Winter attractions include an international ice-carving competition, sled dog races and northern lights viewing. (Fairbanks is considered the best place on earth to view the northern lights.) Summer activities include the Golden Days celebration, Tanana Valley Fair (the state's oldest)

and the World Eskimo-Indian Olympics held annually in July (*see also* World Eskimo-Indian Olympics).

Alaskaland Pioneer Park is a 44-acre park offering a gold rush town, historic buildings, food, small shops, entertainment and a Native Village Museum with live demonstrations of Native culture and crafts.

Fairbanks also offers river rafting, sternwheeler riverboat tours, gold rush sites and dog mushing and is a good jumping-off spot for the Alaska Railroad, Denali National Park and Preserve and remote wilderness areas. For information, contact the Fairbanks Convention and Visitors Bureau, 550 First Ave., Fairbanks 99701; (800) 327-5774, or e-mail info@ explorefairbanks.com. Visit the Web site at www.explorefairbanks.com.

Ferries (SEE ALSO BOATING AND CRUISES)

The Marine Highway System, within the state Department of Transportation and Public Facilities, provides year-round scheduled ferry service for passengers and vehicles to communities in southeastern and southcentral, and seasonal service in southwestern Alaska. Monthly sailings in the summer connect the southeastern Alaska ferry system with southcentral and southwestern Alaska.

A fleet of seven ferries on the southeastern system connects Bellingham, WA, and Prince Rupert, British Columbia, with the southeastern Alaska ports of Hyder/ Stewart, Ketchikan, Metlakatla, Hollis, Petersburg, Wrangell, Kake, Sitka, Angoon, Pelican, Hoonah, Tenakee Springs, Juneau, Haines and Skagway. These southeastern communities (with the exception of Hyder, Haines and Skagway) are accessible only by boat, ferry or airplane. The seven vessels of the southeastern system are the *Aurora, Columbia, Kennicott, LeConte, Malaspina, Matanuska* and *Taku.*

With the addition of the *Kennicott* in summer 1998, the *Malaspina* began service as a day boat between Juneau, Skagway and Haines.

Southwest and southcentral Alaska are served by two ferries. The *Tustumena* serves

The ferry Aurora with a commercial fishing boat. Courtesy of Alaska Division of Tourism.

Seward, Port Lions, Kodiak, Homer and Seldovia, with limited summer service to Chignik, False Pass, Akutan, Sand Point, King Cove, Cold Bay and Dutch Harbor. The *Bartlett* provides service between Valdez and Cordova with summer service to Whittier and whistle stops at Chenega Bay and Tatitlek.

Scheduled state ferry service to southeastern Alaska began in 1963; ferry service to Kodiak Island began in 1964. The first three ferries of the Alaska ferry fleet were the *Malaspina, Matanuska* and *Taku*.

Reservations are required for all sailings. Rates for senior citizens and for passengers with disabilities are available. Contact the Alaska Marine Highway System, 1591 Glacier Ave., Juneau 99801-1427; phone (907) 465-3941; or (800) 642-0066 (U.S. and Canada). For details, read the *Marine Highway News*, published May 1; or check this Web site: www.state.ak.us/~Amhshome.html.

Nautical Miles Between Ports

Southeastern System

Bellingham–Ketchikan	595
Prince Rupert–Ketchikan	91
Ketchikan–Metlakatla	16
Ketchikan–Hollis	40
Hollis–Petersburg	123
Hollis–Wrangell	100
Ketchikan–Wrangell	89
Wrangell–Petersburg	41
Petersburg–Kake	65
Kake–Sitka	115
Sitka–Angoon	67

Southeastern System *continued*

Angoon–Tenakee	35
Tenakee–Hoonah	49
Angoon–Hoonah	63
Hoonah–Juneau (Auke Bay)	48
Sitka–Hoonah	115
Hoonah–Pelican via South Pass	64
Hoonah–Juneau	48
Haines–Skagway	13
Juneau (Auke Bay)–Haines	68
Petersburg–Juneau (Auke Bay)	123
Petersburg–Sitka	156
Juneau (Auke Bay)–Sitka	132
Juneau–Yakutat	234

Southwestern System

Seward–Cordova	144
Seward–Valdez	144
Cordova–Valdez	74
Valdez–Whittier	78
Seward–Kodiak	185
Kodiak–Port Lions	48
Kodiak–Homer	136
Homer–Seldovia	17
Kodiak–Sand Point via Sitkinak Strait	353
Yakutat–Valdez	286

Alaska State Ferry Data

Aurora (235 feet, 14.5 knots): 250 passengers, 34 vehicles, no cabins. Began service in 1977.

Bartlett (193 feet, 13.6 knots): 190 passengers, 29 vehicles, no cabins. Began service in 1969.

Columbia (418 feet, 17.3 knots): 625 passengers, 134 vehicles, 91 cabins. Began service in 1974.

Kennicott (382 feet, 16.75 knots): 748 passengers, 120 vehicles, 109 cabins. Began service in summer 1998.

LeConte (235 feet, 14.5 knots): 250 passengers, 34 vehicles, no cabins. Began service in 1974.

Malaspina (408 feet, 16.5 knots): 500 passengers, 88 vehicles, 83 cabins. Began service in 1963 and was lengthened and renovated in 1972.

Matanuska (408 feet, 16.5 knots): 500 passengers, 88 vehicles, 108 cabins. Began service in 1963.

Taku (352 feet, 16.5 knots): 450 passengers, 69 vehicles, 44 cabins. Began service in 1963.

Tustumena (296 feet, 13.5 knots): 210 passengers, 36 vehicles, 26 cabins. Began service in 1964.

Embarking Passenger and Vehicle Totals (in thousands) on Alaska Mainline Ferries*

Southeastern System

	Passengers	Vehicles
1987	326.6	83.5
1988	344.2	90.7
1989	344.4	89.8
1990	363.1	94.7
1991	368.8	95.2
1992	372.7	97.2
1993	342.6	92.6
1994	348.0	90.8
1995	332.2	88.9
1996	318.9	87.9
1997	300.6	82.4
1998	303.6	84.3

Southwestern System

	Passengers	Vehicles
1987	52.0	16.5
1988	50.3	16.6
1989	44.2	15.7
1990	50.5	16.5
1991	36.2	12.8
1992	47.8	15.7
1993	48.7	15.7
1994	48.5	15.2
1995	45.4	15.1
1996	46.1	14.8
1997	49.4	15.8
1998	48.3	16.5

*Mainline ports for Southeast are: Bellingham, Prince Rupert, Ketchikan, Wrangell, Petersburg, Sitka, Juneau, Haines and Skagway. Mainline ports for southwestern Alaska are: Cordova, Valdez, Whittier, Homer, Seldovia, Kodiak, Seward and Port Lions.

Fires on Wild Land
The 1999 fire season marked 60 years of fire fighting in Alaska. In 1939, fire guards covered only 4 percent of the area needing protection. Today, no area goes unprotected. Village crews make up the backbone of Alaska's fire-fighting operations.

Fire season starts in April or May, when winter's dead vegetation is vulnerable to any spark. Lightning is the leading cause of wild land fires in Alaska. In June, thunderstorms bring as many as 3,000 lightning strikes a day to the Alaska Interior. By mid-July in a normal year, rainfall in interior Alaska increases.

When wildfires threaten inhabited areas, the Bureau of Land Management's (BLM) Alaska Fire Service (in the northern half of the state) and the State of Alaska Division of Forestry (in the southern half of the state) provide fire protection to lands managed by BLM, National Park Service, U.S. Fish and Wildlife Service, Native corporations and the state.

All land management agencies in Alaska have placed their lands in one of four protection categories—critical, full, modified and limited. These protection levels set priorities for fire fighting.

With its 570,374 square miles of land, Alaska is more than twice the size of Texas. Most of this vast area has no roads and transportation for fire fighters is usually by airplane. Fire camps are remote. Mosquito repellent is a necessity, but headlamps are not required since the midnight sun shines all night. Aircraft bring in all supplies, even drinking water. Radios are the main means of communication with headquarters.

Black spruce burns very quickly. Fire fighters use chain saws to cut the trees and Pulaskis to cut through the underlying vegetation. It is nearly impossible to transport heavy equipment to fires in remote areas.

While investigating a brush fire in the Tongass National Forest, State Troopers discovered a small marijuana patch. According to the *Anchorage Daily News,* one investigating officer said, "I left my business card at the growing site, and I'm hoping they will call me."

Bulldozers are not used because they damage the delicate permafrost layer, leading to dramatic erosion.

Fire fighters don't depend on lookout towers in the wilderness to spot wildfires.

Today, computers detect the ionization from a lightning strike anywhere in the state, determine the latitude and longitude of the strike and display it on a computer screen. Detection specialists then fly to the areas of greatest risk.

When a fire is reported, computers tell the dispatcher which agency manages the land and whether the fire should be aggressively attacked.

Remote automatic weather stations report weather conditions all over Alaska, enabling weather forecasters to predict thunderstorms in any part of the state. Smoke jumpers and fire-retardant airplanes are pre-positioned close to the predicted thunderstorm activity.

The largest single fire ever reported in Alaska burned 5 million acres 74 miles northwest of Galena in 1957. Unusually dry weather in 1990 made it the most severe fire season on record in Alaska. Lightning was the primary cause of more than 900 fires, with an average of 2,000 strikes a day between June 26 and July 5.

Alaska Wildfires

Calendar Year	No. of Fires	Acres Burned
1989	485	68,893*
1990	932	3,189,427*
1991	760	1,667,965*
1992	474	150,057*
1993	869	713,116*
1994	643	265,722
1995	421	43,945
1996	724	599,267
1997	716	2,026,899
1998	413	176,000
1999	486	1,005,428

* Combined AFS (federal) and state coverage

In 1996, dryer than normal conditions made it difficult to control a wildfire that began near Big Lake, 60 miles northwest of Anchorage. Fire spread for more than a week, burning 37,500 acres and destroying 344 buildings valued at $8.8 million. Smoke blanketed Anchorage and the Matanuska-Susitna Valley. Fire crews from the Lower 48 were brought in to help fight the blaze, which threatened populated areas. Alaska wildfires have destroyed more acreage in the past, but none have claimed more property.

Fishing

Commercial

Alaska's abundant and largely pristine fishing grounds have provided a harvest of nearly 50 billion pounds of seafood over the past 10 years, accounting for nearly 55 percent of all domestically produced seafood.

The staggering volume is almost four times more than the next largest seafood-producing state. The Alaska Department of Fish and Game, which oversees certain Alaska commercial harvests, said earnings for fish processors in 1999 were estimated at $2.4 billion. In 1999, the ex-vessel value of Alaska's commercial harvest topped $1.2 billion—up from $924 million in 1998. Ex-vessel refers to prices paid to fishermen.

Commercial fishing's ripple effect is felt beyond the generations of coastal families that have made their living from the sea: In 1999, fish products accounted for 44 percent of Alaska's international exports—outstripping oil and natural gas, at 25 percent, and mining, at 12 percent, which placed second and third respectively.

A University of Alaska Anchorage study concluded in 1991 that the state's seafood industry was the most important private basic industry in Alaska, both in terms of employment and income. More than 75,000 people rely on commercial fishing or seafood processing for all or part of their income, and in many small coastal and river towns, commercial fishing is the top source of income, directly or indirectly. Alaska's fisheries taxes, which cities and boroughs share in, has become a key element of the tax base in many smaller communities.

Alaska's commercial fleet faces complex issues in the next millennium. Scientists have joined with Alaska Native villages to gain a better understanding of continued declining salmon returns in western Alaska—a region heavily dependent on salmon for income and to support subsistence life. And researchers are working to understand how ecosystem changes in the vast Bering Sea affect fish production. Factors under study include global warming, a strong El Niño effect followed by ocean cooling, and exceptional temperatures in the Bering Sea.

Fishing boat in Southeast Alaska. From *Journeys Through the Inside Passage* by Joe Upton.

Value and Volume of Alaska Fish and Shellfish Landings

Year	Value	Volume (in lbs.)
1989	1,332,000,000	5,213,100,000
1990	1,500,000,000	5,920,000,000
1991	1,216,482,000	5,144,800,000
1992	1,577,421,000	5,637,937,000
1993	1,278,000,000	6,010,000,000
1994	1,346,000,000	5,779,000,000
1995	1,396,974,000	5,293,445,000
1996	1,190,576,000	5,012,875,000
1997	1,216,700,000	4,226,000,000
1998	1,183,000,000*	5,054,000,000*
1999	1,209,000,000	4,898,000,000

Source: National Marine Fisheries Service,
   U.S. Department of Commerce
*Source: Alaska Department of Fish and Game

Salmon. The ex-vessel value of Alaska's near-record commercial salmon harvest in 1999 was $363 million, up from $261 million in 1998 and reversing a downward trend of several years. Nearly 900 million pounds of salmon were hauled up.

The harvest of 214 million fish was only the second time that commercial landings topped 200 million fish, state officials noted. In 1995, a record 218 million salmon were taken. Some 146 million pink salmon were harvested in 1999, a new statewide record. Projections for 2000 called for a total harvest of about 153 million fish, including 85 million pinks. These numbers are closer to average levels.

Of the 247 million pounds of sockeye landed in 1999, 138 million pounds were taken from Bristol Bay. Sockeye weighed about 6 pounds each and fetched from 60 cents a pound to $1.90 a pound in 1999, depending on where fish were caught. Commercially landed sockeye are a backbone of the canning industry.

Five species of Pacific salmon inhabit Alaska waters and are commercially harvested: king (also known as chinook); silver (coho); pink (humpback); red (sockeye); and chum (dog salmon).

Shellfish. About 225 million pounds of shellfish were harvested in 1999, for an ex-vessel value of $271 million—an improvement of 1998's value of $215 million.

Much of the shellfish volume and value was accounted for by the Bering Sea opilio crab harvest. Some 194 million pounds worth $174 million to fishermen were taken.

Dive fisheries. Alaska's dive fisheries include the Southeast sea cucumber, the Southeast sea urchin, Yakutat scallops and the Southeast geoduck clam. Some 3.8 million pounds of seafood were taken in commercial dive fisheries in 1999. Value of the harvest was $2.6 million.

Dive fisheries are a relatively new and growing sector of commercial fishing, state regulators say. Management issues on the horizon include sustainable harvest strategies, markets and product quality.

Ex-vessel Value of Alaska's Commercial Fisheries (in millions of dollars)

Species	1992	1993	1994	1995	1996	1997	1998	1999*
Salmon	$575	$390	$482	$481	$365	$248	$261	$363
Shellfish	301	356	314	265	164	161	215	271
Halibut	49	60	85	65	78	111	68	137
Herring	30	17	22	42	64	16	12	15
Groundfish	625	455	443	434	685	652	627	409

* Preliminary figures
Source: Alaska Department of Fish and Game, May 2000
www.cf.adfg.state.ak.us

1999 Final Commercial Salmon Harvest* (in thousands of fish)

Region	King	Sockeye	Coho	Pink	Chum	Total
Southeast	190	1,160	3,570	77,700	14,900	97,520
Central (Prince William Sound, Cook Inlet, Kodiak, Chignik and Bristol Bay)	130	39,020	790	59,460	11,230	110,630
Arctic–Yukon–Kuskokwim	100	80	40	0	220	440
Western (Alaska Peninsula and Aleutian Islands)	10	4,730	250	8,440	870	14,300
Total	430	44,990	4,650	145,600	27,220	222,890

* Preliminary figures
Source: Alaska Department of Fish and Game, May 2000
www.cf.adfg.state.ak.us

Herring. Much of Alaska's commercial herring is harvested as sac roe, a longtime delicacy in Japan where consumption has begun to taper. The 1999 herring sac roe harvest was nearly 38 tons and valued at $14 million. Southeast's winter food and bait harvest of herring added another 1,010 tons to the 1999 harvest.

Relied on by earliest Alaska Natives for food, herring are found in commercial quantities from Dixon Entrance in Southeast as far north as Norton Sound. Traditional dried herring is still savored in some Bering Sea villages; Southeast Alaska Natives consume herring eggs.

Halibut. Alaska's commercial halibut season is federally regulated and runs from March 15 through Nov. 15. An additional fishery quota program imposed in 1995 limits the number of halibut permit holders and ended "derby" style fishing that had boats awaiting numerous

openings of just 24 hours to 48 hours.

Halibut are targeted in three zones: the Bering Sea region; Southeast; and the Gulf of Alaska, which accounts for most of the catch. Figures from the National Marine Fisheries Service show that some 67 million pounds of halibut were taken in Alaska in 1998, an increase over 1997's 64 million pounds. The value of the 1998 harvest was $71 million.

Groundfish. Commercially harvested groundfish in Alaska include Pacific cod, rockfishes, sablefish and pollock. By far the largest catch is pollock, much of it taken in the Bering Sea. The fisheries are regulated by the National Marine Fisheries Service.

In all, some 3.9 billion pounds of groundfish were hauled up in 1998; of that, 2.7 billion pounds was pollock. The harvest was about 8 percent greater than 1997ís volume, and was valued at $385 million.

Pacific cod accounted for 5.6 million

pounds in 1998 and was valued at $87 million, the fisheries service said. Volume was down 16 percent over 1997.

Alaska's harvest of rockfishes declined by 40 percent, to 70 million pounds. The harvest was valued at $33 million, off 31 percent.

Some 33.5 million pounds of sablefish were taken in 1998, a drop of 5 percent. Much of the harvest was exported to Japan. The fish were valued at $80 million.

Alaska's billion-dollar groundfish industry has been retooled from early days when it was dominated by foreign-flagged ships, followed by an era of joint-ventures, to today's domestic fleet. The fishery was altered again following passage of the American Fisheries Act in 1998, which authorized the buyout of nine large factory trawlers and divided the pollock harvest between in-shore processors and at-sea processors. The act also instituted cooperative fishing programs. Changes were aimed at blunting some of the race for fish.

Virtually nowhere in the industry has the race for fish been as frenzied as for Alaska's groundfish; over the past decade, the number of harvesting permits has increased by 700 percent, in part explained as the industry moved to a domestic fleet. Not so long ago, pollock and cod were considered low-value species. While rockfish or Pacific cod are worth many times pollock's value, the sheer volume of Alaska's pollock catch now drives the value of this fishery.

Conservation issues are complex as the fleet and fishery managers work to retain a sustainable yield. Some experts say too many boats are chasing too few fish. Highly efficient trawlers emphasize fishing speed and volume. Once a year-round fishery, Alaska's groundfish seasons today have shrunk to a few weeks a year as vessels attain quotas in shorter time.

Still other authorities worry that Alaska fisheries may be headed for biological devastation that has struck New England waters, where overfishing was a factor. Efforts to reduce accidental by-catch waste of species such as halibut, salmon and crab are ongoing. Concerns over illegal fishing, effects of concentrated harvesting during spawning season and habitat pollution persist as well.

Sport

The Alaska Department of Fish and Game has established five regulatory zones, each with its own sportfishing rules. Anglers are advised to consult the *Alaska Sport Fishing Regulations* summary for areas they plan to fish. Summaries may be ordered online at SFregs@fishgame.state.ak.us or by writing to the department at P.O. Box 25526, Juneau 99802-5526, or by inquiring at sportfishing offices in the state.

In 2000, regulations were grouped into

Alaska State Record Trophy Fish

Species	Min. Wt.	Lbs./oz.	Year	Location	Angler
Arctic Char/					
Dolly Varden	10 lbs.	19/12.5	1991	Noatak River	Ken Ubben
Brook Trout*	3 lbs.				
Burbot	8 lbs.	24/12	1976	Lake Louise	George R. Howard
Chum Salmon	15 lbs.	32/0	1985	Caamano Point	Frederick Thynes
Coho Salmon	20 lbs.	26/0	1976	Icy Strait	Andrew Robbins
Cutthroat Trout	3 lbs.	8/6	1977	Wilson Lake	Robert Denison
Grayling	3 lbs.	4/13	1981	Ugashik	Paul F. Kanitz
Halibut	250 lbs.	459/0	1996	Unalaska Bay	Jack Tragis
King Salmon	**	97/4	1985	Kenai River	Lester Anderson
Lake Trout	20 lbs.	47/0	1970	Clarence Lake	Daniel Thorsness
Lingcod	45 lbs.	70/0	1996	Sitka Sound	Howard Motoyoshi
Northern Pike	15 lbs.	38/0	1991	Innoko River	Jack Wagner
Pink Salmon	8 lbs.	12/9	1974	Moose River	Steven A. Lee
Rainbow Trout/					
Steelhead	15 lbs.	42/3	1970	Bell Island	David White
Rockfish	18 lbs.	37/2	1995	Passage Canal	Colin Gamble
Sheefish	30 lbs.	53/0	1986	Pah River	Lawrence E. Hudnall
Sockeye Salmon	12 lbs.	16/0	1974	Kenai River	Chuck Leach
Whitefish	4 lbs.	9/0	1989	Tozitna River	Al Mathews

* This species was added in 1995; no entries to date
** King salmon minimum weight for Kenai River is 75 lbs; for rest of state, 50 lbs.
Source: Alaska Department of Fish and Game Trophy Fish Program

these zones: Arctic-Yukon-Kuskokwim-Tanana-Upper Copper and Upper Susitna Rivers; Bristol Bay-Lower Kuskokwim; Alaska Peninsula-Aleutian Islands-Kodiak Island; Kenai Peninsula-Cook Inlet-Susitna drainage-Prince William Sound-Resurrection Bay; Southeast-Yakutat.

Regulations. A sportfishing license is required for residents and nonresidents 16 years of age or older. Alaska residents age 60 or older who have been resident one year or more do not need a sportfishing license as long as they remain residents. A special identification card is issued for this exemption.

Anglers rarely fish all of Alaska in a lifetime; the state has more coastline than all of the Lower 48 states and more than 100,000 lakes. Alaska's salmon sportfishing is deservedly renown, although some urban Alaska streams have seen reductions in recent years. Conservation-minded anglers should note that while many stocks of Pacific salmon are in trouble in other states, all five species found in Alaska are at healthy levels. In general, king salmon fishing occurs in spring and ends in midsummer; sockeye, pink and chum seasons are next, followed by silver salmon

Top Ten Trophy King Salmon

1. 97 lbs., 4 oz (Kenai River, 1985)
2. 95 lbs., 10 oz. (Kenai River, 1990)
3. 92 lbs., 4 oz. (Kenai River, 1985)
4. 91 lbs., 10 oz. (Kenai River, 1988)
5. 91 lbs., 4 oz. (Kenai River, 1987)
6. 91 lbs. (Kenai River, 1995)
7. 90 lbs., 4 oz. (Kenai River, 1995)
8. 89 lbs., 3 oz. (Kenai River, 1987)
9. 89 lbs., 1 oz. (Kenai River, 1995)
10. 89 lbs. (Kenai River, 1994)

Source: Alaska Department of Fish and Game Trophy Fish Program

in late summer and fall. Out-of-state anglers may call (800) 874-8202 for Alaska information.

Resident sportfishing licenses cost $15, valid for the calendar year issued (nonresident, $100; 1-day nonresident, $10; 3-day nonresident, $20; 7-day nonresident, $39; 14-day nonresident, $50). A resident is a person who has maintained a permanent place of abode within the state for 12 consecutive months and has continuously maintained a voting residence in the state. Military personnel on active duty permanently stationed in the state, and their dependents, can purchase a nonresident military sportfishing license ($15).

An additional stamp is required for those wishing to fish for king salmon. Cost for residents is $10. Nonresidents may purchase a king stamp that's good for the calendar year for $100. Other options are: 1-day nonresident, $10; 3-day nonresident, $20; 7-day nonresident, $30; 14-day nonresident, $50; military, $20.

Nearly all sporting goods stores in Alaska sell fishing licenses. They are also available by mail from the Alaska Department of Revenue, Fish and Game License Section, P.O. Box 25525, Juneau 99802-5525. Or refer to the Sport Fish Division Web site at www.admin.adfg.state.ak.us/license or call toll free at 1-877-9FISHAK.

Fish Wheel
The fish wheel is a handcrafted, wooden machine fastened to a river shore and propelled by current which floats on a log raft and scoops up fish heading upstream to spawn. Widely used

Fish wheel on the Tanana River. From The Alaska Heritage Seafood Cookbook by Ann Chandonnet.

for subsistence salmon fishing along stretches of Alaska's largest rivers, the fish wheel provides a way of catching salmon without injuring them. Contrary to popular belief, Alaska Natives did not invent the fish wheel. Non-Natives first introduced the fish wheel on the Tanana River in 1904. Soon after, it appeared on the Yukon River, where it was used by both settlers and Natives. It first appeared on the Kuskokwim in 1914, when prospectors introduced it for catching salmon near Georgetown.

Today, subsistence fishing with the use of a fish wheel is allowed on the Tanana River, the Copper River and the Kuskokwim River, as well as the Yukon River and its tributaries. There are 166 limited-entry permits for the use of fish wheels by commercial salmon fishermen on the Yukon River system—the only district where both commercial and subsistence fishermen use fish wheels. Fishing times with the wheels are regulated.

Prior to its appearance in Alaska, the fish wheel was used on the East Coast, on the Sacramento River in California and on the Columbia River in Washington and Oregon.

Furs and Trapping
The major sources of harvested Alaska furs are the Yukon and Kuskokwim Valleys.

The Arctic provides limited numbers of arctic fox, wolverine and wolf but the Gulf Coast areas and Southeast are more productive. Southeast Alaska is a good source of mink and otter.

Trapping is seasonal work, and most trappers work summers at fishing or other employment. Licenses are required for trapping. (*See* Hunting section for license fees.)

State-regulated furbearers are beaver, coyote, red fox (includes cross, black or silver color phases), arctic fox (includes white or blue), lynx, marmot, marten, mink, muskrat, river (land) otter, squirrel (parka or ground, flying and red), weasel, wolf and wolverine. Very little harvest or use is made of parka squirrels and marmots.

Prices for raw skins are widely variable

and depend on the buyer, quality, condition and size of the fur.

Pelts accepted for purchase are beaver, coyote, lynx, marten, mink, muskrat, otter, red and white fox, red squirrel, weasel (ermine), wolf and wolverine. Check with a buyer for current market prices.

Geography (SEE MAP,
PAGES 8–9. SEE ALSO GLACIERS AND ICE FIELDS; LAKES; MOUNTAINS; POPULATIONS AND ZIP CODES; REGIONS OF ALASKA; AND RIVERS)

State capital: Juneau.

State population: 622,000

Land area: 570,374 square miles, or about 365 million acres—largest state in the union; one-fifth the size of the Lower 48. Alaska is larger than the three next largest states combined.

Area per person: Approximately 0.92 square mile per person.

Diameter: East to west, 2,400 miles; north to south, 1,420 miles.

Coastline: 6,640 miles, point to point; as measured on the most detailed maps available, including islands, Alaska has 33,904 miles of shoreline—twice the length of the Lower 48. Estimated tidal shoreline, including islands, inlets and shoreline to head of tidewater, is 47,300 miles.

Adjacent salt water: North Pacific Ocean, Bering Sea, Chukchi Sea, Arctic Ocean.

Alaska–Canada border: 1,538 miles long; length of boundary between the Arctic Ocean and Mount St. Elias, 647 miles; Southeast border with British Columbia and Yukon Territory, 710 miles; water boundary, 181 miles.

Geographic center: 63°50' north, 152° west, about 60 miles northwest of Mount McKinley.

Northernmost point: Point Barrow, 71°23' north.

Southernmost point: Tip of Amatignak Island, Aleutian Chain, 51°13'05" north.

Easternmost and westernmost points: It all depends on how you look at it. The 180th meridian—halfway around the world from the prime meridian at Greenwich, England, and the dividing line between east and west longitudes—passes through Alaska. According to one view, Alaska has both the easternmost and westernmost spots in the country! The westernmost is Amatignak Island, 179°10' west; and the easternmost, Pochnoi Point, 179°46' east. On the other hand, if you are facing north, east is to your right and west to your left. Therefore, the westernmost point is Cape Wrangell, Attu Island, 172°27' east; and the easternmost is near Camp Point, in southeastern Alaska, 129°59' east.

Tallest mountain: Mount McKinley, 20,320 feet, and the tallest mountain in North America. Alaska has 39 mountain ranges, containing 17 of the 20 highest peaks in the United States.

In an unprecedented crime wave, the *Valdez Vanguard* reported, "Juveniles were reported spreading Turtle Wax uphostery cleaner on a sidewalk." The newspaper also conducted a man-on-the-street interview by asking, "If the Valdez City Council enacts a $5-per-day RV tax, would you visit Valdez again?" An Ohio resident replied, "No, it would not be worth the money."

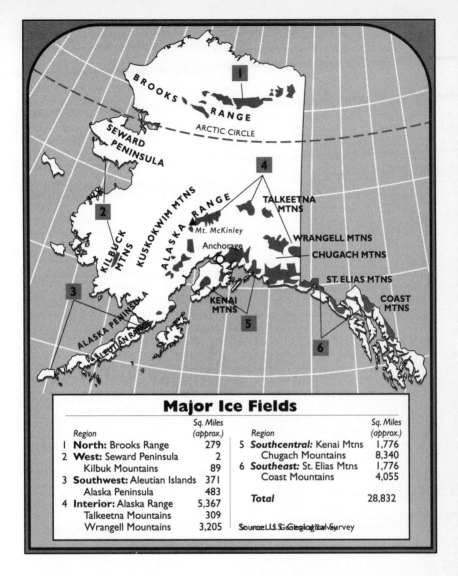

Major Ice Fields

Region	Sq. Miles (approx.)	Region	Sq. Miles (approx.)
1 **North:** Brooks Range	279	5 *Southcentral:* Kenai Mtns	1,776
2 **West:** Seward Peninsula	2	Chugach Mountains	8,340
Kilbuk Mountains	89	6 *Southeast:* St. Elias Mtns	1,776
3 **Southwest:** Aleutian Islands	371	Coast Mountains	4,055
Alaska Peninsula	483		
4 **Interior:** Alaska Range	5,367	**Total**	28,832
Talkeetna Mountains	309		
Wrangell Mountains	3,205	Source: U.S. Geological Survey	

Largest natural freshwater lake: Iliamna, 1,150 square miles. Alaska has more than 3 million lakes more than 20 acres in size.

Longest river: Yukon, 1,875 miles in Alaska; 2,298 total. There are more than 3,000 rivers in the state. The Yukon River ranks third in length of U.S. rivers, behind the Mississippi and Missouri Rivers.

Largest island: Kodiak, in the Gulf of Alaska, 3,588 square miles. There are 1,800 named islands in the state, 1,000 of which are located in Southeast Alaska.

Largest city in population: Anchorage, population 259,391.

Largest city in area: Sitka, with 4,710 square miles, 1,816 square miles of which is water. Juneau is second, with 3,108 square miles.

Glaciers and Ice Fields

The greatest concentrations of glaciers are in the Alaska Range, Wrangell Mountains and the coastal ranges of the Chugach, Coast, Kenai and St. Elias Mountains, where annual precipitation is high. All of Alaska's well-known glaciers fall within these areas. The distribution of glacier ice is shown on the map on page 77.

Glaciers cover approximately 29,000 square miles—or 5 percent—of Alaska, which is 128 times more area covered by glaciers than in the rest of the United States. There are an estimated 100,000 glaciers in Alaska, ranging from tiny cirque glaciers to huge valley glaciers.

Glaciers are formed where, over a number of years, more snow falls than

Beached icebergs along Barry Arm. From *Alaska's Prince William Sound: A Traveler's Guide* by Marybeth Holleman. Photo by the author.

melts. Alaska's glaciers fall roughly into five general categories: alpine, valley, piedmont, ice fields and ice caps. Alpine (mountain and cirque) glaciers head high on the slopes of mountains and plateaus. Valley glaciers are an overflowing accumulation of ice from mountain or plateau basins. Piedmont glaciers result when one or more glaciers join to form a fan-shaped ice mass at the foot of a mountain range. Ice fields develop when large valley glaciers interconnect, leaving only the highest peaks and ridges to rise above the ice surface. Ice caps are smaller glaciers perched on plateaus.

Alaska's better-known glaciers accessible by road are: Worthington (Richardson Highway), Matanuska (Glenn Highway), Exit (Seward Highway), Portage (Seward Highway) and Mendenhall (Glacier Highway). In addition, Childs and Sheridan Glaciers may be reached by car from Cordova, and Valdez Glacier, also accessible by car, is only a few miles from the town of Valdez. The sediment-covered terminus of Muldrow Glacier in Denali National Park and Preserve is visible at a distance along several miles of the park road.

Many spectacular glaciers in Glacier Bay National Park and Preserve, in Kenai Fjords and in Prince William Sound are visible from tour boats or flightseeing.

Glacier ice often appears blue to the eye because it absorbs all the colors of the spectrum except blue, which is scattered back.

About three-fourths of all the fresh water in Alaska is stored as glacial ice. This is many times greater than the volume of water stored in all the state's lakes, ponds, rivers and reservoirs.

• Longest tidewater glacier in North America is Hubbard, 76 miles long (heads in Canada). In 1986, Hubbard rapidly advanced and blocked Russell Fiord near Yakutat. Later in the year, the ice dam gave way.

• Longest glacier is Bering (including Bagley Icefield), more than 100 miles long.

• Southernmost active tidewater glacier in North America is LeConte.

• Greatest concentration of tidewater-calving glaciers is in Prince William Sound, with 20 active tidewater glaciers.

• Largest piedmont lobe glacier is Malaspina, 850 square miles; the Malaspina Glacier complex (including tributary glaciers) is approximately 2,000 square miles in area. The largest glacier is the Bering Glacier complex, about 2,250 square miles in size, which includes Bagley Icefield.

• La Perouse Glacier in Glacier Bay National Park is the only calving glacier in North America that discharges icebergs directly into the open Pacific Ocean.

• There are more than 750 glacier-dammed lakes in Alaska; the largest at present is 28-square-mile Chakachamna Lake west of Anchorage.

• Variegated Glacier, at Russell Fiord in Yakutat Bay, is the most studied glacier in the world. The glacier, which extends 10 miles from its head to its foot, surprised scientists in 1995 by surging (a rise in forward movement) four years ahead of schedule. By the end of summer 1995, the glacier had moved hundreds of yards. Scientists attribute the surge to the movement of water underneath the glacier rather than climatic conditions.

Gold (SEE ALSO
GOLD STRIKES AND RUSHES *AND* MINERALS AND MINING) The largest gold nugget ever found in Alaska was discovered in the summer of 1998. The nugget, weighing

294 troy ounces (24.5 pounds), was found in the Ruby District of northern Alaska. The second-largest nugget, weighing 155 troy ounces, was found Sept. 29, 1903, on Discovery Claim on Anvil Creek, Nome District. The nugget was 7 inches long, 4 inches wide and 2 inches thick.

Four other large nuggets have been found in Alaska, one of which also came from the Discovery Claim on Anvil Creek in 1899. It was the largest Alaska nugget found up to that time, weighing 82.1 troy ounces, and was 6¼ inches long, 3¼ inches wide, 1⅜ inches thick at one end and ½ inch thick at the other.

In 1914, the third-largest nugget mined, weighing 138.4 troy ounces, was found near Discovery Claim on Hammond River, Wiseman District. Three of the top five nuggets have been discovered within the last 16 years, including one from Lower

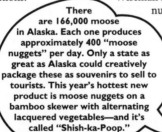

There are 166,000 moose in Alaska. Each one produces approximately 400 "moose nuggets" per day. Only a state as great as Alaska could creatively package these as souvenirs to sell to tourists. This year's hottest new product is moose nuggets on a bamboo skewer with alternating lacquered vegetables—and it's called "Shish-ka-Poop."

Gold Rush Centennial

In the summer of 1896, while prospecting on Rabbit Creek in Canada's Yukon Territory, George Carmack took out a $5 pan of gold—at a time when 10 cents a pan was considered a worthwhile find. Carmack renamed the creek Bonanza and staked claims for himself and his two partners.

When word reached the rest of the world the following spring, more than 100,000 gold seekers from all over the world set off for the Klondike. Many took routes through Alaska or eventually stampeded to Alaska strikes.

Centennial events celebrating Northern gold rushes began in 1997, and many continue through 2004. A sample of events for the year 2000:

March 13–14: Chatanika Days. Winter festival featuring outhouse races, long-john contest and more in gold mining town, 30 miles northeast of Fairbanks. (907) 389-2164.

June, weekend closest to summer solstice: Nome celebrates 24 hours of daylight with a Midnight Sun Festival: a parade with a gold rush theme, a bank holdup, dart tournament, street dance and mini-triathlon. (907) 443-5535.

June to August: Three-Day Gold Rush Adventure. Five Valdez tour companies and the Valdez Museum team up to give the modern traveler an opportunity to relive the excitement of 1897–99 and the Copper River Gold Rush. (907) 835-4731.

In Eagle, take the Daily Walking Tour that includes six restored gold-rush-era buildings. (907) 547-2325.

June to August through 2001: Rent a cabin near the gold rush town of Council, where the Three Lucky Swedes mined for gold before their big discovery in Nome. Fish in the Niukluk River. Advance reservations required. (907) 443-5535.

July 4: Independence Day. Communities throughout the state host parades, games and other fun events. In Skagway, a re-enactment of Soapy Smith's Wake is part of the activities. Check local visitor information centers for particulars.

Sept. 10–11: Klondike Trail of '98 Road Relay, Skagway. A 110-mile footrace begins in Skagway in the evening and ends in Whitehorse, Yukon, on the following afternoon. Ten-member teams compete in this event that follows the Klondike Highway. (403) 668-4236.

For more information, contact the Alaska Gold Rush Centennial Task Force, (907) 269-8721; the Juneau Convention and Visitors Bureau, (907) 586-2201; or the Skagway Convention and Visitors Bureau, (907) 982-2855. The Alaska Division of Tourism has a complete schedule of Alaska's Gold Rush Centennial events. Phone (907) 465-2010; e-mail GoNorth@Commerce.state.ak.us. Dawson has scheduled a "Decade of Centennials" through 2002. Visit the Klondike Gold Rush National Historic Park Web site at www.nps.gov/klgo/. ✳

Glacier Creek, Kantishna District, in 1984, weighing 91.8 troy ounces, and the other from Ganes Creek, Innoko District, in 1986, weighing 122 troy ounces.

If you are interested in gold panning, sluicing or suction dredging in Alaska— for fun or profit—you'll have to know whose land you are on and familiarize yourself with current regulations.

Panning, sluicing and suction dredging on private property, established mining claims and Native lands is considered trespassing unless you have the consent of the owner. On state and federal lands, contact the managing agency for current restrictions on mining. On Native-owned

Stampeders and their supplies at Dyea, about 1898. From *Alaska's History* by Harry Ritter.

lands, contact the tribal council of the village or the Native corporation well in advance of your visit.

You can pan for gold for a small fee by visiting one of the gold-panning resorts in Alaska. Commercial resorts rent gold pans and let you try your luck on gold-bearing creeks and streams on their property.

If you want to stake a mining claim, the state Department of Natural Resources has a free booklet, *Regulations and Statutes Pertaining to Mining Rights of Alaska Lands,* obtained by calling the department offices in Juneau, (907) 465-2400; Fairbanks, (907) 451-2790; or Anchorage, (907) 762-2518. A general government source for information about property is www.dggs.dnr.state.ak.us.

Following are volumes (in troy ounces) and value figures for recent years of Alaska gold production.

Gold Production in Alaska, 1990–99

Year	Vol. (in troy oz.)	Value
1990	231,700	$89,204,000
1991	243,900	88,291,800
1992	262,530	88,463,000
1993	191,265	68,640,800

Year	Vol. (in troy oz.)	Value
1994	182,100	70,300,000
1995	141,882	56,043,390
1996	161,565	62,622,594
1997	590,516	207,287,000
1998	594,111	174,597,000
1999	509,000	144,858,300

The following chart shows the fluctuation in the price of gold (1991–99) after the gold standard was lifted in 1967. Note that these are average annual prices and do not reflect the yearly high or low prices.

Average Annual Price of Gold, per Troy Ounce

1934 to 1967	$ 35.00
1991	362.03
1992	337.00
1993	354.00
1994	386.00
1995	395.00
1996	387.60
1997	330.76
1998	293.88
1999	278.70

Source: Alaska Division of Geological and Geophysical Survey's annual Alaska Mineral Industry reports

Gold Strikes and Rushes

1848—First Alaska gold discovery at Russian River on Kenai Peninsula

1861—Stikine River near Telegraph Creek, British Columbia; Wrangell

1872—Cassiar district in Canada (Stikine headwaters country)

1872—Near Sitka

1874—Windham Bay near Juneau

1880—Gold Creek at Juneau

1886—Fortymile discovery

1887—Yakutat areas and Lituya Bay

1893—Mastodon Creek, starting Circle City

1895—Sunrise district on the Kenai Peninsula

1896—Klondike strike, Bonanza Creek, Yukon Territory, Canada

1896—Council (Seward Peninsula)

1898—Anvil Creek near Nome; Atlin district

1898—Hope and Sunrise on Turnagain Arm

1898—British Columbia

1899—Nome beaches

1900—Porcupine rush out of Haines

1902—Fairbanks (Felix Pedro, Upper Goldstream Valley)

1905—Kantishna Hills

1906—Innoko

1907—Ruby

1908—Iditarod

1913—Chisana

1913—Marshall

1914—Livengood

Golf

The Municipality of Anchorage maintains two golf courses—the Anchorage Golf Course on O'Malley Road, an 18-hole all-grass course offering views of the Chugach Range, the city and, on a clear day, Mount McKinley; and a 9-hole course (artificial turf greens) at Russian Jack Springs located at Boniface Parkway and Debarr Road. Tanglewood Lakes Golf Club offers a 9-hole all-grass course.

Two military courses are open to the public—Eagle Glen Golf Course (18 holes) at Elmendorf Air Force Base, and the 18-hole Moose Run Golf Course (the oldest golf course in Alaska) at Fort Richardson.

Palmer Municipal Golf Course (18 holes) has a driving range, clubhouse, and rental clubs and carts.

Fairbanks offers the 9-hole Fairbanks Golf and Country Club west of the downtown area, the 9-hole Chena Bend Golf Course located at Fort Wainwright, and North Star Golf Club at 4.5 mile Steese Highway north of Fairbanks.

Mendenhall Golf Course in Juneau (9 holes) has a driving range, rental clubs and glacier views.

Every March, Kodiak holds the Pillar Mountain Golf Classic, an irreverent par-70 1-hole match up the side of 1,400-foot Pillar Mountain.

Among Alaska's newest golf course is Muskeg Meadows, opened in 1998 in Wrangell. It is a 9-hole, 36-acre regulation course and driving range. A tournament is held there annually in April.

During the summer months, golfers may tee off as late as 10 P.M. Die-hard golfers play in the winter using brightly painted balls. At the annual Lake Louise winter game in Wasilla, played on lake ice, golfers use orange balls that are highly visible on the snow and ice. Nome hosts the Bering Sea Ice Classic Golf Tournament in March and additional golf tournaments in September.

Alaska's northernmost golf course is in Coldfoot, featuring three holes, a driving range and rental clubs. Herds of musk-oxen are allowed to "play through."

Other golf courses can be found throughout the state, including Birch Ridge in Soldotna and Settlers Bay in Knik. An occasional private campground will offer putting greens or mini-golf for guests.

Government (SEE ALSO COURTS AND GOVERNMENT OFFICIALS) Alaska is represented in the U.S. Congress by two senators and one representative. The capital of Alaska is Juneau.

A governor and lieutenant governor are elected by popular vote for four-year terms on the same ticket. The governor is given extensive powers under the constitution, overseeing 15 major departments: Administration, Commerce and Economic Development, Community and Regional Affairs, Corrections, Education, Environmental Conservation, Fish and Game, Health and Social Services, Labor, Law, Military and Veterans Affairs, Natural Resources, Public Safety, Revenue, and Transportation and Public Facilities.

The Legislature is bicameral, with 20 senators elected from 14 senate districts for four-year terms, and 40 representatives from 27 election districts for 2-year terms. Under the state constitution, redistricting is done every 10 years, after the reporting of the decennial federal census. The latest redistricting occurred in 1991. The judiciary consists of a state supreme court, court of appeals, superior court, district courts and magistrates.

Alaska is unique among the 50 states because most of its land mass has not been organized into political subdivisions equivalent to the county form of government. Local government is by a system of organized boroughs, much like counties in other states. Several areas of the state are not included in any borough because of sparse population. Boroughs generally provide a more limited number of services than cities.

There are two classes. First- and second-class boroughs have three mandatory powers: education, land use planning, and tax assessment and collection. The major difference between the two classes is in how they may acquire other powers. Both classes have separately elected borough assemblies and school boards. All boroughs may assess, levy and collect real and personal property taxes. They may also levy sales taxes.

Incorporated cities are small units of local government, serving one community. There are two classes. First-class cities, generally urban areas, have six-member councils and a separately elected mayor. Taxing authority is somewhat broader than for second-class cities and responsibilities are broader. A first-class city that has adopted a home rule charter is called a home rule city; adoption allows the city to revise its ordinances within lawful limits. Second-class cities, generally places with fewer than 400 people, are governed by a seven-member council, one of whom serves as mayor. Taxing authority is limited. A borough and all cities located within it may unite

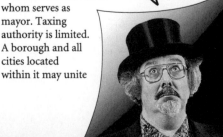

Experienced winter seal hunters wisely take SPAM® on the polar ice pack because SPAM® doesn't freeze!

in a single unit of government called a unified municipality.

There are 246 federally recognized tribal governments in Alaska and one community (Metlakatla, originally an Indian reservation) organized under federal law.

In 2000, there were 16 organized boroughs and unified home rule municipalities: three unified home rule municipalities, five home rule boroughs, seven second-class boroughs.

Alaska's 149 incorporated cities include 12 home rule cities, 21 first-class cities and 116 second-class cities.

Borough Addresses and Contacts

Aleutians East Borough. P.O. Box 349, Sand Point 99661; (907) 383-5334.

Municipality of Anchorage. Mayor's Office or Manager's Office, P.O. Box 196650, Anchorage 99519; (907) 343-4431.

Bristol Bay Borough. Borough Clerk, P.O. Box 189, Naknek 99633; (907) 246-4224.

Denali Borough. Mayor, P.O. Box 480, Anderson 99744; (907) 683-1330.

Fairbanks North Star Borough. Clerk, P.O. Box 71267, Fairbanks 99707; (907) 459-1000.

Haines Borough. Borough Secretary, P.O. Box 1209, Haines 99827; (907) 766-2611.

City and Borough of Juneau. City-Borough Manager, 155 S. Seward St., Juneau 99801; (907) 586-5240.

Kenai Peninsula Borough. Borough Clerk, 144 N. Binkley St., Soldotna 99669; (907) 262-4441.

Ketchikan Gateway Borough. Borough Manager, 344 Front St., Ketchikan 99901; (907) 225-6625.

Kodiak Island Borough. Borough Mayor or Borough Clerk, 710 Mill Bay Road, Kodiak 99615; (907) 486-5736.

Lake and Peninsula Borough. P.O. Box 495, King Salmon 99613; (907) 276-3421.

Matanuska–Susitna Borough. Borough Manager, 350 E. Dahlia Ave., Palmer 99645-6488; (907) 745-4801.

North Slope Borough. Borough Mayor, P.O. Box 69, Barrow 99723; (907) 852-2611.

Northwest Arctic Borough. P.O. Box 1110, Kotzebue 99752; (907) 442-2500.

City and Borough of Sitka. Administrator, 304 Lake St., Room 104, Sitka 99835; (907) 747-3294.

City and Borough of Yakutat. P.O. Box 160, Yakutat 99689; (907) 784-3323.

Government Officials

Russian Alaska

Emperor Paul of Russia grants the Russian-American Company an exclusive trade charter in Alaska.

Chief Manager	Dates Served
Alexander Andrevich Baranov	1799–1818
Leontil Andreanovich Hagemeiste	January–October 1818
Semen Ivanovich Yanovski	1818–1820
Matxei I. Muravief	1820–1825
Peter Egorovich Chistiakov	1825–1830
Baron Ferdinand P. von Wrangell	1830–1835
Ivan Antonovich Kupreanof	1835–1840
Adolph Karlovich Etolin	1840–1845
Michael D. Tebenkof	1845–1850
Nikolai Y. Rosenberg	1850–1853
Alexander Ilich Rudakof	1853–1854
Stephen Vasili Voevodski	1854–1859
Ivan V. Furuhelm	1859–1863
Prince Dmitri Maksoutoff	1863–1867

Territory of Alaska

United States purchases Alaska from Russia in 1867; U.S. Army is given jurisdiction over Department of Alaska.

Army Commanding Officers	Dates Served
Bvt. Maj. Gen. Jefferson C. Davis	Oct. 18, 1867–Aug. 31, 1870
Bvt. Lt. Col. George K. Brady	Sept. 1, 1870–Sept. 22, 1870
Maj. John C. Tidball	Sept. 23, 1870–Sept. 19, 1871
Maj. Harvey A. Allen	Sept. 20, 1871–Jan. 3, 1873
Maj. Joseph Stewart	Jan. 4, 1873–April 20, 1874
Capt. George R. Rodney	April 21, 1874–Aug. 16, 1874
Capt. Joseph B. Campbell	Aug. 17, 1874–June 14, 1876
Capt. John Mendenhall	June 15, 1876–March 4, 1877
Capt. Arthur Morris	March 5, 1877–June 14, 1877

U.S. Army troops leave Alaska in 1877; the highest-ranking federal official left in Alaska is the U.S. collector of customs. The Department of Alaska is put under control of the U.S. Treasury Department.

U.S. Collectors of Customs	Dates Served
Montgomery P. Berry	June 14, 1877–Aug. 13, 1877
H. C. DeAhna	Aug. 14, 1877–March 26, 1878
Mottrom D. Ball	March 27, 1878–June 13, 1879

In 1879 the U.S. Navy is given jurisdiction over the Department of Alaska.

Navy Commanding Officers	Dates Served
Capt. L. A. Beardslee	June 14, 1879–Sept. 12, 1880
Comdr. Henry Glass	Sept. 13, 1880–Aug. 9, 1881
Comdr. Edward Lull	Aug. 10, 1881–Oct. 18, 1881
Comdr. Henry Glass	Oct. 19, 1881–March 12, 1882
Comdr. Frederick Pearson	March 13, 1882–Oct. 3, 1882
Comdr. Edgar C. Merriman	Oct. 4, 1882–Sept. 13, 1883
Comdr. Joseph B. Coghlan	Sept. 15, 1883–Sept. 13, 1884
Lt. Comdr. Henry E. Nichols	Sept. 14, 1884–Sept. 15, 1884

Congress provides civil government for the new District of Alaska in 1884; on Aug. 24, 1912, territorial status is given to Alaska. The U.S. president appoints territorial governors.

Presidential Appointment	Dates Served
John H. Kinkead (President Arthur)	July 4, 1884–May 7, 1885
Alfred P. Swineford (President Cleveland)	May 7, 1885–April 20, 1889
Lyman E. Knapp (President Harrison)	April 20, 1889–June 18, 1893
James Sheakley (President Cleveland)	June 18, 1893–June 23, 1897
John G. Brady (President McKinley)	June 23, 1897–March 2, 1906
Wilford B. Hoggatt (President Theodore Roosevelt)	March 2, 1906–May 20, 1909
Walter E. Clark (President Taft)	May 20, 1909–April 18, 1913
John F.A. Strong (President Wilson)	April 18, 1913–April 12, 1918
Thomas Riggs Jr. (President Wilson)	April 12, 1918–June 16, 1921
Scott C. Bone (President Harding)	June 16, 1921–Aug. 16, 1925
George A. Parks (President Coolidge)	Aug. 16, 1925–April 19, 1933
John W. Troy (President Franklin Roosevelt)	April 19, 1933–Dec. 6, 1939
Ernest Gruening (President Franklin Roosevelt)	Dec. 6, 1939–April 10, 1953

(Continued)

B. Frank Heintzleman (President Eisenhower)	April 10, 1953–Jan. 3, 1957
Mike Stepovich (President Eisenhower)	April 8, 1957–Aug. 9, 1958

In 1906, Congress authorizes Alaska to send a voteless delegate to the House of Representatives.

Delegate to Congress	Dates Served
Frank H. Waskey	1906–1907
Thomas Cale	1907–1909
James Wickersham	1909–1917
Charles A. Sulzer	1917–contested election
James Wickersham	1918, seated as delegate
Charles A. Sulzer	1919, elected; died before taking office
George Grigsby	1919, elected in a special election
James Wickersham	1921, seated as delegate, having contested election of Grigsby
Dan A. Sutherland	1921–1930
James Wickersham	1931–1933
J. Dimond	1933–1944
E. L. Bartlett	1944–1958

Unofficial delegates to Congress to promote statehood, elected under a plan first devised by Tennessee. The Tennessee Plan delegates were not seated by Congress but did serve as lobbyists.

Senator	Dates Served
William Egan	1956–1958
Ernest Gruening	1956–1958

Representative	Dates Served
Ralph Rivers	1956–1958

State of Alaska

Alaska becomes a state on Jan. 3, 1959, and sends two senators and one representative to the U.S. Congress.

Elected Governor	Dates Served
William A. Egan	Jan 3. 1959–Dec. 5, 1966
Walter J. Hickel*	Dec. 5, 1966–Jan. 29, 1969
Keith H. Miller*	Jan 29, 1969–Dec. 7, 1970
William A. Egan	Dec. 7, 1970–Dec. 2, 1974
Jay S. Hammond	Dec. 2, 1974–Dec. 6, 1982
Bill Sheffield	Dec. 6, 1982–Dec. 1, 1986
Steve Cowper	Dec. 1, 1986–Dec. 3, 1990
Walter J. Hickel	Dec. 3, 1990–Dec. 5, 1994
Tony Knowles	Dec. 5, 1994–

*Hickel resigned before completing his first full term as governor to accept the position of Secretary of the Interior. He was succeeded by Miller.

Correspondence Addresses:
    The Hon. Tony Knowles, Office of the Governor, P.O. Box 110001, Juneau 99811. Gov. Knowles's e-mail address is office_of_the_governor@gov.state.ak.us; his Web site can be found at www.gov.state.ak.us/gov/home2.html.
    The Hon. Fran Ulmer, Office of the Lieutenant Governor, P.O. Box 110015, Juneau 99811.

U.S. Congressional Delegation

Elected Senator	Dates Served
E. L. Bartlett	1958–1968
Ernest Gruening	1958–1968
Mike Gravel	1968–1980
Ted Stevens	1968–
Frank H. Murkowski	1980–

Representative	Dates Served
Ralph Rivers	1958–1966
Howard Pollock	1966–1970
Nicholas Begich	1970–1972
Donald E. Young	1972–

Correspondence Addresses:
The Honorable Ted Stevens, U.S. Senate, 522 Hart Bldg., Washington, D.C. 20510. E-mail Senator_stevens@stevens.senate.gov.
The Honorable Frank H. Murkowski, U.S. Senate, 709 Hart Bldg., Washington, D.C. 20510. E-mail@murkowski.senate.gov.
The Hon. Donald E. Young, House of Representatives, 2331 Rayburn House Office Bldg., Washington, D.C. 20515. E-mail don.young@mall.house.gov.

Alaska State Legislature

Members of the Alaska Legislature as of the close of the 22nd legislative session (May 2000) are listed on page 88. During sessions, members of the legislature receive mail at the State Capitol, Juneau

Just as the $80 million tunnel to Whittier opened, a former tour bus driver released a book about "The Strangest Town In Alaska." One Whittier resident quoted in the *Anchorage Daily News* said, "If a city council meeting ends without gunfire, it's a success."

99801-1182. Direct general e-mail to www.legis.state.ak.us/ or to a specific legislator by typing Senator OR Representative_First name_Lastname@ legis.state.ak.us.

House of Representatives

District 1: Bill Williams (D)
District 2: Ben Grussendorf (D)
District 3: Beth Kerftula (D)
District 4: Bill Hudson (R)
District 5: Albert Kookesh (D)
District 6: Alan Austerman (R)
District 7: Gail Phillips (R)
District 8: Gary "Lee" Davis (R)
District 9: Harold Smalley (D)
District 10: Joseph Green (R)
District 11: Norman Rokeberg (R)
District 12: Andrew Halcro (R)
District 13: Ethan Berkowitz (D)
District 14: Lisa Murkowski (R)
District 15: Eric Croft (D)
District 16: J. Allen Kemplen (D)
District 17: John Cowdery (R)
District 18: Con Bunde (R)
District 19: Jerry Sanders (R)
District 20: Brian Porter (R)
District 21: Sharon Cissna (D)
District 22: Ramona Barnes (R)
District 23: Eldon Mulder (R)
District 24: Pete Kott (R)
District 25: Fred Dyson (R)
District 26: Vic Kohring (R)
District 27: Scott Ogan (R)
District 28: Beverly Masek (R)
District 29: John Davies (D)
District 30: Tom Brice (D)
District 31: Jim Whitaker (R)
District 32: John Coghill Jr. (R)
District 33: Gene Therriault (R)
District 34: Jeannette James (R)
District 35: John Harris (R)
District 36: Carl Morgan (R)
District 37: Reggie Joule (D)
District 38: Richard Foster (D)
District 39: Mary Kapsner (D)
District 40: Carl Moses (D)

Alaska Senate

District A: Robin Taylor (R)
District B: Kim Elton (D)
District C: Jerry Mackie (R)

Alaska Senate (continued)

District D: John Torgerson (R)
District E: Jerry Ward (R)
District F: Drue Pearce (R)
District G: Loren Leman (R)
District H: Johnny Ellis (D)
District I: Sean Parnell (R)
District J: Dave Donley (R)
District K: Tim Kelly (R)
District L: Randy Phillips (R)
District M: Rick Halford (R)
District N: Lyda Green (R)
District O: Gary Wilken (R)
District P: Pete Kelly (R)
District Q: Mike Miller (R)
District R: Georgianna Lincoln (D)
District S: Al Adams (D)
District T: Lyman Hoffman (D)

Highways (SEE ALSO ALASKA HIGHWAY AND DALTON HIGHWAY) As of January 1998, the state Department of Transportation and Public Facilities estimated total public road mileage in Alaska at 12,673 centerline miles, including those in national parks and forests (1,186). The state also operates 2,775 miles of ferry routes.

The chart on page 90 lists each major highway in Alaska, its route number, the year the highway opened to vehicle traffic and its total length within Alaska (most of the Alaska Highway, Haines Highway and Klondike Highway 2 lie within Canada). Also indicated is whether the highway is open all year or closed in winter.

Highways in Alaska range from six-lane paved freeways to one-lane dirt and gravel roads.

Approximately 30 percent of the roads in the Alaska highway system are paved. The following major highways are all or partially gravel: Steese (Alaska Route 6), Taylor (Alaska Route 5), Elliott (Alaska Route 2), Dalton (Alaska Route 11) and Denali (Alaska Route 8). Alaska's relative lack of roadway is accentuated by a comparison to Austria, a country only one-eighteenth the size of Alaska but with nearly twice as many miles of road.

Although cruise traffic to Alaska is growing by leaps and bounds, road traffic

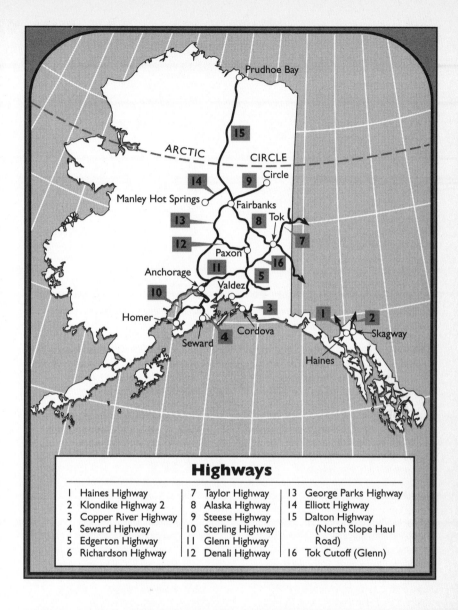

Highways

1 Haines Highway	7 Taylor Highway	13 George Parks Highway
2 Klondike Highway 2	8 Alaska Highway	14 Elliott Highway
3 Copper River Highway	9 Steese Highway	15 Dalton Highway
4 Seward Highway	10 Sterling Highway	(North Slope Haul
5 Edgerton Highway	11 Glenn Highway	Road)
6 Richardson Highway	12 Denali Highway	16 Tok Cutoff (Glenn)

from Outside is on the decline. The number of visitors crossing Alaska–Canada borders dropped 6 percent to 12 percent in 1997, a figure that varied depending on the location of the border crossing.

For weather and updated road conditions, travelers may call (800) 478-7675 for a recorded message that includes avalanche warnings and weight restrictions on the Alaska highway system.

Hiking
Developed trails suitable for all ability levels may be found near Alaska's larger cities and towns. However most of Alaska's public recreation lands are wilderness. Trails are nonexistent and

Major Highways in Alaska

Alaska Route	Year Opened	Total Length (miles) in Alaska Paved	Gravel	Open
Alaska 2	1942	198		All year
Copper River ...... 10 *		12	38	Apr.–Oct.
Dalton........... 11	1974		415	All year
Denali 8	1957	21.4	113	Apr.–Oct.
Edgerton.......... 10	1923	33		All year
Elliott............. 2	1959	30	122	All year
George Parks 3	1971	324		All year
Haines 7	1947	44		All year
Klondike 2	1978	15		All year
Richardson 4	1923	363		All year
Seward/Glenn....... 9&1	1951	305		All year
Steese 6	1928	44	112	All year
Sterling 1	1950	138		All year
Taylor 5	1953	23	135	Apr.–Oct.
Tok Cutoff......... 1	1940	122		All year

*Construction on the Copper River Highway—which was to link up with Chitina on the Edgerton—was halted by the 1964 Good Friday earthquake, which damaged the Million Dollar Bridge. Some Cordovans are now lobbying for its completion.

hikers must chart their own course using topographic maps and a compass. Using both maps and tide tables, it is also possible to hike along ocean shorelines at low tide.

Hikers in Alaska must plan for cold, wet and rapidly changing weather. Take rain gear. If staying overnight in the backcountry, carry a tent, backpacking stove, first-aid kit and emergency flares. Snow can be encountered in any season.

Plan to bring everything you need with you. Some businesses rent canoes and kayaks, but few rent personal gear such as backpacks. Backcountry guides often furnish equipment on escorted expeditions.

Bears inhabit most of Alaska. Read all bear safety information and follow safe procedures for camping and hiking in bear country. You must be completely self-sufficient and responsible for your own safety. (*See* Bears)

Information on hiking in Alaska's national parks and monuments is available from the Alaska Public Lands Information Centers: 605 W. Fourth Ave., Suite 105, Anchorage 99501, (907) 271-2737; 250 Cushman St., Suite 1A, Fairbanks 99701, (907) 456-0527; P.O. Box 359, Tok 99780, (907) 883-5667; and 50 Main St., Ketchikan 99901, (907) 228-6220; or from park headquarters for the area you're interested in. (*See* National Parks, Preserves and Monuments)

The Alaska Division of Parks (*see* State Park System) has information on hiking on the lands managed by that agency.

History (SEE ALSO GOLD STRIKES AND RUSHES AND RUSSIAN ALASKA)

11,000–6,000 years ago—Humans inhabit southeastern, Aleutians, Interior and northwestern Arctic Alaska.

6,000 years ago—Most recent migration from Siberia across the land bridge. Earliest migration believed to have taken place up to 20,000 years ago.

5,000–3,000 years ago—Humans inhabit the Bering Sea Coast.

1725—Vitus Bering sent by Peter the Great to explore the North Pacific.

1741—On a later expedition, Bering and Alexei Chirikof, in separate ships, sight Alaska. Chirikof probably sees land on July 15, a day ahead of his leader, who was perhaps 300 miles or more to the north. Georg Steller goes ashore on Kayak Island, becoming the first European known to have set foot on Alaska soil.

1743—Russians begin concentrated hunting of sea otter, continuing until the species is almost decimated.

1772—A permanent Russian settlement is established at Unalaska.

1774–94—Explorations of Alaska waters by Juan Perez, James Cook and George Vancouver.

1784—First Russian settlement is established on Kodiak Island at Three Saints Bay.

1794—George Vancouver sights Mount McKinley.

1799—Alexander Baranov establishes the Russian post known today as Old Sitka. A trade charter is granted to the Russian-American Company.

1821—Russians prohibit trading in Alaska waters by other nations, making the Russian-American Company the sole trading firm.

1824–42—Russian exploration of the mainland leads to the discovery of the Kuskokwim, Nushagak, Yukon and Koyukuk Rivers.

1837—Father Herman, last survivor of the original Russian missionaries to Alaska, dies on Spruce Island near Kodiak.

1845—The Missionary School at Sitka opens, offering the study of the Aleut, Tlingit and Eskimo languages, medicine and Latin.

1847—Fort Yukon is established by Hudson's Bay Company.

1848—American whalers first enter the Arctic Ocean through Bering Strait.

1853—Russian explorer-trappers find the first oil seeps in Cook Inlet.

1855—The U.S. Navy explores the North Pacific around the Aleutian Islands and the Bering Sea.

1859—Baron Edouard de Stoeckl, minister and chargé d'affaires of the Russian delegation to the United States, is given authority to negotiate the sale of Alaska.

Looking Back

1896

Copper Center was founded as a government agriculture experiment station.

1860—Russians estimate Native Alaskan Christians at 12,000, with 35 chapels, 9 churches, 17 schools and 3 orphanages in 43 communities.

1866—Alaska's first newspaper, *The Esquimeaux,* is published in manuscript at Libbyville.

1867—United States under President Andrew Johnson buys Alaska from Russia for $7.2 million; the treaty is signed March 30 and formal transfer takes place on Oct. 18 at Sitka. Fur seal population begins to stabilize. U.S. Army is given jurisdiction over the Department of Alaska the following year.

1869–70—The *Alaska Times,* the first newspaper to be printed in Alaska, is published in Sitka.

1872—Gold is discovered near Sitka.

1873—Frederick Schwatka conducts a military reconnaisance of Alaska's Interior.

1878—First salmon canneries established at Klawock and Old Sitka.

1882—First commercial herring fishing begins. U.S. Navy destroys the Tlingit village of Angoon.

1884—An Organic Act gives Alaska its first civil government.

1885—Lieutenant Henry Allen explores the Copper River.

1891—First oil claims staked in Cook Inlet area.

1897–1900—Klondike gold rush in Yukon Territory; heavy traffic through Alaska on the way to the goldfields.

1898—Gold is discovered on Nome beaches. Frank Reid shoots con artist Soapy Smith in Skagway. U.S. Geological Survey begins mapping Alaska.

1902—First oil production, at Katalla. Telegraph from Eagle to Valdez is completed.

1906—Peak gold production year. Alaska is granted a nonvoting delegate to Congress; governor's office moves from Sitka to Juneau.

1911—Copper production begins at Kennicott.

1912—Territorial status for Alaska; first territorial Legislature is convened the following year. Mount Katmai erupts.

1913—First airplane flight in Alaska, at Fairbanks; first automobile trip from Fairbanks to Valdez.

1914—President Woodrow Wilson authorizes construction of the Alaska Railroad.

1916—First bill proposing Alaska statehood is introduced in Congress. Peak copper production year.

1917—Creation of Mount McKinley National Park. Founding of Wasilla.

1918—Worldwide epidemic of Spanish flu decimates Alaska's Native population. Creation of Katmai National Monument.

1922—First pulp mill starts production at Speel River near Juneau.

1923—President Warren Harding drives spike completing the Alaska Railroad.

1930—The first "talkie" motion picture is shown in Fairbanks, featuring the Marx Brothers in *The Cocoanuts*.

1935—Matanuska Valley Project, which moves farming families to Alaska, begins. First Juneau-to-Fairbanks flight.

1936—All-time record salmon catch in Alaska—126.4 million fish. Black Rapids Glacier advances 3 miles in three months, coming within a half mile of the Richardson Highway.

1937—Nell Scott is the first woman appointed to the Alaska Legislature.

1940—Military buildup in Alaska; Fort Richardson, Elmendorf Air Force Base are established. Alaska's population includes about 40,000 non-Native Alaskans and 32,000 Natives. Pan American Airways inaugurates twice-weekly service between

Seattle, Ketchikan and Juneau, using Sikorsky flying boats.

1942—Dutch Harbor is bombed and Attu and Kiska islands are occupied by Japanese forces. Alaska Highway is built—first overland connection to Lower 48.

1943—Japanese forces are driven from Alaska.

1953—Oil well is drilled near Eureka, on the Glenn Highway, marking the start of modern oil history.

1957—Kenai oil strike.

1958—Statehood measure is passed by Congress; statehood is proclaimed officially on Jan. 3, 1959; first general election is held.

1963—State ferry service to Southeast Alaska begins.

1964—Good Friday earthquake of March 27 causes heavy damage throughout the Gulf Coast region; 131 people are killed.

1967—Fairbanks flood.

1968—Oil and gas discoveries at Prudhoe Bay on the North Slope; $900 million North Slope oil lease sale the following year; pipeline proposal follows.

1970—Federal government sets aside 500,000 acres for Chugach State Park.

1971—Congress approves Alaska Native Claims Settlement Act, granting title to 40 million acres of land and providing more than $900 million in payment to Alaska Natives.

1973—The first 1,100-mile sled dog race begins March 3, following part of an old dog team mail route blazed in 1910; it's called the Iditarod Trail Sled Dog Race.

1974—Trans-Alaska pipeline receives final approval; construction buildup begins.

1975—Population and labor force soar with construction of pipeline. Alaska gross products hits $5.8 billion—double the 1973 figure.

1976—Voters select Willow area for new capital site.

1977—Completion of the trans-Alaska oil pipeline from Prudhoe Bay to

In Fairbanks, it is illegal for a moose to walk on a sidewalk. The pre-World War I ordinance was created because of a local bar owner who liked to get his pet moose drunk. The moose then stumbled around town annoying the residents. So if it was illegal for a moose to walk on a sidewalk, the animal could not get into the bar to drink.

Valdez; shipment of first oil by tanker from Valdez to Puget Sound.

1978—A 200-mile offshore fishing limit goes into effect. President Jimmy Carter withdraws 56 million acres of federal lands in Alaska to create 17 new national monuments. Congress designates the Iditarod as a National Historic Trail.

1979—State of Alaska files suit to halt the withdrawal of 56 million acres of Alaska land by President Carter under the Antiquities Act.

1980—Special session of the Alaska Legislature votes to repeal the state income tax and provides for refunds of 1979 taxes. Legislature establishes a Permanent Fund as a repository for one-fourth of all royalty oil revenues for future generations. Census figures show Alaska's population grew by 32.4 percent during the 1970s. The Alaska National Interest Lands Conservation Act of 1980 puts 53.7 million Alaska acres into the national wildlife refuge system, parts of 25 rivers into the national wild and scenic rivers system, 3.3 million acres into national forest lands and 43.6 million acres into national park land.

1981—Legislature puts on the ballot a constitutional amendment proposal to limit state spending. Secretary of the Interior James Watt initiates plans to sell oil and gas leases on 130 million acres of Alaska's nonrestricted federal land and announces a tentative schedule to open 16 offshore areas of Alaska as part of an intense national search for oil and gas on the outer continental shelf.

1982—Vote for funds to move state capital from Juneau to Willow is defeated. First Permanent Fund dividend checks of $1,000 each are mailed to every six-month resident of Alaska.

1983—All Alaska, except westernmost Aleutian Islands, moves to Alaska Standard Time, one hour ahead of Pacific Standard Time. Record-breaking salmon harvest in Bristol Bay. Building permits set a record at just under $1 billion.

1984—State of Alaska celebrates its 25th birthday.

1985—Anchorage receives the U.S. bid for the 1994 Olympics. Iditarod Trail Sled

Dog Race is won by Libby Riddles, the first woman to win in the history of the race.

1986—Mount Augustine in lower Cook Inlet erupts. World Championship Sled Dog Race held during Fur Rendezvous is canceled for the first time for lack of snow. Iditarod Trail Sled Dog Race is again won by a woman, Susan Butcher of Manley.

1987—Iditarod Trail Sled Dog Race is won by Susan Butcher for the second consecutive year.

1988—The Iditarod Trail Sled Dog Race is won by Susan Butcher for the third year in a row. Anchorage loses its bid for the 1994 Olympics to Norway.

1989—Worst oil spill in U.S. history occurs in Prince William Sound when the *Exxon Valdez* runs aground. Record-breaking cold hits entire state, lasting for weeks. Soviets visit Alaska, and the Bering Bridge Expedition crosses the Bering Strait by dogsled and skis.

1990—Valdez sets a new record for snowfall. Susan Butcher wins her fourth Iditarod Trail Sled Dog Race. Election upset as Walter J. Hickel becomes governor.

1991—Fairbanks sets a new record for snowfall. Rick Swenson claims fifth Iditarod win.

1992—Alaska celebrates 50th anniversary of the Alaska Highway. One of Alaska's oldest newspapers, the *Anchorage Times,* shuts down. Mount Spurr erupts.

1993—The Department of Fish and Game announces a plan to allow aerial hunting of wolves. Springtime comes early

Residential street in Fairbanks in the early 1900s. From Alaska's History by Harry Ritter.

Matanuska colonists arriving at Palmer Station, 1935. From Alaska's History *by Harry Ritter.*

to the Interior, with the second-warmest April on record.

1994—Diseased herring appear in Prince William Sound for the second season. Exxon is found guilty of reckless-ness in the 1989 oil spill in Prince William Sound. Alaska skier Tommy Moe is a gold medalist at the Olympic Games in Norway.

1995—Two Anchorage residents are killed by a grizzly along a trail in a popular hiking area of Chugach State Park.

1996—Princess Tours' Denali Lodge burns down in March but is rebuilt by June. Alaska's worst wildfire destroys $8.8 million in homes and other buildings.

1997—Legislature approves 71-cent tax increase per cigarette pack. ARCO Alaska and British Petroleum announce plans to develop two more North Slope oil fields.

> A recent edition of the *Archdiocesan News* announced that "The Prison Ministry office has an Independent **STUD** program." What do I have to do to get into Prison?

1998—Falling oil prices force state to use budget reserve funds. El Niño plays havoc with the weather.

1999—The state struggles to define and institute a new subsistence policy. BP-Amoco buys out competitor ARCO Alaska. Joe Redington Sr., father of the Iditarod Trail Sled Dog Race, dies at his home in Knik.

Holidays in 2001

New Year's Day . . . . Jan. 1
Martin Luther King Day . . . . Jan. 15
Presidents' Day
—holiday . . . . Feb. 19
—traditional . . . . Feb. 22
Seward's Day* . . . . March 30
Memorial Day
—holiday . . . . May 28
—traditional . . . . May 30
Independence Day . . . . July 4
Labor Day . . . . Sept. 3
Alaska Day** . . . . Oct. 18
Veterans Day . . . . Nov. 11
Thanksgiving Day . . . . Nov. 22
Christmas Day . . . . Dec. 25

*Seward's Day commemorates the signing of the treaty by which the United States bought Alaska from Russia, signed on March 30, 1867.

**Alaska Day is the anniversary of the formal transfer of the territory and the raising of the U.S. flag at Sitka on Oct. 18, 1867.

Homesteading (See also

Land Use) Until 1995, any Alaska resident of at least one year, 18 years or older and a U.S. citizen, had a chance to receive up to 40 acres of nonagricultural land or up to 160 acres of agricultural land nearly free. To receive title the homesteader was required to pay a $10 application fee and either survey or reimburse the state for survey costs, brush and stake the parcel boundary, build a dwelling, and occupy and improve the land in certain ways within specific time frames. This is called "proving up" on the homestead.

The last available parcel was won in a lottery in early 1997.

The State Homestead Act also allowed homesteaders to purchase parcels at fair market value without occupying or improving the property. In this category, some subdivision lots are left from a 1995 auction; nonresidents may purchase these parcels.

Many of the original homesteaders were veterans who came to Alaska during the late 1940s and early 1950s. They had to brush up their boundaries within 90 days after issuance of the entry permit, complete an approved survey of the land within two or five years (depending on purchase option), erect a habitable permanent dwelling on the homestead within three years, and live on the parcel for 25 months within five years. If the parcel was classified for agricultural use, homesteaders labored mightily to clear and put into production or cultivation 25 percent of the land within five years.

Hooligan

Smelt, also known as eulachon or candlefish, are "ooligan" in southeastern Alaska. The Tlingit dried these oily little fish, inserted a twisted spruce bark wick and used them as candles. The Tlingit caught the 9-inch fish in great numbers, ripened them for several days to speed the release of the oil from the flesh and then rendered their oil in baskets or cooking pots. The flavor and color of the oil or "grease" were determined by the length of time the fish ripened. The oil was stored in bulb kelp "jars" corked with wooden plugs or in bentwood boxes. Some of the oil was traded with Interior people by packing it over timeworn paths which became known as "grease trails." The Tlingit considered hooligan vital to their diet and gallons of the oil were consumed during the winter as a nutritious dip for dried foods.

Hooligan, now considered a subsistence or sport catch only, are caught by dip-netting as they travel upriver to spawn. Hooligan resemble trout in general structure and have a distinctive odor and taste. The flesh is ivory colored, extremely perishable and should be cooked or pickled the same day it is caught.

Native bowl used for hooligan grease. From The Alaska Heritage Seafood Cookbook by Ann Chandonnet.

Hospitals and Health Facilities (*See*

ALSO PIONEERS' HOMES) Alaska has numerous hospitals, nursing homes and other health care facilities.

For a list of emergency medical services, contact the Office of Emergency Medical Services, Division of Public Health, Dept. of Health and Social Services, P.O. Box 110616, Juneau 99811-0616.

Municipal, Private and State Hospitals, Clinics and Specialty Facilities

Anchorage
Alaska Psychiatric Institute (89 beds), 2900 Providence Drive, 99508.
Alaska Regional Hospital (238 beds), 2801 DeBarr Road, P.O. Box 143889, 99514-3889.
Alaska Surgery Center, 4001 Laurel St., 99508-5396.
Charter North Behavioral Health System (74 beds), 2530 DeBarr Road, 99508.
Providence Alaska Medical Center (303 beds), 3200 Providence Drive, P.O. Box 196604, 99519-6604.

Cordova
Cordova Community Medical Center (23 beds), 602 Chasa Ave., P.O. Box 160, 99574.

Fairbanks
Fairbanks Memorial Hospital (166 beds), 1650 Cowles St., 99701.

Glennallen
Cross Roads Medical Center, P.O. Box 5, 99588.

Homer
South Peninsula Hospital (40 beds), 4300 Bartlett St., 99603.

Juneau
Bartlett Regional Hospital (55 beds), 3260 Hospital Drive, 99801.

Ketchikan
Ketchikan General Hospital (92 beds),
3100 Tongass Ave., 99901.

Kodiak
Providence Kodiak Medical Center
(44 beds), 1915 E. Rezanof Drive,
99615.

Palmer
Valley Hospital (36 beds), P.O. Box 1687,
515 E. Dahlia, 99645.

Petersburg
Petersburg Medical Center (25 beds),
P.O. Box 589, 103 Fram St., 99833.

Seward
Providence Seward Medical Center
(six beds), P.O. Box 365, 417 First Ave.,
99664.

Sitka
Sitka Community Hospital (23 beds),
209 Moller Drive, P.O. Box 500,
99835.

Soldotna
Central Peninsula General Hospital
(62 beds), 250 Hospital Place,
99669.

Valdez
Valdez Community Hospital (15 beds),
P.O. Box 550, 911 Meal St., 99686.

Wrangell
Wrangell Medical Center (eight beds), P.O.
Box 1081, 99929.

U.S. Public Health Service Hospitals and Clinics

Anchorage
Alaska Native Medical Center (140 beds),
4315 Diplomacy Drive, 99508.

Barrow
Samuel Simmonds Memorial Hospital
(14 beds), P.O. Box 29, 99723-0029.

Bethel
Yukon–Kuskokwim Delta
Regional Hospital (50
beds), P.O. Box 287,
99559.

Dillingham
Kanakanak Hospital (15 beds),
P.O. Box 130, 99576.

Fairbanks
Chief Andrew Isaac Health Center, 1408
19th St., 99701.

Juneau
SEARHC Medical Clinic, 3245 Hospital
Drive, 99801.

Ketchikan
KIC Tribal Health Clinic, 3289 Tongass
Ave., 99901.

Kodiak
Kodiak Area Native Association, 3449
Rezanof Drive E., 99615.

Kotzebue
Maniilaq Health Center (22 beds), P.O.
Box 43, 99752.

Metlakatla
Annette Island Service Unit, P.O. Box 439,
99926.

Nome
Norton Sound Regional (36 beds), P.O.
Box 966, 5 Bering St., 99762.

Sitka
SEARHC Mount Edgecumbe Hospital
(78 beds), 222 Tongass Drive,
99835.

Military Hospitals

Eielson Air Force Base
Eielson Air Force Base Clinic,
354 MDG/SG, 3349 Central Ave., Suite
1M07, Eielson AFB 99702-2399.

Elmendorf AFB
Headquarters Third Medical Group,

5955 Zeamer Ave., Elmendorf AFB,
99506-3700.

Fort Greely
Fort Greely Health Clinic, 96508.

Fort Richardson
U.S. Army Troop Medical Clinic,
99505.

Fort Wainwright
Bassett Army Community Hospital,
99703.

Ketchikan
Coast Guard Dispensary, 1300 Stedman
St., 99901.

Kodiak
USCG Integrated Support Command,
Rockmore-King Medical Clinic, P.O.
Box 195002, 99619-5002.

Sitka
U.S. Coast Guard Air Station, 611 Airport
Road, 99835.

Nursing Homes

Anchorage
Mary Conrad Center (89 beds), 9100
Centennial Drive, 99504.
Providence Extended Care Center
(224 beds), 4900 Eagle St., 99503.

Fairbanks
Denali Center (90 beds), 1510 19th Ave.,
99701.

Juneau
St. Ann's Care Center (44 beds), 415 Sixth
St., 99801.

Ketchikan
General Hospital Long Term Care
Unit (46 beds), 3100 Tongass Ave.,
99901.

Seward
Wesley Rehabilitation and Care Center
(66 beds), P.O. Box 430, 431 First Ave.,
99664.

Soldotna
Heritage Place (45 beds), 232 Rockwell
Ave., 99669.

Chemical Dependency Treatment Centers

Alaska has 17 chemical dependency
centers located in Anchorage, Eagle River,
Fairbanks, Juneau, Palmer, Sitka and
Wasilla. For details call the Alaska State
Medical Association (907) 562-0304.

Hostels Alaska has 10 Hostelling

International member hostels located in the
following communities:
  Alyeska International Home Hostel,
P.O. Box 10-4099, Anchorage 99510;
(907) 783-2099. Located 40 miles south of
Anchorage in Girdwood.
  Anchorage International Hostel, 700 H
St., Anchorage 99501; (907) 276-3635.
Located on the corner of Seventh and
H Streets. Fax (907) 276-7722. E-mail:
hianch@alaska.net Web: www.alaska.net/~
hianch
  Hostelling International, Mile 3 Oil
Well Road, P.O. Box 39083, Ninilchik
99639; (907) 567-3905.
  Juneau International Hostel, 614
Harris St., Juneau 99801; (907) 586-9559.
Located four blocks northeast of the
capitol building. E-mail: juneauhostel@
gci.net
  Ketchikan Youth Hostel, P.O. Box
8515, Ketchikan 99901; (907) 225-3319.
Located in United Methodist Church,
Grant and Main Streets.
  Sheep Mountain Lodge, HCO 3,
Box 8490, Palmer 99645; (907) 745-5121.
Located at Mile 113.5 of the Glenn
Highway. Fax (907) 745-5120. E-mail:
sheepmtl@alaska.net
  Sitka Youth Hostel, P.O. Box 2645,
Sitka 99835; (907) 747-8661. Located in
United Methodist Church, Edgecumbe
and Kimsham Streets.
  Skagway Home Hostel, P.O. Box 231,
Skagway 99840; (907) 983-2131. Located
on Third Avenue near Main Street.
  Tok International Youth Hostel, P.O.
Box 532, Tok 99780. Located 1 mile south

of Mile 1322.5 of the Alaska Highway on Pringle Drive. (907) 883-3745.

The hostels in Alyeska, Anchorage, Juneau, Skagway and Seward are open year-round. All others are open only in the summer. All of the hostels accept reservations by mail. Opening and closing dates, maximum length of stay and hours vary.

Hostels are available to anyone with a valid membership card issued by one of the associations affiliated with Hostelling International. Membership is open to all ages. A valid membership card, which ranges from $10 to $250 (life), entitles a member to use hostels.

Hostel memberships and a guide to American Youth Hostels can be purchased from the state office (Alaska Council, AYH, Box 240347, Anchorage 99524; (907) 243-3844), national office (American Youth Hostels, 1332 I St. NW, Suite 800, Washington, D.C. 20005) or from most local hostels.

Hot Springs The Alaska

Division of Geological and Geophysical Surveys identifies 124 geothermal areas in the state that include hot springs, fumaroles, geothermal wells or a combination of these. Most geothermal areas (56) occur along the Aleutian volcanic arc, 19 are located in the Southeast panhandle and 49 are scattered throughout mainland Alaska. Most are inaccessible by automobile.

Of the state's 124 geothermal areas, only 19 have experienced any sort of development, and only six hot spring areas provide resort facilities. Resorts

with swimming pools, changing rooms, restaurants and lodging are found at Chena Hot Springs (a 62-mile drive east from Fairbanks) and Circle Hot Springs (136 miles northeast by road from Fairbanks). Although not accessible by road, Bell Island Hot Springs (40 air miles northeast of Ketchikan and accessible by boat) and Melozi Hot Springs (200 air miles northwest of Fairbanks) have lodging, pool and accommodations. Less developed is Manley Hot Springs in the small community of the same name at the end of Elliott Highway (160 miles west of Fairbanks). The hot springs are privately owned and a primitive bathhouse is used primarily by local residents. Manley Hot Springs Resort is located near the springs, but its waters are supplied from a geothermal well. The resort does have a pool, restaurant and lodging facilities. Ophir Hot Springs (about 50 miles southwest of Aniak) has a private hunting camp with accommodations and an aboveground hot pool.

There are 11 additional springs with cabins and/or bathing tubs and changing facilities. Most of these are accessible only by boat, plane, snowmobile, dog team, ATV or on foot. Among them is the community of Tenakee Springs on Chichagof Island in southeastern Alaska, which maintains an old bathhouse near the waterfront for public use. The state Marine Highway System provides ferry service to Tenakee Springs. Chief Shakes Hot Springs, near Wrangell, and White Sulfur Hot Springs and Goddard Hot Springs, both near Sitka, all have Forest Service cabins and are accessible by boat or floatplane. Tolovana Hot Springs, 45 miles northwest of Fairbanks, features two cabins and a hot tub. Reservations are required. Visitors can soak and photograph the old buildings that were once an orphanage at Pilgrim Hot Springs, 60 miles from Nome, accessible by road in summer only. Also on the Seward Peninsula is Serpentine Hot Springs, a winter destination by snowmobile from Nome.

Other springs include Baranof Hot Springs on Baranof Island. Kanuti Hot Springs is about 10 miles west of the Dalton Highway near Caribou Mountain. These springs are used primarily by skiers and mushers in the winter.

A map featuring most of the thermal areas in Alaska can be purchased for $5 from the Alaska Division of Geological and Geophysical Surveys, 794 University Ave., Suite 200, Fairbanks 99701-3645. For a map or more information, call (907) 451-5010 or visit the Web site at www.dggs.dnr.state.ak.us/. E-mail for publications is dggspubs@ dnr.state.ak.us.

Hunting
There are 26 game management units in Alaska with a wide variety of seasons and bag limits. Current copies of the *Alaska State Hunting Regulations* with maps showing game unit boundaries are available from the Alaska Department of Fish and Game (P.O. Box 25526, Juneau 99802) or from Fish and Game offices and sporting goods stores throughout the state.

Regulations. A hunting or trapping license is required for all residents and nonresidents with the exception of Alaska residents under 16 or older than 60. A special identification card is issued for the senior citizen exemption.

A resident hunting license (valid for the calendar year) costs $25; trapping license (valid until September 30 of the year following the year of issue), $15; hunting and trapping license, $39; hunting and sportfishing license, $39; hunting, trapping and sportfishing license, $53.

Both male and female Dall sheep grow horns. From Alaska's Mammals *by Dave Smith (text) and Tom Walker (photographs).*

A nonresident (U.S. citizen) hunting license (valid for the calendar year) costs $85; hunting and sportfishing license, $185; hunting and trapping license, $250. Non-U.S. citizens pay $300 for a hunting license.

Military personnel stationed in Alaska may purchase a fishing license for $15, a small-game hunting license for $25, and a small-game hunting and sportfishing license for $39. Military personnel must purchase a nonresident hunting license at full cost ($85) and pay nonresident military fees for big-game tags (one-half the nonresident rate), unless they are hunting big game on military property.

Licenses may be obtained from any designated issuing agent, via the Internet at www.admin.adfg.state.ak.us/license, by calling 1-877-9FISHAK, or by mail from the Alaska Department of Fish and Game, Licensing Division, P.O. Box 25525, Juneau 99802; (907) 465-2376.

Big-game tags and fees are required for residents hunting musk-oxen and brown/grizzly bear and for nonresidents and noncitizens hunting any big-game animal. These nonrefundable, nontransferable, locking tags (valid for the calendar year) must be purchased prior to the taking of the animal. A tag may be used for any species for which the tag fee is of equal or less value. Fees quoted below are for *each* animal.

All residents (regardless of age), nonresidents and aliens intending to hunt brown/grizzly bear must purchase tags (resident, $25; nonresident, $500; alien, $650). Residents, nonresidents and aliens are also required to purchase musk-oxen tags (resident, $500 each bull taken on Nunivak Island, $25 each cow from Nelson Island or in Arctic National Wildlife Refuge; nonresident, $1,100; alien, $1,500).

Nonresident tag fees for other big game animals: deer, $150; wolf, $30; black bear, $225; elk or goat, $300; caribou, $325; moose, $400; bison, $450; sheep, $425.

Nonresident alien tag fees for other big game animals: deer, $200; wolf, $50; black bear, $300; elk or goat, $400; caribou, $425; moose, $500; bison, $650; and sheep, $550.

Nonresidents hunting brown/grizzly bear, Dall sheep or mountain goat are required to have a guide or be accompanied by an Alaska resident relative over 19 within the second degree of kinship (includes parents, children, sisters or brothers). Nonresident aliens hunting big game must have a guide. A list of registered Alaska guides is available for $5 from the Department of Commerce, Division of Occupational Licensing, Big Game Commercial Services Board, P.O. Box 11806, Juneau 99811-0806.

Residents and nonresidents 16 or older hunting waterfowl must have a signed federal migratory bird hunting stamp (duck stamp) and a signed state waterfowl conservation stamp. The Alaska duck stamp is available from agents who sell hunting licenses or by mail from the Alaska Department of Fish and Game, Licensing Section.

Trophy Game. Record big game in Alaska as recorded by the Boone and Crockett Club (www.boone-crockett.org/).

Black bear: Skull $14^{12}/_{16}$ inches long, $8^{14}/_{16}$ inches wide (1975).

Brown bear (coastal region): Skull $17^{15}/_{16}$ inches long, $12^{13}/_{16}$ inches wide (1952).

Grizzly bear: (Three-way tie) Skull $17^{6}/_{16}$ inches long, $9^{12}/_{16}$ inches wide (1970); skull $16^{14}/_{16}$ inches long, $10^{4}/_{16}$ inches wide (1982), skull $17^{3}/_{16}$ inches long, $9^{5}/_{16}$ inches wide (1991).

Polar bear: Skull $18^{1}/_{2}$ inches long, $11^{7}/_{16}$ inches wide (1963). It is illegal for anyone but an Alaska Eskimo, Aleut or Indian to hunt polar bear in Alaska.

Bison: Right horn $21^{2}/_{8}$ inches long, base circumference 16 inches; left horn $23^{2}/_{8}$ inches long, base circumference 15 inches; greatest spread $35^{3}/_{8}$ inches (1925).

Barren Ground caribou: Right beam $50^{6}/_{8}$ inches, 24 points; left beam $40^{1}/_{8}$ inches, 23 points (1987).

Moose: (Alaska-Yukon) Right palm length $54^{4}/_{8}$ inches, width $22^{2}/_{8}$ inches; left palm length $53^{6}/_{8}$ inches, width $21^{4}/_{8}$ inches; right antler 19 points, left 15 points; greatest spread $65^{1}/_{8}$ inches (1994).

Rocky Mountain goat: Right horn 12 inches long, base circumference

6⁴/₈ inches; left horn 12 inches long, base circumference 6⁴/₈ inches (1949).

Musk-ox: Right horn 29⁷/₈ inches; left horn 29⁶/₈ inches; tip-to-tip spread 29⁵/₈ inches (1996).

Dall sheep: Right horn 48⁵/₈ inches long, base circumference 14⁵/₈ inches; left horn 47⁷/₈ inches long, base circumference 14³/₄ inches (1961).

Hypothermia (SEE ALSO CHILL FACTOR)

Hypothermia develops when the body is exposed to cold and cannot maintain normal temperatures. In an automatic survival reaction, blood flow to the extremities is shut down in favor of preserving warmth in the vital organs. As internal temperature drops, judgment and coordination become impaired. Hypothermia leads to stupor, collapse and death. Immersion hypothermia occurs in cold water.

Hypothermia can occur at any season. To prevent hypothermia, always bring warmer clothing, even in relatively warm summer months. Dress in layers, including inner layers that give warmth even when wet. Keep your energy up by eating snacks and drinking warm beverages.

Travel outdoors with a partner, or in groups, to watch one another for early signs of hypothermia such as shivering, fatigue, stumbling, aimless wandering or irrationality.

Victims of hypothermia should be sheltered from wind and weather and brought indoors as soon as possible.

Ice (SEE GLACIERS AND ICE FIELDS; ICEBERGS; ICE FOG; ICEWORM; AND NENANA ICE CLASSIC)

Icebergs (SEE ALSO GLACIERS AND ICE FIELDS)

Icebergs are formed in Alaska wherever glaciers reach salt water or a freshwater lake. Some accessible places to view icebergs include Glacier Bay, Icy Bay, Yakutat Bay, Taku Inlet, Endicott Arm, portions of northern Prince William Sound (College Fiord, Barry Arm, Columbia Bay), Mendenhall Lake and Portage Lake.

If icebergs contain little or no sediment, approximately 75 percent to 80 percent of their bulk may be underwater. The more sediment an iceberg contains, the greater its density, and an iceberg containing large amounts of sediment will float slightly beneath the surface. Glaciologists of the U.S. Geological Survey believe that some of these "black icebergs" may actually sink to the bottom of a body of water. Since salt water near the faces of glaciers may be liquid to temperatures as low as 28°F, and icebergs melt at 32°F, some of these underwater icebergs may remain unmelted indefinitely.

Alaska's icebergs are small compared to the icebergs found near Antarctica and Greenland. One of the largest icebergs ever recorded in Alaska was formed in May 1977, in Icy Bay. Glaciologists measured it at 346 feet long, 297 feet wide and 99 feet above the surface of the water.

Sea Ice. Seawater typically freezes at −1.8°C or 28.8°F. The first indication that seawater is freezing is the appearance of frazil—tiny needlelike crystals of pure ice—in shallow coastal areas of low current or areas of low salinity such as near the mouths of rivers. Continued freezing turns the frazil into a soupy mass called grease ice and eventually into an ice crust approximately 4 inches thick. More freezing, wind and wave action thicken the ice and break it into ice floes ranging from a few feet to several miles across. In the Arctic Ocean, ice floes can be 10 feet thick. Most are crisscrossed with 6- to 8-foot-high walls of ice caused by the force of winds.

Alaska has one of the highest cremation rates in the nation, and the reason became apparent at the Valdez cemetery last January. The hole in the frozen ground was not large enough for the handmade casket. The only alternative was to stand up the deceased in the grave, but since the casket was symmetrical, no one knew which end was up. A friend at the ceremony said, "If he went head first, he may have wanted everyone to kiss something goodbye."

Sea salt that is trapped in the ice during freezing is leached out over time, making the oldest ice the least saline. Meltwater forming in ponds on multi-year-old ice during summer months is a freshwater source for native marine life.

Refreezing of meltwater ponds and the formation of new ice in the permanent ice pack (generally north of 72° north latitude) begins in mid-September. While the ice pack expands southward, new ice freezes to the coast (shorefast ice) and spreads seaward. Where the drifting ice pack grinds against the relatively stable shorefast ice, tremendous walls or ridges of ice are formed, some observed to be 100 feet thick and grounded in 60 feet of water. They are impenetrable by all but the most powerful icebreakers. By late March the ice cover has reached its maximum extent, approximately from Port Heiden on the Alaska Peninsula in the south to the northern Pribilof Islands and northwestward to Siberia. In Cook Inlet, sea ice usually no more than 2 feet thick can extend as far south as Anchor Point and Kamishak Bay on the east and west sides of the inlet, respectively. The ice season usually lasts from mid-November to April.

The Navy began observing and fore-casting sea ice conditions in 1954 during construction of defense sites along the Arctic coast. In 1969, the National Weather Service began a low-profile sea ice reconnaissance program, which expanded greatly during the summer of 1975 when, during a year of severe ice, millions of dollars of materials had to be shipped to Prudhoe Bay. Expanded commercial fisheries in the Bering Sea also heightened the problem of sea ice for crabbing and bottom fish trawling operations. In 1976, headquarters for a seven-days-a-week ice watch was established at Fairbanks; it was moved to Anchorage in 1981.

The National Weather Service operates a radio facsimile broadcast service that makes current ice analysis charts, special oceanographic charts and standard weather charts available to the public via standard radios equipped with "black box" receivers. Commercial fishing operators, particularly in the Bering Sea, use the radio-transmitted charts to steer clear of problem weather and troublesome ice formations. More information is available from the National Weather Service in Kodiak or Anchorage.

Ice Fog

Ice fog develops when air just above the ground becomes so cold it can no longer retain water vapor and tiny, spherical ice crystals form. Ice fog is most common in arctic and subarctic regions in winter when clear skies create an air inversion, trapping cold air at low elevations. It is most noticeable when pollutants are suspended in the air inversion.

Iceworm

Although often regarded as a hoax, iceworms actually exist. These small, threadlike, segmented black worms, usually less than 1 inch long, thrive in temperatures just above freezing. Observers as far back as the 1880s reported that at dawn or dusk, or on overcast days, the tiny worms, all belonging to the genus *Mesenchytraeus,* may literally carpet the surface of glaciers. When sunlight strikes them, ice worms burrow back down into the ice; temperatures above 75°F kill them.

The town of Cordova commemorates its own version of the iceworm each

The Iceworm Festival parade is held in Cordova in February. **Courtesy of Alaska Division of Tourism.**

February with an Iceworm Festival when a 100-foot-long, multilegged "iceworm" leads a parade down Main Street. Other activities include an arts and crafts show, ski events, contests, dances, and honorary king and queen.

Iditarod Trail Sled Dog Race (SEE ALSO DOG MUSHING AND YUKON QUEST INTERNATIONAL SLED DOG RACE)

Two of the longest sled dog races in the world take place in Alaska: the Yukon Quest and the Iditarod. The first Iditarod Trail Sled Dog Race, conceived and organized by the late Joe Redington Sr., of Knik, and the late Dorothy Page, of Wasilla,

was run in 1967 and covered only 56 miles. The race was lengthened in 1973, and the first ever 1,100-mile sled dog race began in Anchorage on March 3, 1973, and ended April 3 in Nome. Of the 34 who started the race, 22 finished. The Iditarod has been run every year since. In 1997, the Iditarod Trail Sled Dog Race marked its 25th anniversary.

In 1976, Congress designated the Iditarod as a National Historic Trail. The official length of the Iditarod National Historic Trail System, including northern and southern routes, is 2,350 miles.

Following the old dog team mail route blazed in 1910 from Knik to Nome, the race route crosses two mountain ranges, follows

Iditarod Trail Sled Dog Race 2000 Results

Place	Musher	Days	Hrs.	Min.	Day	Arrival Time
1.	Doug Swingley	09	00	58	3/14	10:58
2.	Paul Gebhardt	09	06	04	3/14	16:04
3.	Jeff King	09	08	44	3/14	18:14
4.	Ramy Brooks	09	09	20	3/14	19:20
5.	Charlie Boulding	09	11	16	3/14	21:16
6.	Rick Mackey	09	13	35	3/14	23:35
7.	Martin Buser	09	14	55	3/15	00:55
8.	Rick Swenson	09	15	09	3/15	01:09
9.	Mitch Seavey	09	19	13	3/15	05:15
10.	Bill Cotter	09	20	55	3/15	06:55
11.	Ramey Smyth	09	22	08	3/15	08:08
12.	Hans Gatt	09	22	57	3/15	08:57
13.	Bruce Lee	10	01	23	3/15	11:23
14.	Zach Steer	10	01	44	3/15	11:44
15.	John Barron	10	01	53	3/15	11:53
16.	Tim Osmar	10	02	27	3/15	12:27
17.	Juan Alcina	10	02	34	3/15	12:34
18.	Sonny King	10	03	58	3/15	13:58
19.	Linwood Fiedler	10	04	01	3/15	14:01
20.	DeeDee Jonrowe	10	04	24	3/15	14:24
21.	Vern Halter	10	05	34	3/15	15:34
22.	John Baker	10	05	48	3/15	15:48
23.	Jon Little	10	07	44	3/15	17:44
24.	Ed Iten	10	08	54	3/15	18:54
25.	Harald Tunheim	10	12	04	3/15	22:04
26.	David Sawatzky	10	13	14	3/15	23:14
27.	Tony Willis	10	13	33	3/15	23:33
28.	Mike Williams	10	19	29	3/16	05:29
29.	Raymie Redington	11	00	22	3/16	10:22
30.	Aaron Burmeister	11	03	35	3/16	13:35

Winners and Times

Year	Musher	Days	Hrs.	Min.	Sec.	Prize
1989	Joe Runyan, Nenana	11	05	24	3	$50,000
1990	Susan Butcher, Manley	11	01	53	23	50,000
1991	Rick Swenson, Two Rivers	12	16	34	39	50,000
1992	Martin Buser, Big Lake	10	19	17	15	50,000
1993	Jeff King, Denali Park	10	15	38	15	50,000*
1994	Martin Buser, Big Lake	10	13	02	39	50,000**
1995	Doug Swingley, Simms, MT	09	02	42	19	52,500
1996	Jeff King, Denali Park	09	05	43	13	50,000
1997	Martin Buser, Big Lake	09	08	30	45	50,000†
1998	Jeff King, Denali Park	09	05	52	00	51,000†
1999	Doug Swingley, Lincoln, MT	09	14	31	00	60,000†
2000	Doug Swingley, Lincoln, MT	09	00	58	06	60,000†**

*Does not include $3,000 in silver ingots for reaching the halfway checkpoint first.
**Does not include $2,500 in gold nuggets for first musher to reach Unalakleet.
†Does not include Dodge truck.

the Yukon River for about 150 miles, runs through several Bush villages and crosses the pack ice of Norton Sound.

Strictly a winter trail because the ground is mostly spongy muskeg swamps, the route attracted national attention in 1925 when sled dog mushers, including the famous Leonhard Seppala, relayed 300,000 units of life-saving diphtheria serum to epidemic-threatened Nome. As the airplane and snowmobile replaced the sled dog team, the trail fell into disuse. Thanks to Redington and Page, the trail has been assured a place in Alaska history.

Each year the Iditarod takes a slightly different course, using an alternate southern route in odd years (see map next page). The route is traditionally described as 1,049 miles long (selected because Alaska is the 49th state), but the actual distance run each year is close to 1,100 miles.

In 2000, 81 mushers began the race; 12 were scratched and one withdrew. For more information write the Iditarod Trail committee, P.O. Box 870800, Wasilla 99687. Web site is www.iditarod.com.

Igloo The word igloo, meaning snowhouse, is from northern and eastern Eskimo (Inupiaq *iglu* or "house"). The

stereotypical igloo is a snow block structure that could be built quickly as a temporary trail shelter for arctic Alaska and Canada Eskimos. Igloos are constructed in a spiral with each tier leaning inward at a greater angle. The entrance is a tunnel with a cold trap. A sleeping platform raises sleepers off the cold floor, while a vent at the top allows fresh air for ventilation and an ice window admits light.

Most Alaska indigenous dwellings were sod igloos, dome- or Quonset-shaped structures whose roof was supported with wood or whale bones and covered with insulating sod. (*See also* Barabara)

Information Sources

Agriculture. State Division of Agriculture, P.O. Box 949, Palmer 99645.

Alaska Natives. Alaska Federation of Natives, 1577 C St., Suite 201, Anchorage 99501.

Boating, Canoeing and Kayaking. Alaska Department of Transportation and Public Facilities, 3132 Channel Drive, Juneau 99801-7898, (907) 465-3900; State of Alaska, Division of Parks and Outdoor Recreation, 3601 C St., Suite 1200, Anchorage 99503, (907) 269-8704.

Business. Alaska Department of Community and Economic Development,

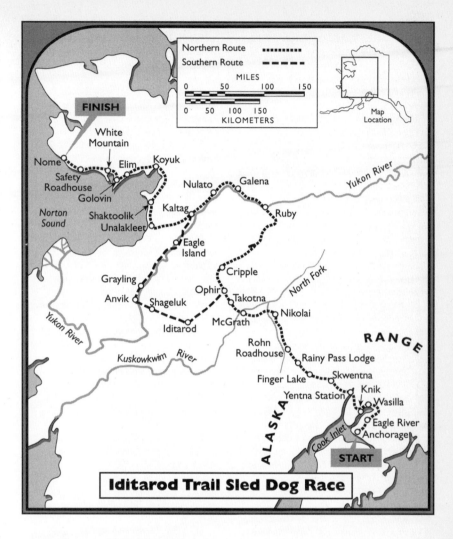

Iditarod Trail Sled Dog Race

Map legend:
- Northern Route
- Southern Route

MILES
0 50 100 150

0 50 100 150
KILOMETERS

Map Location

FINISH

White Mountain

Nome
Safety Roadhouse
Golovin
Elim
Koyuk
Nulato
Galena
Kaltag
Ruby
Shaktoolik
Unalakleet
Norton Sound
Eagle Island
Grayling
Cripple
Anvik
Ophir
Takotna
Shageluk
Nikolai
Iditarod
McGrath
North Fork
Yukon River
Kuskokwim River
Rohn Roadhouse
Rainy Pass Lodge
Finger Lake
Skwentna
Yentna Station
Knik
Wasilla
Eagle River
Anchorage
Cook Inlet
START
ALASKA RANGE

P.O. Box 110800, Juneau 99811-0801, http://www.dced.state.ak.us. State Chamber of Commerce, 217 Second St., Juneau 99801.

Census Data. Alaska Department of Labor, Research and Analysis, P.O. Box 107018, Anchorage 99510, (907) 269-4860.

Customs. U.S., (907) 474-0307.

Directory Assistance. (907) 555-1212.

Disabled Access. Challenge Alaska, (907) 783-2925. Outdoor recreation programs for persons with disabilities. Sea kayaking, adaptive skiing.

Dog Mushing. Alaska Dog Mushers Association, P.O. Box 662, Fairbanks 99707.

Education. Alaska Department of Education, 801 W. 10th St., Suite 200, Juneau 99801, (907) 465-2800.

Elderly. Division of Senior Service, 3601 C St., Suite 310, Anchorage 99503, (907) 269-3666; elsewhere, (800) 478-9969.

Environmental Conservation. Department of Environmental Conservation, 410 Willoughby Ave., Suite 105, Juneau 99801, (907) 465-5065.

Ferry System. Alaska Marine Highway, (800) 642-0066.

Gold Panning. Alaska Miners Association, 3305 Arctic Blvd., Anchorage 99503, (907) 563-9229.

Health. State Department of Health and Social Services, Division of Public Health, P.O. Box 110601, Juneau 99811-0601, (907) 465-3090.

Highway Information. Alaska State Troopers (for emergencies), (907) 269-5511; Alaska State Highway System, (800) 478-7675.

Historical Archives. Alaska State Archives, P.O. Box 6, Juneau 99811; National Archives, 654 W. Third Ave., Anchorage 99501; University of Alaska Archives, 3211 Providence Drive, Anchorage 99508.

Housing. Association of Alaska Housing Authorities, 4300 Boniface Pkwy., Anchorage 99504, (907) 338-3970.

Hunting and Fishing Regulations. State Department of Fish and Game, P.O. Box 25526, Juneau 99811, (907) 465-2376.

Job Opportunities. Job Service, 3301 Eagle, Anchorage 99503, (907) 269-4800; State Employment Service, P.O. Box 25509, Juneau 99802, (907) 465-5934.

Job Opportunities for People with Disabilities. ASSETS, Inc., 2330 Nichols St., Anchorage 99508; (907) 279-6617.

Labor. State Department of Labor, P.O. Box 21149, Juneau 99802, (907) 465-2700.

Land. Alaska Public Lands Information Centers, 605 W. Fourth Ave., Suite 105, Anchorage 99501, (907) 271-2737; 250 Cushman St., Suite 1A, Fairbanks 99701, (907) 451-7352; P.O. Box 359, Tok 99780, (907) 883-5677; Bureau of Land Management, 222 W. Seventh Ave., No. 13, Anchorage 99513; State Division of Lands, P.O. Box 107005, Anchorage 99510; 50 Main St., Ketchikan 99901, (907) 228-6220; Web site: www.nps.gov/aplic/center

Law. Department of Law, P.O. Box 110300, Juneau 99811, (907) 465-2133.

Legal Assistance. Alaska Legal Services, Anchorage (800) 478-9999.

Legislature. Legislative Information Office, 716 W. Fourth Ave., Suite 200, Anchorage 99501, (907) 258-8111.

Libraries. Alaska State Library, 344 W.

Third Ave., Anchorage 99501.

Maps (topographic). U.S. Geological Survey, 4230 University Drive, Room 101, Anchorage 99508; 101 12th Ave., Room 126, Fairbanks 99701.

Military. Department of the Air Force, Headquarters, Alaskan Air Command, Elmendorf Air Force Base 99506; Department of the Army, Headquarters, U.S. Army Alaska, 600 Richardson Drive, P.O. Box 5900, Fort Richardson 99505; State Department of Military and Veterans Affairs, Box 5800, Fort Richardson 99505; Department of Transportation, U.S. Coast Guard, 17th Coast Guard District, P.O. Box 3-5000, Juneau 99802.

Mines and Petroleum. Alaska Miners Association, 3305 Arctic Blvd., No. 202, Anchorage 99503, (907) 563-9229. Web site: www.alaskaminers.org. State Division of Geological and Geophysical Surveys, 764 University Ave., Suite 200, Fairbanks 99707, (907) 451-5001.

Natural Resources. Department of Natural Resources, 400 Willoughby Ave., Juneau 99801, (907) 465-2400.

Permanent Fund Dividend. P.O. Box 110460, Juneau 99811, (907) 465-2323.

Public Safety. Department of Public Safety, P.O. Box 111200, Juneau 99811, (907) 465-4322.

Resorts/Lodges. Alaska National Park Connection, P.O. Box 221011, Anchorage 99522; (888) 277-2757. Hotline connects you with lodging and tour experts at Denali, Glacier Bay, Katmai, Kenai Fjords and Wrangell–St. Elias. E-mail: wingsong@alaska.net.

Revenue. Department of Revenue, P.O. Box 110400, Juneau 99811-0400, (907) 465-2300.

River Running. Bureau of Land Management, 222 W. Seventh Ave., Anchorage 99513, (907) 271-5960; National Park Service, 2525 Gambell St., Anchorage 99503; U.S. Dept. of the Interior, Fish and Wildlife Service, 1011 E. Tudor Road, Anchorage 99503, (907) 786-3487.

Stranded Residents: Association for Stranded Rural Alaskans in Anchorage, 2606 C St., Suite 2B, Anchorage 99503; (907) 272-0643.

Tourism Information. Alaska Tourism Marketing Council, 3601 C St., Suite 700, Anchorage 99503, (907) 269-8182; Alaska Visitors Association, 3201 C St., Suite 403, Anchorage 99503; (907) 561-5733. Visit the Web site at www.travelalaska.com or www.state.ak.us/tourism.

Veterans Affairs. Department of Military and Veterans Affairs, P.O. Box 5800, Fort Richardson 99505, (907) 428-6003.

Weather Information: National Weather Service, Anchorage, (907) 936-2525. Web site: http://alaska.net /~nwsfoanc. Motorist and Recreation Areas, (907) 936-2626; Marine and Boating, (907) 936-2727; General, (907) 266-5105.

Inuit Circumpolar Conference
Started in Barrow in 1977, the Inuit Circumpolar Conference brings together Inuit from Greenland, Canada, Alaska and Chukotka (Russia) to address common concerns regarding environment, human rights, health and economic development. The ICC is prominent in national and international arenas, including the United Nations and circumpolar initiatives such as the eight-nation Arctic Environmental Protection Strategy. In Alaska, the ICC has supported international Native-to-Native agreements on managing shared wildlife resources such as polar bears.

National offices in each of the four countries represented by the ICC carry on the work of the organization, which is directed by triennial general assemblies, the sites of which rotate among countries. The next assembly will be held in Canada in 2001 and will bring together more than 1,000 Inuit from around the Arctic.

Islands
Southeastern Alaska contains about 1,000 of the state's 1,800 named islands, rocks and reefs; several thousand remain unnamed. The Aleutian Island chain, stretching southwest from the mainland, contains more than 200 islands.

Of the state's 10 largest islands, six are in southeastern Alaska. Of the remainder,

Unimak is in the Aleutians, Nunivak and St. Lawrence are in the Bering Sea off the western coast of Alaska, and Kodiak is in the Gulf of Alaska (*see* map, pages 8–9). The state's 10 largest islands, according to U.S. Geological Survey figures, are:

1. Kodiak, 3,588 sq. mi.
2. Prince of Wales, 2,731 sq. mi.
3. Chichagof, 2,062 sq. mi.
4. St. Lawrence, 1,780 sq. mi.
5. Admiralty, 1,709 sq. mi.
6. Baranof, 1,636 sq. mi.
7. Nunivak, 1,600 sq. mi. (estimate)
8. Unimak, 1,600 sq. mi.
9. Revillagigedo, 1,134 sq. mi.
10. Kupreanof, 1,084 sq. mi.

Ivory
Eskimos traditionally carved sea mammal ivory to make such implements as harpoon heads, dolls and ulu (fan-shaped knife) handles. For the past century however most carvings have been made to be sold. Etching on ivory originally was done with hand tools and the scratched designs were filled in with soot. Today power tools supplement the hand tools and carvers may color the etching with India ink, graphite, hematite or commercial coloring.

The large islands of the Bering Sea— St. Lawrence, Little Diomede and Nunivak—are home to the majority of Alaska's ivory carvers. Eskimos from King Island, renowned for their carving skill, now live in Nome.

Walrus. From *Alaska's Mammals* by Dave Smith (text) and Tom Walker (photographs).

The bulk of the ivory used today comes from walrus tusks and teeth seasoned for a few months. Old walrus ivory, often mistakenly called fossil ivory, is also  used. This ivory has been buried in the ground or left on beaches for years; contact with various minerals has changed it from white to tan or any of a multitude of colors. Some highly prized old ivory exhibits rays of deep blue or areas of brown and gold that shine. Most old ivory comes from ancient sites or beaches on St. Lawrence Island and is sold by the pound to non-Native buyers, generally for use in some kind of artwork.

Mastodon tusks are often unearthed in the summer by miners or found eroding on river cutbanks where they have been buried for thousands of years. Although these tusks are enormous and their colorations often beautiful, the material cannot be used efficiently because it dries and then separates into narrow ridges.

Various federal prohibitions govern the collection of old walrus, mammoth and mastodon ivory. These materials may be gathered from private or reservation lands, but may not be traded or sold if found on public lands. The taking of fresh walrus ivory is illegal for non-Natives, in accordance with the Marine Mammal Protection Act of 1972.

Walrus may be taken only by Alaska Natives (Aleuts, Eskimos and Indians) who dwell on the coast of the North Pacific Ocean or the Arctic Ocean and rely on the animals for subsistence or for the creation and sale of Native handicrafts or clothing.

Raw walrus ivory and other parts can be sold only by an Alaska Native to an Alaska Native within Alaska, or to a registered agent for resale or transfer to an Alaska Native within the state. Only authentic Native-processed ivory articles of handicrafts or clothing may be sold or transferred to a non-Native, or sold in interstate commerce.

Beach ivory, which is found on the beach within one-quarter mile of the ocean, may be kept by anyone. This ivory must be registered by all non-Natives with the U.S. Fish and Wildlife Service (USFWS) or the National Marine Fisheries Service within 30 days of discovery. Beach-found ivory must remain in the possession of the finder even if carved or scrimshawed.

Carved or scrimshawed walrus ivory (authentic Native handicraft) or other marine mammal parts made into clothing or other authentic Native handicrafts may be exported from the United States to a foreign country, but the exporter must first obtain a permit from the USFWS. Even visitors from the Lower 48 simply traveling through, or stopping in Canada on their way home, are required to have a USFWS export and/or transit permit. Cost is $25. Mailing the carved ivory home will avoid the need for an export/transit permit. Importation of walrus or other marine mammal parts is illegal except for scientific research purposes or for public display once a permit is granted. Because of ecological sensitivity to the use of elephant ivory, many carvers are switching to whale-bone, recycled from the skeletons of harvested species.

For further information contact: Special Agent-in-Charge, U.S. Fish and Wildlife Service, 1011 E. Tudor Road, Anchorage 99503, (907) 786-3311; or Senior Resident, U.S. Fish and Wildlife Service, 1412 Airport Way, Fairbanks 99701, (907) 456-0239.

Jade Most Alaska jade is found near the Dall, Shungnak and Kobuk Rivers, and Jade Mountain, all north of the Arctic Circle. The stones occur in various shades of green, brown, black, yellow,

The police blotter of the *Seward Phoenix Log* contained the following entries: "7:22 P.M. Caller advised his dog, Trixy, had run away after he removed her collar to give her a bath. 8:03 P.M. Trixy found hiding in the bathroom. She didn't want a bath." The Seward Police Department always gets their man.

white and even red. The most valuable are those that are marbled black, white and green. Gem-quality jade, about one-fourth of the total mined, is used in jewelry making. Fractured jade is used for clock faces, tabletops, bookends and other items. Jade is the Alaska state gem.

Juneau Located on scenic
Gastineau Channel, Juneau is the capital of Alaska. Established in 1880 as a mining camp, it was originally called Harrisburg after Richard Harris, who with his partner, Joseph Juneau, discovered gold and staked their claim in 1880. The camp quickly boomed.

Under Russian rule, the seat of government was at Sitka—with no official "capital." In 1900 Congress moved this seat to Juneau, but Juneau did not become the capital (i.e., where the legislature convenes) until 1912. In 1974, Alaskans voted to move the state capital closer to the state's population center, selecting a site between Anchorage and Fairbanks at Willow. Juneau remained the capital after funding for the transfer of government to Willow was defeated by voters in 1982. Of Southeast Alaska's 60,000 residents, half live in Juneau, Alaska's third-largest city.

Juneau is accessible only by boat, ferry or plane. No roads lead into or out of town. Often called "a little San Francisco," Juneau is tucked at the foot of Mount Juneau. The climate is wet and mild, with summer average daily maximum temperatures of 63°F and winter average daily minimum temperatures of 20°F. Average annual snowfall is about 92 inches in the downtown area.

Sights include the historic shopping district, the Red Dog Saloon, the State and City Museum, the Gastineau Salmon Hatchery, the State Office Building and the Governor's Mansion. Helicopter tours of the Juneau Icefield and tours to Glacier Bay National Park are popular activities, as are fishing, hiking and Inside Passage cruises.

In the summer of 1999, some 595,959 cruise passengers visited Juneau. A popular attraction in Juneau is the Mount Roberts Tramway, a 2,000-foot scenic ride in a spacious gondola.

Additional information is available from the Juneau Convention and Visitors Bureau, 134 Third St., Juneau 99801; (907) 586-2201. E-mail: info@travel juneau.com. or view the visitor guide at www.traveljuneau.com. For a free Juneau Vacation Planner, call (888) 581-2201.

Kodiak Kodiak, the oldest
European settlement in Alaska, is located on Kodiak Island in the Gulf of Alaska, 252 air miles south of Anchorage and the Kenai Peninsula. Known as Alaska's "Emerald Isle," 100-mile-long Kodiak Island and its main city are accessible only by boat, ferry or plane.

After 7,500 years of Alutiiq occupation, Kodiak Island (the second-largest island in the U.S.) was "discovered" by Russian explorer Stephen Glotov in 1763. The town of Kodiak served as Russian Alaska's first capital city until 1804. In 1912, Kodiak was caught in drifting ash from the eruption of Novarupta Volcano on the Alaska Peninsula, which buried the town under 18 inches of pumice. On March 27, 1964, the biggest earthquake to shake North America (measuring 9.2 on the Richter scale) hit the Kodiak area and set off a tsunami (a seismic sea wave) that virtually destroyed downtown Kodiak, its fishing fleet, processing plants and more than 150 homes.

Today, nearly 14,000 residents inhabit the Kodiak Island Borough. Commercial fishing is the island's main industry, with 2,600 vessels and an annual harvest exceeding $80 million— making Kodiak one of the top five commercial fishing ports in the U.S. Timber activities and tourism are also important segments of the local economy. Kodiak is home to the U.S. Coast Guard's base for North Pacific operations, the nation's largest.

The city of Kodiak has two museums, the Baranov and the Alutiiq Museum and Archaeological Respository. The Baranov

Museum displays many items from the Russian era. The Alutiiq Museum, opened in 1995, chronicles the 8,000-year history of the indigenous Alutiiq people and the advent of the Russian fur trade. Icons, rare paintings and handmade brassworks can be seen at the Russian Orthodox Church.

It is estimated that more than 3,000 Kodiak bears inhabit the island. Kodiak National Wildlife Refuge (accessible only by floatplane or boat) was established in 1941 to preserve the natural habitat of the bear. Bears can be observed feeding on salmon during the summer in remote parts of the refuge.

For free maps, brochures, hunting and fishing information, contact the Kodiak Island Convention and Visitors Bureau, 100 Marine Way, Kodiak 99615; (907) 486-4782. Or point your browser to www.kodiak.org/kodiak.

Kuspuk
A *kuspuk* is an Eskimo woman's parka, often made with a loosely cut back so that an infant may be carried piggyback-style. Parkas are made from seal, marmot, ground squirrel, rabbit or fox skins; traditionally, the fur lining faces inward. The ruffs are generally made of wolverine or wolf fur. An outer shell, called a *qaspeg*, is worn over a fur parka to keep it clean and to reduce wear. This outer shell is usually made of brightly colored corduroy, cotton print or velveteen-like material, and may be trimmed with rickrack.

Woman in a kuspuk with her child, fishing through the ice. From The Alaska Heritage Seafood Cookbook by Ann Chandonnet.

Labor and Employer Organizations
Alaska has local branches of dozens of unions, including unions for longshoremen, carpenters, restaurant employees, pulp and paper workers, electrical workers, aerospace workers, fire fighters, teachers and others. For details, consult the *Alaska Labor Union Directory* of the Alaska State AFL-CIO; (907) 258-6284.

Lakes
There are 94 lakes with surface areas of more than 10 square miles among Alaska's more than 3 million lakes. According to the U.S. Geological Survey, the 10 largest natural freshwater lakes in square miles are: Iliamna, 1,150; Becharof, 458; Teshekpuk, 315; Naknek, 242; Tustumena, 117; Clark, 110; Dall, 100; Upper Ugashik, 75; Lower Ugashik, 72; and Kukaklek, 72.

Land Use
(SEE ALSO HIGHWAYS; NATIONAL FORESTS; NATIONAL PARKS, PRESERVES AND MONUMENTS; NATIONAL WILD AND SCENIC RIVERS; NATIONAL WILDERNESS AREAS; NATIONAL WILDLIFE REFUGES; NATIVE PEOPLES; AND STATE PARK SYSTEM) At first glance it seems odd that such a huge area as Alaska has not been more heavily settled. Thousands of acres of forest and tundra, miles and miles of rivers and streams, hidden valleys, bays, coves and mountains are spread across an area so vast that it staggers the imagination. Yet more than two-thirds of the population of Alaska remains clustered around two major centers of commerce, Anchorage and Fairbanks.

Visitors flying over the state are impressed by immense areas showing no sign of humanity. Current assessments indicate that approximately 160,000 acres of Alaska have been cleared, built on or otherwise directly altered by people, either by settlement or resource development, including mining, pipeline construction and agriculture. In comparison to the 365 million acres of land that make up the total of the state, the settled or altered area amounts to less than one-twentieth of 1 percent.

There are several reasons for this lack of development in Alaska. Frozen for long periods in the Arctic, much of the land cannot support quantities of people or industry. Where the winters are "warm," the mountains, glaciers, rivers and oceans prevent easy access for commerce and trade.

The status of land is constantly changing, especially in Alaska. In most places, the free market affects patterns of land ownership but in Alaska, all land ownership patterns until recently were the result of a century-long process of a single landowner, the United States government.

The Statehood Act in 1958 signaled the beginning of a dramatic shift in land ownership patterns. It authorized the state to select 104 million of the 365 million acres of land and inland waters in Alaska. (Under the Submerged Lands Act, the state has title to submerged lands under navigable inland waters.) In passing the Statehood Act, Congress cited economic independence and the need to open Alaska to economic development as the primary purposes for large Alaska land grants.

Alaska Native Claims Settlement Act. The issue of the Native claims in Alaska was resolved with the passage of the Alaska Native Claims Settlement Act (ANCSA) on Dec. 18, 1971. This act of Congress provided for the creation of Alaska Native village and regional corporations and gave the Alaska Eskimos, Aleuts and Indians nearly $1 billion and the right to select 44 million acres from a land pool of some 115 million acres.

Immediately after the settlement act passed, and before Native lands and National Interest Lands were selected, the state filed to select an additional 77 million acres of land. In September 1972, the litigation initiated by the state was resolved by a settlement affirming state selection of an additional 41 million acres.

Section 17 of the settlement act, in addition to establishing a Joint Federal–State Land Use Planning Commission, directed the secretary of the interior to withdraw from public use up to 80 million acres of land in Alaska for study as possible national parks, wildlife refuges, forests, and wild and scenic rivers. These were the National Interest Lands Congress was to

decide upon, as set forth in Section 17(d)(2) of the settlement act, by Dec. 18, 1978. The U.S. House of Representatives passed a bill (HR39) that would have designated 124 million acres of national parks, forests and wildlife refuges, and designated millions of acres of these and existing parks, forests and refuges as wilderness. Although a bill was reported out of committee, it failed to pass the Senate before Congress adjourned.

In November 1978, the secretary of the interior published a draft environmental impact supplement, which listed the actions that the executive branch of the federal government could take to protect federal lands in Alaska until the 96th Congress could consider the creation of new parks, wildlife refuges, wild and scenic rivers and forests. In keeping with this objective, the secretary of the interior, under provisions of the 1976 Federal Land Policy and Management Act, withdrew about 114 million acres of land in Alaska from most public uses. On Dec. 1, 1978, President Jimmy Carter, under the authority of the 1906 Antiquities Act, designated 56 million acres of these lands as national monuments.

In February 1980, the House of Representatives passed a modified HR39. In August 1980, the Senate passed a compromise version of the Alaska lands bill that created 106 million acres of new conservation units and affected 131 million acres in Alaska. In November 1980, the House accepted the Senate version of the Alaska National Interest Lands Conservation Act (ANILCA), which President Carter signed into law on Dec. 2, 1980. This also is known as the d-2 lands bill or the compromise HR39. (*See also* National Forests; National Parks, Preserves and Monuments; National Wild and Scenic

The long-awaited tunnel to Whittier opened to road traffic on June 7, 2000. In a great use of $80 million tax dollars, we can now drive directly to a town that nobody ever wanted to go to in the first place.

Rivers; National Wilderness Areas; *and* National Wildlife Refuges)

Land use in Alaska will continue to be a disputed and complex subject for some time. Implementation of the d-2 bill, and distribution of land to the Native village and regional corporations, the state of Alaska and private citizens in the state will require time. Much of this work is being done by the Bureau of Land Management, which also surveys federal land before a patent is issued. The passage of ANILCA set the stage for long-term management of resources, and the BLM is now moving to establish fish, wildlife and recreation resources as critical and necessary ingredients in a multiple-use mix. Debate continues over issues such as Native sovereignty and subsistence hunting and fishing rights.

Acquiring Land for Private Use.
The easiest and fastest way to acquire land for private use is by purchase from the private sector, through real estate agencies or directly from individuals. Because of speculation, land claim conflicts and delays involving Native, state and federal groups, however, private land is considered by many people to be in short supply and often is very expensive.

Private land in Alaska, excluding land held by Native corporations, is estimated to be more than 1 million acres, but less than 1 percent of the state. Much of this

land passed into private hands through the federal Homestead Acts and other public land laws, as well as land disposal programs of the state, boroughs or communities. Most private land is located along Alaska's limited road network. Compared to other categories of land, it is highly accessible and constitutes some of the prime settlement land.

All laws related to homesteading on federal land (as opposed to state land) in Alaska were repealed as of 1986. Federal land is not available for homesteading or trade and manufacturing sites. (*See also* Homesteading)

Following are programs for the sale of state land.

Auction: Alaska has been selling land by public auction since statehood. The state may sell full surface rights, lease of surface or subsurface rights, or restricted title at an auction. There is a minimum bid of fair market value and the high bidder is the purchaser. Participants must be 18.

Homesite: The homesite program was passed in 1977 by the state legislature. Under its provisions, each Alaska household is eligible for up to five acres. A person who has a homesite entry permit, purchase contract or patent may not apply for another homesite, and neither can any member of that person's household. The land is free, but the individual must pay the cost of the application filing fee ($10), survey and platting, and appraisal, if purchasing. Persons enrolled in this program must live on the homesite for 35 months within seven years of entry and construct a permanent, single-family dwelling on the site within five years. (This is called "proving up" on the land.) After the dwelling is completed and approved by the division, the permit holder may purchase the land at fair market value at the date of purchase. The occupancy requirement is then waived.

Remote Parcels: This remote parcel program replaced the old open-to-entry program. It permitted entry to designated areas to stake a parcel of 5, 20 or 40 acres, depending on the area, and to lease the area for five years with the option of a five-year renewal.

The remote parcel program ended July 1, 1984, when it was replaced by the

Looking Back

1867

The United States purchased Alaska from Russia for $7.2 million.

1983 homesteading bill. Alaskans leasing remote parcels, but who have not yet purchased them, may obtain patent under a remote parcel lease agreement.

Lottery: One year of residency is required to participate in the lottery program. Successful applicants are determined by a drawing and pay the appraised fair market value of the land. They repay the state over a period of up to 20 years, with interest set at the current federal land loan bank rate. Lotteries require a 5 percent down payment.

The state offered 100,000 acres of land to private ownership in each fiscal year from July 1, 1979, to July 1, 1982. Disposal levels since then have been based on an annual assessment of the demand.

On April 1, 1983, the Department of Natural Resources discontinued a program that provided Alaska residents who were registered voters a 5-percent-per-year-of-residency discount (up to $25,000) on the sale of land purchased from the state. Recent legislation has changed U.S. military veteran benefits. A 90-day service now qualifies the veteran. Formerly, 15-year veteran residents had been eligible for up to $37,500 on this one-time program.

Following is the amount of land owned by various entities as of 1999:

Alaska Land Ownership

Owner	Acreage (millions of acres)
State	90.1
U.S. Bureau of Land Management	86.9
U.S. Fish and Wildlife	72.4
National Park Service	52.9
Native	37.4
Forest Service	22.5
Military and other federal	2.3
Other Private (besides Native)	1.0

Source: U.S. Bureau of Land Management

Information and applications for state programs are available from the Department of Natural Resources Public Information Office:

Northern Region, 3700 Airport Way, Fairbanks 99709.

Northwest Alaska. From *A Place Beyond* by Nick Jans.

Southcentral Region, 3601 C St., Suite 200, Anchorage 99503.

Southeastern Region, 400 Willoughby Ave., Suite 400, Juneau 99801.

Languages (SEE ALSO IGLOO; MASKS; NATIVE PEOPLES; AND PARKA)

Besides English, Alaska's languages include 20 Native American languages. Fifteen of these Native languages are at risk of extinction: Han, Haida, Eyak, Tanana, Tlingit, Dena'ina (or Tanaina), Ahtna, Ingalik, Holikachuk, Tsimshian, Koyukon, Upper Kuskokwim, Upper Tanana, Kutchin and Aleut. The Eskimo language group—Yupik, Central Yupik, Siberian Yupik and Inupiaq—is widely spoken by many Natives in western and northern Alaska.

Mammals (SEE ALSO BEARS; MUSK-OXEN; AND WHALES AND WHALING)

Large Land Mammals. Black Bear: Highest densities are found in Southeast, Prince William Sound and southcentral coastal mountains and lowlands. Black bears also occur in interior and western Alaska, but are absent from Southeast islands north of Frederick Sound (primarily Admiralty, Baranof and Chichagof) and the Kodiak archipelago. They are not commonly found west of about Naknek Lake on the Alaska Peninsula, in the

Caribou calf. From *Caribou: Wanderer of the Tundra* by Tom Walker.

Aleutian Islands or on the open tundra sloping into the Bering Sea and Arctic Ocean. (*See also* Bears)

Brown/Grizzly Bear: These large omnivores are found in most of Alaska except for Southeast islands south of Frederick Sound or in the Aleutians (except for Unimak Island). (*See also* Bears)

Polar Bear: There are two groups in Alaska's Arctic rim: an eastern group found largely in the Beaufort Sea and a western group found in the Chukchi Sea between Alaska and Siberia. The latter group are the largest polar bears in the world. Old males can exceed 1,500 pounds. (*See also* Bears)

American Bison: In 1928, 23 bison were transplanted from Montana to Delta Junction to restore Alaska's bison population which had died out some 500 years before. Today, several hundred bison graze near Delta Junction; other herds range at Farewell, at Chitina and along the lower Copper River.

Barren Ground Caribou: There are at least 13 distinct caribou herds, with some overlapping ranges: Adak, Alaska Peninsula, Arctic, Beaver, Chisana, Delta, Kenai, McKinley, Mentasta, Mulchatna, Nelchina, Porcupine and Fortymile. Porcupine and Fortymile herds range into Canada. The Western Arctic herd

numbers about 450,000, the state's largest. Hunters of the 50 villages along its migration route take about 20,000 caribou annually for meat.

Sitka Black-tailed Deer: Sitka black-tailed deer range the coastal rain forests of southeastern Alaska. They have been successfully transplanted to the Yakutat area, Prince William Sound, and Kodiak and Afognak Islands.

Roosevelt Elk: Alaska's only elk occur on Raspberry and Afognak Islands, the result of a 1928 transplant of 105 Roosevelt elk from the Olympic Peninsula in Washington state. Other transplant attempts have failed.

Moose: Moose occur from the Unuk River in Southeast to the Arctic Slope, but are most abundant in second-growth birch forests, on timberline plateaus and along major rivers of Southcentral and Interior. They are not found on islands in Prince William Sound or the Bering Sea, on most major islands in Southeast or on Kodiak or the Aleutians groups.

Mountain Goat: These white-coated animals are found in mountains throughout Southeast, and north and west along coastal mountains to Cook Inlet and Kenai Peninsula. They have been successfully transplanted to Kodiak and Baranof Islands.

Musk-Oxen: These shaggy, long-haired mammals were eliminated from Alaska by hunters by 1865. The species was reintroduced and first transplanted to Nunivak Island, and from there to the Arctic Slope around Kavik, Seward Peninsula, Cape Thompson and Nelson Island. (*See also* Musk-Oxen)

Reindeer: Introduced from Siberia just before the 20th century, reindeer roamed much of the Bering Sea Coast region but are now confined to St. George and Nunivak Islands and the Seward Peninsula.

Dall Sheep: The only white, wild sheep in the world, Dall sheep are found in all major mountain ranges in Alaska except the Aleutian Range south of Iliamna Lake.

Wolf: Wolves are protected and managed as big game and valuable furbearers. Wolves are found throughout Alaska except Bering Sea islands, some

Southeast and Prince William Sound islands, and the Aleutian Islands. The wolf succeeds in a variety of climates and terrains. Because some biologists believe wolves must be culled to maintain caribou herd populations, controversial wolf kills, in which wolves are hunted by air, have taken place.

Wolverine: Shy, solitary creatures, wolverines are found throughout Alaska and on some Southeast islands. They are not abundant in comparison with other furbearers.

Furbearers. Beaver: These large vegetarian rodents are found in most of mainland Alaska from the Brooks Range to the middle of the Alaska Peninsula. Abundant in some major mainland river drainages in the Southeast and on Yakutat forelands, they have also been successfully transplanted to the Kodiak area. Beaver dams are sometimes destroyed to allow salmon upstream; however, beavers can rebuild their dams quickly and usually do so on the same site.

Coyote: The coyote is a relative newcomer to Alaska, showing up shortly after the turn of the century, based on reports from old-timers and records. They are not abundant statewide, but are common in Tanana, Copper, Matanuska and Susitna river drainages and on Kenai Peninsula. The coyote is found as far west as Alaska Peninsula and the north side of Bristol Bay. Coyotes are increasingly seen near Anchorage.

Fox: *Arctic* (white and blue phases): Arctic foxes are found almost entirely along the Arctic coast as far south as the northwestern shore of Bristol Bay. They have been introduced to the Pribilof and Aleutian Islands, where the blue color phase, most popular with fox farmers, predominates. The white color phase occurs naturally on Saint Lawrence and Nunivak Islands. *Red:* Its golden fur coveted by trappers, the red fox is found throughout Alaska except for most areas of Southeast and around Prince William Sound.

Lynx: These shy night-prowlers' main food source is the snowshoe hare. The lynx is found throughout Alaska, except on the Yukon–Kuskokwim Delta, southern Alaska Peninsula and along coastal tidelands. It is relatively scarce along the northern Gulf Coast and in southeastern Alaska.

Hoary Marmot: Present throughout most of the mountain regions of Alaska and along the Endicott Mountains east into Canada, the hoary marmot lives in the high country, especially the warm slopes near and above timberline.

Marten: The marten must have climax spruce forest to survive; its habitat ranges throughout timbered Alaska, except north of the Brooks Range, on treeless sections of the Alaska Peninsula, and on the Yukon–Kuskokwim Delta. It has been successfully introduced to Prince of Wales, Baranof, Chichagof and Afognak Islands in this century.

Muskrat: Muskrats are found in greatest numbers around lakes, ponds, rivers and marshes throughout all of mainland Alaska south of the Brooks Range except for the Alaska Peninsula west of the

In June 1999, a grizzly bear took up residence on the fairways of the Kenai golf course. What rules of the sport apply in a case like this? According to golf course employee Robert Speakman, "You just let him play through."

Ugashik lakes. They were introduced to Kodiak, Afognak and Raspberry Islands. Muskrats were traditionally an important early spring subsistence food for Native Alaskans.

River otter: A member of the weasel family, the river otter occurs throughout the state except on Aleutian Islands, Bering Sea islands and the Arctic coastal plain east of Point Lay. It is most abundant in southeastern Alaska, in Prince William Sound coastal areas and on the Yukon–Kuskokwim Delta. It is sometimes called the "land otter" to distinguish it from the sea otter.

Raccoon: The raccoon is not native to Alaska and is considered an undesirable addition because of its 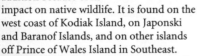 impact on native wildlife. It is found on the west coast of Kodiak Island, on Japonski and Baranof Islands, and on other islands off Prince of Wales Island in Southeast.

Squirrel: *Northern flying:* These small nocturnal squirrels are found in interior, southcentral and southeastern Alaska where coniferous forests are sufficiently dense to provide suitable habitat. *Red:* These tree squirrels inhabit spruce forests, especially along rivers, from Southeast north to the Brooks Range. They are not found on the Seward Peninsula, Yukon–Kuskokwim Delta and Alaska Peninsula south of Naknek River.

Weasel: Least weasels and short-tailed weasels are found throughout Alaska, except for the Bering Sea and Aleutian Islands. Short-tailed weasels are brown with white underparts in summer, becoming snow-white in winter (designated ermine).

Other Small Mammals. Bat: There are five common bat species in Alaska.

Northern Hare (Arctic Hare or Tundra Hare): This large hare inhabits western and northern coastal Alaska, weighs 12 pounds or more and measures 2½ feet long.

Snowshoe Hare (or Varying Hare): In winter, these animals become pure white; in summer, their coats are grayish to brown. The snowshoe hare occurs throughout Alaska except for the lower portion of Alaska Peninsula, the Arctic coast and most islands; it is scarce in southeastern Alaska. Cyclic population highs and lows of hares occur roughly every 10 years. Their big hind feet, covered with coarse hair in winter, act as snowshoes for easy travel over snow.

Brown Lemming: Lemmings are found throughout northern Alaska and the Alaska Peninsula; they are not present in Southeast, Southcentral or the Kodiak archipelago.

Collared Lemming: Resembling large meadow voles, collared lemmings range from the Brooks Range north and from the lower Kuskokwim River drainage north.

Northern Bog Lemming (sometimes called Lemming Mice): These tiny mammals, rarely observed, occur in meadows and bogs across most of Alaska.

Deer Mouse: These rodents inhabit timber and brush in southeastern Alaska.

House Mouse: Extremely adaptive, familiar house mice are found in Alaska seaports and large communities in southcentral Alaska.

Meadow Jumping Mouse: These mice can jump 6 feet and are found in the southern third of Alaska from the Alaska Range to the Gulf of Alaska.

Collared Pika: Members of the rabbit family, pikas are found in central and southern Alaska; they are most common in the Alaska Range.

Porcupine: These slow-moving rodents prefer forests and inhabit most wooded regions of mainland Alaska.

Norway Rat: The Norway rat came to Alaska on whaling ships in the mid-1800s, thriving in Aleutian ports (the Rat Islands group is named for the Norway rats). They are now found in virtually all Alaska seaports, and in Anchorage and Fairbanks and other population centers with open garbage dumps.

Shrew: Seven species of shrew range in Alaska.

Meadow Vole (or Meadow Mouse): Extremely adaptive, there are seven species of meadow vole attributed to Alaska that range throughout the state.

Red-backed Vole: The red-backed vole prefers cool, damp forests and is found throughout Alaska from Southeast to Norton Sound.

Woodchuck: These large, burrowing squirrels, also called groundhogs, are found in the eastern Interior between the Yukon and Tanana Rivers, from east of Fairbanks to the Alaska–Canada border.

Bushy-tailed Woodrat: Commonly called pack rats because they tend to carry off objects to their nests, woodrats are found along the mainland coast of southeastern Alaska.

Marine Mammals. Marine mammals found in Alaska waters are: **dolphin** (Grampus, Pacific white-sided and Risso's); **Pacific walrus; porpoise** (Dall and harbor); **sea otter; seal** (harbor, larga, northern elephant, northern fur, Pacific bearded

or *oogruk*, ribbon, ringed and spotted); **Steller sea lion;** and **whale** (Baird's beaked or giant bottlenose, beluga, blue, narwhal, bowhead, Cuvier's beaked or goosebeaked, fin or finback, gray, humpback, killer, minke or little piked, northern right, pilot, sei, sperm and Bering Sea beaked or Stejneger's beaked). (*See also* Whales and Whaling)

The Marine Mammal Protection Act, passed by Congress on Dec. 21, 1972, provided for a complete moratorium on the taking and importation of all marine mammals. The purpose was to protect population stocks of marine mammals that "are, or may be, in danger of extinction or depletion as a result of man's activities." Congress further found that marine mammals have "proven themselves to be resources of great international significance, aesthetic and recreational as well as economic, and it is the sense of the Congress that they should be protected and encouraged to develop to the greatest extent feasible commensurate with sound policies of resource management and that the primary objective of their management should be to maintain the health and stability of the marine ecosystem. Whenever consistent with this primary objective, it should be the goal to obtain an optimum sustainable population keeping in mind the carrying capacity of the habitat."

The U.S. Fish and Wildlife Service (Department of the Interior) is responsible for the management of polar bears, sea otters and walrus in Alaska. The National Marine Fisheries Service (Department of Commerce) is responsible for the management of all other marine mammals. The state of Alaska assumed management of walrus in April 1976, and relinquished it back to the USFWS in July 1979.

Masks (SEE ALSO NATIVE ARTS AND CRAFTS)

Masks are integral to the cultures of the Eskimos, coastal Indians and Aleuts of Alaska.

Eskimo. Eskimo masks rank among the finest tribal art in the world. Ceremonialism and the mask-making that accompanied it were highly developed and practiced widely by the time the first Russians established trading posts in southeastern Alaska in the early 1800s.

Shaman used masks during certain ceremonies, sometimes in conjunction with wooden puppets, in ways that frightened and entertained participants. Dancers wore religious masks in festivals that honored the spirits of animals and birds to be hunted or that needed to be appeased. Each spirit was interpreted in a different mask and each mask was thought to have a spirit, or *inua,* of its own. This *inua* tied the mask to the stream of spiritual beliefs present in Eskimo religion. Not all masks were benign; some were surrealistic pieces that represented angry or dangerous spirits. Some had moving parts.

In 1996, the Anchorage Museum of History and Art held a notable exhibit "Agayuliyararput Our Way of Making Prayer: The Living Tradition of Yup'ik Masks," to demonstrate the interest of Yup'ik people in preserving their past and carrying the vital tradition of mask-making into the future. The exhibit went on to tour the Lower 48 in 1997.

Indian. Several types of masks existed among the Tlingit and other coastal Indians of Alaska, including simple single-face masks, occasionally having an elaborately carved totemic border; a variation of the face mask with the addition of moving parts; and transformation masks, which have several faces concealed within the first.

Tlingit mask

Masked dancers were accompanied by a chorus of tribal singers who sang songs associated with the masks and reflecting the wealth of the host. Masks were the critical element in portraying the relationship of the tribe with spirits and projecting their power to spellbind their audiences.

Masks were always created to be worn, but not all members of the tribe held sufficient status or power to wear them. Ceremonial use of masks generally took place in the fall or winter, when the spirits of the other world were said to be nearby.

Northwest Coast Indian mask-makers primarily used alder, though red and yellow cedar were used at times.

Aleut. Examples of masks used on various islands of the Aleutian Chain for shamanistic and ceremonial purposes are reported as early as the mid-18th century. Some of these early masks represented animals. Many were apparently destroyed after use. Aleut legends maintain that some masks were associated with ancient inhabitants of the region.

On the Shumagin Islands, a group of cavelike chambers yielded important examples of Aleut masks late in the 19th century. A number of well-preserved masks, apparently associated with the burials of Aleut whalers, were found. All of them had once been painted. Some of them had attached ears and tooth grips. Pegs were used for inserting feathers or carved wooden appendages similar to those of Eskimo masks of southern Alaska today. Fragments of composite masks, those decorated with feathers, appendages or movable parts, have been found on Kagamil Island with earlier remains.

Early accounts of masked Aleut dances say each dance was accompanied by special songs. Most masks were apparently hidden in caves or secret places when the ceremony ended.

Today, modern Aleut mask-makers study the old traditions and reproduce masks from museum collections or create contemporary variants in clay, glass and even chrome.

McNeil River State Game Sanctuary

Photographers, naturalists, wildlife enthusiasts and researchers come to McNeil River State Game Sanctuary in Southwestern Alaska for the opportunity to view the world's largest concentration of brown bears in their natural habitat. The Alaska Department of Fish and Game (ADF&G) manages the sanctuary's unique bear-viewing program, which allows visitors to watch the brown bears as they congregate to feed on migrating salmon. Small groups are escorted to a viewing area by an ADF&G guide and are limited to 10 visitors a day. Despite the number of bears and the presence of humans, there have been no injuries to bears or humans in the 23 years of the program.

All visitors must apply for a permit to visit the sanctuary. In 1999, almost 1,200 people applied for one of 280 permits awarded by lottery. Applications are available after January 1 and due March 1 for the upcoming visitor season. Contact the Alaska Department of Fish and Game, Division of Wildlife Conservation, 333 Raspberry Road, Anchorage 99518-1599, Attention: McNeil River.

Statistics on the bears in the sanctuary have been compiled since 1976:

Most bears seen at one time at McNeil Falls—68

Most bears seen in one day at McNeil Falls—105

Most salmon seen caught in one day by one bear—90

Most salmon seen caught in one year by one bear—1,012

Most salmon seen caught in one year at McNeil Falls—15,455

Medal of Heroism

By a law enacted in 1965, the Alaska governor is authorized to award, in recognition of valorous and heroic deeds, a state medal of heroism to those who have saved a life or, at risk to their lives, have served the state or community on behalf of the health, welfare or safety of others. The heroism medal is not necessarily given every year, and may be awarded posthumously. It was last awarded in 1996. Following are recipients of the Alaska Medal of Heroism:

Albert Rothfuss (1965), Ketchikan. Rescued a child from drowning in Ketchikan Creek.

Randy Blake Prinzing (1968), Soldotna. Saved two lives at Scout Lake.

Nancy Davis (1971), Seattle. A flight attendant who convinced an alleged hijacker to surrender.

Jeffrey Stone (1972), Fairbanks. Saved two youths from a burning apartment.

Gilbert Pelowook (1975), Savoonga. An Alaska state trooper who aided plane crash victims on St. Lawrence Island.

Residents of Gambell (1975). Provided aid and care for plane crash victims on St. Lawrence Island.

George Jackinsky (1978), Kasilof. Rescued two persons from a burning aircraft.

Mike Hancock (1980), Lima, Ohio. In 1977, rescued a victim of a plane crash that brought down high-voltage lines.

David Graham (1983), Kenai. Rescued a person from a burning car.

Robert Larson (1983), Anchorage. An employee of the Department of Public Safety who flew through hazardous conditions to rescue survivors of the crash that took John Stimson's life.

John Stimson (1983), Cordova. A first sergeant in the Division of Fish and Wildlife Protection who died in a helicopter accident during an attempt to rescue others.

Esther Farquhar (1984), Sitka. Tried to save other members of her family from a fire in their home; lost her life in the attempt.

Darren Olanna (1984), Nome. Died while attempting to rescue a person from a burning house.

Billy Westlock (1986), Emmonak. Rescued a youngster from the Emmonak River.

Lieutenant Commander Whiddon, Lieutenant Breithaupt, ASM2 Tunks, AD1 Saylor and **AT3 Milne (1987)**, Sitka. U.S. Coast Guard personnel rescued a man and his son from their sinking boat during high seas.

The Army and Air National Guard (1988), Gambell, Savoonga, Nome and Shishmaref. Searched for seven missing walrus hunters from Gambell.

Evans Geary, Johnny Sheldon, Jason Rutman, Jessee Ahkpuk Jr. and **Carl Hadley (1989)**, Buckland. These youths rescued two friends who, while skating on a frozen pond, had fallen through the ice.

Robert Cusack (1991), Lake Iliamna. Rescued a woman and a child who were trapped inside a floatplane that had crashed and sank in Lake Iliamna.

Clifford Comer, Robert Yerex, Gary Strebe, David Schron and **Jeffery Waite (1992)**, Air Station Kodiak. Coast Guard members rescued a four-man fishing crew in 45-knot winds and 35-foot seas.

Clyde Aketachunak (1994), Kotlik. Awarded posthumously after Aketachunak died in an attempt to save 6-year-old Jennifer Prince from drowning in Kotlik Slough in July 1993.

Sgt. David Lancaster (1994), formerly of Fort Richardson, and **Tom Burgess (1994)**, North Pole. Two men saved the lives of passengers on a tour bus that was involved in a head-on collision on the Parks Highway in July 1993.

Eric Pentilla, Randy Oles, Walter Greaves and **Jerry Austin (1994)**. Four men were involved in the rescue of seven missionaries whose plane crashed in the Bering Sea when returning from Russia in August 1993.

Travis Bennett (1994), North Pole. Bennett was 14 when he waded into the Chena River to save the life of Debbie Peterson, who was drowning, in July 1994.

Mike Olsen, Rusty Shaub, Kevin Kramer and **George Coulter (1994)**. These four men rescued the survivors of an

Metric Conversions (approximate)

	When you know:	You can find:	If you multiply by:
Length	inches	millimeters	25.4
	feet	centimeters	30.5
	yards	meters	0.9
	miles	kilometers	1.6
	millimeters	inches	0.04
	centimeters	inches	0.4
	meters	yards	1.1
	kilometers	miles	0.6
Temperature	degrees Fahrenheit	degrees Celsius	5/9 (after subtracting 32)
	degrees Celsius	degrees Fahrenheit	9/5 (then add 32)

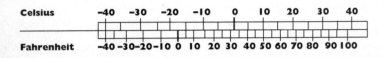

Mileage Chart

Driving Mileage Between Principal Points	Anchorage, AK	Dawson City, YT	Dawson Creek, BC	Fairbanks, AK	Haines, AK	Homer, AK	Prince Rupert, BC	Seattle, WA	Skagway, AK	Valdez, AK	Whitehorse, YT
Anchorage, AK		515	1608	358	775	226	1605	2435	832	304	724
Dawson City, YT	515		1195	393	578	741	1192	2022	435	441	327
Dawson Creek, BC	1608	1195		1486	1135	1834	706	827	992	1534	884
Fairbanks, AK	358	393	1486		653	584	1483	2313	710	284	602
Haines, AK	775	578	1135	653		1001	1132	1962	359	701	251
Homer, AK	226	741	1834	584	1001		1831	2661	1058	530	950
Prince Rupert, BC	1605	1192	706	1483	1132	1831		1033	989	1531	881
Seattle, WA	2435	2022	827	2313	1962	2661	1033		1819	2361	1711
Skagway, AK	832	435	992	710	359	1058	989	1819		758	108
Valdez, AK	304	441	1534	284	701	530	1531	2361	758		650
Whitehorse, YT	724	327	884	602	251	950	881	1711	108	650	

airplane crash in Taku Inlet in July 1994.

(Louis R.) Rick Gottwald (1995), Juneau. Docked in Juneau's Harris Harbor, Gottwald noticed flames coming from a boat tied up at an adjacent dock. He swam 50 feet to the burning boat and saved an intoxicated man who was onboard.

Trooper Rose Edgren (1995), Delta Junction. Responding to a domestic violence call, Edgren and her partner were fired upon. Pushing her partner to safety, Edgren returned fire, shot the attacker and then administered lifesaving first aid.

Sam Hoger (1996), Eagle River. While visiting New Orleans for a karate competition, Hoger rescued a 10-year-old boy from drowning. After a night in the hospital, the rescued boy went on to win a bronze medal in his event.

Microbreweries
As in many parts of the United States, limited-edition stouts, ales and beers are a trend in Alaska. Many of the breweries offer dining and window observation of the brewing process. Others offer tours and samples.

Alaskan Brewing & Bottling Company, 5429 Shaune Drive, Juneau 99801; tours and samples available.

Borealis Brewery, 349 E. Ship Creek Ave., Anchorage 99501.

Cusack's Brewpub, 598 W. Northern Lights Blvd., Anchorage 99503.

Glacier Brew House, 737 W. Fifth Ave., Anchorage 99501.

Midnight Sun Brewing Company, 7329 Arctic Blvd., Anchorage 99518.

Moose's Tooth Pub & Pizzeria, 3300 Old Seward Highway, Anchorage 99503.

Raven's Ridge, 5690 Supply Road, Fairbanks 99701.

Snow Goose Restaurant/ Sleeping Lady Brewing Co., 717 W. Third Ave., Anchorage 99501.

Military
Until the rapid escalation of war in Europe in 1940–41, Congress saw little need for a strong military presence in the territory of Alaska. Spurred by World War II and a growing realization

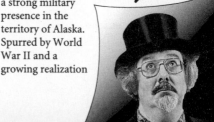

A slightly intoxicated Anchorage idiot tried to rob an adult bookstore by running off with the entire cash register instead of just taking the $200 that was inside the machine. Anchorage police solved the case quickly—the register's tape trailed out behind the thief, and the cops followed it right to his door.

that Alaska could shorten the route to Asia for friend and foe, the government built and still maintains units of the Air Force, Army, Navy and Coast Guard at dozens of installations across the state and on floating units in Alaska waters.

All branches of the military in Alaska are part of the Alaskan Command (ALCOM). ALCOM is charged with maintaining air sovereignty, deploying forces for worldwide contingencies as directed by the commander-in-chief, Pacific Command, providing support to federal and state authorities during civil emergencies, and conducting joint training for the rapid deployment of combat forces. The combined forces of ALCOM include nearly 21,000 Air Force, Army, Navy and Coast Guard personnel, guardsmen and reservists.

At the state level are Air National Guard and Army National Guard units.

U.S. Army. The Alaska District of the U.S. Army Corps of Engineers designs and constructs buildings, runways, roads, utilities and other facilities for the Army, Air Force and National Guard in Alaska. The District develops and regulates water resources and has an increasing workload in environmental restoration. Elmendorf's 437,060-square-foot medical center was completed in 1999. It has a day-to-day bed capacity of 40, but may accommodate 156 beds in an emergency.

District headquarters are located at Elmendorf Air Force Base. Construction field offices are located at Forts Richardson and Wainwright. A project office has been established for Elmendorf's $160 million new medical center. A fifth office is located at the Chena River Lakes Flood Control project near Fairbanks. The Regulatory Branch has field offices in Juneau and Fairbanks.

District staff includes 20 Army engineer officers and 400 civilians representing skills in engineering, architecture, the natural sciences, real estate, contracting and administration.

The United States Army Alaska became the primary Army unit in Alaska upon the inactivation of the 6th Infantry Division (Light) in July 1994. The inactivation of the 6th and the activation of U.S. Army Alaska also marked the return of Army headquarters in the state from Fort Wainwright (Fairbanks) to Fort Richardson (Anchorage). The brigade task force commander, a colonel, and his staff are located at Fort Wainwright. The senior Army commander in Alaska, a major general, is at Fort Richardson.

Besides combat and combat support forces at those two posts, the U.S. Army Alaska has research facilities and training grounds at Fort Greely. The Alaska-based soldiers must be prepared to move quickly to support other troops as needed. In 1990–91, more than 200 Alaska-based soldiers were deployed to the Persian Gulf.

The primary element of U.S. Army Alaska is the light infantry brigade task force, named the 172nd Infantry Brigade (Separate). The 172nd is headquartered with most of its forces at Fort Wainwright. The brigade's 1st Battalion, 501st Parachute Infantry Regiment is stationed at Fort Richardson.

In addition, the 59th Signal Battalion oversees all Army communications in the state; the Northern Warfare Training Center at Fort Greely trains soldiers, guard members and representatives from other services in arctic combat and survival; and the Cold Regions Test Center, also at Fort Greely, tests equipment for cold-weather use.

The Army in Alaska conducts mid-winter training exercises each year for its soldiers and participates in multiservice exercises. Besides unit-level training in Alaska, soldiers train at the Joint Readiness Training Center at Fort Polk, LA, the Yakima Training Center in Washington state and at the National Training Center at Fort Irwin, CA. Soldiers also participate in exercises in Thailand and Guam.

United States Army helicopters are stationed at Fort Wainwright and Fort Greely. Year-round training is conducted with infantry and support units with Blackhawk (UH-60) and Chinook (CH-47) helicopters under demanding arctic conditions. Medical evacuations of military and civilians in need are performed by the 68th Medical Company, which participates in the Military Assistance to Safety and Traffic (MAST) program. The 68th is stationed at Fort Wainwright and has a small team at Fort Greely. The High Altitude Rescue Team (HART) flies specially equipped Chinook helicopters in support of rescues on Mount McKinley and other remote peaks. Army helicopters also transport and train with the Alaska National Guard throughout the state.

U.S. Air Force. The 11th Air Force (AF) helps maintain air superiority in Alaska and supports Alaska-based ground forces, and combat-ready air forces.

The commander of the 11th AF is the senior military officer in Alaska and also serves as the commander of the Alaskan Command and the Alaskan North American Aerospace Defense Region (NORAD).

The largest subordinate units in the 11th AF are the 3rd Wing at Elmendorf AFB, near Anchorage, and 354th Fighter Wing at Eielson AFB, near Fairbanks.

The 3rd Wing provides air defense and air superiority in Alaska, as well as supporting PACAF during contingencies in the Pacific Command area of responsibility. The 3rd is equipped with F-15C/D Eagles and F-15E Strike Eagles. The wing's F-15C/D aircraft stand active air defense alert 24 hours a day, year-round, in support of the NORAD mission.

Military airlift in Alaska is provided by the 3rd Wing's 517th Airlift Squadron at Elmendorf, with C-130 and C-12 aircraft. The 962nd Airborne Warning and Control Squadron flies the E-3 Sentry, a modified Boeing 707 equipped with a 30-foot-diameter rotodome mounted above the fuselage. The E-3 can direct friendly fighter aircraft to intercept and identify unknown aircraft as they enter U.S. airspace and also augment existing ground-based radar systems during peacetime by

Captain Randy Acord, an Army Air Force engineer flight test officer in World War II, holds the prop of a twin-engine P-38 fighter at Ladd Field near Fairbanks in 1944. From Heroes of the Horizon *by Gerry Bruder.*

providing a survivable airborne radar platform during hostilities.

The 354th Fighter Wing uses the F-16 to provide close air support and battlefield air interdiction requirements of the 6th Infantry Division (Light) and Pacific Air Forces worldwide mobility commitments. The OA-10 Thunderbolt II provides forward air control for joint U.S. Army and Air Force contingencies.

Remote locations of the 11th AF are operated by the 611th Air Support Group at Elmendorf AFB. These locations include Galena and King Salmon airports, Eareckson Air Force Station on Shemya Island and a network of 18 Air Force radar sites throughout Alaska.

Other major Air Force components in Alaska include the Air Mobility Command, Air Force Space Command and Air Force Intelligence Agency. When mobilized, the state's Air National Guard becomes an integral part of Alaskan Command's Air Force component. The Guard maintains KC-135 Tankers, C-130s and air rescue HH-60 Pavehawk helicopters.

Navy and Marine Corps. U.S. Navy officers and enlisted personnel are assigned to the Alaskan Command Headquarters staff. As Naval Component of the Alaskan Command, U.S. Naval Forces Alaska (USNAVAK), is composed of seven active-duty U.S. Navy personnel assigned to the USNAVAK staff. They are supplemented by U.S. Coast Guard personnel from the 17th Coast Guard District staff as needed. There are no Marines assigned to the Alaskan Command Headquarters or units.

The Navy and Marine Corps have commands and detachments located in Anchorage. Commands located in Anchorage include the Naval Security Group Activity; Military Sealift Command Office; Naval Reserve Center; Personnel Support Detachment, Company E, 4th Recon Battalion, 4th Marine Division; as well as several other small detachments.

U.S. Coast Guard. The U.S. Coast Guard has been a part of Alaska since the mid-1800s, when it patrolled the extensive and unforgiving coastline with the wooden sailing and steam ships of its predecessor, the Revenue Cutter Service. Since those early days, the service has changed names and wooden ships have been replaced by today's fleet of ships, boats and aircraft, operated and maintained by Alaska's Coast Guard men and women.

The 17th Coast Guard District encompasses the entire state of Alaska, or 45,000 miles of coastline—more than all other states combined. The Coast Guard performs its many missions in Alaska with 2,000 military and civilian employees at 44 units and detachments. The district headquarters is located in Juneau, and the largest Coast Guard base in the country is in Kodiak.

Major responsibilities in Alaska include enforcing the 200-mile fisheries conservation zone where the majority of the fish caught are sold to foreign countries. Search and rescue in Alaska is another task performed by Coast Guard units. The service maintains aids to navigation, including Long-Range Aids to Navigation (LORAN) lighthouses and buoys. Protecting the marine environment against pollution is also a major responsibility. The Coast Guard served as the Federal On-Scene Coordinator for the cleanup of the *Exxon Valdez* oil spill. The Coast Guard has three marine safety offices and five marine safety detachments as well as a Vessel Traffic System in Valdez to maintain the safety of the marine and coastal environment.

The Coast Guard also has an active role in the defense of Alaska. The District Commander is designated the Naval Component Commander for the Alaskan Command in addition to his responsibility as Commander, Maritime Defense Command One Seven. The Alaskan Command Naval component commander's mission complements that of Maritime Defense Command One Seven.

National Guard. The Department of Military and Veterans Affairs includes the Alaska Army National Guard and the Air National Guard. The guard performs a wide range of missions including security, search and rescue, reconnaissance, airlift, transportation, logistics, aerial refueling, drug interdiction and youth support. Guard units also respond to emergencies or disasters. About 1,300 full-time employees work for the Alaska National Guard at some 76 locations across the state.

The guard's headquarters and the Rescue Coordination Center of the Alaska Air National Guard are at Camp Denali near Anchorage. The Alaska Air Guard has about 2,000 members. The 176th Wing, home of the 144th Airlift Squadron and the

210th Rescue Squadron, is at Kulis ANG Base; the 168th Air Refueling Wing is assigned to Eielson AFB; and the 206th Combat Communications Squadron is at Elmendorf AFB.

The Alaska Army National Guard has its headquarters at Camp Denali. Of the nearly 2,000 soldiers assigned, most are members of the 207th Infantry Group (Scout). Battalion headquarters are at Nome, Bethel, Wasilla, Anchorage and Juneau. Training sites include Camp Denali, Bryant Army Guard Heliport, Camp Carroll and Stewart River near Nome.

The guard is committed to several youth programs, especially the Alaska National Guard Youth Academy—ChalleNGe Program for drop-outs or youth-at-risk ages 16 to 18.

Military Population. Military services are a major industry in Alaska and have a significant impact on the Alaska economy. The total population of the military forces in Alaska as of September 1999 was 20,786 service members, plus approximately 35,400 family members. Population figures include Air Force, Army, Navy and Marine Corps active-duty members, plus members of Alaska's Air National Guard and Alaska's Army National Guard. Alaska was also home to 32 Canadian forces.

Minerals and Mining

(*SEE ALSO* COAL; GOLD; OIL AND GAS; *AND* ROCKS AND GEMS*)* The sum of exploration and development investment in Alaska and the value of minerals produced exceeded $1 billion in 1999 for the fourth consecutive year. Contrary to the worldwide trend, exploration expenditures in the state in 1998, at $57.1 million, almost matched the $57.8 million invested in 1997. Due to completion of the production-rate-increase project at the Red Dog zinc-lead mine early in the year, development expenditures in 1998 were down from $168.4 million in 1997 to only $55.4 million.

The loss of development activity in 1998 was counterbalanced by increased

Alaska Copper

In late summer 1900, a team of adventurous prospectors operating 200 miles north of the Gulf of Alaska along the Chitina River (a tributary of the Copper River) stumbled upon a massive cliff of green rock. When they analyzed samples, they discovered the ore was 70 percent copper and included some silver and gold as well. They had uncovered one of the earth's richest copper reserves. . . . Before the mine closed in 1938 it produced 1 billion pounds of copper and 9.7 million ounces of silver worth a combined $300 million—a dollar sum practically equal to that produced by gold. —Harry Ritter, *Alaska's History*

production of zinc and lead, though the increased production was itself offset by metal prices that were considerably lower than in 1997. The total value of Alaska mineral production in 1998 was $920.2 million, with $814.4 million in metals, $71.4 in industrial material such as rock, sand and gravel, and $35.4 million in coal.

Metal production accounted for 88 percent of the total 1998 production, with 549,348 tons of zinc valued at $505.4 million; 594,191 ounces of gold valued at $174.6 million; 14.9 million ounces of silver valued at $82.2 million; 102,887 tons of lead with a value of $49.4 million; and 1,900 tons of copper valued at $2.9 million. Between 1997 and 1998, zinc prices declined 22 percent, lead prices 14 percent and gold prices 11 percent.

The Red Dog Mine near Kotzebue produced most of the lead and zinc, as well as about 5 million ounces of silver, while the Greens Creek Mine near Juneau produced the balance of the lead and zinc, about 9 million ounces of silver, and about 60,000 ounces of gold. Red Dog produces about 80 percent of the U.S. zinc, and about 6 percent of the world total. Greens Creek produces 33 percent of the U.S. silver, and about 8 percent of the world total.

Most of the gold in Alaska in 1998 was from the Fort Knox open-pit, hard-rock mine near Fairbanks, where almost exactly 1,000 ounces daily were produced, for a total of 365,320 ounces. About 30,000 ounces were produced at the Illinois Creek open-pit, hard-rock mine near Galena, and a further 40,000 ounces were mined at the Nixon Fork underground mine near McGrath. About 100 placer gold mines statewide produced an additional 95,300 ounces, with seven large mines producing 75 percent of the total.

A small amount of copper was produced as a by-product at both the Greens Creek and the Nixon Fork mines.

The Usibelli Mine near Healy produced the only coal in the state in 1999, and exported about 326,000 tons of the total 1.1 million tons to Korea, with the remainder firing seven power plants throughout the interior of the state, including a state-of-the-art, clean coal power plant.

Sealaska Corp. shipped a small amount of high-quality calcium carbonate in 1998 from the Calder limestone deposit on Prince of Wales Island, following several years of development, potentially heralding a new industry for Southeast Alaska.

Several exploration projects show promise of becoming the mines for the future. At the Kensington Mine north of Juneau all permits are in place, but modifications have been proposed to allow for profitable mining even at the depressed prices of 1999.

Canadian researchers on the tundra found that mosquitos could drain half of an unprotected person's blood supply in two hours! Last summer, when an incoming tourist to Alaska announced he was going to a remote bear-viewing lodge, a local resident asked if he had brought bug dope with him. The tourist replied, "I'm staying in a $1,000 a night lodge—I don't think they'll have bugs."

The mine is projected to produce about 200,000 ounces of gold a year. At Donlin Creek near Iditarod, drilling in 1998 increased the resource to 11.5 million ounces of gold, and at the Shotgun prospect 100 miles to the south, a gold resource of 1 million ounces is anticipated. In the Interior, the True North gold prospect about 8 miles from the Fort Knox Mine has a gold reserve of 1.3 million ounces, the nearby Gil prospect has a resource of 450,000 ounces, and the Ryan Lode Mine to the west has a resource of more than 1 million ounces. The Pogo gold prospect northeast of Delta Junction has a gold reserve of 5 million ounces, but unlike the low-grade Fort Knox Mine (0.024 ounces of gold per ton), Pogo has a grade 20 times that, at 0.52 ounces per ton. This rich deposit, containing more than 5.6 million ounces of gold and more projected, has created a claim-staking rush from Fairbanks to the Canadian border and beyond.

Several companies have been exploring for polymetallic deposits containing gold, silver, copper, lead and zinc along the north flank of the Alaska Range from Tok to Healy. These prospects such as Dry Creek and Rumble Creek resemble the Wolverine deposit in the Yukon.

About 9,000 state mining claims and 3,000 state prospecting sites were located in 1999, bringing the total active claims to about 50,000. About 1,500 new federal claims were staked, mainly in Southeast, with the total active federal claims numbering about 8,000.

Mosquitoes
Alaska's ubiquitous mosquito is sometimes jokingly referred to as the state bird. At least 25 species of mosquito are found in Alaska (the number may be as high as 40), the females of all species feeding on people, other mammals or birds. Males and females eat plant sugar, but only the females suck blood, which they use for egg production. The itch that follows the bite comes from an anticoagulant injected by the mosquito. No Alaska mosquitoes carry diseases. The insects are present from April through September in many areas of the state. Out

Headnets provide some protection from thick clouds of mosquitoes. From The Alaska River Guide by Karen Jettmar.

in the Bush they are often at their worst in June, tapering off in July. The mosquito menace usually passes by late August and September. From Cook Inlet south, the bugs concentrate on coastal flats and forested valleys. In the Aleutian Islands, mosquitoes are absent or present only in small numbers. The most serious mosquito infestations occur in moist areas of slow-moving or standing water, such as fields, bogs and forests of interior Alaska, from Bristol Bay eastward.

Mosquitoes are most active at dusk and dawn; low temperatures and high winds decrease their activity. Mosquitoes can be controlled by draining their breeding areas or spraying with approved insecticides. When traveling in areas of heavy mosquito infestations, it is wise to wear protective clothing, carefully screen living areas and tents, and use a good insect repellent.

Mountains
Of the 20 highest mountains in the United States, 17 are in Alaska, which has 19 peaks over 14,000 feet. (*See* map on pages 128–29)

Mount McKinley

Mount McKinley in the Alaska Range is the highest mountain on the North American continent. The South Peak is 20,320 feet high; the North Peak has an elevation of 19,470 feet. The mountain was named in 1896 for William McKinley of Ohio, who was the Republican candidate for president. An earlier name had been Denali, an Athabascan word meaning "the high one." The state of Alaska officially renamed the mountain Denali in 1975 and the state Geographic Names Board claims the proper name for the mountain is Denali. However, the federal Board of Geographic Names has not taken any action and congressional legislation has been introduced to retain the name McKinley in perpetuity.

Mount McKinley is within Denali National Park and Preserve. The park entrance is about 237 miles north of Anchorage and 121 miles south of Fairbanks via the George Parks Highway. A 90-mile gravel road runs west from the highway through the park; vehicle traffic on the park road is restricted. The park is also accessible via the Alaska Railroad and by aircraft.

The mountain and its park are one of the top tourist attractions in Alaska. The finest times to see McKinley up close are on summer mornings. August is best, according to statistics based on 13 summers of observation by park ranger Rick McIntyre. The mountain is rarely visible the entire day. The best view is from Eielson Visitor Center, about 66 miles from the park entrance and 33 miles northeast of the summit. The center, open from early June through the second week in September, is reached by shuttle bus provided by the park. There is a $21 bus fee for the eight-hour round trip. Discounts are available for children. For more information about Denali National Park, call (907) 683-2294 or (907) 272-7275.

Eleven climbers perished on Mount McKinley in May 1992, making it the deadliest climbing season in the mountain's history. The 11 climbers, including one American mountaineering guide, died in five separate incidents on the mountain. Since 1932, when the National Park Service began keeping records of climbers attempting to reach the summit of Mount McKinley, 87 climbers have been killed on the mountain. Among the deadliest years on the mountain were 1981 and 1989, when six

(Continued on page 130)

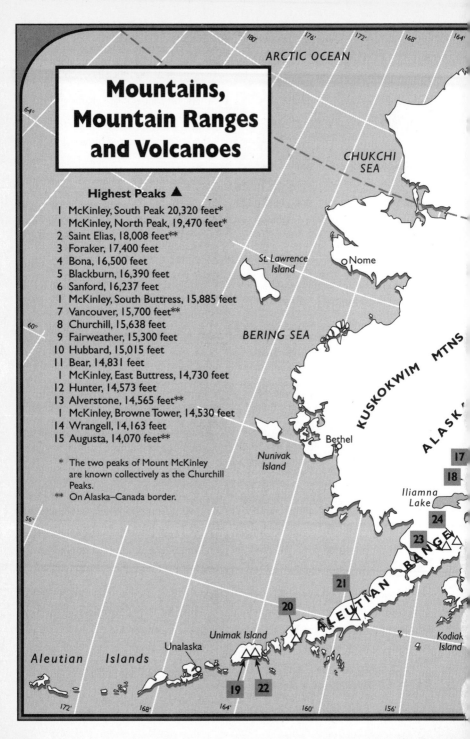

Mountains, Mountain Ranges and Volcanoes

Highest Peaks ▲

1 McKinley, South Peak 20,320 feet*
1 McKinley, North Peak, 19,470 feet*
2 Saint Elias, 18,008 feet**
3 Foraker, 17,400 feet
4 Bona, 16,500 feet
5 Blackburn, 16,390 feet
6 Sanford, 16,237 feet
1 McKinley, South Buttress, 15,885 feet
7 Vancouver, 15,700 feet**
8 Churchill, 15,638 feet
9 Fairweather, 15,300 feet
10 Hubbard, 15,015 feet
11 Bear, 14,831 feet
1 McKinley, East Buttress, 14,730 feet
12 Hunter, 14,573 feet
13 Alverstone, 14,565 feet**
1 McKinley, Browne Tower, 14,530 feet
14 Wrangell, 14,163 feet
15 Augusta, 14,070 feet**

* The two peaks of Mount McKinley are known collectively as the Churchill Peaks.
** On Alaska–Canada border.

ARCTIC OCEAN

CHUKCHI SEA

St. Lawrence Island

Nome

BERING SEA

KUSKOKWIM MTNS

ALASK

Bethel

Nunivak Island

Iliamna Lake

17
18
24
23

21

20

ALEUTIAN RANGE

Unimak Island

Unalaska

Aleutian Islands

19   22

Kodiak Island

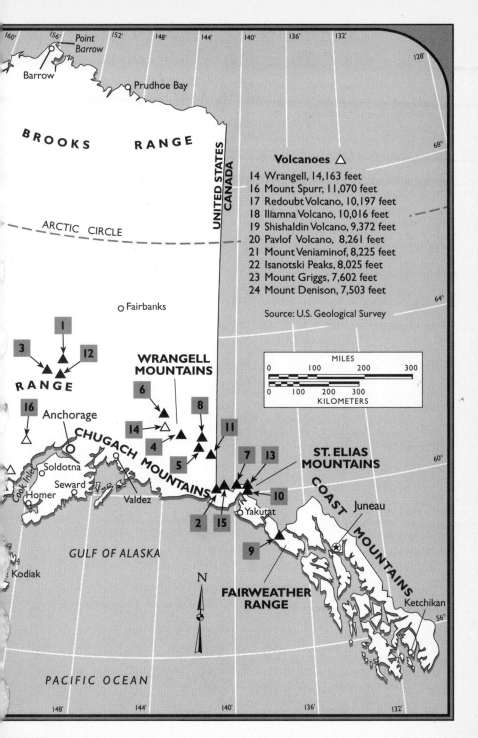

Point Barrow
Barrow
Prudhoe Bay

B R O O K S   **R A N G E**

ARCTIC CIRCLE

UNITED STATES
CANADA

○ Fairbanks

Volcanoes △

14 Wrangell, 14,163 feet
16 Mount Spurr, 11,070 feet
17 Redoubt Volcano, 10,197 feet
18 Iliamna Volcano, 10,016 feet
19 Shishaldin Volcano, 9,372 feet
20 Pavlof Volcano, 8,261 feet
21 Mount Veniaminof, 8,225 feet
22 Isanotski Peaks, 8,025 feet
23 Mount Griggs, 7,602 feet
24 Mount Denison, 7,503 feet

Source: U.S. Geological Survey

MILES

| 0 | 100 | 200 | 300 |

| 0 | 100 | 200 | 300 |

KILOMETERS

R A N G E

**WRANGELL
MOUNTAINS**

Anchorage

CHUGACH MOUNTAINS

Soldotna
Seward
Valdez
Homer
Cook Inlet

**ST. ELIAS
MOUNTAINS**

Yakutat

Juneau

COAST MOUNTAINS

GULF OF ALASKA

Kodiak

N

**FAIRWEATHER
RANGE**

Ketchikan

PACIFIC OCEAN

(Continued from page 127)
mountaineers were killed each of those two years; 1967 and 1980, when eight mountaineers were killed each year, and 1992, when 11 died.

Of the 1,183 climbers taking part in the 1999 mountaineering season, some 508, or 43 percent, reached the summit. Climbers came from 39 countries. Nine major search and rescue missions were logged but there were no fatalities, continuing a trend toward safer climbing on the mountain. In the four years ending 1994, 64 major incidents and 20 deaths were reported; from 1995 to 1999, there were 53 major incidents and 12 deaths.

The third annual Denali Pro Mountaineer of the Year went to Michal Krissak of Slovakia. He was attempting a solo summit of McKinley when he found a semiconscious Japanese climber at 19,500 feet. Krissak abandoned his summit bid and ignored temperatures below zero and great risk to his own life to help the Japanese climber to safety. The award is bestowed by the NPS and Pigeon Mountain Industries.

In 1995, for the first time in park history, climbers were charged a $150 fee to scale the mountain. Rescues in 1998 cost the National Park Service $181,163; military costs were $321,455.

The Park Service now requires climbers to register 60 days before a planned climb. Information on climbing Mount McKinley can be found on the National Park Service Web site at www.nps.gov/dena or call (907) 733-2231.

Mount McKinley Firsts.

1896: Prospector William Dickey names the prominent peak Mount McKinley.

West Buttress Route, Mount McKinley. From To the Top of Denali by Bill Sherwonit.

1902: Alfred H. Brooks, leader of a U.S. Geological Survey party, is the first white man to set foot on McKinley's slopes.

1903: Judge James Wickersham and four others from Fairbanks make the first attempt on the peak.

1910: The Sourdough Expedition makes an attempt; two members reach the summit of the North Peak.

1913: Hudson Stuck's expedition is the first to reach the South Peak.

1932: Bush pilot Joe Crosson makes the first glacier landing on Muldrow Glacier for the Allen Carpé Expedition.

1947: Barbara Washburn is the first woman to reach the summit.

1967: Ray Genet, Dave Johnson and Art Davidson make the first winter ascent.

1979: Mushers Joe Redington Sr. and Susan Butcher mush a team of sled dogs to the summit.

1984: Japanese explorer Naomi Uemura makes the first winter solo ascent but dies during his descent.

1988: Vern Tejas makes the first complete winter solo climb.

1991: Taras Genet, 12, the son of Ray Genet, becomes the youngest person to climb McKinley.

1995: The youngest female to have climbed McKinley is Merrick Johnston, age 12.

1998: The youngest male to have climbed McKinley is Kim Young Sik, age 12.

1998: Japanese adventurer Masatoshi Kuriaki, 25, makes the second complete winter solo climb.

1999: Highest short-haul rescue by the National Park Service Lama helicopter is made from 19,500 feet.

Mukluks
Mukluks are lightweight boots designed to provide warmth in extreme cold. Eskimo mukluks are traditionally made with *oogruk* (bearded seal) skin soles and leg uppers of caribou trimmed with fur.  Athabascan mukluks are traditionally made of moose hide and trimmed with fur and beadwork. Hay inner soles add insulation. The mukluks may be either calf-height or knee-height, with a leather drawstring in a casing around the top to keep out the wind and snow.

Eskimos of long ago sewed all their own clothing, mainly from the skins of animals and seabirds. These mukluks were not worn in winter unless the weather was warm, for they were made from seal leather with the hair removed and *oogruk* soles. The *oogruk* was oiled very heavily to be water-resistant and no fur trim was used on the "water mukluks," as they were called. The skins of large fish, including salmon, were also used to make the water-resistant mukluks.

Any mukluks that have been exposed to water or dampness should be hung in a cool place to dry slowly; sudden heat could shrink them out of shape and make them hard and stiff.

Muktuk
This Eskimo delicacy consists of outer skin layers and attached blubber of a whale. The two species of whale from which muktuk is most often sliced are the bowhead and the beluga, or white whale. The outer skin layers consist of a corky protective layer, the true skin and the blubber. In the case of beluga muktuk, the outer layer is white, the next layer is black and the blubber is pink. It may be eaten fresh, frozen, boiled or fermented.

Museums, Cultural Centers, Exhibits, Historic Parks, Historical Societies and Repositories

Visiting any of the following museums, historic sites, notable exhibits, archives or other repositories offers a look into the rich diversity of Alaska culture and history. Many of the smaller museums are open only June through September.

Adak Community Museum, P.O. Box 5244, Naval Air Station, Adak, FPO Seattle,

WA 98791. Houses World War II memorabilia, wildlife displays and Aleut artifacts.

Alaska Aviation Heritage Museum, 4721 Aircraft Drive, Anchorage 99502; (907) 248-5325. Located on the south shore of Lake Hood, and features 30 vintage aircraft, video and a military aviation gallery. Watch takeoffs and landings from the largest floatplane base in the world.

Alaska Collection, Z. J. Loussac Library, 3600 Denali, Anchorage 99503; (907) 343-2832. Rare books, reference books, state records, microfilm of newspapers, catalogs of photographs at other archives in the state.

Alaska Experience Center, 705 W. Sixth Ave., Anchorage 99501; (907) 276-3730. *Alaska the Great Land* shows hourly on a 180-degree screen; in another exhibit, viewers "experience" a 4.5 earthquake.

Alaska Homestead and Historical Museum, Milepost 1415.4 Alaska Highway, Delta Junction 99737. Large collection of historical farming equipment; guided tours of authentic homestead farm.

Alaska Indian Arts, Inc., P.O. Box 271, Haines 99827; (907) 766-2160. Workshop with totem carvers, silversmiths and printmakers. Chilkat Dancers perform several times each week during the summer.

Alaska Museum of Natural History, 11723 Old Glenn Highway, Eagle River 99577; (907) 694-0819. Largest collection of rocks, minerals and fossils in state; Alaska dinosaur story; store.

Alaska Native Heritage Center, 8800 Heritage Center Drive, Anchorage 99506; (907) 330-8000. Welcome House, contemporary culture and traditional village exhibits, theater and Native Tradition Bearers.

Alaska Public Lands Information Center, 605 W. Fourth, Anchorage 99501; (907) 271-2737. Features extensive displays and information on refuges, forests, parks

Looking Back

1972

The Alaska Center for Documentary Film, an arm of the University of Alaska Museum, began recording the changing cultures of Alaska Natives.

and outdoor recreation lands in Alaska. Video programs and computers permit self-help trip-planning. For on-line information, see www.nps.gov/aplic/center.

Alaska Public Lands Information Center, 250 N. Cushman St., Fairbanks 99701; (907) 456-0527. Provides information on Alaska's state parks, national parks, national forests and wildlife refuges. Free museum featuring films on Alaska, interpretive programs, lectures, exhibits, artifacts, photographs and short video programs on each region of the state.

Alaska Public Lands Information Center, 50 Main St., Ketchikan 99901; (907) 228-6220.

Alaska Public Lands Information Center, Mile 1314 Alaska Highway, P.O. Box 359, Tok 99780; (907) 883-5667.

Alaska Resources Library, 222 W. Seventh Ave., Anchorage 99513; (907) 271-5025. Information on archaeology, Native land claims, environmental and natural resources of Alaska, ornithology and wildlife biology, fisheries biology and cold regions engineering.

Alaska SeaLife Center. P.O. Box 1329, Mile 0 Seward Highway, Seward 99664; (907) 224-3080 or (800) 224-3902. Live marine mammals and seabirds in habitat exhibits. Aquarium, research center and rehab center for marine mammals and seabirds.

Alaska State Archives, Box 6, Juneau 99811. Photographs, documents, state government records.

Alaska State Museum, 395 Whittier St., Juneau 99801-1718; (907) 465-2901. E-mail: jerryh@muskox. alaska.edu. Comprehensive collections on Alaska Natives, art, natural history, gold rush days, archaeology, botany, contemporary gold-mining issues, geology and paleontology. Lectures, guided tours, workshops, films and demonstrations.

Alaska State Troopers Museum, P.O. Box 100280, Anchorage 99510; (907) 770-5050. Exhibits, memorabilia and photographs detailing Alaska law enforcement history.

Alfred Starr Nenana Cultural Center, 415 Riverfront, P.O. Box 1, Nenana 99760; (907) 832-5520. Ice Classics, boat racing, Native Land Claims and Episcopal Church exhibits.

Alpine Historical Park, P.O. Box 266, Sutton 99674, access via Elementary School Road from Glenn Highway. Open-air museum featuring the concrete ruins of the Sutton Coal Washery (1920–22), historical buildings, perennial gardens, and picnic and playground facilities.

Alutiiq Musem and Archaeological Repository, Kodiak Area Native Association, 402 Center St., Kodiak 99615; (907) 486-7004. Repository holds 100,000 artifacts, historic photos and archival documents about Alutiiq culture.

American Bald Eagle Foundation, (Haines Highway and Second St.) P.O. Box 49, Haines 99827; (907) 766-3094. Special programs and lectures explain how birds interact with the environment.

Anchorage Museum of History and Art, 121 W. Seventh Ave., Anchorage 99501; (907) 343-4326. Alaska Gallery dioramas depict 10,000 years of Alaska history. Guided tours with docents available. "Art of the Far North" contains early engravings by artists who accompanied 18th-century explorers and features works of art from travelers, adventurers, early residents and Native artists.

Anvik Historical Society Museum, P.O. Box 110, Anvik 99558; (907) 663-6358. Displays history and archaeology of lower Yukon Athabascan village.

Baranov Museum (Erskine House)/ Kodiak Historical Society, 101 Marine Way, Kodiak 99615; (907) 486-5920. Closed in February. Former Russian fur warehouse from early 1800s, oldest wooden building on the West Coast of the United States. Exhibits offer an overview of Alutiiq, Russian and early American history. National historic landmark.

Begich-Boggs Visitor Center, P.O. Box 129, Girdwood 99587; (907) 783-2326. (*See* Portage Glacier)

Bristol Bay Historical Museum, P.O. Box 43, Naknek 99633; (907) 246-4432. "Living history museum" features regional archaeology, history, ethnology, commercial fishing and canning.

Carrie M. McLain Memorial Museum, P.O. Box 53, Nome 99762; (907) 443-6630. Artifacts, photos and treasures; exhibits include the Nome gold rush featuring more than 6,000 gold rush photos, Eskimo culture and the Bering Land Bridge. Videos on the history of Nome shown during the summer season.

Chugach Heritage Center, Railroad Depot, Seward 99664; (907) 224-5065. Opened May 1998. Storytelling, dancing, slides and videos, master artists at work, exhibits about Chugach peoples.

Circle District Museum/Circle District Historical Society, (Mile 127.7 Steese Highway) P.O. Box 1893, Central 99730. Permanent displays include a period cabin of the mining camps, the first printing press north of Juneau, equipment used in early-day mining and trapping, Yukon Quest Sled Dog Race sled display, research library with archives and photograph collection.

Clausen Memorial Museum, P.O. Box 708, Petersburg 99833; (907) 772-3598. Photos, Norwegian family items, cannery and fisheries items, fox farming, world's record king salmon and other artifacts from area's past.

Collections Museum, Wrangell Chamber of Commerce, Wrangell 99929; (907) 874-3901. A privately owned museum of artifacts including the Bigelow Family collection and the gold rush.

Copper Center Lodge, Drawer J, Copper Center 99673; (907) 822-3245. Historic roadhouse opened in 1898. Museum exhibits, operating fish wheel.

Cordova Historical Museum, P.O.

Box 391, Cordova 99574; (907) 424-6665. Exhibits of art, geology, fisheries and marine articles.

Corrington Museum, (Fifth and Broadway) P.O. Box 382, Skagway 99840; (907) 983-2580. Forty unique ivory exhibits tracing Alaska's history.

Crow Creek Mine, Mile 3.1 Crow Creek Road, Girdwood 99587; (907) 278-8060. National historic site with eight original, fully restored buildings from 1898; daily gold panning, tools.

Delta Historical Society Museum/Big Delta State Historical Park, Mile 275 Richardson/Alaska Highway, Delta Junction 99737; (907) 895-4555. A glimpse of life in interior Alaska, 1904–47, the 10-acre park includes Rika's Roadhouse (built in 1910 and restored in 1986), an important waystation on the Valdez-Fairbanks Trail, sod-roofed museum, ferryman's cabin and other historic structures. Guides are in period costumes.

Dog Mushing Museum, Box 80-136, Fairbanks 99708; (907) 456-6874. Dog sleds, mushing paraphernalia.

Dorothy G. Page Museum and Old Wasilla Townsite Park, P.O. Box 870874, Wasilla 99654; (907) 373-9071. Historic buildings, including first schoolhouse (1917). Eskimo and Athabascan exhibits, gold mining exhibits, "Flying Dentist's" office.

Duncan Cottage Museum, Duncan St., P.O. Box 8, Metlakatla 99926; (907) 886-7363. Tsimshian bentwood boxes, antiques, books, photographs.

Eagle Historical Society and Museum, P.O. Box 23, Eagle 99738; (907) 547-2325. Restored courthouse, customs house and several Fort Egbert buildings. Daily walking tours and historical movies.

Eagle River Nature Center, Mile 12.7 Eagle River Road, Eagle 99738; (907) 694-2108.

Interpretive displays, programs, guided daily hikes, outdoor telescopes, spectacular views. Entrance to walkable section of scenic Iditarod Trail.

Eklutna Historical Park and Heritage House Museum, 16515 Centerfield Drive, Suite 102, Eagle River 99577; (907) 696-2828, located 25 miles north of Anchorage on the Glenn Highway. The park offers 30-minute tours and information about the blending of Athabascan and missionary cultures. Historic photos and objects. Unique grave monuments called spirit houses, and St. Nicholas Russian Orthodox Church.

El Dorado Gold Camp, 1975 Discovery Drive, Fairbanks 99709; (907) 479-7613. Located at Mile 1.3 Elliott Highway, just past Fox, 9 miles north of Fairbanks. Tour of a working gold mine, permafrost tunnel, sluice box, assay office, gold panning.

Elmendorf Air Force Base Wildlife Museum, 4803 Eighth St., Anchorage 99507; (907) 552-2282, enter base through Boniface Parkway Gate. Habitat displays of Alaska wildlife: bear, musk-oxen, Dall sheep, small mammals, extensive displays of fish.

Ester Gold Camp, P.O. Box 109, Ester 99725; (800) 676-6925. Ester Camp was built in 1936 by the Fairbanks Exploration Company to support a large-scale gold dredge operation. It reopened in 1958 as a tourist attraction and is on the National Register of Historic Places.

Fairbanks Exploration Industrial Complex, Illinois St., Fairbanks; (907) 451-1920. Four houses for miners built in 1916 serve as an inn. Visitors may watch gold pans being manufactured and see a machine shop complex where "time stands still."

Fairbanks Historical Preservation Foundation. (*See* SS *Nenana*)

Fraternal Order of Alaska State Troopers,

Alaska ranks No. 1 in households possessing a personal computer, and 52 percent of Anchorage households are connected to the Internet. An e-mail circulated through Alaska which listed the "Official mottos of Alaskan cities." The web posting claimed that Wasilla's slogan was "Wasilla—Where Marijuana is a Vegetable."

320 W. Fifth Ave., Anchorage; (907) 279-5050. Law enforcement history from territorial days to statehood.

Fort Richardson Fish and Wildlife Center, Building 600, Fort Richardson 99505; (907) 384-0437 or 384-0823. Mounted animals and fish: moose family with calves, bear, musk-oxen, birds, wolves and sea mammals. Guided tours by military personnel who specialize in wildlife biology.

Fourth Avenue Theatre, 630 W. Fourth Ave., Anchorage 99501; (907) 257-5600 or (907) 257-5650. Art deco building from the 1940s houses museum photo display of old Anchorage on the lower level. On the main level, free Alaska-theme movies on the big screen. Dinner theater during the summer. Departure point for one-hour trolley tours of Anchorage.

George I. Ashby Memorial Museum/Copper Valley Historical Society, P.O. Box 84, Copper Center 99573; (907) 822-5285. Early mining of gold and copper, church and Native artifacts. Information about the stampeders who unsuccessfully tried to take the Valdez Glacier "All-Alaska" Trail to the Klondike in 1898.

George Otenna Museum, Wales 99783; (907) 664-3671. This Eskimo community of 162 is accessible only by air and dog sled. Museum features contemporary arts and crafts as well as Eskimo artifacts and the history of Wales and the surrounding area. Behind the present village is a burial mound of the Birnirk culture (A.D. 500 to A.D. 900), a National Historic Landmark.

Gold Dredge No. 8, P.O. Box 81941, Fairbanks 99708; (907) 547-6058. Millions of ounces of gold have been extracted by this dredge since 1928—one of two gold dredges in Alaska open to the public. Listed in the National Register of Historic Sites, the dredge is a 250-foot vessel as tall as a five-story building. Exhibits include mastodon and woolly mammoth bones and tusks.

Heritage Library Museum, Northern Lights and C St., Anchorage 99503; (907) 265-2834. Displays of Native baskets, ivory and artifacts; photos, hunting implements, rare books and paintings.

Hoonah Cultural Center/Hoonah Indian Association, P.O. Box 144, Hoonah 99829. Features history and culture of local Tlingit Indians. Displays of Tlingit art and artifacts, totem poles, guided tours.

Hope and Surise Historical and Mining Museum, Second Street, P.O. Box 88, Hope 99605; (907) 782-3740. Historic buildings, gold rush, mining and homesteading memorabilia.

House of Wickersham, 123 Seventh St., Juneau 99801; (907) 586-9001. Built in 1898, the house was the residence of one of Alaska's first federal judges, James Wickersham. Educational tours and permanent collections.

Huslia Cultural Center, P.O. Box 70, Huslia 99746. Beadwork, arts and crafts.

Iditarod Trail Sled Dog Race Headquarters and Museum, Mile 2.2 Knik Road, P.O. Box 870800, Wasilla 99687; (907) 376-5155. Memorabilia, mushing films, full-size replica of checkpoint cabin and cache. Of particular interest are the sleds that Susan Butcher and Joe Redington Sr. used to mush to the top of Mount McKinley.

The Imaginarium Science Discovery Center, 737 W. Fifth Ave., Suite G, Anchorage 99501; (907) 276-3179. Hands-on scientific displays for children, planetarium bubble show, polar bear lair, arctic ecology. Monthly rotating exhibits.

Independence Mine State Historic Park, Hatcher Pass, near Palmer 99645; (907) 745-2827. Features restored gold mine buildings, mining machinery and a visitor center in spectacular mountain setting. Recreational gold panning permitted.

Interior and Arctic Alaska Aeronautical Museum, P.O. Box 70437, Fairbanks 99707.

Inupiat Heritage Center, P.O. Box 749, Barrow 99723; (907) 852-4594. The 24,000-square-foot facility opened June 24, 1998, and houses a climate-controlled collection, library, offices and storage areas for artifacts. Unusual aspects include a

Traditional Room for an "Elders-in-Residence" program and a Skinning Room.

Isabell Miller Museum/Sitka Historical Society, 330 Harbor Drive, Sitka 99835; (907) 747-6455. Located in the Centennial Building near the cruise ship lightering dock, exhibits include Tlingit baskets and carvings; the New Archangel Russian dancers and Noow Tlien Native dancers perform; and a research library of manuscripts and photographs.

Juneau-Douglas City Museum, 155 S. Seward St., Juneau 99801; (907) 586-3572. Videos and exhibits highlight Juneau's colorful history and gold mining heritage; historic downtown walking tour.

Kake Tribal Heritage Foundation, P.O. Box 263, Juneau 99801.

 Kasaan Totem Park, east side of Prince of Wales Island. Reached by charter plane or private boat. Part of a government-sponsored totem restoration program begun in 1937. Contains some examples moved from the Haida village of Old Kasaan.

K'beq Kenaitze Indian Tribe, P.O. Box 988, Kenai 99611; (907) 283-3633. Archives of Kenai branch of Cook Inlet Athabascan Indians.

Kenai Visitors and Cultural Center, 11471 Kenai Spur Highway, P.O. Box 1991, Kenai 99611; (907) 283-1991. Houses all the exhibits from Fort Kenay, plus a large eagle display.

Kennecott Mine, Wrangell–St. Elias National Park, Kennicott 99588; (907) 582-5128. An abandoned copper mine with many buildings perched on steep slopes. Kennicott-McCarthy Wilderness Guides conduct historic tours of the mine and town, which ceased operating in 1938.

Klawock Totem Park/City of Klawock, P.O. Box 113, Klawock 99925. Historic site on west coast of Prince of Wales Island. Reached by air, private boat, state ferry. Park contains 21 totems—both replicas and originals—from the abandoned village of Tuxekan.

Klondike Gold Rush National

Historical Park, P.O. Box 517, Skagway 99840; (907) 983-2921. An unusual unit of this park is the Chilkoot Trail, a 33-mile trek through history, sometimes called "the longest museum in the world." Hundreds of relics such as wagon wheels, coffee pots left behind by the stampeders of '98 remain on the trail. Another unit of this park is in Pioneer Square in Seattle.

Knik Museum, Knik Road, Wasilla 99687; (907) 376-7755. Restored pool hall houses exhibits about fish camps, gold mines, dog mushers.

Kodiak Museum. (*See* Alutiiq Museum and Archaeological Repository)

Kodiak Tribal Council's Barabara, 713 Rezanof Drive, Kodiak 99615; (907) 486-4449. Authentic traditional Alutiiq dwelling (barabara) used to stage presentations by the Kodiak Alutiiq Dancers.

Last Chance Mining Musem, P.O. Box 21264, Juneau 99802; (907) 586-5338. Historic gold rush mining building listed on National Register of Historic Places.

Marine Education Center, Third and Railway, P.O. Box 730, Seward 99664; (907) 224-5261. Interpretive displays about northern seas, Resurrection Bay, marine animals; live saltwater tanks; movies feature whales, salmon and other marine subjects. Operated by the University of Alaska.

Marine Works World War II Mini Museum, 2315 Airport Beach Road, Unalaska 99685; (907) 581-1749. Informal collection of articles from the Aleutian campaign of World War II.

Mascot Saloon Museum, National Park Service, Third and Broadway, Skagway 99840; (907) 983-2921. A typical saloon of 1898.

Mukluk Land, Tok Chamber of Commerce, Tok 99780; (907) 833-5887. A summer display of early mining equipment, some actually operating Alaska Road Commission machinery, old snowmobile collection and gold panning.

Museum of Alaska Transportation and Industry, Mile 47 Parks Highway, Wasilla 99687-0646; (907) 376-1211. Planes, trains, vehicles, tractors, tools. Ten acres of neat old stuff.

Museum of Northern Adventure, Main

St., Talkeetna 99676; (907) 733-2710 or (907) 733-3999. Historic railroad building, exhibits about homesteading, prospecting, wildlife and famous Alaska characters.

NANA Museum of the Arctic, P.O. Box 49, Kotzebue 99752; (907) 442-3747. Collections reflect Eskimo ethnology and natural history of northwestern Alaska; wildlife exhibits, slide show. Cultural heritage demonstrations such as skin sewing, ivory carving, Eskimo dancing, Eskimo blanket toss. Winter hours by appointment.

National Archives, Alaska Region, 654 W. Third Ave., Anchorage 99501; (907) 271-2441. Contains more than 9,000 cubic feet of historical records, among them photographs, maps and architectural drawings, dating from about 1867 to the present. These records were created or received by the federal courts and over 30 federal agencies in Alaska. Both original records and microfilm are available for research.

National Bank of Alaska Heritage Library. (*See* Heritage Library Museum)

Nenana Cultural Center, c/o City of Nenana, P.O. Box 70, Nenana 99760; (907) 832-5520. In log building next to salmon bake. Features Athabascan traditions linking the past to the present.

Nome Historical Park, c/o Nome Convention and Visitors Bureau, Box 240, Nome 99762; (907) 443-5535. Contains a nonworking gold dredge and mining equipment from the gold rush era.

Oil Pipeline Terminus, Valdez 99686; (907) 835-2686. Bus tours of pipeline terminal are available daily, May to September. Reservations suggested. Entry restricted to authorized bus tours only.

Oscar Anderson House, 420 M St., Anchorage 99502; (907) 274-2336. The city's first wood frame house,

built in 1915 by Swedish immigrant Oscar Anderson, was completely restored in 1982. Swedish Christmas celebration.

Palmer Musem, 723 S. Valley Way, Palmer 99645; (907) 745-2880. Colony items, farm implements, flowers and vegetables that thrive in the North.

Pioneer Air Museum, Box 70437, Fairbanks 99707; (907) 451-0037. Located behind Civic Center at Alaskaland. Features antique aircraft and stories of their Alaska pilots, with displays from 1913–48.

The Pioneers of Alaska Museum, (at Alaskaland) Airport Way and Peger Road, Fairbanks 99707; (907) 451-0037. Free guided historical walking tours. Park features Kitty Hensley house, Judge Wickersham house, first Presbyterian Church (1906); re-created Native village, gold rush town and paddle wheel riverboat.

Portage Glacier/Begich-Boggs Visitor Center, P.O. Box 129, Girdwood 99587; (907) 783-2326. Located 55 miles south of Anchorage off the Seward Highway. Exhibits on glaciers and ice caves. Theater shows 20-minute documentary *Voices from the Ice.* Interpretive programs during the summer.

Potter Section House and Historic Park, on Seward Highway, 12 miles south of Anchorage; (907) 345-5014. Alaska Railroad historic site. Chugach State Park headquarters; maps, brochures, interpretive display, rotary snowplow, railroad cars.

Pratt Museum, 3779 Bartlett St., Homer 99603; (907) 235-8635. Natural and cultural history of Kenai Peninsula. Displays include Eskimo, Indian and Aleut tools and clothing dioramas, whale skeletons; marine aquarium; botanical garden.

Rasmusson Library, University of Alaska Fairbanks 99775; (907) 474-7481. Extensive Alaska and Arctic archives and photograph collection available to researchers.

Resurrection Bay Historical Society Museum. (*See* Marine Education Center)

Russian Bishop's House, P.O. Box 738, Sitka 99835; (907) 747-6281. Located on Lincoln Street, a restored residence built in 1842 with private chapel. One of only four Russian log structures remaining in North America. Both a unit of the Sitka National Historical Park and a National Historic Landmark. Exhibits describe Russian America.

Samuel K. Fox Museum (Dillingham Heritage Museum), P.O. Box 330, Dillingham 99576; (907) 842-5610 or (907) 842-5521. Ethno-history museum featuring Yup'ik Eskimo culture of southwestern Alaska through contemporary and traditional arts, crafts and artifacts.

Saxman Totem Park and Tribal House, P.O. Box 8558, Ketchikan 99901. Historic site, 2.5 miles south of town. Park includes totems such as the famous Lincoln Pole, a carving center and Tlingit tribal house. Guided tours available.

Seward Marine Education Center. (*See* Marine Education Center)

Sheldon Jackson Museum, 104 College Drive, Sitka 99835-7657; (907) 747-8981. Located on the campus of Sheldon Jackson College, Alaska's oldest museum has many exhibits of Tlingit artifacts, clothing, beadwork, art and carvings.

Sheldon Museum and Cultural Center, P.O. Box 269, Haines 99827; (907) 766-2366. Exhibits on the Dalton Trail, the overland freight route used to Fort Selkirk in the Klondike; Tlingit culture, Chilkat blankets, pioneer history.

Simon Paneak Memorial Museum, P.O. Box 21085, Anaktuvuk Pass 99721-0085; (907) 661-3413. Display of hunting tools and a description of the Paleo-Indian people who

Looking Back

1996

The 46½-foot "Healing Heart" totem was raised in Craig. It was carved by Tsimshian Stan Marsden in honor of his son; a film about the totem was shown at the Sundance Film Festival.

occupied the Mesa Site in the Brooks Range more than 11,000 years ago.

Sitka National Historical Park Visitor Center, 106 Metlakatla, Sitka 99835; (907) 747-6281. Displays of Tlingit history, totems, artifacts. Totem pole collection contains both original pieces collected 1901–03 and copies of originals lost to time and the elements.

Skagway Historical Museum and Archive, P.O. Box 415, Skagway 99840; (907) 983-2921. Klondike Gold Rush artifacts, library, tours, lectures, store.

Soldotna Historical Society Museum, P.O. Box 1986, Soldotna 99669; (907) 283-8051. Features wildlife museum and historic log village, including last territorial school (1958). Homesteading artifacts and photos.

Southcentral Alaska Museum of Natural History, 11723 Old Glenn Highway, Eagle River 99577; (907) 694-0819. Exhibits embrace geology, biology and anthropology of southcentral Alaska. "Fossil Forest" features elements of a newly discovered duck-billed dinosaur from the Talkeetna Mountains.

Southeast Alaska Indian Cultural Center, 106 Metlakatla, Sitka 99835; (907) 747-8061. Housed in the Sitka National Park Visitor Center; visitors may talk to Native artists at work: beadworkers, carvers, printmakers, silversmiths.

Southeast Alaska Visitor Center, 50 Main St., Ketchikan 99901; (907) 228-6214. Exhibits and videos about public lands and mining. See crystals and marble mined from southeastern Alaska; historic gold rush photos.

SS *Nenana*/**Fairbanks Historical Preservation Foundation,** 2300 Airport Way, Cabin No. 1876, Box 70552, Fairbanks 99707; (907) 456-8848. Located at Alaskaland, a newly restored river steamer, a National Historic Landmark. Compelling 300-foot diorama takes visitors on a 2,400-mile voyage through the years 1847–1932 along the Yukon River system.

Sullivan Roadhouse, P.O. Box 987, Delta Junction 99737; (907) 895-5068. Visitor Center and historic buildings with photos and displays depicting winter Fairbanks to Valdez trail.

Talkeetna Historical Society Museum, P.O. Box 76, Talkeetna 99676; (907) 733-2487. Located one block off Main Street, the Talkeetna Townsite Historic District contains buildings reflecting a small 1917–40 gold mining community. Museum portrays lives of gold miners, early aviators and climbers of Mount McKinley.

Tanana Yukon Historical Society. (*See* House of Wickersham)

Tok Visitor Center, P.O. Box 335, Tok 99780; (907) 883-5887 or 883-5775. At the junction of Alaska and Glenn Highways, displays of Dall sheep, waterfowl, wolf, caribou, fossils and minerals. Open May to October.

Tongass Historical Museum, 629 Dock St., Ketchikan 99901; (907) 225-5600. Collection of Alaskana, Northwest Coast Native materials, photo archives and maritime history displays. Summer exhibit features the historic cannery town of Loring.

Totem Heritage Center, 601 Deermount St., Ketchikan 99901; (907) 225-5900. Large collection of original Tsimshian, Haida and Tlingit totems from the surrounding islands.

Trail of '98 Museum, P.O. Box 415, Skagway 99840; (907) 983-2420. On Broadway. Houses fine collection of gold rush artifacts, all once used by stampeders, and some personal belongings of notorious con man Soapy Smith. Photographs, historical records.

University of Alaska Archives and Manuscripts, Library, University of Alaska, 3211 Providence Drive, Anchorage 99508; (907) 786-1849 (Dennis Walle, archivist). Historic and contemporary papers, records, photographs; some artifacts. Open by appointment to researchers. Catalog of holdings available.

University of Alaska Museum, 907 Yukon Drive, Box 756960, Fairbanks 99775-1200; (907) 474-7505. Five galleries display Alaska's history, Native culture, art, natural phenomena, wildlife, birds, geology and prehistoric past, including the mummy of a 36,000-year-old Steppe bison, and a display on the northern lights. Sculptures, totem poles, a Russian blockhouse and a nature trail with signs identifying local plants. Many special programs.

Valdez Museum and Historical Archive, 217 Egan St., Valdez 99686; (907) 835-2764. Permanent exhibits celebrate the 1898 gold rush route across Valdez Glacier. Restored 1907 Ahrens steam fire engine, log cabin, original Cape Hinchinbrook lighthouse lens, exhibits on the 1964 earthquake, the trans-Alaska oil pipeline and 1989 *Exxon Valdez* oil spill cleanup.

Veniaminov Museum, St. Herman's Russian Orthdox Theological Seminary, Mission Road, Kodiak 99615; (907) 486-3524. Archive of personal items belonging to Ivan Veniaminov (later Bishop Innocent); papers and documents, many in Russian, about Russian America and the Orthodox church in Russian America.

Wasilla–Knik–Willow Creek Historical Society. (*See* Dorothy G. Page Museum)

Wrangell Museum, P.O. Box 1050, Wrangell 99929; (907) 874-3770. Housed in Wrangell's oldest building, displays include items from Wrangell history, Tlingit artifacts and petroglyphs including the oldest known Tlingit houseposts.

Yupiit Piciryarait ("People's Lifeways") Culture Center, P.O. Box 219, Bethel 99559; (907) 543-1819. Located 420 Hoffman Hwy. The museum contains artifacts from the region such as masks, drums, parkas, tools and a kayak.

Mushrooms
More than 500 species of mushroom grow in Alaska and while most are not common enough to be seen and collected readily by the amateur mycophile (mushroom hunter), many edible and choice species shoot up in any available patch of earth. Alaska's giant arc of

mushrooms extends from Southeast's panhandle through Southcentral, the Alaska Peninsula and the Aleutian Chain and is prime mushroom habitat. Interior, western and northern Alaska also support mushrooms in abundance.

Mushroom seasons vary considerably according to temperature, humidity and available nutrients but most occur from June through September. In a particularly cold or dry season, the crop will be scant.

There are relatively few poisonous mushrooms considering the number of species that occur throughout Alaska. Potentially fatal mushrooms, some of which occur in populated areas, include fly agaric (*Amanita muscaria*), poison pax (*Paxillus involutus*) and false morels. Easy-to-identify edible species include hedgehogs (*Hydnum repandum*) and shaggy manes (*Coprinus comatus*). Even edible mushrooms may disagree with one's digestion; the only test for an inedible or poisonous mushroom is positive identification. *If you can't identify it, don't eat it.*

Muskeg
Muskegs are bogs where little vegetation can grow except for sphagnum moss, black spruce, Sitka spruce, dwarf birch, tussocks and a few other shrubby plants. Such swampy areas cover much of Alaska. Nearly half of Alaska—175 million acres—is classified as wetlands. With nearly two-thirds of the nation's wetlands within its borders, Alaska boasts many of the most diverse wildlife habitats in North America. Waterfowl, muskrats, moose and many species of insect depend on wetlands for survival.

Musk-Oxen
Musk-oxen are stocky, shaggy, long-haired mammals of the extreme northern latitudes. They remain in the open through Alaska's long winters. Their name is misleading, for they have no musk gland and are more closely related to sheep and goats than to cattle. Adult males may weigh 500 to 900 pounds, females 300 to 700 pounds. Both sexes have horns

During extremely cold weather, musk-oxen stand still to conserve energy. From Alaska's Mammals by Dave Smith (text) and Tom Walker (photographs).

that droop down from their forehead and curve back up at the tips.

When threatened by wolves or other predators, musk-oxen form circles or lines with their young in the middle. These defensive measures did not protect them from hunters and their guns.

Musk-oxen were eliminated from Alaska in about 1865, when hunters shot and killed the last herd of 13. The species was reintroduced to the territory in the 1930s when 34 musk-oxen were purchased from Greenland and brought to the University of Alaska Fairbanks. In 1935–36, the 31 remaining musk-oxen at the university were shipped to Nunivak Island in the Bering Sea, where the herd eventually thrived. Animals from the Nunivak herd have been transplanted to areas along Alaska's western and northern coasts; at least five wild herds—approximately 3,000 musk-oxen—exist in the state.

The soft underhair of musk-oxen is called qiviut and grows next to the skin, protected by long guard hairs. It is shed naturally every spring. The Musk Ox Development Corp., maintains a herd in Palmer and collects qiviut for the Oomingmak cooperative. The hair is spun into yarn in Rhode Island and sent back to Alaska, where the cooperative arranges for knitters in villages in western Alaska, where jobs are scarce, to knit the yarn into clothing at their own pace.

Each village keeps its own distinct signature pattern for scarves knitted from qiviut. Villagers also produce stoles, tunics, hats and smoke rings, circular scarves that fit around the head like a hood. About 300 women are employed as knitters.

In southcentral Alaska musk-oxen can be viewed from May to September at the musk-oxen farm in Palmer. In the Interior look for them at the university's Research Station on Yankovich Road in Fairbanks; (907) 474-7207.

National Forests (SEE ALSO LAND USE; NATIONAL PARKS, PRESERVES AND MONUMENTS; NATIONAL WILDERNESS AREAS; AND TIMBER) Alaska has two national forests, the Tongass and the

Old Growth

Old-growth forests are "multi-aged." Many age classes of trees are present, from saplings to old-timers, assuring a sustainable cycle of decay and regeneration. Instead of fire, periodic gales, usually from the Southeast, are the major disturbance to our coastal forests.

—Rita O'Clair, Robert Armstrong and Richard Carstensen, *The Nature of Southeast Alaska*

Chugach. The Tongass occupies most of the panhandle, or southeastern portion of the state. The Chugach extends south and east of Anchorage along the southcentral Alaska coast, encompassing most of the Prince William Sound area.

These two national forests are managed by the U.S. Forest Service for a variety of uses. They provide forest products for national and international markets, minerals, recreational opportunities, wilderness experiences and superb scenery and pristine vistas.

Nearly 200 public recreation cabins are maintained in the Tongass and Chugach National Forests. They accommodate visitors from all over the world and are a vacation bargain, including a boat on some freshwater lakes. All Tongass and Chugach National Forest cabins are reserved through the National Recreation Reservation System (NRRS). With this system, once people know which cabin and dates they would like, they can call the toll-free number at (877) 444-6777. International calls can be made (toll call) by dialing (518) 885-3639. Prospective visitors may also go to the NRRS Web site at: www.reserveusa.com to read more about it, check on availability and book over the Internet. The fee system allows users to rent cabins from $15 to $65 a night. (*See also* Cabins)

Wildlife and fisheries are important Forest Service programs in the national forests of Alaska. The Tongass and Chugach National Forests are also home

Wilderness Units in Tongass National Forest

Wilderness Areas Established Dec. 2, 1980, by ANILCA	Acres
Coronation Island Wilderness	19,232
Endicott River Wilderness	98,729
Kootznoowoo Wilderness* (Admiralty Island National Monument)**	955,921
Maurelle Islands Wilderness	4,937
Misty Fiords National Monument**	2,142,243
Petersburg Creek–Duncan Salt Chuck Wilderness	46,777
Russell Fiord Wilderness	348,701
South Baranof Wilderness	319,568
South Prince of Wales Wilderness	90,996
Stikine–LeConte Wilderness	448,926
Tebenkof Bay Wilderness	66,839
Tracy Arm–Fords Terror Wilderness	653,179
Warren Island Wilderness	11,181
West Chichagof–Yakobi Wilderness	264,747

Wilderness Areas Established Nov. 28, 1990, by TTRA	
Chuck River Wilderness	74,298
Karta Wilderness	39,889
Kuiu Wilderness	60,581
Pleasant–Lemesurier–Inian Islands Wilderness	23,096
South Etolin Wilderness	83,371

Total acreage 5,753,211

*Kootznoowoo Wilderness includes 18,486 acres (including 24 acres of non-national forest land) in the Young Lake Addition established by TTRA.
**Designated monuments under ANILCA; first areas so designated in the national forest system. These wildernesses include only the public lands above mean high tide.

National Forest Lands in Alaska	Tongass	Chugach
Total acreage before ANILCA	15,555,388	4,392,646
Total acreage after ANILCA	16,954,713	5,940,040*
Wilderness acreage created	5,753,211	None created
Wilderness study	None created	2,019,999 acres

*This lands act provides for additional transfers of national forest land to Native corporations, the state and the U.S. Fish and Game Department of an estimated 296,000 acres on Afognak Island, and an estimated 242,000 acres to the Chugach Native Corporation.

to some of Alaska's most magnificent wildlife. It is here that the bald eagle and large brown (grizzly) bears may be encountered in large numbers. Five species of Pacific salmon spawn in the rivers and streams of the forests and smaller mammals and waterfowl abound. The Forest Service is charged with the management of this rich habitat. The Alaska Department of Fish and Game manages the wildlife species that this habitat supports.

There are many recreational opportunities in the national forests of Alaska including backpacking, fishing, hunting, photography, boating, nature study and camping, to list just a few. For further information concerning recreational opportunities, contact the U.S. Forest Service office nearest the area you are visiting.

The Alaska National Interest Lands Conservation Act (ANILCA) created approximately 5.5 million acres of wilderness divided into 14 units within the 17-million-acre Tongass National Forest. It also added three new areas to the forest: the Juneau Icefield, Kates Needle and parts of the Barbazon Range, totaling more than 1 million acres. The Tongass Timber Reform Act (TTRA) of 1990 amended ANILCA and designated five additional wilderness areas and an addition to the existing Kootznoowoo Wilderness, as well as 12 Land Use Designation II backcountry semiprimitive roadless areas managed primarily for fish, wildlife and recreation resources.

The lands bill also provided extensive additions to the Chugach National Forest. These additions, covering about 2 million acres, include the Nellie Juan area east of Seward, College Fiord extension, Copper/Rude Rivers addition and a small extension at Controller Bay southeast of Cordova.

The charts on page 142 show the effect of the Alaska Lands Act on the Tongass and Chugach National Forests.

National Historic Places *(See also Archaeology)*

A "place" on the National Register of Historic Places is a district, site, building, structure or object significant for its history, architecture, archaeology or culture. The national register also includes National Historic Landmarks. NHLs are properties given special status by the Secretary of the Interior for their significance to the nation. The register is an official list of properties recognized by the federal government as worthy of preservation. Listing in the register begins with the owner's consent and includes a nomination process with reviews by the State Historic Preservation Office, the Alaska Historical Commission and the Keeper of the National Register. Limitations are not placed on a listed property. The federal government does not attach restrictive covenants to the property or seek to acquire it. For details, consult oha@alaska.net.

Listing in the register means that a property is accorded

> ## The Past Beckons
> Of all American adults planning a trip in 1993, more than 35 percent chose historic or cultural sites as their most desired destination, according to Travelometer. Nearly one-third of those polled by the New York Times in 1993 rated cultural and historic activities as very important in vacation decisions. Respondents also ranked Alaska fifth among the top 10 fantasy vacations. ✬

national recognition for its significance in American history or prehistory. Additional benefits include tax credits on income-producing properties and qualification for federal matching funds for preservation, maintenance and restoration work when such funds are available. Listed properties are guaranteed a full review process for potential adverse effects by federally funded, licensed or otherwise assisted projects. Such a review usually takes place while the project is in the planning stage. Alternatives are sought to avoid damaging or destroying the property.

Southcentral. A.E.C. Cottage No. 25, Anchorage
Alaska Central Railroad Tunnel No. 1, Seward
Alaska Nellie's Homestead, Lawing vicinity
Alex (Mike) Cabin, Eklutna
American Cemetery, Kodiak
Anchorage Cemetery, Anchorage
Anchorage City Hall, Anchorage
Anchorage Depot, Anchorage
Anchorage Hotel, Anchorage
Anderson (Oscar) House, Anchorage
Ascension of Our Lord Chapel, Karluk

> One particularly dumb Anchorage criminal was arrested three years ago for selling cocaine to an undercover Anchorage police officer. He was arrested *again* in January 1998 for selling crack to the same undercover officer. He said he even recognized the cop, but sold it to him anyway. Why do you think they call it "dope"?

Bailey Colony Farm, Palmer
Ballaine House, Seward
Beluga Point Archaeological Site, North
   Shore, Turnagain Arm
Bering Expedition Landing Site NHL,
   Kayak Island
Berry House, Palmer
Brown & Hawkins Store, Seward
Campus Center Site, Anchorage
Cape St. Elias Lighthouse, Kayak Island
Chilkat Oil Company Refinery Site, Katalla
Chisana Historic Mining Landscape
   District, Chisana
Chitina Tin Shop, Chitina
Chugachik Island Archaeological Site,
   Kachemak Bay
Coal Village Site, Kachemak Bay
Cooper Landing Historic District, Cooper
   Landing
Cooper Landing Post Office, Cooper
   Landing
Copper River and Northwestern Railway,
   Chitina vicinity
Cordova Post Office and Courthouse,
   Cordova
Crow Creek Mine, Girdwood
Cunningham-Hall PT–6 NC692W Aircraft,
   Palmer
Dakah De'nin's Village Site, Chitina
David (Leopold) House, Anchorage
Diversion Tunnel, Lowell Creek, Seward
Eklutna Power Plant, Eklutna vicinity
Federal Building–U.S. Courthouse (Old),
   Anchorage
Fourth Avenue Theatre, Anchorage
Gakona Roadhouse, Gakona
Government Cable Office, Seward
Herried House, Palmer
Hirshey Mine, Hope vicinity
Holm (Victor) Cabin, Cohoe
Holy Assumption Russian Orthodox
   Church NHL, Kenai
Holy Resurrection Church, Kodiak
Holy Transfiguration of Our Lord Chapel,
   Ninilchik
Hope Historic District, Hope vicinity
Hyland Hotel, Palmer
Independence Mine Historic District,
   Hatcher Pass
Indian Valley Mine, Girdwood vicinity
Jesse Lee Home, Seward
Kansky's, Nebesna

*Fireweed at sunset, Kennecott Copper Mine.
From Picture Journeys in Alaska's Wrangell–
St. Elias by George Herben.*

KENI Radio Building, Anchorage
Kennecott Mines NHL, McCarthy
   vicinity
Kimball's Store, Anchorage
Kirsch's Place, Talkeetna
Knik Site, Knik vicinity
KOD-171 Archaeological Site, Kodiak
KOD-207 Archaeological Site, Kodiak
KOD-233 Archaeological Site, Kodiak
Kodiak Naval Operating Base (Fort
   Abercrombie and Fort Greely) NHL,
   Kodiak Island
Lauritsen Cabin, Seward Highway
Loussac-Sogn Building, Anchorage
Matanuska Colony Community Center,
   Palmer
McCarthy General Store, McCarthy
McCarthy Power Plant, McCarthy
Middle Bay Brick Kiln, Kodiak
Million Dollar Bridge, Cordova
Moose River Site, Naptowne, Kenai area
Nabesna Gold Mine, Nabesna area
Nativity of Holy Theotokos Church,
   Afognak Island
Nativity of Our Lord Chapel, Ouzinkie
Old St. Nicholas Russian Orthodox Church,
   Eklutna

Palmer Depot, Palmer
Palugvik Archaeological District NHL, Hawkins Island
Patten Colony Farm, Palmer
Pioneer School House, Anchorage
Potter Section House, Anchorage
Protection of the Theotokos Chapel, Akhiok
Puhl House, Palmer
Rebarcheck (Raymond) Colony Farm, Palmer area
Reception Building, Cordova
Red Dragon Historic District, Cordova
Russian-American Company Magazin (Erskine House) NHL, Kodiak
St. Michael the Archangel Church, Cordova
St. Nicholas Chapel, Seldovia
St. Peter's Episcopal Church, Seward
Sts. Sergius and Herman of Valaam Chapel, Ouzinkie
Sts. Sergius and Herman of Valaam Church, English Bay
Selenie Lagoon Archaeological Site, Port Graham vicinity
Seward Depot, Seward
Site Summit, Anchorage
Sunrise City Historic District, Hope
Susitna River Bridge, Alaska Railroad, Talkeetna vicinity
Swetman House, Seward
Tangle Lakes Archaeological District, Paxson vicinity
Teeland's Store, Wasilla
Three Saints Bay Site NHL, Kodiak Island
United Protestant Church, Palmer
Valdez Trail, Copper Bluff Segment, Copper River
Van Gilder Hotel, Seward

Wasilla Community Hall, Wasilla
Wasilla Depot, Wasilla
Wasilla Elementary School, Wasilla
Wendler Building, Anchorage
Yukon Island, Main Site NHL, Yukon Island

Southeast. Admiralty Island CCC, Canoe Route
Alaska Native Brotherhood Hall NHL, Skagway
Alaska Steam Laundry, Juneau
Alaska Totems, Ketchikan
Alaskan Hotel, Juneau
Alexander Lake Shelter Cabin, Admiralty Island
American Flag Raising Site NHL, Sitka
Beaver Lake Dam, Admiralty Island
Bergmann Hotel, Juneau
Big Shaheen Cabin, Admiralty Island
Building No. 29 NHL, Sitka
Burkhart-Dibrell House, Ketchikan
Cable House and Station, Sitka
Cape Spencer Lighthouse, Cape Spencer
Chicken Ridge Historic District, Juneau
Chief Kushakes House, Saxman
Chief Shakes House, Wrangell
Chilkoot Trail and Dyea NHL, Skagway
Davidson Lake Shelter Cabin, Admiralty Island
Davis (J.M.) House, Juneau
Distin Lake Shelter Cabin, Admiralty Island
Duncan (Father William) Cottage, Metlakatla
Eldred Rock Lighthouse, Lynn Canal
Emmons House, Sitka
Etolin Canoe, Etolin Island

First Lutheran Church, Ketchikan
Fort Durham NHL, Taku Harbor, Juneau
  vicinity
Fort William H. Seward NHL, Haines
Frances House, Juneau
Fries Miners Cabins, Juneau
Gilmore Building, Ketchikan
Government Indian School, Haines
Governor's Mansion, Juneau
Gruening (Ernest) Cabin, Juneau
Hanlon-Osbakken House, Sitka
Hasselborg Cabin, Admiralty Island
Hasselborg Lake East Shelter Cabin,
  Admiralty Island
Hasselborg Lake North Shelter Cabin,
  Admiralty Island
Hasselborg Lake South Shelter Cabin,
  Admiralty Island
Holy Trinity Church, Juneau
Jualpa Mining Camp, Juneau
Juneau Downtown Historic District, Juneau
Kake Cannery NHL, Kake
Ketchikan Ranger House, Ketchikan
Klondike Gold Rush National Historic
  Park, Skagway area
Lake Guerin East Shelter Cabin, Admiralty
  Island
Lake Guerin West Shelter Cabin, Admiralty
  Island
MacKinnon Apartments, Juneau
Mayflower School, Douglas
Mills (May) House, Sitka
Mills (W.P.) House, Sitka
Mitchell Bay Shelter Cabin, Admiralty
  Island

Mole Harbor Shelter Cabin, Admiralty
  Island
Murray Apartments and Cottages,
  Sitka
M.V. *Chugach*, Petersburg
New Russia Archaeological Site NHL,
  Yakutat
Old Sitka NHL, Sitka
Pleasant Camp, Haines Highway
Porcupine Historic District, Skagway
  vicinity
Russian Bishop's House NHL, Sitka
St. John the Baptist Church, Angoon
St. Michael the Archangel Cathedral NHL,
  Sitka
St. Nicholas Russian Orthodox Church,
  Juneau
St. Peter's Church, Sitka
St. Phillip's Episcopal Church, Wrangell
Saxman Totem Park, Ketchikan
See House, Sitka
Sheldon Jackson Museum, Sitka
Sitka National Historical Park, Sitka
Sitka Naval Operating Base NHL, Sitka
Sitka Pioneers' Home, Sitka
Sitka Post Office and Courthouse
Skagway and White Pass Historic District
  NHL, Skagway vicinity
Sons of Norway Hall, Petersburg
The Star, Ketchikan
Stedman Thomas Historic District,
  Ketchikan
Thayer Lake East Shelter Cabin, Admiralty
  Island
Thayer Lake North Shelter Cabin,
  Admiralty Island
Thayer Lake South Shelter Cabin,
  Admiralty Island
Totem Bight, Ketchikan
Twin Glacier Camp, Juneau
U.S. Army Corps of Engineers, Storehouse
  No. 3, Portland Canal
U.S. Army Corps of Engineers, Storehouse
  No. 4, Hyder
U.S. Coast and Geodetic Survey House,
  Sitka
Valentine Building, Juneau
Walker-Broderick House, Ketchikan
Wickersham (James) House, Juneau
Windfall Harbor Shelter Cabin, Admiralty
  Island
Ziegler House, Ketchikan

St. Michael the Archangel Cathedral NHL, Sitka

Western. Adak Army and Naval Operating Bases NHL, Adak

Anangula Site NHL, Aleutian Islands

Ananiuliak Island Archaeological District, Aleutian Islands

Aniakchak Bay Historic Landscape District

Anvil Creek Gold Discovery Site, Nome

Archaeological Site 49 AF 3, Katmai National Park and Preserve

Archaeological Site 49 MK 10, Katmai National Park and Preserve

Atka B-24 Liberator, Aleutian Islands

Attu Battlefield and U.S. Army and Navy Airfields NHL, Attu

Brooks River Archaeological District NHL, Katmai National Park and Preserve

Cape Field at Fort Glenn NHL, Aleutian Islands

Cape Krusenstern Archaeological District NHL, Kotzebue vicinity

Cape Nome Mining District Discovery Sites NHL, Nome

Cape Nome Roadhouse, Nome vicinity

Carrighar (Sally) House, Nome

Cathedral of the Holy Ascension of Christ NHL, Unalaska

Chaluka Site NHL, Umnak Island

Christ Church Mission, Anvik

Discovery Saloon, Nome

Dutch Harbor Operating Base and Fort Mears NHL, Aleutian Islands

Elevation of the Holy Cross Church, Naknek

Fairhaven Ditch, Imruk Lake

First Mission House, Bethel

Fort St. Michael Site, Unalakleet vicinity

Fure's Cabin, Katmai National Park and Preserve

Gambell Sites, Gambell

Holy Resurrection Church, Belkofski

Iyatayet Archaeological Site NHL, Norton Sound

Japanese Occupation Site, Kiska NHL, Aleutian Islands

Kaguyak Village Site, Katmai National Park and Preserve

Kijik Historic District, Lake Clark National Park and Preserve

Kolmakov Redoubt Site, Kuskokwim River, Aniak vicinity

Kukak Village, Katmai National Park and Preserve

Norge Storage Site, Teller

Old St. Joseph's Catholic Church, Nome

Old Savonoski Site, Katmai National Park and Preserve

Onion Portage Archaeological District NHL, Noatak vicinity

Pilgrim 100B N709Y Aircraft, Dillingham

Pilgrim Hot Springs, Seward Peninsula

Port Moller Hot Springs Village Site, Alaska Peninsula

Presentation of Our Lord Chapel, Nikolai

Redoubt St. Michael Site, Unalakleet vicinity

S.S. *Northwestern* Shipwreck Site, Unalaska

St. Alexander Nevsky Chapel, Akutan

St. George the Great Martyr Orthodox Church, St. George Island

St. Jacob's Church, Napaskiak

St. John the Baptist Chapel, Naknek

St. John the Theologian Church, Perryville

St. Nicholas Chapel, Ekuk

St. Nicholas Chapel, Igiugig

St. Nicholas Chapel, Nondalton

St. Nicholas Chapel, Pedro Bay

St. Nicholas Chapel, Sand Point

St. Nicholas Church, Kwethluk

St. Nicholas Church, Nikolski

St. Nicholas Church, Pilot Point

St. Seraphim Chapel, Lower Kalskag

St. Sergius Chapel, Chuathbaluk

Sts. Constantine and Helen Chapel, Lime Village

Sts. Peter and Paul Russian Orthodox Church, St. Paul Island

Savonoski River District, Katmai National Park and Preserve

Seal Islands Historic District NHL, Pribilof Islands

Sitka Spruce Plantation NHL, Amaknak Island

Snow Creek Placer Claim No. 1, Nome vicinity

Solomon Roadhouse, Solomon

USA Today reported this Alaska top story of the day: "The state board of fisheries is considering whether to impose seasonal catch limits on tourists."

Takli Island Archaeological District, Katmai
National Park and Preserve
TEMNAC P-38G Lightning Aircraft,
Aleutian Islands
Transfiguration of Our Lord Chapel,
Nushagak
Wales Archaeological District NHL, Wales
vicinity

Interior. Bettles Lodge, Bettles City
Biederman (Ed) Fish Camp, Eagle area
Big Delta Historic District, Delta Junction
Campus Archaeological Site, Fairbanks
Central Roadhouse, Central
Chatanika Gold Camp, Chatanika
Chena Pump House, Fairbanks
Chugwater Archaeological Site, Fairbanks
Clay Street Cemetery, Fairbanks
Coal Creek Mining District, Circle vicinity
Creamer's Dairy, Fairbanks
Curry Lookout, Talkeetna vicinity
Davis (Mary Lee) House, Fairbanks
Discovery Claim, Pedro Creek, Fairbanks
Dry Creek Archaeological Site NHL, Healy
vicinity
Eagle Historic District NHL, Eagle
Ester Camp Historic District, Fairbanks
Ewe Creek Ranger Cabin No. 8, Denali
National Park
Fairview Inn, Talkeetna
F. E. Company Dredge No. 2, Fairabnks
F. E. Company Housing, Fairbanks
F. E. Company Machine Shop, Fairbanks
F. E. Company Manager's House, Fairbanks
Federal Building, U.S. Post Office,
Courthouse (Old), Fairbanks
Goldstream Dredge No. 8, Mile 9, Old
Steese Hwy., Ester
Harding Railroad Car, Alaskaland,
Fairbanks
Igloo Creek Cabin No. 25, Denali National
Park
Immaculate Conception Church, Fairbanks
Joslin (Falcon) House, Fairbanks
The Kink, Fortymile River
Lacey Street Theatre, Fairbanks
Ladd Field NHL (Fort Wainwright),
Fairbanks
Lower East Fork Ranger Cabin No. 9,
Denali National Park
Lower Toklat River Ranger Cabin No. 18,
Denali National Park

*A skier explores the Peters Hills, with Mount
McKinley in the distance. From Alaska's
Accessible Wilderness by Bill Sherwonit.*

Lower Windy Creek Ranger Cabin No. 15,
Denali National Park
Main School, Fairbanks
Masonic Temple, Fairbanks
McGregor (George) Cabin, Eagle vicinity
Mission Church, Arctic Village
Mission House (Old), Fort Yukon
Moose Creek Ranger Cabin No. 19, Denali
National Park
Mount McKinley National Park
Headquarters, Denali National Park
Nenana Depot, Nenana
Oddfellows Hall (First Avenue Bathhouse),
Fairbanks
Rainey's Cabin, Fairbanks
Riley Creek Ranger Cabin No. 20, Denali
National Park
Ruby Roadhouse, Ruby
Sanctuary River Cabin No. 31, Denali
National Park
Slaven (Frank) Roadhouse, Eagle vicinity
Steele Creek Roadhouse, Fortymile
Stern-wheeler SS *Nenana* NHL, Fairbanks
Sullivan's Roadhouse, Delta
Sushana River Ranger Cabin No. 17, Denali
National Park
Talkeetna Historic District, Talkeetna
Tanana Mission, Tanana

Canoers on Wonder Lake with Mount McKinley in the background. From Discover Alaska *by Alaska Northwest Books.*

Taylor (James) Cabins, Eagle vicinity
Teklanika Archaeological District, Denali National Park and Preserve
Thomas (George C.) Memorial Library NHL, Fairbanks
Toklat Ranger Station (Pearson Cabin) No. 4, Denali National Park
Tolovana Roadhouse, Tanana vicinity
Upper East Fork Cabin No. 29, Denali National Park
Upper Savage River Cabin, Denali National Park
Upper Toklat River Ranger Cabin No. 24, Denali National Park
Upper Windy Creek Ranger Cabin No. 7, Denali National Park
Wickersham House, Fairbanks
Woodchopper Roadhouse, Eagle vicinity
Yukon River Lifeways District, Eagle vicinity

Far North. Aluakpak Site, Wainwright vicinity
Anaktuuk Site, Wainwright vicinity
Atanik District, Wainwright vicinity
Avalitkuk Site, Wainwright vicinity
Birnirk Site NHL, Barrow
Gallagher Flint Station Archaeological Site NHL, Sagwon
Ipiutak Archaeological District, Point Hope
Ipiutak Site NHL, Point Hope
Ivishaat Site, Wainwright vicinity
Kanitch, Wainwright vicinity

Leffingwell Camp NHL, Flaxman Island
Napanik Site, Wainwright vicinity
Negilik Site, Barrow
Point Barrow Refuge, Cape Smythe
Prudhoe Bay Oil Field Discovery Site, Deadhorse
Utkeagvik Presbyterian Church Manse, Barrow
Uyagaagruk, Wainwright vicinity
Whaling and Trading Station, Barrow vicinity
Will Rogers–Wiley Post Crash Site, Barrow vicinity

National Parks, Preserves and Monuments

The National Park Service administers approximately 54 million acres of land in Alaska, consisting of 15 units classified as national parks, national preserves and national monuments. The Alaska National Interest Lands Conservation Act of 1980—also referred to as ANILCA (*see* Land Use)—created 10 new National Park Service units in Alaska and changed the size and status of three existing Park Service units: Denali National Park and Preserve (formerly Mount McKinley National Park); Glacier Bay National Monument, now a national park and preserve; and Katmai National Monument, now a national park and preserve. (*See* map, pages 150–51)

In 1999, Alaska's national parks, preserves and monuments attracted 2.1 million visitors.

National parks are traditionally managed to preserve scenic, wildlife and recreational values; mining, cutting of house logs, hunting and other resource exploitation are carefully regulated within park, monument and preserve boundaries, and motorized access is restricted to automobile traffic on authorized roads. However regulations for National Park Service units in Alaska recognize that these units contain lands traditionally occupied and used by Alaska Natives and rural residents for subsistence activities. To
(*Continued on page 152*)

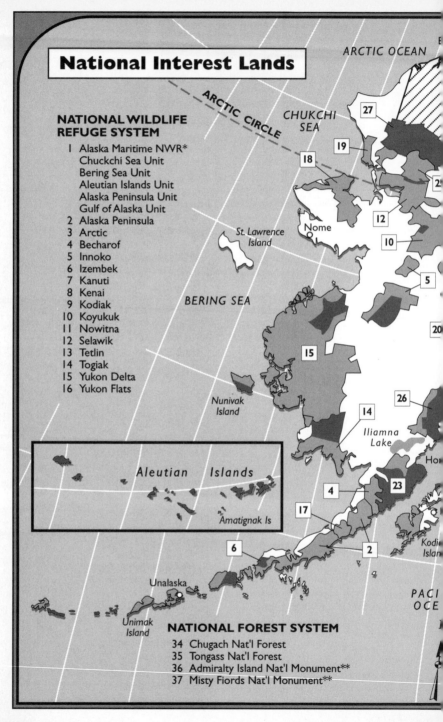

National Interest Lands

NATIONAL WILDLIFE REFUGE SYSTEM

1 Alaska Maritime NWR*
   Chuckchi Sea Unit
   Bering Sea Unit
   Aleutian Islands Unit
   Alaska Peninsula Unit
   Gulf of Alaska Unit
2 Alaska Peninsula
3 Arctic
4 Becharof
5 Innoko
6 Izembek
7 Kanuti
8 Kenai
9 Kodiak
10 Koyukuk
11 Nowitna
12 Selawik
13 Tetlin
14 Togiak
15 Yukon Delta
16 Yukon Flats

NATIONAL FOREST SYSTEM

34 Chugach Nat'l Forest
35 Tongass Nat'l Forest
36 Admiralty Island Nat'l Monument**
37 Misty Fiords Nat'l Monument**

ARCTIC OCEAN

ARCTIC CIRCLE

CHUKCHI SEA

St. Lawrence Island

Nome

BERING SEA

Nunivak Island

Aleutian Islands

Amatignak Is

Iliamna Lake

Unalaska

Unimak Island

Kodiak Island

PACIFIC OCEAN

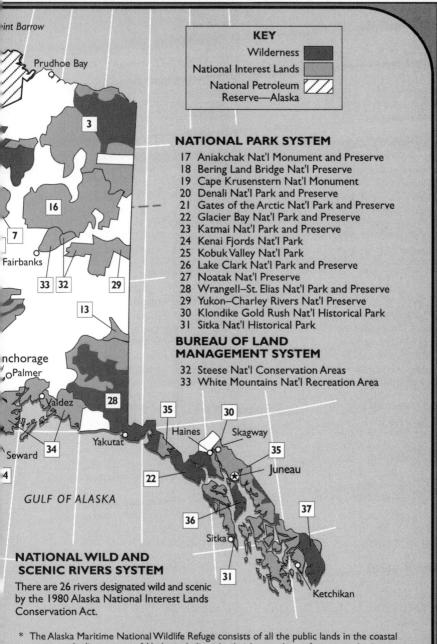

KEY

Wilderness	■
National Interest Lands	■
National Petroleum Reserve—Alaska	▨

int Barrow

Prudhoe Bay

3

16

7

Fairbanks

33 32

29

13

nchorage
oPalmer

Valdez

28

34

Seward

4

Yakutat

GULF OF ALASKA

35

30

Haines

Skagway

35

Juneau

22

36

37

Sitka

31

Ketchikan

NATIONAL PARK SYSTEM

17 Aniakchak Nat'l Monument and Preserve
18 Bering Land Bridge Nat'l Preserve
19 Cape Krusenstern Nat'l Monument
20 Denali Nat'l Park and Preserve
21 Gates of the Arctic Nat'l Park and Preserve
22 Glacier Bay Nat'l Park and Preserve
23 Katmai Nat'l Park and Preserve
24 Kenai Fjords Nat'l Park
25 Kobuk Valley Nat'l Park
26 Lake Clark Nat'l Park and Preserve
27 Noatak Nat'l Preserve
28 Wrangell–St. Elias Nat'l Park and Preserve
29 Yukon–Charley Rivers Nat'l Preserve
30 Klondike Gold Rush Nat'l Historical Park
31 Sitka Nat'l Historical Park

BUREAU OF LAND MANAGEMENT SYSTEM

32 Steese Nat'l Conservation Areas
33 White Mountains Nat'l Recreation Area

NATIONAL WILD AND SCENIC RIVERS SYSTEM

There are 26 rivers designated wild and scenic by the 1980 Alaska National Interest Lands Conservation Act.

* The Alaska Maritime National Wildlife Refuge consists of all the public lands in the coastal waters and adjacent seas of Alaska, including islands, islets, rocks, reefs, capes and spires.

** Admiralty Island and Misty Fiords national monuments are part of the Tongass National Forest, which includes 17 other wilderness areas.

(Continued from page 149)
accommodate these users, management of some parks, preserves and monuments in Alaska provides for subsistence hunting, fishing and gathering activities, and the use of such motorized vehicles as snowmobiles, motorboats and airplanes where these activities are customary. National preserves permit sport hunting.

Information on parks, preserves and monuments is available at the Alaska Public Lands Information Centers: 605 W. Fourth Ave., Suite 105, Anchorage 99501, (907) 271-2737, 250 Cushman St., Suite 1A, Fairbanks 99701, (907) 451-7352; 50 Main St., Ketchikan 99501, (907) 228-6220; and P.O. Box 359, Tok 99780, (907) 883-5677. The Web site for the Alaska Public Lands Information Center is www.nps.gov/aplic/center. Online information is available from the National Park Service (www.nps.gov) for these Alaska parks: Aniakchak (/ania); Bering Land Bridge (/bela); Cape Krusenstern (/cakr); Denali (/dena); Gates of the Arctic (/gaar); Glacier Bay (/glba); Katmai (/katm); Kenai Fjords (/kefj); Klondike Gold Rush (/klgo); Kobuk Valley (/kobu); Lake Clark (/lacl); Noatak (/noat); Sitka (/sitk); Wrangell (/wrst); and Yukon-Charley (/yuch).

Following is a list of National Park Service parks, preserves and monuments. The U.S. Forest Service manages another two national monuments: Admiralty Island National Monument, 937,000 acres; and Misty Fiords National Monument, 2.1 million acres. Both are in Southeast and part of the National Wilderness Preservation System. (*See also* National Wild and Scenic Rivers *and* National Wilderness Areas)

There are two NPS-affiliated areas in Alaska: the Aleutian World War II National Historic Area at Unalaska and the Inupiat Heritage Center in Barrow.

The former was designated in 1996 to interpret, educate and inspire people about the history and the role of the Aleut people and the Aleutian Islands in World War II. The federal government does not own or manage the park, which is overseen by the Ounalashka Corp., a Native village corporation. The NPS provides technical assistance.

The Inupiat Heritage Center is affiliated with the New Bedford Whaling National Historic Park in New Bedford, MA. In the 19th century, more than 2,000 whaling voyages departed New Bedford for the western Arctic. The National Park Service has helped with exhibits and other technical assistance.

National Park Service units are followed by address, acreage and major features or recreations:

Aniakchak National Monument and Preserve, Superintendent, Katmai National Park and Preserve, P.O. Box 7, King Salmon 99613 (603,000 acres). Aniakchak dry caldera.

Bering Land Bridge National Preserve, National Park Service, P.O. Box 220, Nome 99762 (2,785,000 acres). Lava fields, rare plants, archaeological sites, migratory waterfowl.

Cape Krusenstern National Monument, National Park Service, P.O. Box 1029, Kotzebue 99752 (660,000 acres). Archaeological sites.

Denali National Park and Preserve, National Park Service, P.O. Box 9, Denali Park 99755 (6,028,000 acres). Mount McKinley, abundant wildlife.

Gates of the Arctic National Park and Preserve, National Park Service, P.O. Box 74680, Fairbanks 99707 (8,472,000 acres). Brooks Range, wild and scenic rivers, wildlife.

Glacier Bay National Park and Preserve, National Park Service, Bartlett

Looking Back

June 1786

No one lived on St. George Island in the Pribilofs until June 1786, when Captain Gerassim Pribilov left a party of Russian hunters there with provisions for the winter.

Cove, Gustavus 99826 (3,283,000 acres). Glaciers, marine wildlife.

Katmai National Park and Preserve, National Park Service, P.O. Box 7, King Salmon 99613 (4,090,000 acres). Valley of Ten Thousand Smokes, brown bears.

Kenai Fjords National Park, National Park Service, P.O. Box 1727, Seward 99664 (570,000 acres). Fjords, Harding Icefield, Exit Glacier, waterfowl, sea otters.

Klondike Gold Rush National Historical Park, National Park Service, P.O. Box 517, Skagway 99840 (2,721 acres, including 15 restored turn-of-the-century structures). Chilkoot Trail.

Kobuk Valley National Park, National Park Service, P.O. Box 1029, Kotzebue 99752 (1,750,000 acres). Archaeological sites, Great Kobuk Sand Dunes, river rafting.

Lake Clark National Park and Preserve, National Park Service, 4230 University Drive, Suite 311, Anchorage 99508 (4,044,000 acres). Backcountry recreation, fishing, scenery.

Noatak National Preserve, National Park Service, P.O. Box 1029, Kotzebue 99752 (6,574,000 acres). Abundant wildlife, river floating.

Sitka National Historical Park, National Park Service, P.O. Box 738, Sitka 99835 (106 acres). Russian Bishop's House, totems, trails.

Wrangell–St. Elias National Park and Preserve, National Park Service, P.O. Box 439, Copper Center 99573 (13,188,000 acres). Rugged peaks, glaciers, expansive wilderness.

Yukon-Charley Rivers National Preserve, National Park Service, P.O. Box 167, Eagle 99738 (2,523,000 acres). Backcountry recreation, river floating.

National Petroleum Reserve (SEE ALSO OIL AND GAS)

In 1923, President Warren G. Harding signed an executive order creating Naval Petroleum Reserve Number 4 (NPR-4), the last of four petroleum reserves to be placed under control of the U.S. Navy. The secretary of the Navy was charged to "explore, protect, conserve, develop, use and operate the Naval Petroleum Reserves," including NPR-4, on Alaska's North Slope. (*See* map, pages 150–51)

The U.S. Geological Survey (USGS) had begun surface exploration in the area in 1901; following creation of the 23-million-acre reserve, exploration programs were conducted by the Navy. From 1944 to 1953, extensive geological and geophysical surveys were conducted and 36 test wells were drilled. Nine oil and gas fields were discovered; the largest oil field, near Umiat, contains an estimated 70 million to 120 million barrels of recoverable oil. Active exploration was suspended in 1953.

In 1974, the Arab oil embargo, coupled with the knowledge of large petroleum reserves at nearby Prudhoe Bay, brought about renewed interest in NPR-4, and Congress directed the Navy to resume its exploration program.

In 1976, all lands within NPR-4 were redesignated the National Petroleum Reserve Alaska (NPR-A) and jurisdiction was transferred to the Secretary of the Interior. In 1980, Congress authorized the secretary to oversee an expeditious program of competitive leasing of oil and gas tracts in the reserve, clearing the way for private development of the area's resources.

By mid-1983, three competitive bid lease sales, involving 7.2 million acres of NPR-A, had been held. Dates of the sales and the number of acres involved were: January 1982, 1.5 million acres; May 1982, 3.5 million acres; and July 1983, 2.2 million acres. Interest from the oil companies has lessened over the years and leases

> The American Association for Nude Recreation announced that Alaska is the only state without a nudist colony.

expired. Prior to 1999, the last oil lease sale was in 1984, but was canceled when no bids were entered. Currently there are 1,185 active oil and gas leases, covering nearly 2.8 million acres.

The Interior Department, through USGS, continued exploration of NPR-A into the 1980s. Past naval explorations and those conducted by USGS resulted in the discovery of oil at Umiat and Cape Simpson, and several gas fields including Walakpa, Gubic and Point Barrow. The North Slope Borough is developing reserves in the Walakpa field to provide gas for heating and electrical generation for Barrow. The borough plans to drill up to eight wells to produce the gas. Data gathered indicates NPR-A may contain recoverable reserves of 1.85 billion barrels of crude oil and 3.74 trillion cubic feet of natural gas. Such optimistic data fueled bidding in a May 1999 lease sale. Alaska's two largest oil companies at that time, BP Exploration (Alaska) Inc. and ARCO Alaska Inc., won interest in 87 percent of the leases. Bidding on the 5,700-acre blocks between Teshekpuk Lake and the Colville River totaled $105 million.

National Wild and Scenic Rivers (SEE ALSO

RIVERS) The Alaska National Interest Lands Conservation Act (ANILCA) of Dec. 2, 1980, gave wild and scenic river classification to 13 streams within the National Park System, six in the National Wildlife Refuge System and two in Bureau of Land Management Conservation and Recreation areas. (See map, pages 150–51) An additional five rivers are located outside designated preservation units. Twelve more rivers were designated for further study and possible wild and scenic classification.

The criteria for wild and scenic river classification covers more than just float trip possibilities. Scenic features, wilderness characteristics and recreational opportunities that would be impaired by alteration, development or impoundment are also considered.

Rivers are classified into three categories

A kayaker paddles across mirror-smooth Lake Beverley in Wood–Tikchik State Park. From Alaska's Accessible Wilderness by Bill Sherwonit.

under the Wild and Scenic Rivers Act. The wild classification is most restrictive of development or incompatible uses—it stresses the wilderness aspect of the rivers. The scenic classification permits some intrusions upon the natural landscape, and the recreational classification is the least restrictive category. A specified amount of land back from the river's banks is also put in protected status to ensure access, use and the preservation of aesthetic values for the public.

For those desiring to float these rivers, special consideration must be given to put-in and take-out points because most of the designated wild and scenic rivers are not accessible by road. This means that voyagers and their crafts must be flown in and picked up by charter Bush planes. Because Federal Aviation Administration regulations prohibit the lashing of canoes and kayaks to pontoons of floatplanes when carrying passengers, inflatable rafts and folding canvas or rubber kayaks are often more convenient and less expensive to transport.

Further information on rivers and river running can be obtained from the Alaska Public Lands Information Centers: 605 W. Fourth Ave., Suite 105, Anchorage 99501; 250 Cushman St., Suite 1A, Fairbanks 99701; 50 Main St., Ketchikan 99901; and P.O. Box 359, Tok 99780; the U.S. Fish and Wildlife Service, 1011 E. Tudor Road, Anchorage 99503; and the Bureau of Land Management, 222 W. Seventh Ave., No. 13, Anchorage 99513. Information for rivers within park units or managed by the National Park Service is also available from the particular park headquarters. (*See also* National Parks, Preserves and Monuments)

Rivers Within National Park Areas.

Alagnak—Katmai National Preserve

Alatna—Gates of the Arctic National Park

Aniakchak—Aniakchak National Monument; Aniakchak National Preserve

Charley—Yukon–Charley Rivers National Preserve

Chilikadrotna—Lake Clark National Park and Preserve

John—Gates of the Arctic National Park and Preserve

Kobuk—Gates of the Arctic National Park and Preserve

Mulchatna—Lake Clark National Park and Preserve

Noatak—Gates of the Arctic National Park and Noatak National Preserve

North Fork Koyukuk—Gates of the Arctic National Park and Preserve

Salmon—Kobuk Valley National Park

Tinayguk—Gates of the Arctic National Park and Preserve

Tlikakila—Lake Clark National Park and Preserve

Rivers Within National Wildlife Refuges.

Andreafsky—Yukon Delta National Wildlife Refuge

Ivishak—Arctic National Wildlife Refuge

Nowitna—Nowitna National Wildlife Refuge

Selawik—Selawik National Wildlife Refuge

Sheenjek—Arctic National Wildlife Refuge

Wind—Arctic National Wildlife Refuge

General information on rivers not listed in refuge brochures may be obtained from respective refuge offices by addressing queries to refuge managers. Addresses for refuges are given in the brochures.

Rivers Within Bureau of Land Management Units.

Beaver Creek—The segment of the main stem from confluence of Bear and Champion Creeks within White Mountains National Recreation Area to the Yukon Flats National Wildlife Refuge boundary.

Birch Creek—The segment of the main stem from the south side of Steese Highway downstream to the bridge at Milepost 147.

Rivers Outside of Designated Preservation Units.

Alagnak—Those segments or portions of the main stem and Nonvianuk tributary lying outside and westward of Katmai National Park and Preserve.

Delta River—The segment from and including all of the Tangle Lakes to a point one-half mile north of Black Rapids.

Fortymile River—The main stem within Alaska, plus tributaries.

Gulkana River—The main stem from the outlet of Paxson Lake to the confluence with Sourdough Creek; various segments of the west fork and middle fork.

Unalakleet River—Approximately 80 miles of the main stem.

Rivers Designated for Study for Inclusion in Wild and Scenic Rivers System.

Colville River
Etivluk–Nigu Rivers
Kanektok River
Kisaralik River
Koyuk River
Melozitna River
Porcupine River
Sheenjek River (lower segment)
Situk River
Squirrel River
Utukok River
Yukon River (Rampart section)

National Wilderness Areas

(*SEE ALSO* CABINS) Passage of the Alaska National Interest Lands Conservation Act (ANILCA) on Dec. 2, 1980, added millions of acres to the National Wilderness

Preservation System. Administration of these wilderness areas is the responsibility of the agency under whose jurisdiction the land is situated. Agencies that oversee wilderness areas in Alaska include the National Park Service, U.S. Fish and Wildlife Service and the U.S. Forest Service. Although the Bureau of Land Management has authority to manage wilderness in the public domain, no BLM wilderness areas exist in Alaska. (*See* map, pages 150–51)

Passage of the Tongass Timber Reform Act (TTRA) on Nov. 28, 1990, designated an additional 299,721 acres of the Tongass National Forest as wilderness.

Wilderness allocations to different agencies in Alaska are: U.S. Forest Service, approximately 5.7 million acres; National Park Service, approximately 32 million acres; and U.S. Fish and Wildlife Service, approximately 18.7 million acres.

Wilderness, according to the federal Wilderness Act of 1964, is land sufficient in size to enable the operation of natural systems without undue influence from human activities in surrounding areas and should be places in which people are visitors only. Alaska wilderness regulations follow the stipulations of the Wilderness Act as amended by the Alaska lands act. Specifically designed to allow for Alaska conditions, the rules are considerably more lenient about transportation access, human-made structures and use of mechanized vehicles. The primary objective of a wilderness area continues to

The latest nationwide survey showed that Alaskans are the fourth-fattest people in the nation. In spite of this impressive statistic, a sign at a roadside diner outside of Sutton, Alaska, proclaimed, "If you don't eat here, we'll both starve!"

be the maintenance of the wilderness character of the land.

Some characteristics of Alaska wilderness areas:

• Fishing, hunting and trapping continue on lands within the national forests, national wildlife refuges and national park preserves. National park wilderness does not allow sport hunting or sport or commercial trapping.

• Subsistence uses including hunting, fishing, trapping, berry gathering and use of timber for cabins and firewood may be allowed but are not permitted in all wilderness areas. Contact the particular land manager for limits on subsistence activity.

• Public recreation or safety cabins in wilderness areas in national forests, national wildlife refuges and national park preserves continue to be maintained and may be replaced. A limited number of new public-use cabins may be added if needed.

• Existing special-use permits on all national forest wilderness lands for cabins, homesites or similar structures may continue. Use of temporary campsites, shelters and other temporary facilities and equipment related to hunting and fishing on national forest lands will continue.

• Fish habitat enhancement programs, including planting of vegetation, construction of buildings, fish weirs, fishways, spawning channels and other accepted means of maintaining, enhancing and rehabilitating fish stocks, may be allowed in national forest wilderness areas.

• Special-use permits for guides and outfitters operating within wilderness areas in the national forests and national wildlife refuges are allowed.

• Private, state and Native lands surrounded by wilderness areas are guaranteed access through the wilderness area.

• Use of fixed-wing airplanes, motorboats, snowmachines and nonmotorized methods of surface transportation for traditional activities and for access to villages and homesites is allowed to continue.

National Wildlife Refuges

(*See* map, pages 150–51)

Congress has designated 16 National Wildlife Refuges in Alaska, totaling 77 million acres. The refuges have 10 designated wilderness areas and six rivers designated National Wild and Scenic Rivers. At just under 20 million acres each, both the Arctic National Wildlife Refuge and the Yukon Delta National Wildlife Refuge are among the largest wildlife refuges in the world. Refuges are managed by the U.S. Fish and Wildlife Service's Region 7 at 1011 E. Tudor Road, Anchorage 99503.

National wildlife refuges in Alaska were established to conserve fish and wildlife populations and habitats in their natural diversity. Refuges are open to the public for many noncommercial recreational and subsistence uses including wildlife observation, photography, boating, camping and hiking. Hunting, fishing and trapping are allowed in accordance with state regulations and those set by the Federal Subsistence Board.

Visitors are encouraged to contact the refuge manager for information on special closures or other special conditions. Commercial guiding, air taxi operations and other commercial uses may be authorized by special permit. Subsistence activities are permitted, as is the use of snowmachines, motorboats and other nonmotorized surface transportation methods for traditional activities. With adequate snow cover, recreational snowmachining is allowed on the Kenai Refuge. Transportation in off-road vehicles, including all-terrain vehicles, motorcycles and airboats, is not permitted.

Most refuges are in remote areas—only the Kenai and Tetlin Refuges are accessible from the highway system. Airplane access is allowed but helicopter access requires a permit and must be determined compatible with refuge purposes.

Refuge managers may be contacted at their field headquarters listed below or use the Region 7 home page on the Internet at www.r7.fws.gov.

National Wildlife Refuge administrative addresses are followed by acreage and predominant wildlife:

Alaska Maritime National Wildlife Refuge, 2355 Kachemak Drive, Suite 101, Homer 99603 (3.4 million acres). Seabirds, sea lions, sea otters, harbor seals, walrus, whales.

Alaska Peninsula National Wildlife Refuge, P.O. Box 277, King Salmon 99613 (3.5 million acres). Brown bears, caribou, moose, sea otters, bald eagles, peregrine falcons, wolves, wolverines, migrating whales.

Arctic National Wildlife Refuge, 101 12th Ave., P.O. Box 20, Fairbanks 99701 (19.5 million acres). Caribou, polar bears, grizzly bears, wolves, Dall sheep, peregrine falcons, musk-oxen, snowy owls.

Becharof National Wildlife Refuge, P.O. Box 277, King Salmon 99613 (1.2 million acres). Brown bears, bald eagles, caribou, moose, salmon.

Innoko National Wildlife Refuge, P.O. Box 69, McGrath 99627 (3.8 million acres). Migratory waterfowl, beaver, lynx, marten, moose.

Izembek National Wildlife Refuge, P.O. Box 127, Cold Bay 99571 (303,094 acres). Black brant (coastal geese), brown bears.

Kanuti National Wildlife Refuge, 101 12th Ave., P.O. Box 11, Fairbanks 99701 (1.4 million acres). Waterfowl.

Kenai National Wildlife Refuge, Box 2139, Soldotna 99669 (1.9 million acres). Moose, salmon, mountain goats, Dall sheep, bears, lynx, wolves.

Kodiak National Wildlife Refuge, 1390 Buskin River Road, Kodiak 99615 (1.9 million acres). Brown bears, black-tailed deer, bald eagles, river otters.

Koyukuk National Wildlife Refuge, P.O. Box 287, Galena 99741 (3.5 million acres). Wolves, bears, moose, waterfowl.

Nowitna National Wildlife Refuge, P.O. Box 287, Galena 99741 (1.5 million acres). Migratory waterfowl, moose, bears, furbearers.

Selawik National Wildlife Refuge, P.O. Box 270, Kotzebue 99752 (2.1 million acres). Caribou, migratory birds.

Tetlin National Wildlife Refuge,

P.O. Box 779, Tok 99780 (700,053 acres). Migratory waterfowl, Dall sheep, moose, bears, ptarmigan.

Togiak National Wildlife Refuge, P.O. Box 270, Dillingham 99576 (4.1 million acres). Caribou, walrus, seabirds, moose.

Yukon Delta National Wildlife Refuge, P.O. Box 346, Bethel 99559 (19.1 million acres). Migratory birds, musk-oxen and reindeer are found on Nunivak Island.

Yukon Flats National Wildlife Refuge, 101 12th Ave., P.O. Box 264, Fairbanks 99701 (8.6 million acres). Waterfowl, moose, bears.

Native Arts and Crafts (SEE ALSO BALEEN; BASKETS; BEADWORK; IVORY; MASKS; NATIVE PEOPLES; POTLATCH; SKIN SEWING; AND TOTEMS)

Traditional arts and crafts of Alaska's Natives were produced for ceremonial and utilitarian reasons. These objects were not thought of as art in the Western sense but as pieces and designs to fulfill specific needs. Native art also reflected spiritual values and the environment each group inhabited. Alaska Natives are known for their ingenious use and manipulation of natural materials to supply life's needs: Roots, bark, grasses, wood, fur, quills, skins, feathers, and the sea's resources are still used to produce containers, clothing, hunting implements, ceremonial regalia and many other items.

Today, most Native utilitarian objects are modern adaptations using plastic, metal and glass. But many traditional Native designs and natural materials are still used to create ceremonial objects, and Alaska Native arts and crafts are widely sought by collectors, museums and tourists. This new market has proven beneficial to Native artists and to Native culture as it moves from a subsistence lifestyle to a cash economy.

The Inupiat and Yup'ik Eskimo people, like other Alaska Native groups, are divided geographically and linguistically. Because their coastal environment offers few forest resources, the Eskimo people have learned

to rely on the tundra and the sea. The Inupiat of northern Alaska are known for making objects out of sea mammal parts—especially walrus ivory, baleen and whale bone. Their ivory carving and scrimshaw work is world renowned. More contemporary work in which stiff baleen is coiled into elegant baskets is gaining recognition.

The Yup'ik of western Alaska also utilize sea mammals in their art. In addition, they rely heavily on the coastal rye grass for their intricate coiled baskets and mat work. Yup'ik ceremonial masks—carved primarily of driftwood, assembled and painted—are distinctive in the global tribal mask-making tradition. Both the Inupiat and Yup'ik groups produce warm, beautiful clothing using the furs and skins of land and sea mammals.

The Aleut people of the Aleutian Islands also make attractive baskets from rye grass but they use a twining technique. The Aleut are known for their traditional capes made of sea mammal gut and painted bentwood hunting hats and visors.

The Athabascan Indians of Alaska's Interior live in a region abundant with

Traditional Native Distribution

forest and river resources. They make decorative beaded clothing and other items, often on tanned, smoked moosehide; birch bark is formed into lightweight canoes, baby cradles and containers. Athabascans are also known for their skill sewing skins into clothing.

The Tlingit, Haida and Tsimshian people of southeastern Alaska are part of the Pacific Northwest Coast Indian culture, which extends down the coast of British Columbia and into Washington state. Each member of this culture is given at birth his or her own totemic crest—an animal form representing the family clan. These crests are reproduced in many art forms such as elaborate ceremonial regalia; carvings in wood, metal or stone; paintings or prints; and jewelry. The carvers of the Northwest Coast, best known for monumental totem poles, record legendary happenings and

honor important people or events. Artwork adheres to a complex, formal design system and is highly stylized and dramatic. Fine Northwest Coast pieces such as carved and painted wooden hats, rattles, masks and bentwood boxes are sought worldwide by collectors and museums.

Native Peoples
Alaska's 104,000 Native people make up about 17 percent of the state's total population. Of those, the majority are Eskimo, Indian and Aleut. Although many live in widely scattered villages along the coastline and great rivers of Alaska, about 24,000 Natives lived in Anchorage as of 1998. Fairbanks had a Native population of 6,100.

At the time Europeans came in contact with the Natives of Alaska in 1741, Russians estimated the Native population at 100,000. The Eskimo, Indian and Aleut people lived within well-defined regions: There was little mixing of ethnic groups. All were hunting and gathering people who did not practice agriculture.

In southeastern Alaska, the herring, salmon, deer and other plentiful foods permitted the Haida and Tlingit Indians to settle in permanent villages and develop a culture rich in art. The Athabascans lived chiefly in the Interior. They migrated from one seasonal subsistence camp to another to take advantage of seasonal abundance of fish, waterfowl and other game. The coastal Eskimo and Aleut subsisted primarily on the rich resources of the rivers and the sea.

Alaska's Tsimshian Indians moved in 1887 from their former home in British Columbia to Annette Island in Southeast Alaska, under the Rev. William Duncan, an Anglican. About 1,700 Tsimshian now live in Metlakatla. They are primarily fishermen, as are most Southeasterners.

Approximately 1,700 Haida live in Alaska, about 300 of whom live in Hydaburg on the south end of Prince of Wales Island. It is believed they migrated to Alaska from interior Canada in the 1700s. The Haida excel at totem carving and are noted for skilled working of wood, bone, shell, stone and silver.

Today, about 9,400 Tlingit (KLINK-it) live throughout Alaska. The Tlingit, who migrated west from what is now Canada before the first European contact, commercially dominated the interior Canadian Indians, trading eulachon oil, copper pieces and Chilkat blankets for various furs and beaded clothing. Like the Haida and Tsimshian, Tlingit are part of the totem culture; totems provide a record of major events in family or clan history.

Athabascan Indians, who number approximately 11,700 in Alaska, occupied the vast area of Alaska's Interior. They were nomadic people whose principal sources of food were caribou, moose and fish. Hard times and famines were frequent for all Athabascans except the Tanaina and Ahtna groups who lived along the Gulf of Alaska and could rely on salmon.

The Eskimo have traditionally lived in villages along the harsh Bering Sea and Arctic Ocean coastlines, and along a thin strip of the Gulf of Alaska coast, including Kodiak Island. They took berries, salmon, waterfowl, ptarmigan and a few caribou but it was the sea and its whales, walruses and seals that provided the foundation for their existence. Houses were barabaras— dwellings built partially underground and covered with sod.

The Aleut have traditionally lived on the Alaska Peninsula and along the Aleutian Chain. When the Russians reached the Aleutians in the 1740s, practically every island was inhabited. Decimated by contact with whites, only a few Aleut settlements remain, including two established by Russians on the Pribilof Islands, St. Paul and St. George.

The Aleut lived in permanent villages, taking advantage of sea life and land mammals

Alaskans now spend $957 million each year to catch 6,346,098 sport fish. That's $150.80 per fish! You'd save time, money and automobile wear and tear if you simply stood in a cold shower for 6 hours, burned a $100 bill, and went out for salmon and champagne at the best restaurant in town!

John Charlie, in decorated moosehide dance clothes, and his grandfather, Neil Charlie. From Children of the Midnight Sun *by Tricia Brown (text) and Roy Corral (photographs).*

for food. Their original dwellings were large, communal structures housing as many as 40 families. After Russian occupation they lived in smaller houses, many adopting the Russian-style log cabin. Today many Aleuts are commercial fishermen.

Rapid advances in communications, transportation and other services to remote villages have altered Native life in Alaska. Economic changes, from a subsistence to a cash economy, culminated in the passage of the Alaska Native Claims Settlement Act in 1971. It gave Alaska Natives $962.5 million and 44 million acres of land as compensation for the loss of lands historically occupied or used by their people.

Native Regional Corporations

Twelve in-state regional business corporations were formed under the 1971 Alaska Native Claims Settlement Act to manage money and land received from the government. (*See* map, page 162) A 13th corporation was organized for those Natives residing outside Alaska. Following is a list of corporations and the area or region each administers:

Ahtna Inc. (Copper River Basin), P.O. Box 649, Copper Center 99588, or 406 W. Fireweed Lane, Anchorage 99503.

Aleut Corp. (Aleutian Islands), 1 Aleut Plaza, 4000 Old Seward Highway, Suite 300, Anchorage 99503.

Arctic Slope Regional Corp. (Arctic Alaska), P.O. Box 129, Barrow 99723, or 301 Arctic Slope Ave., Anchorage 99501.

Bering Straits Native Corp. (Seward Peninsula), P.O. Box 1008, Nome 99762.

Bristol Bay Native Corp. (Bristol Bay area), P.O. Box 198, Dillingham 99576, or P.O. Box 100220, Anchorage 99510.

Calista Corp. (Yukon–Kuskokwim Delta), P.O. Box 408, Bethel 99559, or 601 W. Fifth Ave., Suite 200, Anchorage 99501.

Chugach Alaska Corp. (Prince William Sound), 560 E. 34th Ave., Suite 200, Anchorage 99503.

Cook Inlet Region Inc. (Cook Inlet region), 2525 C St., Anchorage 99503.

Doyon, Ltd. (interior Alaska), 201 First Ave., Suite 200, Fairbanks 99701.

Koniag Inc. (Kodiak area), 4300 B St., Suite 407, Anchorage 99503.

NANA Regional Corp. (Kobuk region), P.O. Box 49, Kotzebue 99752, or 1001 E. Benson Blvd., Anchorage 99508.

Sealaska Corp. (southeastern Alaska), One Sealaska Plaza, Suite 400, Juneau 99801.

Thirteenth Regional Corp. (outside Alaska), 4370 NE Halsey St., Suite 130, Portland, OR 97213.

Regional Nonprofit Corporations.

Aleutian–Pribilof Islands Association Inc. (Aleut Corp.), 201 E. Third Ave., Anchorage 99501.

Association of Village Council Presidents (Calista Corp.), P.O. Box 219, Bethel 99559.

Bristol Bay Native Association (Bristol Bay Native Corp.), P.O. Box 237, Dillingham 99756.

Central Council of Tlingit–Haida

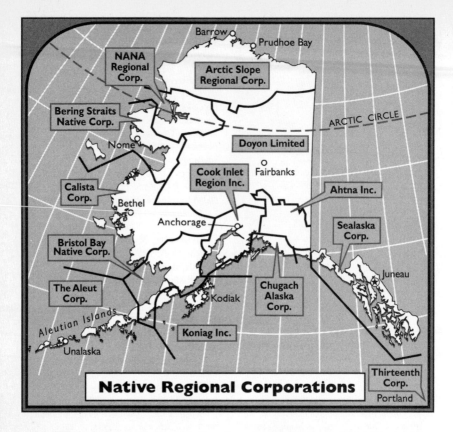

Native Regional Corporations

Indian Tribes (Sealaska Corp.), 1 Sealaska Plaza, Suite 200, Juneau 99801.

Cook Inlet Tribal Council Inc. (Cook Inlet Region, Inc.), 670 W. Fireweed Lane, Anchorage 99503.

Copper River Native Association (Ahtna Inc.), Drawer H, Copper Center 99573.

Inupiat Community of the Arctic Slope (Arctic Slope Regional Corp.), P.O. Box 437, Barrow 99723.

Kawerak, Inc. (Bering Straits Native Corp.), P.O. Box 948, Nome 99762.

Kodiak Area Native Association (Koniag, Inc.), P.O. Box 172, Kodiak 99615.

Maniilaq (formerly Mauneluk) Association (NANA Regional Corp.), P.O. Box 256, Kotzebue 99752.

North Pacific Rim Native Association (Chugach Alaska Corp.), 560 E. 34th Ave., Anchorage 99503.

Ounalashka Corp. (Aleut Corp.), P.O. Box 149, Unalaska 99685.

Tanana Chiefs Conference (Doyon Ltd.), 201 First Ave., Fairbanks 99701.

Other Native Organizations.
Alaska Eskimo Whaling Commission, P.O. Box 570, Barrow 99723.

Alaska Federation of Natives, 1577 C St., Anchorage 99501.

Alaska Native Brotherhood, P.O. Box 112, Juneau 99801.

Alaska Native Commission on Alcoholism and Drug Abuse, P.O. Box 4-2463, Anchorage 99509.

Alaska Native Cultural Arts Exchange, 117 W. Fourth Ave., Anchorage 99501.

Alaska Native Foundation, 3305 Arctic Blvd., Anchorage 99503.

Alaska Native Health Board, 4201 Tudor Centre Drive, Anchorage 99508.

Bristol Bay Area Health Corp., P.O. Box 130, Dillingham 99576.

Central Council of Tlingit and Haida Indian Tribes of Alaska, One Sealaska Plaza, Suite 200, Juneau 99801.

Eyak Corp., P.O. Box 340, Cordova 99574.

Fairbanks Native Association Inc., 310 First Ave., Fairbanks 99701.

Interior Village Association, 127 1/2 Minnie St., Fairbanks 99701.

Inuit Circumpolar Conference, Barrow 99723.

Norton Sound Health Corp., P.O. Box 966, Nome 99762.

Qawalangin (Sons of the Sea Lion), P.O. Box 334, Unalaska 99685, is the federally recognized tribal government of the Unangan (Aleut) people of Unalaska.

Southeast Alaska Regional Health Corp., P.O. Box 2800, Juneau 99803.

Yukon–Kuskokwim Health Corp., P.O. Box 528, Bethel 99559.

Yupiktat Bista (a branch of the Association of Village Council Presidents), Bethel 99559.

Native Village Corporations.

In addition to the 13 regional corporations managing money and land received as part of the Alaska Native Claims Settlement Act, eligible Native villages were required to form corporations and to choose lands made available by the settlement act by December 1974. The 203 Native villages that formed village corporations eligible for land and money benefits are listed under their regional corporation.

Ahtna Inc.: Cantwell, Chistochina, Chitina, Copper Center, Gakona, Gulkana, Mentasta Lake, Tazlina.

Aleut Corp.: Akutan, Atka, Belkofski, False Pass, King Cove, Nelson Lagoon, Nikolski, St. George, St. Paul, Sand Point, Unalaska, Unga.

Arctic Slope Regional Corp.: Anaktuvuk Pass, Atkasook, Barrow, Kaktovik, Nuiqsut, Point Hope, Point Lay, Wainwright.

Bering Straits Native Corp.: Brevig Mission, Council, Golovin, Inalik/ Diomede, King Island, Koyuk, Marys Igloo, Nome, St. Michael, Shaktoolik, Shishmaref, Stebbins, Teller, Unalakleet, Wales, White Mountain.

Bristol Bay Native Corp.: Aleknagik, Chignik, Chignik Lagoon, Chignik Lake, Clarks Point, Dillingham, Egegik, Ekuk, Ekwok, Igiugig, Iliamna, Ivanof Bay, Kokhanok, Koliganek, Levelock, Manokotak, Naknek, Newhalen, New Stuyahok, Nondalton, Pedro Bay, Perryville, Pilot Point, Portage Creek, Port Heiden, South Naknek, Togiak, Twin Hills, Ugashik.

Calista Corp.: Akiachak, Akiak, Alakanuk, Andreafsky, Aniak, Atmautluak, Bethel, Bill Moores, Chefornak, Chevak, Chuathbaluk, Chuloonwick, Crooked Creek, Eek, Emmonak, Georgetown, Goodnews Bay, Hamilton, Hooper Bay, Kasigluk, Kipnuk, Kongiganak, Kotlik, Kwethluk, Kwigillingok, Lime Village, Lower Kalskag, Marshall, Mekoryuk, Mountain Village, Napaimiute, Napakiak, Napaskiak, Newtok, Nightmute, Nunapitchuk, Ohogamiut, Oscarville, Paimiut, Pilot

Kate Carmack, a Tagish Tlingit, c.a. 1898, who helped discover the Klondike gold. From Gold Rush Women *by Claire Rudolf Murphy and Jane G. Haigh.*

Station, Pitkas Point, Platinum, Quinhagak, Red Devil, Russian Mission, St. Marys, Scammon Bay, Sheldons Point, Sleetmute, Stony River, Toksook Bay, Tuluksak, Tuntutuliak, Tununak, Umkumiut, Upper Kalskag.

Chugach Natives Inc.: Chenaga, Eyak, Nanwalek, Port Graham, Tatitlek.

Cook Inlet Region Inc.: Chickaloon, Eklutna, Knik, Ninilchik, Seldovia, Tyonek.

Doyon Ltd.: Alatna, Allakaket, Anvik, Beaver, Bettles Field, Birch Creek, Chalkyitsik, Circle, Dot Lake, Eagle, Fort Yukon, Galena, Grayling, Healy Lake,

Holy Cross, Hughes, Huslia, Kaltag, Koyukuk, Manley Hot Springs, McGrath, Minto, Nenana, Nikolai, Northway, Nulato, Rampart, Ruby, Shageluk, Stevens Village, Takotna, Tanacross, Tanana, Telida.

Klukwan Inc.: Klukwan.

Koniag Inc.: Afognak, Akhiok, Kaguyak, Karluk, Larsen Bay, Old Harbor, Ouzinkie, Port Lions, Woody Island.

NANA Regional Corp. Inc.: Ambler, Buckland, Deering, Kiana, Kivalina, Kobuk, Kotzebue, Noatak, Noorvik, Selawik, Shungnak.

Sealaska Corp.: Angoon, Craig, Hoonah, Hydaburg, Kake, Kasaan, Klawock, Saxman, Yakutat.

Shee-Atika Corp.: Sitka.

Nenana Ice Classic

(*SEE ALSO* BREAKUP) The Ice Classic is a gigantic betting pool offering $300,000 in cash prizes to the lucky winner—or winners—who guess the time, to the nearest minute, of the ice breakup on the Tanana River at the town of Nenana. Official breakup time each spring is established when surging ice dislodges a four-legged "tripod" and breaks an attached line, which stops a clock set to Yukon standard time.

Tickets for the classic sell for $2 each, entitling the holder to one guess. Ice Classic officials estimate more than $7 million has been paid to lucky guessers through the years.

The primary intention of the Ice Classic was never as a fund-raiser for the town but as a statewide lottery, officially sanctioned by the first state legislature in one of its earliest actions in 1959.

Over the years the Ice Classic has benefited Nenana. Fifty percent of the gross proceeds goes to the winners. Nenana residents are paid salaries for ticket counting and compilation, and about 15 percent is earmarked for

In the 2000 Nenana Ice Classic, a world record *one hundred forty-four* Alaskans paid money to bet that the ice would go out on April 31st—a day that doesn't even exist! In 1999, only 96 people made the same bet. Alaskans have therefore gotten a whopping 50 percent dumber in the last year!

Nenana Ice Classic, Breakup Times, 1918–2000

April	May	May
20, 1940— 3:27 P.M.	1, 1989— 8:14 P.M.	8, 1930— 7:03 P.M.
20, 1998— 4:54 P.M.	2, 1976—10:51 A.M.	8, 1933— 7:30 P.M.
23, 1993— 1:01 P.M.	2, 1960— 7:12 P.M.	8, 1968— 9:26 P.M.
24, 1990— 5:19 P.M.	3, 1941— 1:50 A.M.	8, 1986— 9:31 P.M.
26, 1995— 1:22 P.M.	3, 1919— 2:33 P.M.	8, 1971—10:50 P.M.
26, 1926— 4:03 P.M.	3, 1947— 5:53 P.M.	9, 1923— 2:00 P.M.
28, 1969—12:28 P.M.	4, 1967—11:55 A.M.	9, 1955— 2:31 P.M.
28, 1943— 7:22 P.M.	4, 1973—11:59 A.M.	9, 1984— 3:33 P.M.
29, 1939— 1:26 P.M.	4, 1944— 2:08 P.M.	10, 1931— 9:23 A.M.
29, 1958— 2:56 P.M.	4, 1970—10:37 P.M.	10, 1972—11:56 A.M.
29, 1953— 3:54 P.M.	5, 1957— 9:30 A.M.	10, 1975— 1:49 P.M.
29, 1983— 6:37 P.M.	5, 1961—11:31 A.M.	10, 1982— 5:36 P.M.
29, 1999— 9:47 P.M.	5, 1996—12:32 P.M.	11, 1921— 6:42 A.M.
29, 1994—11:01 P.M.	5, 1987— 3:11 P.M.	11, 1918— 9:33 A.M.
30, 1997—10:28 A.M.	5, 1929— 3:41 P.M.	11, 1920—10:45 A.M.
30, 1936—12:58 P.M.	5, 1946— 4:40 P.M.	11, 1985— 2:36 P.M.
30, 1980— 1:16 P.M.	5, 1963— 6:25 P.M.	11, 1924— 3:10 P.M.
30, 1942— 1:28 P.M.	6, 1977—12:46 P.M.	12, 1927— 5:42 A.M.
30, 1934— 2:07 P.M.	6, 1974— 3:44 P.M.	12, 1922— 1:20 P.M.
30, 1978— 3:18 P.M.	6, 1950— 4:14 P.M.	12, 1952— 5:04 P.M.
30, 1951— 5:54 P.M.	6, 1928— 4:25 P.M.	12, 1937— 8:04 P.M.
30, 1979— 6:16 P.M.	6, 1954— 6:01 P.M.	12, 1962—11:23 P.M.
30, 1981— 6:44 P.M.	6, 1938— 8:14 P.M.	13, 1948—11:13 A.M.
May	7, 1925— 6:32 P.M.	14, 1992— 6:26 A.M.
1, 2000—10:47 A.M.	7, 1965— 7:01 P.M.	14, 1949—12:39 P.M.
1, 1991—12:04 A.M.	8, 1959—11:26 A.M.	15, 1935— 1:32 P.M.
1, 1932—10:15 A.M.	8, 1966—12:11 P.M.	16, 1945— 9:41 A.M.
1, 1956—11:24 A.M.		20, 1964—11:41 A.M.

upkeep of the Nenana Civic Center and as donations to the local visitors center, the library and special events at the high school.

The Internal Revenue Service also gets a chunk of withholding taxes on the payroll and a bite of each winner's share. In 2000, 18 winners split the pot, giving them $18,611 each.

Another pool, the Kuskokwim Ice Classic, has been a tradition in Bethel since 1924. Initially, it was said that the winner was paid 20 fish or 20 furs but stakes are considerably higher now and the winner receives 40 percent of the total ticket sales.

Breakup times for the Nenana Ice Classic from 1918 through 2000 are arranged in order of day and time of breakup (see chart).

Newspapers and Periodicals *(Rates are subject to change)* **Alaska Angler,** Box 83550, Fairbanks 99708. Bimonthly. Annual rate: $49.

Alaska Bar Rag, 510 L St., No. 602, Anchorage 99501. Bimonthly. Annual rate: $25

Alaska Bushmaster, 301 Calista Court, Suite B, Anchorage 99518. Monthly. Free.

Alaska Business Monthly, P.O. Box 241288, Anchorage, 99524-1288. Monthly. Annual rate: $21.95.

Alaska Contractor, 401 W. International Airport Road, Suite 11, Anchorage 99518. Four times a year. Free.

Alaska Designs, P.O. Box 103115, Anchorage, 99510-3115; Monthly (except

August). Annual rate: $36 for non-members; Free for members.

Alaska Digest, 3002 Spenard Road, No. 1, Anchorage 99503. Nine issues a year. Free.

Alaska Directory of Attorneys, 203 W. 15th Ave., Suite 102, Anchorage 99501. Biannually. Annual rate: $70.

Alaska Equipment Trader, 4220 B St., Suite 210, Anchorage 99503. Monthly. Annual rate: $12.

The Alaska Geographic Society, P.O. Box 93370, Anchorage 99509. Quarterly. Annual rates: $49; outside the U.S., $59

Alaska Hunter, P.O. Box 83550, Fairbanks 99708. Monthly. Annual rate: $49.

Alaska International Trade Directory, P.O. Box 112955, Anchorage 99511-2955. Annually. Free.

Alaska Journal of Commerce, 4220 B St., Suite 210, Anchorage 99513. Weekly. Annual rate: $30.

Alaska Justice Forum, 3211 Providence Drive, Anchorage 99508. Quarterly. Free.

ALASKA magazine, 619 E. Ship Creek Ave., Suite 329, Anchorage 99501. Ten issues a year. Subscriptions: $24; Outside the U.S.: $30.

Alaska Media Directory, 6828 Cape Lisburne Loop, Anchorage 99504-3958. Annually. Annual rate $88.

AlaskaMen, 205 E. Dimond Blvd., Suite 522, Anchorage 99518. Bimonthly. Subscriptions: (800) MY-AKMEN.

Alaska Military Weekly, 4220 B St., Suite 210, Anchorage 99503. Weekly. Free.

Alaska Miner, 3305 Arctic Blvd., Suite 202, Anchorage 99503. Monthly. Mailed to members of Alaska Miners Association only.

Alaska Miners Association Handbook and Service Directory, 3305 Arctic Blvd., Suite 202, Anchorage 99503. Annually. Mailed to members of Alaska Miners Association only.

Alaska Native Directory, 3002 Spenard Road, Anchorage 99503. Updated regularly. Annual rate: $157.50.

Alaska Pet News, P.O. Box 4083, Palmer 99645. Monthly. Annual rate: $18.

Alaska Post, 600 Richardson Drive, Fort Richardson 99505-5900.Weekly. Free.

Alaska Resource Guide, P.O. Box 201741, Anchorage 99520-1741. Annually. Annual rate $14.95 plus shipping and handling.

Alaska Snow Rider, 1801 Crescent Drive, Anchorage 99508. Monthly, September to April. Free.

Alaska Star, 16941 N. Eagle River Loop, Eagle River 99577. Weekly. Annual rate: $25.

Alaska Transporter, 501 W. Northern Lights Blvd., Suite 100, Anchorage 99503. Annually. Free to the trade.

Alaska Wellness Magazine, 911 W. 19th Ave., Anchorage 99503-1704. Bimonthly. Annual rate $15.

Alaska Women Speak, P.O. Box 92842, Anchorage 99509-2842. Quarterly. Annual rate: $16.

Alaskan, 134th Public Affairs Team, P.O. Box 5800, Anchorage 99505. Quarterly. Free to members of the Army National Guard.

Alaskan Southeaster, 9301 Glacier Highway, Suite 200, Juneau 99801. Monthly. Annual rate: $28.

The All-Alaska Weekly, P.O. Box 70970, Fairbanks 99707. Weekly. Annual rate: $24.

Anchorage Chamber of Commerce Newsletter, 441 W. Fifth Ave., Suite 300, Anchorage 99501. Monthly. Free to members only.

Anchorage Daily News, P.O. Box 149001, Anchorage 99514-9001. Daily. Annual rates: Anchorage home delivery, $135; second-class mail, $390.

Anchorage Press, P.O. Box 241841, Anchorage 99524-1841. Weekly. Free locally. Mailed subscriptions: $30 (in state), $70 (out of state).

Anchorage Visitors Guide, 524 W. Fifth Ave., Anchorage 99501. Home page: www.alaska.net/~acvb. April and October. Free.

Arctic Sounder, P.O. Box 290, Kotzebue 99752. Weekly. Annual rates: Second class mail, $45; first class, $90.

Boat Broker, 1910 Alex Holden Way,

Juneau 99801. Monthly. Free to Southeast communities; $10 mailed.

Bristol BayTimes, P.O. Box 1770, Dillingham 99576. Weekly. Annual rates: Second-class mail, $45; first class, $90.

Bush Blade, P.O. Box 168, Anchor Point 99556. Monthly. Annual rate: $7.50.

Business News Alaska, P.O. Box 233101, Anchorage 99523-3101. Monthly. Annual rate: $24.

Capital City Weekly, 1910 Alex Holden Way, Juneau 99801. Weekly. Annual rates: Home delivery, free; $52 if mailed.

Captn Jackis Tide & Current Almanac, P.O. Box 65119, Port Ludlow, WA 98365-0119. Annually. $14.95.

The Chamber, 401 W. International Airport Road, Suite 11, Anchorage 99518. Four times a year. Free.

Chilkat Valley News. P.O. Box 630, Haines 99827. Weekly. Annual rates: $36 in Haines; $42 mailed in state.

Chugiak/Eagle River Business and Service Directory, P.O. Box 770353, Eagle River 99577; Biannually. Free.

Clarion Dispatch, P.O. Box 3009, Kenai 99611. Weekly. Free.

COAST, 702 W. 32nd Ave., Suite 203, Anchorage 99503. Monthly. Free.

Commercial Buyers Guide, P.O. Box 112955, Anchorage 99511-2955. Annually. Free.

Cordova Times, P.O Box 200, Cordova 99574. Weekly. Annual rates: $45 second class mail; $90 first class.

Cuisine Scene, 702 W. 32nd Ave., Suite 203, Anchorage 99503. Biannually. Free.

Current Drift, P.O. Box 210430, Anchorage 99521-0430. Monthly. Free to members of Alaska Boating Association.

Daily Sitka Sentinel, P.O. Box 799, Sitka 99835. Monday through Friday. Annual rate: $80.

Delta Wind, P.O. Box 986, Delta Junction 99737. Biweekly. Rate: 85 cents per issue.

Denali Summer Times, P.O. Box 40, Healy 99743. Annually. Free.

Dillingham/Southwest Alaska Visitor's Guide, P.O. Box 1770, Dillingham 99576; Annually. Free.

Dutch Harbor Fisherman, Box 920472, Dutch Harbor 99692. Weekly. Annual rates: Second class $45; first class $90.

Eastside Pulse, Southside Pulse, and **Westside Pulse,** P.O. Box 92896, Anchorage 99509-2896. Monthly. Free.

Fairbanks Daily News-Miner, P.O. Box 70710, Fairbanks 99707. Daily. Annual rates: $294 Fairbanks; $306 Alaska; $334 out of Alaska.

Fairbanks Magazine, 921 Woodway, Fairbanks 99709. June through October. Rate: $2.25 per issue.

The Frontiersman, 5751 E. Mayflower Court, Wasilla 99654. Twice weekly. Annual rates: $40 Mat-Su; $65.60 Alaska; $70.60 outside Alaska.

Goldpanner, 3112 Broadway Ave., Unit 18A, Eielson AFB 99702-1895. Weekly. Free.

Greatland Bushmailer, 3110 Spenard Road, Anchorage 99503. Monthly. Free to rural villages.

Guidelines, 2207 Spenard Road, Suite 201, Anchorage 99503. Quarterly. Free to members.

Homer Alaska Tribune, 601 E. Pioneer Ave., Suite 109, Homer 99603. Weekly. Annual rate: $30.

Homer News, 3482 Landings St., Homer 99603. Weekly. Annual rate: $35 Kenai Peninsula Borough.

Hot Sheet, 1910 Alex Holden Way, Juneau 99801. Weekly. Free.

Island News, P.O. Box 19430, Thorne Bay 99919. Weekly. Annual rate: $55.

Juneau Empire, 3100 Channel Drive, Juneau 99801-7814. Monday through Friday and Sunday. Annual rate: $125.

Kaniqsirugut News, P.O. Box 966, Nome 99762. Four times a year. Free.

On Aug. 2, the police blotter of the **Valdez Vanguard** reported this heinous crime: "The giant Pixie fishing lure from South Central Hardware was taken and put into the mouth of the big salmon at the Hook, Line, and Sinker tackle shop."

Ketchikan Daily News, P.O. Box 7900, Ketchikan 99901. Monday through Saturday. Annual rate: $122 local.

Kodiak Daily Mirror, 1419 Selig, Kodiak 99615. Monday through Friday. Annual rates: $96; $132 mailed in state.

The Local Paper, 516 Stedman, Ketchikan 99901. Weekly. Free.

Marine Highway News, 3100 Channel Drive, Juneau 99801. Annually. Free.

Marine Yellow Pages, 15311 NE Ninth St., Redmond, WA 98052. Annually. Free.

The MILEPOST®, Morris Communications, 619 E. Ship Creek Ave., Suite 329, Anchorage 99501. Annually. 2000 edition: $24.95

Mukluk News, P.O. Box 90, Tok 99780. Bimonthly. Annual rate: $20.

Mushing, P.O. Box 149, Ester 99725. Web site: www.polarnet.com/users/mushing. Bimonthly. Annual rate: $24.

The Nicklesaver, 500 Main St., Unit C, Wasilla 99687. Weekly. Free.

The Nome Nugget, P.O. Box 610, Nome 99762. Weekly. Annual rate: $55.

Nome Visitors Guide, 301 Calista Court, Suite B, Anchorage 99518. Annually. Free.

Northcountry Companion Traveler's Guide, P.O. Box 336, Glennallen 99588. Annually. Free.

Northern Light, 3211 Providence Drive, Anchorage 99508. Weekly. Free.

On Board, 411 W. First Ave., Anchorage 99501. Annually. Free

Peninsula Clarion, P.O. Box 3009, Kenai 99611. Sunday through Friday. Annual rate: $78.

Pennysaver, 1001 Northway Drive, Anchorage 99508. Weekly. Free.

Petersburg Pilot, P.O. Box 930, Petersburg 99833. Weekly. Annual rate: $40.

July 1946

The "hell town" of Nome has lost its frontier character and become too "doggone civilized," old-timers complained. For the first time in its history, Nome's churches outnumbered its saloons.

Petroleum News, P.O. Box 233101, Anchorage 99523-3101. Monthly. Annual rate: $35.95.

Prince William Sound Visitor's Guide, 301 Calista Court, Suite B, Anchorage 99508. Annually. Free.

Real Estate Now, 702 W. 32nd Ave., Suite 203, Anchorage 99503. Biweekly. Free

Real Estate This Week, 741 Sesame St., Suite 100, Anchorage 99503. Weekly. Free.

Sealaska Shareholder, 1 Sealaska Plaza, Suite 400, Juneau 99801-1276. Five times a year. Free to shareholders.

Senior Voice, 325 E. Third Ave., Suite 300, Anchorage 99501. Monthly. Annual rate: $12.

Seward Phoenix-Log, P.O. Box 89, Seward 99664. Weekly. Annual rates: $45 second class; $90 first class.

Seward Visitor's Guide, P.O. Box 89, Seward 99664. Annually. Free.

Skagway News, P.O. Box 498, Skagway 99840-0498. Biweekly. Annual rate: $30.

Sourdough Sentinel, Third Wing, Public Affairs, 6920 12th St., Elmendorf Air Force Base 99506. Weekly. Free.

Southeast Empire, 3100 Channel Drive, Juneau 99801-7814. Semimonthly. Free.

Sun Star, P.O. Box 756640, Fairbanks 99775-6640. Weekly. Annual rate: $20.

Trade Winds, 401 W. International Airport Road, Suite 11, Anchorage 99518. Quarterly. Free.

True North magazine, Journalism and Public Communications Department, University of Alaska Anchorage, 3211 Providence Drive, Anchorage 99508. Annually. Free.

Tundra Drums, Box 868, Bethel 99559. Weekly. Annual rate: $45.

Turnagain Times, P.O. Box 1044, Girdwood 99587. Semimonthly. Annual rate: $18.

Unalaska/Dutch Harbor Visitor's

Guide, 301 Calista Court, Suite B, Anchorage 99518. Annually. Free.

Valdez Star, P.O. Box 2949, Valdez 99686. Weekly. Annual rate: $45.

Valdez Vanguard, P.O. Box 98, Valdez 99686-0098. Weekly. Annual rates: $45 second class; $90 first class.

Valley Sun, 5751 E. Mayflower Court, Wasilla 99654. Weekly. Free to Matanuska-Susitna Borough box holders.

Welcome to Alaska and the Mat-Su Valley, 401 W. International Airport Road, Suite 11, Anchorage 99518. Semiannually. Free.

Wrangell Sentinel and *Wrangell Guide,* P.O. Box 798, Wrangell 99929. Weekly. Annual rate: $32.

Wrangell-St. Elias News, McCarthy, Box MXY, Glennallen 99588. Bimonthly. Annual rate: $10.

Nome
Located on the shores of Norton Sound on the Seward Peninsula's south coast, Nome (population 3,615) is the transportation and commercial center for northwestern Alaska. Nome owes its name to a misinterpretation of "? name" on a chart in 1850. The question mark was taken as a "C" for cape, and the "A" in "name" was read as an "O." Originally the settlement was named Anvil City when gold was found in the Anvil Creek area in the summer of 1898.

The real gold stampede to Nome began in June 1899, when an estimated 30,000 miners rushed to Nome to stake claims and pitch their tents along the beaches of the Bering Sea Coast. That year, Nome was the largest city in the Alaska Territory. Miners quickly fled when their claims didn't pay, and by 1906 most of the gold and the prospectors were gone.

The mean average daily temperature in winter is −8°F and summer temperatures range from 40°F to 50°F. Mean annual snowfall, occurring from late September through early June, is 53 inches.

A 3,350-foot-long granite wall built by the U.S. Army Corps of Engineers protects Nome from the sea. It is 65 feet wide at the base, 16 feet wide at its top, and 18 feet above mean low water.

Although not connected by road to the rest of the state, Nome boasts more than 300 miles of road in the area—the second-largest city road system in the state. There is no winter maintenance of the roads.

The city of Nome has several schools, including the Northwest College, and the distinction of having the state's oldest first-class school district. It also offers many churches, a library and museum containing more than 6,000 photographs of the gold rush, Eskimo history and the Bering Land Bridge; and a historical park with a nonworking gold dredge and mining equipment from the gold rush days. For a fee, visitors may still try their luck panning the sands of the Nome beaches.

Throughout the year Nome offers many festivals and celebrations including its most famous event—the finish of the Iditarod Trail Sled Dog Race. There's the Bering Sea Ice Classic Golf Tournament played on the frozen Bering Sea in March; a Polar Bear Swim on Memorial Day; a Midnight Sun Festival in June, featuring a raft race on the Nome River with many a strange craft taking part; a 12.5-mile run to the top of 1,977-foot Anvil Mountain on July 4; and a Labor Day Bathtub Race. Other celebrations include a reindeer fair, snowmobile races, snowshoe, softball games and the largest state basketball tournament.

The city today is a jumping-off point for flights to Russia (only an hour-long flight away), surrounding Bush villages and tours of the Arctic. For details, consult Nome's Web site: www.alaska.net/~nome.

No-see-ums
The words describe a small biting two-winged midge. In its usual swarms this tiny, gray-black, silver-winged gnat is a most persistent pest and annoys all creatures. The insect is difficult to see when traveling solo. While no-see-ums don't transmit disease, their bites are irritating. Protective clothing, netting and a good repellent are recommended while in dense brush or near still-water ponds. Tents and recreational vehicles should be well screened.

Oil and Gas (SEE ALSO PIPELINE AND NATIONAL PETROLEUM RESERVE)

Alaska's first exploratory oil well was drilled in 1898 on the Iniskin Peninsula, Cook Inlet, by Alaska Petroleum Company. Oil was encountered in this first hole at about 700 feet but a water zone beneath the oil strata cut off the oil flow. Total depth of the well was approximately 1,000 feet.

The first commercial oil discovery was made in 1902 near Katalla, near the mouth of the Bering River east of Cordova. This field produced until 1933.

As early as 1921, oil companies surveyed land north of the Brooks Range for possible drilling sites. In 1923, the federal government created Naval Petroleum Reserve Number 4 (now known as National Petroleum Reserve Alaska; see National Petroleum Reserve), a 23 million-acre area of Alaska's North Slope. Wartime needs speeded up exploration. In 1944, the Navy began drilling operations on the petroleum reserve and continued until 1953, but made no oil discoveries which were economic. Between 1981 and 1984, the U.S. Department of the Interior leased oil and gas tracts in the reserve but none are active today.

Today, virtually all of Alaska's oil is produced from two regions, North Slope and Cook Inlet.

Discovered in 1968, Prudhoe Bay was the first commercial North Slope oil field to produce oil. Commercial production began in 1977, when Alyeska Pipeline Service Co. completed the pipeline between Valdez and Prudhoe Bay. Between discovery of oil and the start of commercial production, operators produced and refined small amounts of oil and gas for fuel to run the field equipment, and injected the residual oil back into the reservoir. North Slope fields produced a total of 13.8 billion barrels by the end of 1999, 81 percent of it from Prudhoe Bay, 13 percent from Kuparuk and 6 percent from other fields.

Three North Slope satellite developments began production in 1993: Point McIntyre, by far the largest; North Prudhoe Bay State; and West Beach. Other new satellites are the Niakuk pool, which began producing in 1994, and the Midnight Sun, which started in 1998. Milne Poine, a Kuparuk River field development, increased production in late 1994 and 1995. Other new Kuparuk River developments are: Tarn, which started production in July 1998; Tabasco, in April 1998; and West Sak, in late 1997. These recent additions have somewhat offset regional decline in oil production.

Recent exploration has resulted in several discoveries that should contribute to North Slope production. The Colville River field, discovered in 1994, is the largest of these and will begin production late in 2000. Various satellite developments are being evaluated throughout the North Slope. New additions can only partially limit the decline at Prudhoe and the other larger oil fields.

Companies first discovered Cook Inlet oil at Swanson River on the Kenai Peninsula in 1957 and began production in 1959. In 1962, the first offshore oil in Cook Inlet was discovered, making the inlet one of three successful areas in the United States for offshore oil production. Currently there are 15 production platforms in Cook Inlet, one of which produces only gas.

Regional production in Cook Inlet peaked in 1970 at 230,000 barrels daily

Fossil Fuel

Scientists don't know exactly how oil is formed but most believe that today's oil and gas were yesterday's marine microorganisms. As the tiny creatures died, their bodies collected on the seafloor, where they were covered with sediment. Eventually the sediment hardened into rock; over time, many layers of sediment could have been deposited. Heat and pressure from the covering rock layers are thought to have combined with bacterial processes to transform the sea creatures into petroleum. —Susan Ewing, *The Great Alaska Nature Factbook* ✸

(83 million barrels a year) and subsequently declined to 29,910 barrels a day in 1999. By the end of 1998 Cook Inlet fields had produced 1.2 billion barrels of oil, 48 percent of this from McArthur River, 18 percent from Swanson River and 34 percent from the other fields. Two fields, West McArthur River and Sunfish (Tyonek Deep), were discovered in 1991. West McArthur River began production in 1993 and contributed 5.8 million barrels.

Gas production from the Cook Inlet continues at significant levels with 180 billion cubic feet produced during 1999.

The Tyonek Deep reservoir in the North Cook Inlet Unit is under development by Phillips. First production is planned for 2000. In addition, Forcenergy is planning to develop the West Foreland gas reservoir and Redoubt Shoals Oil Field. Several companies are exploring for coalbed methane in the Matanuska Valley.

Projected Reserves and Production. The Division of Oil and Gas (DO&G) estimates that Alaska's total reserves are: oil, 6.2 billion barrels; gas, 34 trillion cubic feet.

North Slope fields hold 99 percent of the oil and 91 percent of the state's gas reserves. The balance are in Cook Inlet.

Reserve estimates of oil for North Slope fields have increased through the years. In January 1986, Prudhoe Bay had produced 4.4 billion barrels and reserves were

5.8 billion barrels. By January 1998 the field had produced nearly 10 billion barrels and reserves were estimated at 2.8 billion barrels. Much of the increase in ultimate recovery was due to improved technology, such as increased horizontal drilling and enhanced oil recovery. Technology may further increase future reserve estimates, but the main variables in recovering oil will be the perceived oil prices and the cost of production.

North Slope oil production peaked in 1988 at 2 million barrels a day and subsequently declined to 1.2 million barrels a day by 1998. The DO&G estimates that combined production from operating fields and to-be-developed fields will decline to 435,000 barrels a day in the year 2019.

Cook Inlet fields will continue to produce well into the century, however production is estimated to decline to 7,000 barrels a day by 2003. Cumulative production between 1997 and 2003 will be an estimated 50.5 million barrels.

Gas. All Alaska gas is produced from the North Slope, mostly from the Prudhoe Bay area, and from Cook Inlet, the same two regions that produce the state's oil. The production regimes of the two regions are very different because their markets are very different. The primary market for North Slope gas is neighboring Barrow as fuel for home heating oil production and related facilities. Most of the extracted gas is

injected back into the
reservoirs. That gas is
available for sale if
and when a market
develops. North Slope fields had produced
a cumulative net 3.6 trillion cubic feet by
the end of 1998.

The Alaska Natural Gas Transportation
System, a gas pipeline, was authorized
by the federal government in 1977 but
construction has not begun and a completion date not set for the foreseeable future
due to problems in financing the $40 billion
project. Most industry observers say that
the proposed gas pipeline is the most viable
idea for transporting North Slope gas to
Valdez for shipment to market. Gas
production in the North Slope is expected
to increase for the next several years and has
become an increasingly greater proportion
of the field production.

Cook Inlet fields, however, lie near two
gas-processing plants and the Anchorage
and Kenai commercial markets. Nearly all
extracted gas has been consumed and very
little has been injected. Regional production
reached an all-time high of 215 billion cubic
feet a year in 1998. Cook Inlet fields had
produced a cumulative net 5.6 trillion cubic
feet by the end of 1998.

Since 1987, Alaska and Texas have
alternated as the No. 1 state in oil production. As of 1997 the top five oil-producing
states are: Texas, Alaska, Louisiana,
California and Oklahoma. Alaska currently
provides about 15 percent of the nation's
domestic production of oil.

In fiscal 1998, the state of Alaska
received $7.96 million in royalties (includes
previous revisions and settlements) from
its oil and gas resources; approximately
78 percent of its unrestricted revenue
comes from petroleum taxes and royalties.
Since 1965, the state has collected about
$47 billion in unrestricted oil and gas
revenues. When the price of oil dropped in
early 1986, oil industry employment
declined and state government was in
a more tenuous fiscal situation. Oil prices
had improved by early 1990, but by then
Prudhoe Bay production had begun to
decline. In January 1994, crude oil prices

sunk to a 10-year low although they
recovered midyear. The state's oil and gas
industry absorbed major layoffs in 1994
and 1995.

The oil industry received some good
news in 1995 when the federal ban on
exporting Alaska oil was lifted. Oil
companies began exports in 1996. The
Far East is the major international market
for Alaska oil.

In 2000, BP Amoco struck a $30 billion
deal with Atlantic Richfield Co., dramatically changing the playing field for "Big
Oil." (*See* Yearly Highlights)

Oil and gas leasing on state land in
Alaska is managed by the Department of
Natural Resources, Division of Oil and Gas.
The Secretary of the Interior is responsible
for establishing oil and gas leasing on
federal lands in Alaska, including the outer
continental shelf. In 1986, Chevron, in
partnership with a Native corporation,
completed its well at Kaktovik on the
coastal plain of the Arctic National Wildlife
Refuge. The land was obtained in a swap
with the U.S. Department of the Interior
but Congress will have to approve any
further development within the boundaries
of the refuge.

Alaska Oil and Natural Gas Liquid Production

Year	Oil*	Natural Gas**
1988	738.1	400.415
1989	684.0	403.920
1990	647.3	412.121
1991	656.3	442.317
1992	627.3	449.126
1993	577.9	455.835
1994	568.9	469.041
1995	541.6	499.008
1996	544.2	490.591
1997	507.714	481.910
1998	450.8	473.650

*Millions of barrels
**Billions of cubic feet

Source: Alaska Department of Natural Resources,
Division of Oil & Gas

Oil Spill Prince William Sound
was the site of the largest oil spill in U.S.

history when the 987-foot *Exxon Valdez* tanker, carrying a full cargo of 53 million gallons of crude oil, struck Bligh Reef on March 24, 1989. Before the tanker leak could be stopped, more than 270,000 barrels, or more than 11.3 million gallons, of crude oil oozed into Prince William Sound. The oil, which poured out of the tanker at a rate of 42,488 barrels an hour, contaminated more than 1,500 miles of coastline in Prince William Sound, the Gulf of Alaska and lower Cook Inlet.

Shortly before the collision, the captain had changed course, veering from the normal shipping lane to avoid icebergs. At the time the tanker hit the reef, however, the third mate was piloting the tanker.

Within 15 hours of the spill, skimmer ships began to vacuum oil off the water's surface; booms were set up strategically to prevent the oil spill from contaminating salmon fisheries. Other fishing vessels assisted in attempts to capture oiled and wounded wildlife and transport those animals to rehabilitation centers.

Four days after the spill, the oil slick covered a 300-square-mile area, hitting islands, beaches and fish hatcheries throughout the sound, an area known for its rich commercial herring and salmon hatcheries. Oil from the tanker also was found to have fouled beaches on the Alaska Peninsula, almost 600 miles from the spill site.

Cleanup involved armies of crews, who tried scrubbing rocks by hand to washing the shore rocks with highly pressurized hot water. Bioremediation was another cleanup technique; it involved applying fertilizer to oiled shorelines to accelerate oil-metabolizing bacteria. Winter storms scoured many beaches throughout the oil spill area. Cleanup efforts resumed in the spring of 1990 and continued into 1992.

Thousands of marine mammals, birds and other wildlife perished as a result of the oil spill. Carcasses of 1,011 sea otters were recovered from the sound in 1989, and estimates of the number of otters that died range from about 3,500 to 5,500. About 31,000 birds were reported to have been killed.

But scientists believe these figures represent only a fraction of the total loss, since many birds were thought to have floated out to sea; still others sank or simply have not been found. Preliminary figures fix the loss at between 350,000 and 390,000 birds, according to a report by federal agencies including the U.S. Department of Fish and Wildlife, in charge of damage assessment and restoration.

Exxon Corp. accepted responsibility on March 25, 1989. More than 29,000 claims were filed for damages related to the oil spill. Many of the claims were from fishermen, canneries, Natives and business owners whose livelihood was curtailed by the oil spill. In 1989, the red salmon season was canceled in Prince William Sound.

The state sued Exxon and Alyeska Pipeline Service Co. in 1989; Exxon countersued, alleging that state officials had hampered cleanup

Looking Back

1977

The trans-Alaska oil pipeline from Prudhoe Bay to the ice-free port of Valdez on Prince William Sound was completed. The 800-mile pipeline carries oil over two mountain ranges and 350 rivers and streams.

Tucson's *Arizona Daily Star* reported: "Residents of [Anchorage] own approximately 50,000 dogs—each of which expels an average of three-quarters of a pound of poop daily. That adds up to 37,500 pounds each and every day. Well, now. Enjoy your breakfast." Who says there's no such thing as bad publicity?

efforts. In October 1991, the state and the federal government settled their suits with Exxon, splitting $1.25 billion. Of this amount, $900 million in civil damages is to be paid over a 10-year period ending in September 2001.

In 1994, Exxon and 3,500 Alaska Natives reached an agreement in which Exxon agreed to pay $20 million for loss of subsistence hunting. Also that year a jury awarded commercial fishermen $286.8 million in damages. And a federal jury ordered Exxon to pay $5 billion in punitive damages. Litigation continues today as Exxon appeals the punitive damage award.

It is estimated that Exxon spent about $2.5 billion on the cleanup. During its peak, 11,000 people worked on the cleanup, using 1,400 vessels and 85 aircraft. Environmental monitoring continues.

Exxon released its own scientific study on the oil spill in mid-1993, which concluded that no significant effects on the shoreline persist.

For further information, contact the Exxon Valdez Oil Spill Trustee Council, 645 G St., Anchorage 99501; (907) 278-8012. Other contacts: Alaska Resources Library and Information Services, 3150 C St., Suite 100, Anchorage 99503-3916, (907) 272-7547; Exxon Mobil, 5959 Las Colinas Blvd., Irving, TX 75039-2298, (972) 444-1000.

Parka

Pronounced "PAR-kee" and sometimes spelled "parky," this over-the-head garment worn by Eskimos was one of their main pieces of clothing. Parka styles, materials used and ornamentation (such as pieced calfskin or beadwork trim) varied from village to village. The cut of parkas also changed from north to south.

The work parka was worn with the skin on the outside and the fur inside. Work parkas were meant to be serviceable, not beautiful. Often worn with pants made from skins, they provided excellent protection from the cold. These parkas usually used a secondhand worn ruff. Very poor persons did not have ruffs on their parkas at all, and if a person owned a parka without a ruff, he or she was given a ruff to use. When that person died, the ruff was cut off the parka and returned to the original owner.

A fancy parka, reserved for special occasions, used the skin of the male ground squirrel, which produces large gray pelts. These decorated parkas had intricate fancywork with wolverine tassels and trims

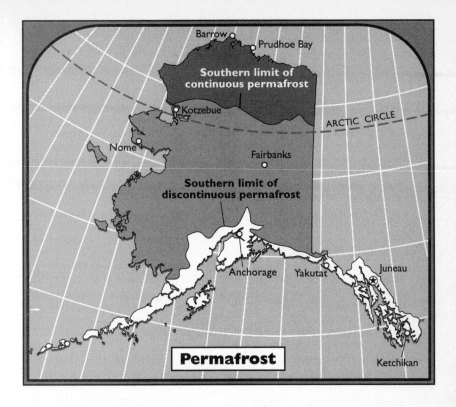

Southern limit of
continuous permafrost

Barrow

Prudhoe Bay

ARCTIC CIRCLE

Kotzebue

Nome

Fairbanks

Southern limit of
discontinuous permafrost

Anchorage   Yakutat   Juneau

Permafrost

Ketchikan

and were topped with a wide wolf ruff, made in layers so the ruff stood out from the face. The fancy parka had furs inside and out. Wealth was judged by the quality of a wearer's best parka.

The Aleut rain parka was made from *oogruk* (bearded seal) intestine. Instead of a fur ruff around the face of the hood, the rain parka had a folded *oogruk* piece which served as a sinew drawstring casing.

Eskimos used many animals skins for parkas including seal, reindeer, caribou and ground squirrel. Wolf and wolverine were prized for ruffs. Also used to make parkas were skins from the wolf fish and bird skins—leaving the feathers on the outside—including those of murre, cormorants and diving fish ducks.

Permafrost
Permafrost is defined as ground that remains frozen for two or more years. In its continuous form,

permafrost underlies the entire Arctic region to depths of 2,000 feet. In broad terms, continuous permafrost occurs north of the Brooks Range and in the alpine region of mountains, including those of the Lower 48.

Discontinuous permafrost occurs south of the Brooks Range and north of the Alaska Range. Much of the Interior and parts of southcentral Alaska are underlain by discontinuous permafrost.

Permafrost affects many buildings and natural bodies. It influences construction in the Arctic because building on it may cause the ground to thaw and if the ground is ice-rich, structures will sink. Arctic and subarctic rivers typically carry 55 percent to 65 percent of the precipitation that falls onto their watersheds, roughly 30 percent to 40 percent more than rivers of more temperate climates. Consequently, northern streams are prone to flooding and carry high silt loads. Permafrost is responsible for the thousands of shallow lakes dotting the arctic tundra because groundwater is held on the surface.

A tunnel excavated in permafrost near Fox, north of Fairbanks, during the early 1960s is maintained cooperatively by the University of Alaska Fairbanks and the U.S. Army Cold Regions Research and Engineering Laboratory. One of the few such tunnels in the world, it offers unique research opportunities on a 40,000-year-old accumulation of sediments and ice.

The tunnel is open to the public from June 1 through Aug. 31 each year, by appointment only, through the CRREL office.

Permanent Fund

In 1976, state voters approved a constitutional amendment to establish the Alaska Permanent Fund. This provides that a percentage of all mineral lease rentals, royalties, royalty sales proceeds, federal mineral revenue-sharing payments and bonuses be placed in a permanent fund. Essentially a trust fund for all Alaskans, money in the principal must be invested and cannot be spent without a vote of the people. Income from the permanent fund is available for appropriation by the legislature.

In 1980, the legislature established a permanent fund dividend payment program that provides distribution of approximately one-half of the fund's earnings (interest dividends and capital gains) among the people of Alaska. Eligible residents were to receive a $50 dividend for each year of residency since 1959. The U.S. Supreme Court declared the 1980 program unconstitutional on the grounds that it discriminated against short-term residents, and in 1982 a new state program was signed into law. Under that plan, an initial $1,000 dividend was paid to applicants who had lived in the state for at least six months prior to applying. Since then, dividends have been distributed each year to every resident who applies by March 31 and qualifies. The amount is decided by adding together the fund's net income for the last five years, multiplying that number by 21 percent, and dividing that number in half.

If Alaska's permanent fund were a Fortune 500 company, it would rank in the top 3 percent in terms of net income. It is one of the 75 largest pools of money in the country, and the only fund that pays dividends to residents. In 1999, the permanent fund produced more net income for the state than unrestricted oil revenues. In fiscal 1999, the permanent fund earned $2.5 billion, growing to a value of $26.4 billion, and paid record dividends of $1,769.84. Its total rate of return was 9.49 percent, bolstered by a 19 percent return on its U.S. stock investments, which comprised 36 percent of total allocations.

Pioneers' Homes

The first pioneers' home was established

in Sitka in 1913 for "indigent prospectors and others who have spent their years in Alaska." Of the thousands of stampeders who came north between 1896 and 1900, 933 men and women submitted applications. However the home was not open to women until 1950; upon statehood in 1959, it was opened to Natives.

Currently six state-supported pioneers' homes offer assisted-living care for some 600 older Alaskans. The homes offer a range of service levels, providing assistance with activities of daily living, intermittent health care and recreation depending upon residents' needs, with an emphasis on care of individuals with Alzheimer's disease and related disorders. Applicants must be 65 years of age or older, must have lived continuously in Alaska for one year immediately preceding application, must have a need for the services provided in the homes and, if able, must pay rent established by the Department of Administration.

For additional information about pioneers' homes, contact the Director of the Division of Alaska Longevity Programs, P.O. Box 110211, Juneau 99811-0211; (907) 465-4400.

Sitka Pioneers' Home

Anchorage Pioneers' Home, 923 W. 11th Ave., Anchorage 99501; (907) 276-3414.

Fairbanks Pioneers' Home, 2221 Eagan Ave., Fairbanks 99701; (907) 456-4372.

Juneau Pioneers' Home, 4675 Glacier Highway, Juneau 99801; (907) 780-6422.

Ketchikan Pioneers' Home, 141 Bryant, Ketchikan 99901; (907) 225-4111.

Palmer Pioneers' Home, 250 E. Fireweed, Palmer 99645; (907) 745-4241.

Sitka Pioneers' Home, 120 Katlian St., Sitka 99835; (907) 747-3213.

Pipeline
The trans-Alaska oil pipeline designer, builder and operator is Alyeska Pipeline Service Co., which previous to the April 2000 merger between BP-Amoco and ARCO was a consortium of seven oil companies:

BP Pipelines (Alaska), Inc., 50.01 percent

ARCO Transportation Alaska, Inc., 22.29 percent

Exxon Pipeline Co., 20.34 percent

Mobil Alaska Pipeline Co., 3.08 percent

Amerada Hess Pipeline Corp., 1.5 percent

Phillips Alaska Pipeline Corp., 1.42 percent

Unocal Pipeline Co., 1.36 percent

The new make-up of consortium numbers and percentages were not available at press time.

Pipeline length: 800 miles; slightly less than half that length is buried, the remainder is on 78,000 above-ground supports, located 60 feet apart and built in a flexible zigzag pattern. There are more than 800 river and stream crossings. Normal burial of pipe was used in stable soils and rock; above-ground pipe—insulated and jacketed—was used in thaw-unstable permafrost areas.

Thermal devices prevent thawing around vertical supports. The pipeline has 151 stop-flow valves.

Pipe: Specially manufactured coated pipe with zinc anodes installed to prevent corrosion. Size is 48 inches in diameter, with thickness from 0.462 to 0.562 inch.

Cost: $8 billion, which includes terminal at Valdez but excludes interest on money raised for construction.

Amount of oil pumped through pipeline: At the end of 1999, 13.8 billion barrels of crude oil. The current flow represents about 15 percent of the total U.S. oil production. At any one moment, there are about 9 million barrels of oil in the line.

Operations: Control center at Valdez terminal and 11 operating pump stations along the line monitor and control pipeline.

Pipeline throughput: An average of 1.15 million barrels a day in early 1999.

Estimated crude oil reserves recoverable on the North Slope: Approximately 3.6 billion barrels as of early 1999.

Terminal: 1,000-acre site at Port Valdez, northernmost ice-free harbor in the United States, with 18 tanks providing storage capacity of 9.2 million barrels of oil.

Valdez ship-loading capacity: 110,000 barrels an hour for each of three berths; 80,000 barrels per hour for one berth.

Length and cost of pipeline haul road built by Alyeska: 360 miles, from the Yukon River to Prudhoe Bay; $150 million.

Yukon River bridge: First bridge (2,290 feet long) to span the Yukon in Alaska.

Important dates: July 1968, Prudhoe Bay oil field discovery confirmed; **1970**, lawsuits filed to

Anchorage's population of 4,000 Canada geese produce an incredible 16,920 pounds of droppings per day, and everyone has an opinion on goose excrement. In one day, the migratory bird biologist in charge of the city's goose problem was called both a "goose murderer" and "a sop to the animal rights activists." When your area of expertise is goose poop, your self esteem is going to suffer.

The trans-Alaska oil pipeline 15 miles south of Livengood in the late 1970s. From *Alaska's History* by Harry Ritter.

halt construction, Alyeska Pipeline Service Co. formed; **Nov. 16, 1973,** presidential approval of pipeline legislation; **April 29, 1974,** construction begins on North Slope Haul Road (now the Dalton Highway) and is completed 154 days later; **March 27, 1975,** first pipe installed at Tonsina River; **June 20, 1977,** first oil leaves Prudhoe Bay, reaches Valdez terminal July 28; **Aug. 1, 1977,** first tanker load of oil shipped aboard the SS *ARCO Juneau*; **June 13, 1979,** tanker number 1,000 (SS *ARCO Heritage*) sails; **July 15, 1983,** 3 billionth barrel of oil leaves pump station; **Sept. 15, 1986,** 5 billionth barrel of oil leaves pump station; **Feb. 16, 1988,** 6 billionth barrel arrives at the marine terminal; **May 2, 1988,** *Chevron Mississippi* is 8,000th tanker to load crude oil at marine terminal; **March 24, 1989,** *Exxon Valdez* tanker runs aground after departing the marine terminal and spills more than 11 million gallons of North Slope crude into Prince William Sound; **Dec. 28, 1992,** *ARCO California,* 12,000th tanker to load; **March 1994,** 10 billionth barrel is pumped from the North Slope into the pipeline; **April 1996,** 22,000-gallon spill from defective valve.

Joint Pipeline Office: Because of concerns about spills from and corrosion of the trans-Alaska oil pipeline, the Joint Pipeline Office was established in 1990. The office is composed of nine state and federal regulatory and management agencies. Each agency has responsibilities either for issuing permits or for monitoring the operation and environmental safety of any and all pipelines operating in Alaska.

State agencies represented in the office include the Department of Natural Resources, the Department of Environmental Conservation, the Department of Fish and Game, and the Office of the Governor, Division of Governmental Coordination.

Place Names

Alaska has a rich international heritage of place names. Throughout the state, names of British (Barrow), Spanish (Valdez), Russian (Kotzebue), French (La Perouse), American (Fairbanks) and Native Alaskan (Sitka) origin dot the map. Some Alaska place names are quite common. There are about 70 streams called Bear Creek in Alaska (not to mention Bear Bay, Bear Bluff, Bear Canyon, Bear Cove and Bear Draw) and about 50 called Moose Creek. Many place names have an unusual history. Moose Pass is said to derive its name from a 1903 incident when a mail carrier driving a dog team had difficulty gaining the right-of-way from a large moose.

Poisonous Plants

(*SEE ALSO* MUSHROOMS) Alaska has few poisonous plants, compared to the number of species growing here. Nonetheless, some extremely poisonous plants thrive. Baneberry *(Actaea rubra),* water hemlock *(Cicuta douglasii* and *C. mackenzieana),* fly agaric mushroom *(Amanita muscaria),* monkshood *(Aconitum* species) and false hellebore *(Veratrum* species) are the most dangerous. Be sure you have properly identified plants before harvesting for food.

Alaska has no poison ivy or poison oak, found in almost all other states, but our cow parsnip produces a photo-reactive chemical which can cause blisters and burns.

Political Parties

A recognized political party in Alaska is an organized group that represents a political program and either nominates a candidate for governor who received at least 3 percent of the total votes cast for governor in the preceding general election, or has registered enough voters to equal 3 percent of the votes cast for governor in the last election. Until it qualifies as a political party under this definition, an independent political group may field candidates for statewide and districtwide offices by filing nominating petitions.

Alaska's six political parties are:

Alaskan Independence Party, Chairman Mark Chryson, P.O. Box 70007, Fairbanks 99707; (907) 376-8285.

Democratic Party of Alaska, State Chair Christopher Cook, P.O. Box 200445, Anchorage 99520; (907) 344-9888.

Green Party of Alaska, Chairman Soren Wuerth, 3180 Amber Bay Loop, Anchorage 99515; (907) 274-7336

Libertarian Party, Chairman Len Karpinski, (907) 248-4367.

Republican Moderate Party, Chairman Ray Metcalfe, (907) 344-4514.

Republican Party of Alaska, Chairman Tom McKay, 1001 W. Fireweed Lane, Anchorage 99503; (907) 276-4467.

Populations and Zip Codes

According to the Alaska Department of Labor and Workforce Development, many areas of Alaska gained population in the past decade.

Between 1990 and 1997, Alaska's population increased by 11 percent, compared to a 4.7 percent increase in the U.S. population. The greatest overall growth occurred in Anchorage which accounted for 42 percent of the state's population in 1999. Only the Yakutat Borough lost population over the 1990–94 period.

Populations for cities and communities in the following lists are taken from the Alaska Department of Labor figures for July 1, 1999. Entries lacking zip codes are communities without a U.S. post office. Population numbers also are available online at www.labor.state.ak.us/research/pop/pop.htm.

(NA=Not Available)

The 2000 Anchorage Telephone Book caused a flap when the cover photo was found to be a composite of Mount Hunter (150 miles north) and Bird Point (30 miles south.) This continued a tradition from 1987 when the phone book cover presented the Anchorage coastline with vivid blue water instead of the usual mucky brownish-gray. At that time, an Anchorage Telephone Utility spokesman said, "We're going to make our city beautiful, one way or another."

Community	Year Incorporated	Population	Zip
Adak Station	1972	106	96505
Akhiok (AH-key-ok)	1972	101	99615
Akiachak (ACK-ee-a-chuck)	—	560	99551
Akiak (ACK-ee-ack)	1970	338	99552
Akutan (ACK-oo-tan)	1979	408	99553
Alakanuk (a-LACK-a-nuk)	1969	658	99554
Aleknagik (a-LECK-nuh-gik)	1973	187	99555
Alexander	—	39	99695
Allakaket (alla-KAK-it)	1975	187	99720
Ambler	1971	286	99786
Anaktuvuk Pass (an-ak-TOO-vuk)	1957	314	99721
Anchor Point	—	1,227	99556
Anchorage (municipality)*	1920	259,391	99510
Eastchester Station	—	—	99501
Fort Richardson	—	—	99505
Elmendorf Air Force Base	—	—	99506
Mountain View	—	—	99508
Spenard Station	—	—	99509
Downtown Station	—	—	99510
South Station	—	—	99511
Alyeska Pipeline Company	—	—	99512
Federal Building	—	—	99513
Anderson	1962	517	99744
Angoon	1963	576	99820
Aniak (AN-ee-ack)	1972	604	99557
Annette	—	45	99926
Anvik	1969	93	99558
Arctic Village	—	138	99722
Atka	1988	105	99502
Atmautluak (at-MAUT-loo-ack)	1976; dissolved 1996	296	99559
Atqasuk	1983	274	99791
Attu Coast Guard Station	—	24	99502
Auke Bay	—	NA	99821
Barrow	1959	4,438	99723
Beaver	—	126	99724
Bethel	1957	5,471	99559
Bettles City	1985	26	99726
Big Delta	—	511	99737
Big Lake	—	2,162	99652
Birch Creek	—	35	99790
Brevig Mission	1969	279	99785
Buckland	1966	428	99727
Butte	—	2,699	NA
Cantwell	—	166	99729
Cape Yakataga	—	NA	99574
Central	—	62	99730
Chalkyitsik (chawl-KIT-sik)	—	102	99788
Chase	—	55	NA
Chefornak (cha-FOR-nack)	1974	416	99561

*Includes Eklutna

Community	Year Incorporated	Population	Zip
Chenega	—	69	99574
Chevak	1967	763	99563
Chickaloon	—	212	99674
Chicken	—	17	99732
Chignik	1983	103	99564
Chignik Lagoon	—	68	99565
Chignik Lake	—	136	99564
Chiniak	—	75	99548
Chistochina	—	52	99615
Chitina (CHIT-nah)	—	94	99566
Chuathbaluk (chew-ATH-ba-luck)	1975	105	99557
Chugiak (CHOO-gee-ack)	—	*	99567
Circle	—	89	99733
Circle Hot Springs	—	35	NA
Clam Gulch	—	113	99568
Clarks Point	1971	68	99569
Clear	—	NA	99704
Coffman Cove	1989	228	99950
Cohoe	—	602	99669
Cold Bay	1982	71	99571
Coldfoot	—	18	99701
College	—	12,122	99708
Cooper Landing	—	285	99572
Copper Center	—	553	99573
Copperville	—	194	NA
Cordova**	1909	2,435	99574
Covenant Life	—	67	NA
Craig	1922	2,136	99921
Crooked Creek	—	137	99575
Crown Point	—	91	NA
Cube Cove	—	139	99850
Deadhorse	—	2	99734
Deering	1970	148	99736
Delta Junction	1960	889	99737
Denali National Park	—	NA	99755
Dillingham	1963	2,302	99576
Diomede (DY-o-mede)	1970	136	99762
Dot Lake	—	101	99737
Douglas	1902	NA	99824
Dry Creek	—	115	NA
Dutch Harbor	1942	NA	99692
Eagle	1901	152	99738
Eagle River	—	*	99577
Eagle Village	—	32	NA
Edna Bay	—	55	99825
Eek	1970	281	99578
Egegik (EEG-gah-gik)	1985	117	99579
Eielson Air Force Base	—	4,751	99702
Ekwok (ECK-wok)	1974	125	99580

*The population of Chugiak–Eagle River is counted as one unit, with 28,600 residents.
**Includes Eyak since 1993

Community	Year Incorporated	Population	Zip
Elfin Cove	—	50	99825
Elim (EE-lum)	1970	306	99739
Emmonak (ee-MON-nuk)	1964	818	99581
Ester	—	240	99725
Evansville	—	24	99726
Fairbanks (city)	1903	31,697	9970–
Main Office	—	—	99701
Eielson Air Force Base	—	4,751	99702
Fort Wainwright	—	—	99703
Main Office Boxes	—	—	99706
Downtown Station	—	—	99707
College Branch	—	—	99708
Salcha	—	—	99714
False Pass	1990	48	99583
Ferry	—	74	NA
Flat	—	12	99584
Fort Greely	—	635	99790
Fort Wainwright	—	—	99703
Fort Yukon	1959	570	99740
Fox	—	332	99712
Fox River	—	439	NA
Fritz Creek	—	2,097	99603
Gakona (ga-KOH-na)	—	22	99586
Galena (ga-LEE-na)	1971	563	99741
Gambell	1963	668	99742
Game Creek	—	50	NA
Girdwood	—	NA	99587
Glennallen	—	494	99588
Gold Creek	—	NA	99695
Golovin (GAWL-uh-vin)	1971	141	99762
Goodnews Bay	1970	256	99589
Grayling	1969	184	99590
Gulkana	—	90	99586
Gustavus (ga-STAY-vus)	—	377	99826
Haines	1910	1,775	99827
Halibut Cove	—	71	99603
Hamilton	—	0	NA
Happy Valley	—	401	99950
Harding Lake	—	30	99714
Healy	—	646	99734
Healy Lake	—	61	NA
Hobart Bay	—	48	99850
Hollis	—	111	99950
Holy Cross	1968	247	99602
Homer	1964	4,154	99603
Hoonah	1946	877	99829
Hooper Bay	1966	1,028	99604
Hope	—	130	99605
Houston	1966	836	99694
Hughes	1973	61	99745

The Changing Faces of Anchorage

The minority population in Alaska's largest city is growing quickly and the number is projected to jump within the next decade from one in four to nearly one in three, notes Anchorage statistician Sue Fison. The number of Hispanics has increased nearly four times faster than that of whites since 1990. The growth rate for Asians is more than twice that of whites.

Natives and African Americans each accounted for about 7 percent of Anchorage's population in 1995. Asians, primarily Filipino, Korean and Japanese, made up 5.7 percent of the city's population. Hispanics are estimated to represent about 5.4 percent of Anchorage's population, says Fison. Anchorage's minority population is smaller proportionately and significantly different than that of the rest of the United States; The largest minority group in Anchorage is Native Americans, who account for less than 1 percent of the nation's population.

These population changes are likely to play a larger role in the city's future, Fison says. Some impacts are already clear; Retailers have altered their stocks to reflect the population, devoting space to Asian and Hispanic foods, for example. Other impacts are evolving as minority communities form a political presence. ✴

Community	Year Incorporated	Population	Zip
Huslia (HOOS-lee-a)	1969	272	99746
Hydaburg	1927	369	99922
Hyder	—	126	99923
Icy Bay	—	NA	99695
Iguigig	—	62	99613
Iliamna (ill-ee-YAM-nuh)	—	93	99606
Indian	—	NA	99540
Ivanof Bay	—	29	99502
Jakolof Bay (Red Mountain)	—	40	99603
Juneau (city/borough)	1900	30,189	99801
Main Office	—	—	99801
Main Office Boxes	—	—	99802
Mendenhall Station	—	—	99803
State Government Offices	—	—	99811
Kachemak (CATCH-a-mack)	1961	419	99603
Kake	1952	745	99830
Kaktovik (kack-TOE-vik)	1971	259	99747
Kalifonsky	—	338	99669
Kalskag	1975	NA	99607
Kaltag	1969	254	99748
Karluk	—	41	99608
Kasaan (Ka-SAN)	1976	48	99924
Kasigluk (ka-SEEG-luk)	1982; dissolved 1996	528	99609
Kasilof (ka-SEE-loff)	—	548	99610
Kasitsna Bay	—	NA	99695
Kenai (KEEN-eye)	1960	7,005	99611
Kenny Lake	—	507	99695
Ketchikan	1900	8,320	99901
Kiana (Ky-AN-a)	1964	398	99749
King Cove City	1947	691	99612

Community	Year Incorporated	Population	Zip
King Salmon	—	499	99613
Kipnuk (KIP-nuck)	—	573	99614
Kivalina	1969	366	99750
Klawock (kla-WOCK)	1929	673	99925
Klukwan	—	136	99827
Knik	—	483	99687
Kobuk	1973	94	99751
Kodiak	1940	6,893	99615
U.S. Coast Guard Station	—	1,831	99619
Kokhanok (KO-ghan-ock)	—	163	99606
Koliganek (ko-LIG-a-neck)	—	205	99576
Kongiganak (kon-GIG-a-nuck)	—	359	99559
Kotlik	1970	579	99620
Kotzebue (KOT-sa-bue)	1958	2,932	99752
Koyuk	1970	280	99753
Koyukuk (KOY-yuh-kuck)	1973	101	99754
Kupreanof (ku-pree-AN-off)	1975	24	99833
Kwethluk (KWEETH-luck)	1975	698	99621
Kwigillingok (kwi-GILL-in-gock)	—	360	99622
Lake Minchumina (min-CHOO-min-a)	—	38	99757
Larsen Bay	1974	137	99624
Lazy Mountain	—	1,109	NA
Levelock (LEH-vuh-lock)	—	131	99625
Lignite	—	131	NA
Lime Village	—	62	99627
Loring	—	NA	99950
Lower Kalskag	1969	310	99626
Lutak	—	53	NA
Manley Hot Springs	—	88	99756
Manokotak (man-a-KO-tack)	1970	399	99628
Marshall	1970	318	99585
McCarthy	—	37	99588
McGrath	1975	423	99627
McKinley Park	—	169	99755
Meadow Lakes	—	5,232	NA
Mekoryuk (ma-KOR-ee-yuk)	1969	193	99630
Mendeltna	—	80	NA
Mentasta Lake	—	125	99780
Metlakatla	1944	1,472	99926
Meyers Chuck	—	30	99903
Minto	—	248	99758
Moose Creek	—	677	99705
Moose Pass	—	118	99631
Mosquito Lake	—	94	NA
Mountain Village	1967	766	99632
Naknek (NACK-neck)	—	624	99633
Nanwalek (formerly English Bay)	—	170	99695
Napakiak (NAP-uh-keey-ack)	1970	363	99634
Napaskiak (na-PASS-kee-ack)	1971	406	99559
Naukati Bay	—	164	99950

Community	Year Incorporated	Population	Zip
Nelson Lagoon	—	87	99571
Nenana (nee-NA-na)	1921	348	99760
New Stuyahok (STU-ya-hock)	1972	475	99636
Newhalen	1971	178	99606
Newtok	1976; dissolved 1997	284	99559
Nightmute	1974	230	99690
Nikiski	—	3,038	99635
Nikolaevsk	—	488	99556
Nikolai	1970	105	99691
Nikolski	—	39	99638
Ninilchik (Nin-ILL-chick)	—	687	99639
Noatak (NO-uh-tack)	—	423	99761
Nome	1901	3,615	99762
Nondalton	1971	224	99640
Noorvik	1964	632	99763
North Pole	1953	1,616	99705
Northway	—	113	99764
Northway Junction	—	116	NA
Northway Village	—	103	NA
Nuiqsut (noo-IK-sut)	1975	486	99789
Nulato	1963	381	99765
Nunapitchuk (NU-nuh-pit-CHUCK)	1982	471	99641
Old Harbor	1966	276	99643
Olga Bay	—	NA	99697
Ophir	—	NA	99695
Oscarville	—	64	99695
Ouzinkie (oo-ZINK-ee)	1967	256	99644
Palmer	1951	4,151	99645
Paxson	—	30	99737
Pedro Bay	—	36	99647
Pelican	1943	137	99832
Perryville	—	102	99648
Petersburg	1910	3,415	99833
Pilot Point	1992	77	99649
Pilot Station	1969	544	99650
Pitkas Point	—	146	99658
Platinum	1975	43	99651
Pleasant Valley	—	584	NA
Point Baker	—	51	99927
Point Hope	1966	794	99766
Point Lay	—	217	99759
Polk Inlet	—	16	NA
Port Alexander	1974	86	99836
Port Alice	—	4	99950
Port Alsworth	—	88	99653
Port Clarence	—	22	99762
Port Graham	—	178	99603
Port Heiden	1972	125	99549
Port Lions	1966	243	99550
Port Protection	—	50	99950

Community	Year Incorporated	Population	Zip
Portage Creek	—	18	NA
Primrose	—	62	NA
Prudhoe Bay	—	47	99734
Quinhagak (QUIN-a-gak)	1975	595	99655
Rampart	—	66	99767
Red Devil	—	44	99656
Red Dog	—	55	NA
Ridgeway	—	2,382	NA
Rowan Bay	—	0	99850
Ruby	1973	184	99768
Russian Mission	1970	311	99657
St. George	1983	143	99591
St. Marys/Andreafsky	1967	475	99658
St. Michael	1969	381	99659
St. Paul	1971	673	99660
Salamatof	—	1,122	99611
Salcha	—	387	99714
Sand Point	1966	842	99661
Savoonga (suh-VOON-guh)	1969	653	99769
Saxman	1930	371	99901
Scammon Bay	1967	484	99662
Selawik (SELL-a-wick)	1977	767	99770
Seldovia	1945	284	99663
Seward	1912	3,010	99664
Shageluk (SHAG-a-look)	1970	140	99665
Shaktoolik (shack-TOO-lick)	1969	218	99771
Sheldon Point	1974	149	99666
Shishmaref (SHISH-muh-reff)	1969	556	99772
Shungnak (SHOONG-nack)	1967	255	99773
Sitka (City)	1963/1971	8,681	99835
Skagway	1900	825	99840
Skwentna	—	72	99667
Slana	—	55	99586
Sleetmute	—	103	99668
Soldotna	1967	4,140	99669
South Naknek	—	132	99670
Stebbins	1969	524	99671
Sterling	—	6,138	99472
Stevens Village	—	92	99774
Stony River	—	35	99557
Sutton	—	470	99674
Takotna (Tah-KOAT-nuh)	—	48	99675
Talkeetna (Tal-KEET-na)	—	363	99676
Tanacross	—	86	99776
Tanana (TAN-a-nah)	1961	301	99777
Tatitlek	—	105	99677
Telida	—	2	99695
Teller	1963	266	99778
Tenakee Springs	1971	93	99841
Tetlin	—	89	99779

Community	Year Incorporated	Population	Zip
Thorne Bay	1982	582	99919
Togiak (TOE-gee-yack)	1969	841	99678
Tok (TOKE)	—	1,235	99780
Toksook Bay	1972	513	99637
Tonsina	—	47	99573
Trapper Creek	—	344	99683
Tuluksak (tu-LOOK-sack)	1970; dissolved 1997	443	99679
Tuntutuliak (TUN-too-TOO-li-ack)	—	350	99680
Tununak	1975; dissolved 1997	331	99681
Twin Hills	—	76	99576
Two Rivers	—	660	99716
Tyonek (ty-O-neck)	—	160	99682
Ugashik	—	8	99695
Unalakleet (YOU-na-la-kleet)	1974	805	99684
Unalaska (UN-a-LAS-ka)	1942	4,178	99685
Upper Kalskag/Kalskag	1975	261	NA
Valdez (val-DEEZ)	1901	4,164	99686
Venetie (VEEN-a-tie)	—	232	99781
Wainwright	1962	545	99782
Wales	1964	170	99783
Wasilla (wah-SIL-luh)	1974	5,213	99687
Whale Pass	—	62	99950
White Mountain	1969	197	99784
Whitestone Logging Camp	—	118	NA
Whittier	1969	280	99693
Willow	—	507	99688
Wiseman	—	20	99790
Womens Bay	—	675	NA
Wrangell	1903	2,549	99929
Yakutat (YAK-a-tat)	1948/1992	729	99689

Last year's combined commercial and sport harvests of pink salmon, chinook salmon, chum salmon, sockeye salmon, coho salmon, and pollock in Alaska totalled 1,299,951,857 fish! If they were laid end to end, they would stretch 403,883 miles! The line would go around the earth 16.25 times, or to the moon and 69 percent of the way back! And I caught *six feet* of 'em!

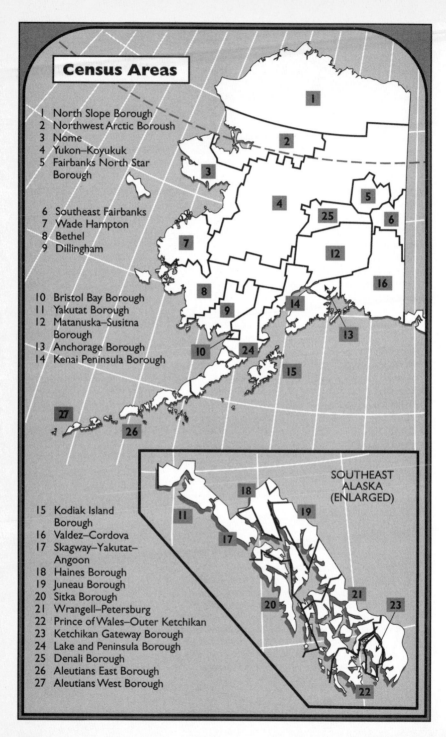

Census Areas

1 North Slope Borough
2 Northwest Arctic Boroush
3 Nome
4 Yukon–Koyukuk
5 Fairbanks North Star
   Borough

6 Southeast Fairbanks
7 Wade Hampton
8 Bethel
9 Dillingham

10 Bristol Bay Borough
11 Yakutat Borough
12 Matanuska–Susitna
    Borough
13 Anchorage Borough
14 Kenai Peninsula Borough

15 Kodiak Island
    Borough
16 Valdez–Cordova
17 Skagway–Yakutat–
    Angoon
18 Haines Borough
19 Juneau Borough
20 Sitka Borough
21 Wrangell–Petersburg
22 Prince of Wales–Outer Ketchikan
23 Ketchikan Gateway Borough
24 Lake and Peninsula Borough
25 Denali Borough
26 Aleutians East Borough
27 Aleutians West Borough

SOUTHEAST
ALASKA
(ENLARGED)

Population by Census Areas

Key	Census Area	1970	1980	1990	1999
	Alaska	302,583	401,851	550,043	622,000
1	North Slope Borough	3,451	4,199	5,979	7,413
2	Northwest Arctic Borough	4,048	4,831	6,113	6,873
3	Nome Census Area	5,749	6,537	8,288	9,311
4	Yukon–Koyukuk	7,045	6,471	6,681	6,372
5	Fairbanks North Star Borough	45,864	53,983	77,720	83,773
6	Southeast Fairbanks	4,308	5,676	5,913	6,283
7	Wade Hampton	3,917	4,665	5,791	7,060
8	Bethel	8,917	10,999	13,656	16,167
9	Dillingham	2,510	3,232	4,012	4,731
10	Bristol Bay Borough	1,147	1,094	1,410	1,258
11	Yakutat Borough	385	563	705	729
12	Matanuska–Susitna Borough	6,509	17,816	39,683	55,694
13	Anchorage Municipality	126,385	174,431	226,338	259,391
14	Kenai Peninsula Borough	16,586	25,282	40,802	48,952
15	Kodiak Island Borough	9,409	9,939	13,309	13,989
16	Valdez–Cordova Census Area	4,979	8,348	9,952	10,333
17	Skagway–Yakutat–Angoon	2,792	3,478	4,385	3,541
18	Haines Borough	1,401	1,680	2,117	2,475
19	Juneau Borough	13,556	19,528	26,751	30,189
20	Sitka Borough	6,073	7,803	8,588	8,681
21	Wrangell–Petersburg	4,920	6,167	7,042	7,137
22	Prince of Wales–Outer Ketchikan	3,782	3,822	6,278	6,589
23	Ketchikan Gateway Borough	10,041	11,316	13,828	13,961
24	Lake and Peninsula Borough	1,362	1,384	1,668	1,791
25	Denali Borough	NA	1,402	1,792	1,871
26	Aleutians East Borough	1,301	1,643	2,464	2,151
27	Aleutians West Census Area	6,533	6,125	9,478	5,285

Source: Alaska Department of Labor, July 1, 1999

Growth of Alaska's Major Cities

City	1900	1920	1940	1950	1970	1980	1999**
Anchorage*	NA	1,856	4,229	11,254	48,081	174,431	259,391
Barrow	NA	NA	NA	NA	2,104	2,207	4,438
Cordova	NA	955	938	1,165	1,164	1,879	2,435
Fairbanks	NA	1,155	3,455	5,771	14,771	22,645	31,697
Juneau	1,864	3,058	5,729	5,956	6,050	19,528	30,189
Kenai	290	332	303	321	3,533	4,324	7,005
Ketchikan	459	2,458	4,695	5,305	6,994	7,198	8,320
Kodiak	341	374	864	1,710	3,798	4,756	6,893
Nome	12,488	852	1,559	1,876	2,357	2,301	3,615
Petersburg	NA	879	1,323	1,619	2,042	2,821	3,415
Seward	NA	652	949	2,114	1,587	1,843	3,010
Sitka	1,396	1,175	1,987	1,985	6,075	7,803	8,681
Valdez	315	466	529	554	1,005	3,079	4,164
Wrangell	868	821	1,162	1,263	2,029	2,184	2,549

*Includes Eklutna
**Source: Alaska Department of Labor, Research and Analysis Section, July 1, 1999

Potlatch

Potlatch This Native gathering, primarily an Indian custom, is held to commemorate major life events. Traditional Native foods are served, songs and dances are performed and gifts are distributed to attendees. A funeral potlatch might include the giving away of the deceased's possessions to relatives or to those who had shown kindness to the deceased.

Before the U.S. and Canadian governments outlawed the practice in the 1880s, potlatches were a focal point of Native society. The host family might give away all its possessions to demonstrate its wealth to the guests. Each guest in turn would feel obliged to hold an even more sumptuous potlatch. The outlawing of potlatches resulted in the disintegration of many aspects of Native culture. Potlatch restrictions were repealed in 1951.

Radio Stations

Radio Stations Alaska's radio stations broadcast a variety of music, talk shows, and religious and educational programs. Many radio stations in Alaska also broadcast personal messages, long a popular and necessary form of communication in Alaska—especially in the Bush. To accommodate these messages—and radio's unique role in providing vital weather information to fishermen and hunters—the United States and Canada agreed to grant some Alaska radio stations international communication status. The "clear channel" status provides protection against interference from foreign broadcasters. Personal messages are heard on:

Anchorage, KYAK's Bush Pipeline
Barrow, KBRW's Tundra Drum
Bethel, KYUK's Tundra Drums
Dillingham, KDLG's Bristol Bay Messenger
Fairbanks, KIAK's Pipeline of the North
Galena, KIYU's Yukon Wireless
Glennallen, KCAM's Caribou Clatter
Haines, KHNS's Listener Personals
Homer, KBBI's Bay Bush Lines
Ketchikan, KRBD's Muskeg Messenger; KTKN's Public Service Announcements
Kodiak, KVOK's Highliner Crabbers
Kotzebue, KOTZ's Messages
McGrath, KSKO's Messages
Nome, KICY's Ptarmigan Telegraph; KNOM's Hot Lines
North Pole, KJNP's Trapline Chatter
Petersburg, KFSK's Muskeg Messages; KRSA's Channel Chatters
Sitka, KCAW-FM's Muskeg Messages
Soldotna, KSRM's Tundra Tom Tom
Wrangell, KSTK-FM's Radiograms

Statewide. APRN, 810 E. Ninth Ave., Anchorage 99501.
Bush Radio Network, Box 91941, Anchorage 99509.

Anchorage. KADX-FM 94.7 MHz; 2509 Ide St., 99503.
KAFC-FM 93.7 MHz; P.O. Box 210389, 99521.
KASH 1080 kHz; 3601 C St., Suite 290, 994503.
KASH-FM 107.5 MHz; 800 E. Dimond Blvd., Suite 3-370, 99515.
KATB-FM 89.3 MHz; P.O. Box 210389, 99521.
KAXX 1020 kHz; 2509 Ide St., 99503.
KBFX-FM 100.5 MHz; 800 E. Dimond Blvd., Suite 3-320, 99515.
KBRJ-FM 104.1 MHz; 9200 Lake Otis Pkwy., 99507.

Money magazine's annual survey tries to find the best place to live in the U.S. The weather category contains a subcategory, "the number of days with *some* sunshine." Even 1 or 2 minutes a day counts as *some* sunshine. Of the 300 largest cities in the U.S., Anchorage was rated number 300.

KBYR 700 kHz; 1007 W. 32nd Ave., 99503.

KEAG-FM; KOOL-FM 97.3 MHz; 9200 Lake Otis Pkwy., 99507.

KENI 650 kHz; 800 E. Dimond Blvd., Suite 3-320, 99515.

KFAT-FM 92.9 MHz; 11259 Tower Road, 99515.

KFQD 750 kHz; **KWHL-FM** 106.5 MHz; 9200 Lake Otis Pkwy., 99507.

KGOT-FM 101.3 MHz; 800 E. Dimond Blvd., Suite 3-370, 99515.

KHAR 590 kHz; 9200 Lake Otis Pkwy., 99507.

KKRO-FM 102.1 MHz; 11259 Tower Road, 99515.

KLEF-FM 98.1 MHz; 3601 C St., Suite 290, 99503.

KMXS-FM 103.1 MHz; 9200 Lake Otis Pkwy., 99507.

KNBA-FM 90.3 MHz; 818 E. Ninth Ave., 99501-3826.

KNIK-FM 105.3 MHz; 907 E. Dowling Road, Suite 24, 99518.

KQEZ-FM 92.1 MHz; 11259 Tower Road, 99515.

KRPM-FM 96.3 MHz; 11259 Tower Road, 99515.

KRUA-FM 88.1 MHz; 3211 Providence Drive, 99508.

KSKA-FM 91.1 MHz; 3877 University Drive, 99508.

KTZN 550 kHz; 800 E. Dimond Blvd., Suite 3-370, 99515.

KYMG-FM 98.9 MHz; 800 E. Dimond Blvd., Suite 3-370, 99515.

Barrow. KBRW 680 kHz; **KBRW-FM** 91.9 MHz; P.O. Box 109, 99723.

Bethel. KYKD-FM 100.1 MHz; P.O. Box 2428, 99559.

KYUK 640 kHz; Pouch 468, 99559.

Chevak. KCUK 88.1 kHz; 985 KSD Way, 99563.

Cordova. KCDV-FM 100.9 MHz; Box 60, 99574.

KLAM 1450 kHz; P.O. Box 60, 99574.

Dillingham. KDLG 670 kHz; P.O. Box 670, 99576.

KRUP 99.1 MHz; P.O. Box 157, 99576.

Fairbanks. KAKQ-FM 101.1 MHz; 546 Ninth Ave., 99701.

KCBF 820 kHz; **KXLR-FM** 95.9 MHz; 1060 Aspen St., 99709.

KFAR 660 kHz; **KWLF-FM** 98.1 MHz; P.O. Box 70910, 99707.

KIAK 970 kHz; **KIAK-FM** 1025 MHz; 546 Ninth Ave., Suite 200, 99701.

KSUA-FM 91.5 MHz; P.O. Box 750113, 99775-0113.

KUAC-FM 89.9 MHz; University of Alaska, P.O. Box 755620, 99775-5620.

KUWL-FM 103.9 MHz; P.O. Box 70910, 99707.

KWLF-FM 98.1 MHz; P.O. Box 70910, 99707.

Fort Yukon. KZPA-FM 900 MHz; P.O. Box 50, 99740.

Galena. KIYU 910 kHz; P.O. Box 165, 99741.

Glennallen. KCAM 790 kHz; P.O. Box 249, 99588.

Haines/Klukwan/Skagway. KHNS-FM 102.3 MHz; P.O. Box 1109, Haines 99827.

Homer. KBBI 890 kHz; 3913 Kachemak Way, 99603.

KGTL 620 kHz; **KWVV-FM,** 103.5 MHz; P.O. Box 109, 99603.

KPEN-FM 101.7 MHz; P.O. Box 109, 99603.

KWVV-FM 103.5 MHz; P.O. Box 109, 99603.

Juneau. KINY 800 kHz; 1107 W. Eighth St., Suite 2, 99801.

KJNO 630 kHz; 3161 Channel Drive, Suite 2, 99801.

KSUP-FM 106.3 MHz; 107.9 kHz; 1107 W. Eighth Ave., Suite 2, 99801.

KTKU-FM 105.1 MHz; 3161 Channel Drive, Suite 2, 99801.

KTOO-FM 104.3 MHz; 360 Egan Drive, 99801.

Kenai. KDLL 91.9 kHz; Box 2111, 99611.
  KPEN-FM 101.7 MHz; P.O. Box 109, Homer 99603.
  KZXX 980 kHz; 6672 Kenai Spur Road, 99611.

Ketchikan. KFMJ 99.9 kHz; 516 Stedman St., 99901.
  KGTW-FM 106.7 MHz; 526 Stedman St., 99901.
  KRBD-FM 105.9 MHz; 123 Stedman St., 99901.
  KTKN 930 kHz; **KGTW-FM** 106.7 MHz; 526 Stedman St., 99901.

Kodiak. KMXT-FM 100.1 MHz; 620 Egan Way, 99615.
  KRXX-FM 101.1 MHz; P.O. Box 708, 99615.
  KVOK 560 kHz; P.O. Box 708, 99615.

Kotzebue. KOTZ 720 kHz; P.O. Box 78, 99752.

McCarthy. KXKM-FM 89.7 MHz; P.O. Box 467, Valdez 99686.

McGrath. KSKO 870 kHz; P.O. Box 70, 99627.

Naknek. KAKN-FM 100.9 MHz; P.O. Box 214, 99633.

Nenana. KIAM 630 kHz; P.O. Box 474, 99760.

Nome. KICY 850 kHz; **KICY-FM** 100.3 MHz; P.O. Box 820, 99762-0820.
  KNOM 780 kHz; P.O. Box 988, 99762.

North Pole. KJNP 1170 kHz; **KJNP-FM** 100.3 MHz; P.O. Box 56359, 99705.

Petersburg. KFSK-FM 100.9 MHz; P.O. Box 149, 99833.
  KRSA 580 kHz; P.O. Box 650, 99833.

St. Paul. KUHB-FM 91.9 MHz; P.O. Box 905, 99660.

Sand Point. KSDP 830 kHz; P.O. Box 328, 99661.

Seward. KSWD 950 kHz; **KPFN-FM** 105.9 MHz; P.O. Box 230004, 99523.

Sitka. KCAW-FM 104.7 MHz; 2-B Lincoln St., 99835.
  KIFW 1230 kHz; **KSBZ-FM** 103.1 MHz; 611 Lake St., 99835.

Soldotna. KKIS-FM, 96.5 MHz; HC2, P.O. Box 852, 99669.
  KSLD 1140 kHz; HC2, P.O. Box 852, 99669.
  KSRM 920 kHz; **KWHQ-FM** 100.1 MHz; HC2, P.O. Box 852, 99669.

Talkeetna. KTNA-FM, 88.5 MHz; P.O. Box 300, 99676.

Unalakleet. KNSA 930 kHz; P.O. Box 178, 99684.

Valdez. KCHU 770 kHz; P.O. Box 467, 99686.
  KVAK 1230 kHz; P.O. Box 367, 99686.

Wasilla. KMBQ-FM 99.7 MHz; 851 E. Westpoint, Suite 212, 99654.

Whittier. KCHU-FM 88.3 MHz; P.O. Box 467, Valdez 99686.

Wrangell. KSTK-FM 101.7 MHz; P.O. Box 1141, 99929.

Yakutat. KJFP-FM 103.9 MHz; P.O. Box 388, 99689.

Railroads (SEE ALSO SKAGWAY)

The Alaska Railroad is the northernmost railroad in North America and was for many years the only one owned by the federal government. Ownership has been transferred to the state. The ARR rolls on 470 miles of mainline track from the ports of Seward and Whittier to Anchorage, Cook Inlet and Fairbanks in the Interior.

The Alaska Railroad began in 1912

when Congress appointed a commission to study transportation problems in Alaska. In March 1914, the president authorized railroad lines in the territory of Alaska to connect open harbors on the southern coast of Alaska with the Interior. The Alaska Engineering Commission surveyed railroad routes in 1914 and, in April 1915, President Woodrow Wilson announced the selection of a route from Seward north 412 miles to the Tanana River (where Nenana is now located), with branch lines to Matanuska coal fields. The main line was later extended to Fairbanks. Construction of the railroad began in 1915 from a wilderness construction camp on Cook Inlet. Almost overnight, a tent city of 2,000 sprang up and Anchorage was born.

On July 15, 1923, President Warren G. Harding drove in the golden spike at Nenana, signifying completion of the railroad.

The railroad offers year-round passenger and freight service. The ARR features flag-stop service along the Anchorage-to-Fairbanks corridor, as well as summer express trains to Denali National Park and Preserve and beyond to Fairbanks. Passenger service is daily between mid-May and mid-September, and in winter weekly service is available between Anchorage and Fairbanks. One-day excursions between Anchorage, Seward and Whittier are provided daily, mid-May to early September. In 1999, a record 672,000 passengers rode the Alaska Railroad. For more information contact the Alaska Railroad, P.O. Box 107500, Anchorage 99510; (800) 544-0552; www.alaskarailroad.com.

The privately owned White Pass & Yukon Route provided a narrow-gauge link between Skagway, Alaska, and Whitehorse, Yukon. When it was built—1898 to 1900—it was the farthest north any railroad had operated in North America. The railway maintained one of the steepest railroad grades in North America, climbing to 2,885 feet at White Pass in only 20 miles of track.

The White Pass & Yukon Route provided both passenger and freight service until 1982, when it suspended service until 1988. Currently, the route provides daily passenger service only. Contact the White Pass & Yukon Route, P.O. Box 435, Skagway 99840, or call toll free (800) 343-7373. E-mail: info@whitepass.net or check the WP&YR Web page at www.whitepassrailroad.com.

Regions of Alaska

(SEE MAP, PAGES 8–9)

Southeast. Southeast, Alaska's panhandle, stretches approximately 500 miles from Icy Bay, northwest of Yakutat, to Dixon Entrance at the U.S.–Canada border beyond the southern tip of Prince of Wales Island. Massive ice fields, glacier-scoured peaks and steep valleys, more than a thousand named islands and numerous unnamed islets and reefs characterize this vertical world where few flat expanses break the steepness. Spruce, hemlock and cedar cover many mountainsides and are harvested as timber.

Average temperatures range from 50°F to 60°F in July and from 20°F to 40°F in January. Average annual precipitation varies from 80 inches to more than 200 inches. The area receives from 30 inches to 200 inches of snow in the lowlands and more than 400 inches in the high mountains.

The region's economy revolves around fishing and fish processing, timber and tourism. Mining has increased with development of a world-class molybdenum mine near Ketchikan.

Airplanes and boats are principal means of transportation. Only three communities in Southeast are connected to the road system: Haines, via the Haines Highway to the Alaska Highway at Haines Junction; Skagway, via Klondike Highway 2 to the Alaska Highway; and Hyder, to the continental road system via the Cassiar Highway in British Columbia. Juneau, on the Southeast mainland, is the state capital; Sitka, on Baranof Island, was the capital of Russian America.

Southcentral/Gulf Coast. The Southcentral/Gulf Coast region curves 650 miles north and west of Southeast to Kodiak Island. About two-thirds of the state's residents live in the arc between the Gulf of Alaska on the south and the Alaska Range on the north, the region commonly called Southcentral. On the region's eastern boundary, only the Copper River valley breaches the mountainous barrier of the Chugach and St. Elias Mountains. On the west rise lofty peaks of the Aleutian Range. Within this mountainous perimeter course the Susitna and Matanuska Rivers.

The irregular plain of the Copper River lowland has a colder climate than the other major valley areas. The January average for Kenny Lake is –2°F. The January average for the Talkeetna airport is 10°F. July temperatures average 50°F to 60°F in the region.

Regional precipitation ranges from a scant 17 inches annually in drier areas to more than 76 inches a year at Thompson Pass in the coastal mountains.

Vegetation varies from the spruce-hemlock forests of Prince William Sound to mixed spruce and birch forests in the Susitna Valley to tundra in the highlands of the Copper River–Nelchina Basin.

Alaska agriculture historically has been most thoroughly developed in the Matanuska Valley. The state's dairy industry is centered there and at a project at Point MacKenzie, across Knik Arm from Anchorage. Vegetables thrive in the area, which is well known for its giant cabbages.

Hub of the state's commerce, transportation and communications is Anchorage, on a narrow plain at the foot of the Chugach Mountains, and bounded by Knik Arm and Turnagain Arm, offshoots of Cook Inlet. The population of Alaska's largest city is closely tied to shifts in the state's economy.

Alaska's major banks, oil companies and the Alaska Railroad have headquarters in Anchorage. The city's port handles most of the shipping in and out of the state. Valdez, to the east of Anchorage on Prince Willam Sound, is the southern terminal of the trans-Alaska oil pipeline, which transports oil from Prudhoe Bay on the North Slope.

Interior. Great rivers have forged a broad lowland, known as the Interior, in the central part of the state between the Alaska Range on the south and the Brooks Range on the north. The Yukon River carves a swath across the entire state. In the Interior, the Tanana, Porcupine, Koyukuk and several other rivers join with the Yukon to create summer and winter highways. South of the Yukon, the Kuskokwim River rises in the hills of the western Interior before beginning its meandering course across the Bering Sea coast region.

Winter temperatures in the Interior commonly drop to –50°F or colder. Ice fog sometimes hovers over Fairbanks and other low-lying communities when the temperature falls below zero. Controlled by the extremes of a continental climate, summers usually are warmer than in any other region; high temperatures can climb to 90°F. The climate is semiarid, with about 12 inches of precipitation recorded annually.

Immense forests of birch and aspen bring vibrant green and gold to the Interior's landscape. Spruce covers many of the slopes and cottonwoods thrive near river lowlands. But in northern and western reaches of the Interior, the North American taiga gives way to tundra. In highlands above tree line and in marshy lowlands, grasses and shrubs replace trees.

Gold lured the first large influx of non-Natives to Alaska's Interior. From 1903 to 1910, the largest community in the region was the booming gold-mining camp of Fairbanks. Now the city on the banks of the Chena River is a transportation and supply center for eastern and northern Alaska. The main campus of the University of Alaska overlooks the city.

About 100 miles east of Fairbanks, farmers at the Delta project work to build a foundation for agriculture based on barley. At Healy, southwest of Fairbanks, the state's only operating coal mine produces coal used to generate electricity for the Interior. The rest of the Interior relies primarily on a subsistence economy, sometimes combined with a cash economy where fishing or seasonal government jobs are available.

Arctic. Beyond the Brooks Range, more than 80,000 square miles of tundra interlaced with meandering rivers and countless ponds spread out along the North Slope. In far northwestern Alaska, the Arctic curves south to take in Kotzebue and other villages of the Kobuk and Noatak River drainages.

Short, cool summers and temperatures only between 30°F and 40°F allow the permanently frozen soil to thaw just a few inches. Winter temperatures range well below zero but the Arctic Ocean moderates temperatures in coastal areas. Severe winds sweep along the coast and through mountain passes. Cold and wind often drop the chill-factor temperature far below the actual temperature. Most areas receive less than 10 inches of precipitation a year but

Small boy with king salmon, early 1920s. From *Alaska's History* by Harry Ritter.

the terrain is wet in summer because of little evaporation and frozen ground.

Traditionally the home of Inupiat Eskimos, the Arctic was inhabited by few non-Natives until oil was discovered at Prudhoe Bay in the 1960s. Today the region's economy is focused on Prudhoe Bay and neighboring Kuparuk oil fields. Petroleum-related jobs support most of the region's residents. Subsistence hunting and fishing fill any economic holes left by the oil industry.

The largest Inupiat Eskimo community in the world, Barrow is the center of commerce and government activity for the region. Airplanes, the major means of transportation, fan out from there to the region's far-flung villages.

The Dalton Highway, formerly called the North Slope Haul Road, connects the Arctic with the Interior. The 416-mile road is

The *Wall Street Journal* ranked Juneau with Chernobyl as one of the world's worst vacation destinations. About the same time, an internet list of "Official mottos of Alaskan cities" claimed that Juneau's slogan was "Who Says Government Stiffs and Slackjaw Yokels Don't Mix?"

open to the public all the way to Deadhorse. Permits are no longer required to drive the highway. (*See* Dalton Highway)

Western/Bering Sea Coast. Western Alaska extends along the Bering Sea coast from the Arctic Circle south to where the Alaska Peninsula joins the mainland near Naknek on Bristol Bay. Home of Inupiat and Yup'ik Eskimos, the region centers around the immense Yukon–Kuskokwim River Delta, the Seward Peninsula to the north and Bristol Bay to the south.

Summer temperatures range from about 30°F to about 60°F. Winter readings generally range from just above zero to near 30°F. Wind chill lowers temperatures considerably. Total annual precipitation is about 20 inches; northern regions are drier.

Much of the region is covered with tundra, although a band of forest covers the hills on the eastern end of the Seward Peninsula and Norton Sound. In the south near Bristol Bay the tundra once again gives way to forests. In between the marshy flatland of the great Yukon–Kuskokwim Delta spreads out for more than 200 miles.

Gold first attracted non-Natives to the hills and creeks of the Seward Peninsula. To the south, only a few anthropologists and wildlife biologists entered the world of the Yup'ik Eskimos of the delta. At the extreme south, the world's largest sockeye salmon run drew fishermen to the riches of Bristol Bay.

The villages of western Alaska are linked by air and water, dogsled and snow-machine. Commerce on the delta radiates from Bethel, largest community in western Alaska. To the north, Nome dominates commerce on the Seward Peninsula, while several fishing communities rely on the riches of Bristol Bay.

Southwestern/Alaska Peninsula and Aleutians. Southwestern Alaska includes the Alaska Peninsula and Aleutian Islands. From Naknek Lake, the peninsula

By Any Other Name . . .

The name Alaska is probably an abbreviation of Unalaska, derived from the original Aleut word agunalaksh, which means "the shores where the sea breaks its back."

—Corey Ford,
Where the Sea Breaks Its Back ✦

curves southwest about 500 miles to the first of the Aleutian Islands; the Aleutians continue south and west more than 1,000 miles. Primarily a mountainous region with about 50 volcanic peaks, only on the Bering Sea side of the peninsula does the terrain flatten out.

More than 200 islands, roughly 5,500 square miles in area, form the narrow arc of the Aleutians, which separate the North Pacific from the Bering Sea. Nearly the entire chain is in the Alaska Maritime National Wildlife Refuge. Unimak Island, closest to the Alaska Peninsula mainland, is 1,000 miles from Attu, the most distant island. Five major island groups make up the Aleutians, all of which are treeless except for a few scattered stands that have been transplanted.

The Aleutian climate is cool. Summer temperatures range to about 50°F and winter readings reach 20°F or colder. Winds are almost constant and fog is common. Precipitation ranges from 21 inches to more than 80 inches annually. The peninsula's climate is somewhat warmer than the islands' in summer and cooler in winter.

Aleuts, original inhabitants of the chain, still live at Atka, Atka Island; Nikolski, Umnak Island; Unalaska, Unalaska Island; Akutan, Akutan Island; and False Pass, Unimak Island.

The quest for furs first drew Russians to the islands and peninsula in the 1700s. The traders conquered the Aleuts and forced them to hunt marine mammals. After the United States purchased Alaska in 1867, fur traders switched their efforts to fox farming. Many foxes were turned loose on the islands, where they flourished and destroyed native wildlife. With the collapse of the fur market in the 1920s and 1930s, the islands were left to themselves. This relative isolation was broken during World War II when Japanese military forces bombed Dutch Harbor and landed on Attu and Kiska Islands. The United States military retook the islands, and after the war the government resettled Aleuts living in the western Aleutians to villages in the eastern Aleutians, closer to the mainland.

Today fishing provides the main economic base for the islands and the peninsula. Many Aleuts go to Bristol Bay or Unalaska to fish commercially in summer.

Religion

Nearly every religion practiced in American society is found in Alaska. Anchorage alone has nearly 200 churches and temples. Following is a list of addresses for some of the major ones:

Alaska Baptist Convention, 1750 O'Malley Road, Anchorage 99516.

Alaska Moravian Church, Bethel 99559.

Anchorage Friends Church (Native), 1227 E. 75th Ave., Anchorage 99503.

Assemblies of God District Council, 1048 W. International Airport Road, Anchorage 99502.

Baha'i Faith, 13501 Brayton Drive, Anchorage 99516.

Christian Church of Anchorage, 8050 Old Seward Hwy., Anchorage 99518.

Christian House of Prayer Alaska, 3721 E. 84th Ave., Anchorage 99502.

Christian Science Church, 1347 L St., Anchorage 99501.

Church of God, 1711 S. Bragaw St., Anchorage 99508.

Church of Jesus Christ of Latter-day Saints, 13111 Brayton Drive, Anchorage 99516.

Congregation Beth Sholom, 7525 E. Northern Lights Blvd., Anchorage 99504.

Episcopal Diocese of Alaska, 1205 Denali Way, Fairbanks 99701.

Evangelical Lutheran Church of America, 1847 W. Northern Lights Blvd., Anchorage 99502.

Islamic Center of Alaska, 5630 Silverado Way, Anchorage 99518.

Jehovah's Witnesses, 2301 Strawberry Road, Anchorage 99507.

Lubavitch Jewish Center of Alaska, Congregation Shomrei Ohr, 1210 E. 26th Ave., Anchorage 99508.

Orthodox Church, Diocese of Alaska, Chancery, 513 E. 24th Ave., Anchorage 99504.

Presbyterian Churches, 616 W. 10th Ave., Anchorage 99501.

Roman Catholic Arch-diocese of Anchorage, 225 Cordova, Anchorage 99501.

Salvation Army, 726 E. Ninth Ave., Anchorage 99501.

Trinity Christian Reformed Church, 3000 E. 16th Ave., Anchorage 99508.

United Methodist Church, Alaska Missionary Conference, 3402 Wesleyan Drive, Anchorage 99508.

Unity of Anchorage, 10821 Totem Road, Anchorage 99516.

Reptiles

For all practical purposes, reptiles are not found in Alaska outside of captivity. The northern limits of North American reptilian species may be the latitude at which their embryos fail to develop during the summer. Three sightings of a species of garter snake, *Thamnophis sirtalis,* have been reported on the banks of the Taku River and Stikine River.

Rivers

(SEE ALSO NATIONAL WILD AND SCENIC RIVERS *AND* YUKON RIVER) There are more than 3,000 rivers in Alaska. The 10 longest are:

Yukon River— 1,400 miles in Alaska; the remainder is in Canada.

Porcupine River— 555 miles. The Porcupine is a major tributary of the Yukon River.

During the year 2000, wildlife experts announced that porcupines float in water, owls are the only birds who can see the color blue, and polar bears are left-handed. To top it off, *dumblaws.com* proclaimed that it is illegal in Alaska to push a live moose out of a moving airplane.

Rafting on Tatshenshini-Alsek River, Glacier Bay National Park and Preserve. Photo by Karen Jettmar, author of *The Alaska River Guide.*

Koyukuk—554 miles
Kuskokwim—540 miles
Tanana—531 miles
Innoko—463 miles
Colville—428 miles
Noatak—396 miles
Kobuk—396 miles
Birch Creek—314 miles

The major navigable Alaska inland waterways are:

Chilkat—Navigable by shallow-draft vessels to village of Klukwan, 25 miles above mouth.

Kobuk—Controlling channel depth is about 5 feet through Hotham Inlet, 3 feet to Ambler and 2 feet to Kobuk Village, about 210 river miles.

Koyukuk—Navigable to Allakaket by vessels drawing up to 3 feet during normally high river flow and to Bettles during occasional higher flows.

Kuskokwim—Navigable (June 1 to September 30) by 18-foot-draft ocean-going vessels from mouth upriver 65 miles to Bethel. Shallow-draft (4-foot) vessels can ascend river to mile 465. McGrath is at mile 400.

Kvichak—The river is navigable for vessels of 10-foot draft to Alaganak River, 22 miles above the mouth of Kvichak River. Remainder of this river (28 miles) navigable by craft drawing 2 feet to 4 feet, depending on the stage of the river. Drains into Lake Iliamna, which is navigable an additional 70 miles.

Naknek—Navigable for vessels of 12-foot draft for 12 miles with adequate tide. Vessels with 3-foot draft can continue an additional 7.5 miles.

Noatak—Navigable (late May to mid-June) for shallow-draft barges to a point about 18 miles below Noatak village. Shallow-draft vessels can continue on to Noatak.

Nushagak—Navigable (June 1 to August 31) by small vessels of 2½-foot draft to Nunachuak, about 100 miles above the

Glacial Flour

Glacial rivers, such as the Knik River near Anchorage and the Nenana River of the Interior, appear milky from their heavy loads of silt, or "glacial flour," released into the river from melting glaciers. Fish live in the cloudy rivers, but usually move into clearer water to spawn. A Nenana River riverboat captain likes to say that glacial rivers are too dry to drink and too wet to plow.   —Susan Ewing, *The Great Alaska Nature Factbook* ✷

mouth. Shallow-draft, oceangoing vessels can navigate to mouth of Wood River at mile 84.

Porcupine—Navigable to Old Crow, Yukon Territory, by vessels drawing 3 feet, during spring runoff and fall rain floods.

Stikine—Navigable (May 1 to Oct. 15) from mouth 165 miles to Telegraph Creek, British Columbia, by shallow-draft, flat-bottom riverboats.

Susitna—Navigable by stern-wheelers and shallow-draft, flat-bottom riverboats to confluence of Talkeetna River, 75 miles upstream, but boats cannot cross bars at mouth of river. Not navigable by ocean-going vessels.

Tanana—Navigable by shallow-draft (4-foot), flat-bottom vessels and barges from the mouth to Nenana and by smaller river craft to the Chena River 201 miles above the mouth. Craft of 4-foot draft can navigate to Chena River on high water to University Avenue Bridge in Fairbanks.

Yukon—Navigable (June 1 to Sept. 30) by shallow-draft, flat-bottom riverboats from the mouth to near the head of Lake Bennett. It cannot be entered or navigated by oceangoing vessels. Controlling depths are 7 feet to Stevens Village and 3 feet to 5 feet from there to Fort Yukon.

Roadhouses

An important part of Alaska history, roadhouses were modest quarters that offered bed and board to travelers along early-day Alaska trails. Because most travel was done in winter, many roadhouses provided accommodations for sled dog teams. By 1920, there were roadhouses along every major transportation route in Alaska. Most roadhouses have vanished though a few of the historic roadhouses survive, including Gakona Lodge on the Glenn Highway, Paxson Lodge at the junction of the Richardson and Denali Highways, and Talkeetna Roadhouse. The Cape Nome Roadhouse was a major stopover for dog teams and also served as a temporary orphanage. Several roadhouses are included in the National Register of Historic Places. Some historic roadhouses are now museums or occupied by businesses.

Rocks and Gems (SEE ALSO GOLD; JADE; AND MINERALS AND MINING)

Gemstones are not easy to find in Alaska. Rockhounds must hunt for them and often walk quite a distance. The easiest specimens to collect are float-rocks scattered by glaciation. These rocks are found on ocean beaches and railroad beds, and in creeks and rivers all over Alaska. In most rock-hunting areas, every instance of high water, wind, heavy rain and a melting patch of snow and ice uncovers a new layer, so you can hunt in the same area and make new finds.

The easiest gemstones to search out are in the crypto-crystalline group of quartz minerals. These gems have crystals not visible to the naked eye. They are the jaspers, agates, cherts and flints.

Thunder eggs, geodes and agatized wood (all in the chalcedony classification) occur in Alaska. Thunder eggs have a jasper rind enclosing an agate core; harder-to-find geodes usually have an agate rind with a hollow core filled with crystals; agatized

199

and petrified woods come in various colors and often show the plant's growth rings. Sometimes even the bark or limb structure is visible on agatized and petrified woods.

Crystalline varieties of quartz can also be found: amethyst (purple), citrine (yellow), rose quartz (pink), rock crystal (clear) and smoky quartz (brown).

Other gems to search for in Alaska are onyx, feldspar, porphyry, jade, serpentine, soapstone, garnet, rhodonite, sapphire, marble, staurolite, malachite and covelite (blue copper).

Russian Alaska (SEE ALSO BARANOV, ALEXANDER; BERING, VITUS; HISTORY; SEWARD, WILLIAM H.; AND VENIAMINOV, IOANN) Russian presence in Alaska began with the 1741 voyages of Vitus Bering and Alexei Chirikov. Their exploration of the Aleutian Islands and the Alaska mainland spurred dozens of voyages by Russian fur entrepreneurs, or *promyshlenniki*. By the mid-1800s, Russians had explored most of the coast of southern and southwestern Alaska and some of the Interior. Their interest in Alaska lay primarily in exploiting the rich fur resources of the region, especially sea otters and fur seals. In 1799, the Russian post known today as Old Sitka was established. That same year, a trade charter was granted to the Russian-American Company, a monopoly authorized by the czar in 1790 to control activities in Alaska.

During the entire Russian period, from 1741 to 1867, there were rarely more than about 500 Russians in Alaska at any one time. Nevertheless, the Aleut, Eskimo and Indians whom the Russians encountered felt the devastating effects of foreign contact. Native populations declined drastically from introduced diseases. The population of the Aleut people, the first to succumb to Russian occupation, was reduced to less than 20 percent of the precontact level through warfare, disease and starvation. The Tlingit, Haida and Chugach may have been reduced by 50 percent. The Russians also brought to the new land their customs, religion and language, which, through subjugation and the efforts of Orthodox missionaries, brought great changes in traditional technologies, social patterns and religious beliefs.

In 1867, facing increasing competition and frustrated in its efforts to expand, the Russians sold Alaska to the United States for $7.2 million.

One of the foremost legacies of the Russian period is the Russian Orthodox Church, still a vital aspect of Native culture in Southwest, Southcentral and Southeast Alaska. Visitors to Kenai, Kodiak, Sitka and smaller Native communities will see the familiar onion-shaped domes of the Russian Orthodox churches.

Russian Christmas

Russian Christmas is the Russian Orthodox observance of the birth of Christ. It begins on January 7—Twelfth Night, 12 days after Dec. 25.

The holiday, called *Selavi,* is celebrated for seven days, with church services including songs in Slavonic, fireworks and special foods. Part of the tradition involves carrying a star from house to house, caroling, and sharing food and small gifts.

Russian Christmas is observed in cities and towns with Orthodox parishes, such as Akutan, Anchorage, Dillingham, Eklutna, Juneau, Kenai, Kodiak, Lower Kalskag, Naknek, New Stuyahok, Newhalen, Ninilchik, Nushagak, Pedro Bay, St. Paul, St. George, Seldovia and Sitka.

School Districts (SEE ALSO EDUCATION) Alaska's 53 public school districts served 133,047 pre-elementary through 12th grade students in the 1999–2000 school year. There are two types of districts: city and borough school districts and Regional Educational Attendance Areas (REAA). The 34 city and borough school districts are located in municipalities, each contributing funds for the operation of its local schools. City and borough school districts are supported by 65.6 percent state, 26.7 percent local and 7.7 percent federal funding.

The 19 REAAs are in the unorganized boroughs and have no local government to contribute funds to their schools. The REAAs are almost solely dependent upon state funds for school support.

Alaska's total education payroll for 1999 was $788 million—rivaling oil as the state's payroll leader. The statewide average annual wage for classroom teachers was $38,850.

The Alyeska Central School, Alaska Department of Education, 3134 Channel Drive, No. 100, Juneau 99801-7897, provides courses by correspondence to students in grades K–12.

Names and addresses of Alaska's public school districts are available from the Department of Education in Juneau.

Seward Located on Resurrection Bay, on the east coast of the Kenai Peninsula, Seward lies 127 miles south of Anchorage by road or 35 minutes by plane. Population is about 3,000.

The city is named for U.S. Secretary of State William H. Seward, who was instrumental in negotiating the purchase of Alaska from Russia. The city of Seward was founded in 1902 by surveyors for the Alaska Railroad as the ocean terminus of the railroad.

Resurrection Bay is a year-round ice-free harbor, and Seward is an important cargo and fishing port. The Alaska state ferry and many cruise ships call here. The economy of the town is based on tourism, a coal terminal, fisheries and government

offices. Visitors enjoy wildlife and glacier tours, sportfishing expeditions, kayaking, photography safaris, nature cruises, RV parking, hotels, dozens of bed-and-breakfast establishments, art galleries, coffeehouses, canoeing and hiking.

Attractions in the area include Exit Glacier (accessible by trail), Kenai Fjords National Park (set aside in 1980) and Chugach National Forest. From puffins to oystercatchers to bald eagles, more than 100 species of birds abound. Substantial numbers of marine mammals inhabit or migrate through Seward's coastal waters, including sea otters, Steller sea lions, dolphins and Pacific gray whales.

Attractions unveiled in 1998 include the Alaska SeaLife Center and the Chugach Heritage Center.

For information about Kenai Fjords National Park, call (907) 224-3175. Consult the Chamber of Commerce at (907) 224-8051. Web site: www.seward.net/chamber.

Seward, William H.

(*SEE ALSO* RUSSIAN ALASKA) William H. Seward, the man who negotiated the purchase of Alaska from Russia, was born in New York in 1801. He was admitted to the bar in 1822 and eventually became governor of New York for two terms (declining a third). Seward returned to his law practice until 1849, when he was elected to the United States Senate and served for two terms. In 1860 Seward was a candidate for the presidential nomination, but failing to receive it, he then supported Lincoln, whose cabinet he entered as secretary of state, a position he held from 1861 to 1869.

Due to the rapidly declining fur trade and the economizing and streamlining of the St. Petersburg regime, operations such as the Russian-American Company were deemed expendable. The Grand Duke Constantine urged the sale of Alaska to the United States in 1857, but the American Civil War in 1861 forestalled talks.

At the conclusion of the war, the czar's representative began immediate negotiations with Secretary of State Seward, who was eager to buy, and a selling price of $7.2 million was agreed upon—about 2 cents an acre. The treaty was signed on March 30, 1867, and ratified by the Senate on June 20. Formal handover did not occur until October 18.

Newspaper editorials denounced the acquisition of the apparently worthless real estate, ridiculed the agreement as "Seward's folly" and caricatured Alaska as "Walrussia" and "Seward's icebox."

After leaving office in 1869, Seward traveled around the world; he visited Alaska in 1869. He died in 1872.

Shipping Vehicles. Persons
shipping vehicles between Washington and Anchorage are advised to shop around for the carrier that offers the services and rates most suited to the shipper's needs. Not all carriers offer year-round service, and freight charges vary greatly depending upon the carrier and the weight and height of the vehicle. Rates quoted here are only approximate. Sample fares per unit:

northbound, Washington to Anchorage, under 66 inches in height, $1,030; over 66 inches and under 87 inches, $1,318. Southbound, Anchorage to Washington, any unit under 84 inches, $730. Fuel surcharges and terminal handling charges may be applied.

Not all carriers accept rented moving trucks and trailers, and a few of those that do accept them require authorization from the rental company to carry its equipment to Alaska. Check with the carrier and your rental company before booking service.

Make your reservation at least two weeks in advance, and prepare to have the vehicle at the carrier's loading facility two days prior to sailing. Carriers differ on what items they allow to travel inside the vehicle, from nothing at all to goods packaged and addressed separately. Coast Guard regulations forbid the transport of vehicles holding more than one-quarter tank of gas, and none of the carriers listed allows owners to accompany their vehicles in transit. *Remember to have fresh antifreeze installed in your car or truck prior to sailing.*

At a lesser rate, you can ship your vehicle aboard a state ferry to southeastern ports. However you must accompany your vehicle or arrange for someone to drive it on and off the ferry at departure and arrival ports.

Carriers that will ship cars, truck campers, house trailers and motor homes from Anchorage to Seattle/Tacoma include:

The Alaska Railroad, P.O. Box 107500, Anchorage 99510; (907) 265-2490.

CSX Lines, 1717 Tidewater Road, Anchorage 99501; (907) 274-2671, or vehicle rates hotline (907) 263-5900.

Totem Ocean Trailer Express, 2511 Tidewater Ave., Anchorage 99501; (907) 276-5868; (800) 234-8683. In the Seattle/Tacoma area, contact:

A.A.D.A. Systems, P.O. Box 2323, Auburn, WA 98071; (206) 762-7840.

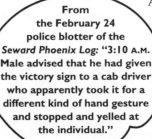

From the February 24 police blotter of the *Seward Phoenix Log:* "3:10 A.M. Male advised that he had given the victory sign to a cab driver who apparently took it for a different kind of hand gesture and stopped and yelled at the individual."

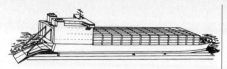

Alaska Railroad, 2203 Airport Way S., Suite 215, Seattle, WA 98134; (206) 624-4234.

CSX Lines, 3600 Port of Tacoma Road, Tacoma, WA 98424; (253) 593-1504

Totem Ocean Trailer Express, P.O. Box 24908, Seattle, WA 98124; (206) 628-4343 or (800) 426-7617 (outside Washington, Alaska and Hawaii).

Vehicle shipment between southeastern Alaska ports and Seattle is provided by:

Alaska Marine Lines, 5615 W. Marginal Way SW, Seattle, WA 98106; (206) 764-8346 or (800) 443-4343 (serves Ketchikan, Wrangell, Petersburg, Sitka, Juneau, Haines, Skagway, Yakutat, Excursion Inlet and Hawk Inlet).

Boyer Alaska Barge Line, 7318 Fourth Ave. S., Seattle, WA 98108; (206) 763-8575 (serves Ketchikan and Wrangell).

For shipping to Bush areas:

Alaska Bush Service, P.O. Box 190827, Anchorage 99519; (907) 344-6690.

Household Goods and Personal Effects. Many moving van lines have service to and from Alaska through their agency connections in most Alaska and Lower 48 cities. To initiate service, contact the van line agents nearest your starting point.

Northbound goods are shipped to Seattle and transferred through a port agent to a waterborne vessel for transportation to Alaska. Few shipments go overland to Alaska. Southbound shipments are processed in a like manner through Alaska ports to Seattle, then on to the destination.

Haul-it-yourself companies provide service to Alaska. It is possible to ship a rented truck or trailer into southeastern Alaska aboard the carriers that accept privately owned vehicles (*see* Vehicles, *preceding*). A few of the carriers sailing between Seattle and Anchorage also carry rented equipment. However shop around for this service because it has not been common practice in the past—rates can be very high if the carrier does not yet have a specific tariff established for this type of shipment. *You will not be allowed to accompany the rented equipment.*

Sitka

The town of Sitka (population 8,779), one of the most scenic of Southeast Alaska's cities, is located on the west side of Baranof Island in the shadow of Mount Edgecumbe, about 95 miles southwest of Juneau.

Tlingit Indians originally occupied the townsite until Alexander Baranov, chief manager of the Russian-American Company, built a trading post and fort in 1799 just north of their settlement. The Indians burned down the fort, and in 1804 Baranov defeated the alliance of local Tlingits, driving them from their settlement and naming the site New Archangel Bay. By 1810, New Archangel was thriving as the capital of Russian Alaska. New Archangel was later renamed Sitka, meaning "by the sea" in the Tlingit language.

Today, tourism and commercial fishing are the mainstays of the town's economy.

The climate of Sitka is mild and wet, with an annual precipitation of 95 inches and an average daily temperature of 33°F in January and 55°F in July.

Among the many sights in Sitka are Castle Hill, where Russia turned Alaska over to the United States in 1867; the Sitka pioneers' home (the first of six pioneers' homes built in Alaska); and Sitka National Historical Park, which reflects both the community's Tlingit heritage and its Russian past with two units: the Fort Site and the Russian Bishop's House. A replica of the old Russian Blockhouse, the original Russian Bishop's House (built in 1842) and the Indian Fort Site are preserved as part of the Sitka National Historical Park.

Visitors can see Sitka's historical roots in St. Michael's Cathedral, which contains priceless icons saved from fire that destroyed the cathedral in 1966. The existing structure was rebuilt from the original plans. The Sheldon Jackson Museum boasts one of the finest collections of Native arts and crafts in Alaska.

Located within walking distance from downtown Sitka is the Alaska Raptor Center, offering self-guided or guided interpretive tours. The facility treats injured birds of prey so they can return to the wild.

Annual events include the Sitka Summer Music Festival, featuring world renowned chamber music, and the Island Institute Writers' Conference in June. Alaska Day Celebration in October celebrates the transfer of Alaska from the Russians. Whale Fest, an annual celebration of Sitka's marine life, takes place the first weekend in November.

Contact the Sitka Convention and Visitors Bureau, Box 1226, Sitka 99835; (907) 747-5940, for more information.

Sitka Slippers
Also known as Alaska tennis shoes, Wrangell sneakers or Petersburg sneakers, Sitka slippers are heavy-duty rubber boots worn by residents of rainy southeastern Alaska.

Skagway (SEE ALSO CHILKOOT TRAIL)

Skagway, population 825, is found at the north end of Taiya Inlet on Lynn Canal in Southeast Alaska, about 90 air miles north of Juneau. The climate at Skagway averages 57°F in summer, 23°F in winter and the city has an annual precipitation of about 30 inches. Skagway serves as a gateway to the Alaska Highway in Southeast Alaska.

Skagway began as a gold-rush town, springing up overnight as fortune-seekers made their way from Skagway, up the White Pass and Chilkoot Trails, to the Yukon goldfields.

In July 1897, Skagway was little more

Looking Back

June 6, 1912

Darkness fell for three days on the Alaska Peninsula when the volcano named Mount Novarupta erupted, spewing 6 cubic miles of earth into the sky. Nearly 2 feet of ash fell on Kodiak, collapsing buildings and polluting water supplies.

than a tent town. Within months the town swelled to more than 20,000, with dance halls and gambling houses, saloons and residences. Frontier Skagway was once described as "hell on earth." Two years later the Klondike gold rush was over, and by 1903 Skagway's population had dwindled to 500.

Today, tourism is Skagway's main economic activity. The town serves the Alaska State Ferry and many cruise ships. More than 690,000 visitors came to Skagway during the summer of 1999.

New for 2000, the White Pass & Yukon Route railway has added a new steam engine, No. 40, from Colorado. (See also Railroads)

Visitors may walk Skagway's historical district, featuring false-fronted buildings and boardwalks of the Klondike Gold Rush National Historical Park. Other attractions include the Trail of '98 Museum and *The Days of 1898 Show with Soapy Smith*, a play that relates the history of the town in the days of one of its most notorious con men.

Prepared hikers can climb the 33-mile Chilkoot Trail, the historic route of the gold seekers over 3,739-foot Chilkoot Pass to Lake Bennett. Relics are still visible along the trail.

For more information on Skagway, consult the Skagway Convention and Visitors Bureau, P.O. Box 1025, Skagway 99840; (907) 983-2855.

Skiing
Both cross-country and downhill skiing are popular forms of outdoor recreation in Alaska from November through May. There are developed ski facilities in several Alaska communities, backcountry powder skiing is available by charter helicopter or ski-equipped aircraft, and cross-country skiing opportunities are

virtually limitless. It is also possible to ski during the summer months by chartering a plane to reach glacier skiing spots.

Several cross-country ski races are held each year. The largest, the Alaska Nordic Ski Cup Series, determines contestants for the Arctic Winter Games and Junior Olympic competitions. The series of five races is held in Anchorage, Homer, Salcha and Fairbanks. The World Masters Cross Country Ski Championships were held in Anchorage in February 1992, and Valdez is now home to the World Extreme Ski Championships in April.

In the 1992 Winter Olympics, Hilary Lindh of Juneau turned all eyes to Alaska when she won the silver medal for the downhill. Lindh's was the first individual-merit Olympic medal ever won by an Alaskan.

"Moe-mania" struck when Alaskan Tommy Moe captured the gold medal in the downhill and silver in the super-giant slalom at the 1994 Olympics in Lillehammer, Norway.

Anchorage. There are two major downhill ski areas in the Anchorage area: Alyeska Resort and Alpenglow at Arctic Valley. Alyeska Resort, 40 miles southeast of Anchorage, is the state's largest ski resort, offering five chair lifts with runs up to a mile long. Chair No. 3 is equipped for night skiing, and a fifth chair lift is reserved for racer training. The resort also has two rope tows and cross-country skiing.

The Westin Alyeska Prince Hotel, a seven-story, 300-room inn opened in 1994, includes six restaurants, an indoor pool, exercise and health facilities, and meeting rooms.

The resort features a new, high-speed gondola capable of carrying 60 passengers at a time to a restaurant high on the slopes.

Alyeska is open year-round, offering skiing from November through April and sightseeing in the summer. Hours of operation depend on daylight, except for chair No. 3.

Alpenglow, a few miles from Anchorage, is owned and operated by the Anchorage Ski Club, a nonprofit corporation. Arctic Valley is open on winter weekends and holidays. Facilities include two double chair lifts, a T-bar/Poma lift combination and three rope tows on beginner slopes.

Several smaller alpine slopes maintained by the municipality of Anchorage include: Far North Bicentennial Park; Russian Jack Springs Park, with rope tows; and Hilltop, south of town, featuring the closest chair lift to the Anchorage area.

There are several popular cross-country ski trails in the Anchorage area in city parks. These include Russian Jack Springs, with nearly 5 miles of trails, all lighted; Kincaid Park, site of the first World Cup and U.S. National races in Alaska and the United States in March 1983, with 24 miles of trails, 6 miles lighted, and a warm-up chalet; Far North Bicentennial Park, with 3 miles of trails, about 2 miles lighted; Hillside Park, with 10.8 miles of trails, 1.5 miles lighted; Tony Knowles Coastal Trail, with 9 miles of trails, none lighted; and Chester Creek Greenbelt, with 6.2 miles of trails, none lighted.

Cross-country skiers also can find trails in Chugach State Park; in Hatcher Pass north of Anchorage and in the Turnagain Pass area; in Chugach National Forest, about 57 miles south of Anchorage; and at Sheep Mountain Lodge along the Glenn Highway. Call the Nordic Skiing Association, (907) 561-0949.

Cordova. The Sheridan Ski Club operates the Mount Eyak Ski Hill about seven blocks from downtown Cordova. The season starts in December and extends until April, depending on snow.

Fairbanks. Cleary Summit and Skiland, about 20 miles from town on the Steese Highway, both privately owned and operated, have rope tows, with a chair lift at Cleary Summit; Birch Hill, located on Fort Wainwright, is mainly for military use; the University of Alaska has a small slope and rope tow; and Chena Hot Springs Resort at Mile 57 on the Chena Hot Springs Road has a small alpine ski area that uses a tractor to transport skiers to the top of the hill.

Popular cross-country ski trails in the Fairbanks area include Birch Hill recreation area, about 3 miles north of town on the Steese Expressway to a well-marked turnoff, then 2 miles in; the University of Alaska Fairbanks, with 26 miles of trails that lead to Ester Dome; Creamers Field trail near downtown; Salcha cross-country ski area, about 40 miles south of town on the Richardson Highway, with a trail system also used for ski races; Two Rivers trail area, near the elementary school at Mile 10 on the Chena Hot Springs Road; and Chena Hot Springs Resort, offering cross-country ski trails for both novice and more experienced skiers.

Kenai Peninsula. Most communities on the lower Kenai have trails or areas for skiing, including Anchor Point, Seldovia and Ninilchik. The best concentration of trails and slopes for Nordic, backcountry and downhill skiing is in the Homer area. Among them are Baycrest–Diamond Ridge, Homestead Trail, Ohlson Mountain and McNeil Canyon. Skiing on glaciers (accessible by helicopter) is possible in the Kenai Mountains across Kachemak Bay from Homer. Ski-joring (cross-country with a dog towing you) is increasingly popular in Homer.

Palmer. Hatcher Pass, site of the Independence Mine State Park, north of Palmer, is an excellent cross-country ski area with several maintained trails. The lodge has a coffee shop and warm-up area. The ski area is open from October through May.

Southeast. Eaglecrest Ski Area on Douglas Island, 12 miles from Juneau, has a 4,800-foot-long chair lift, a Platter Pull lift, a 3,000-foot-long chair lift and a day lodge. Cross-country ski trails are also available. Eaglecrest is open from November to May. A few smaller alpine ski areas are located at Cordova, Valdez, Ketchikan and Homer. All have rope tows.

Skin Sewing (SEE ALSO BEADWORK; MUKLUKS; AND PARKA) The craft of sewing tanned hides and furs was highly developed among Alaska Natives. Although commercially made garments are now often worn by Eskimo villagers, women who are exceptional skin sewers still not only ensure the safety of family members who must face the harsh outdoors, but are regarded as a source of pride for the entire community.

Sewers place great importance on the use of specific materials, some of which are only available seasonally. Winter-bleached sealskin can only be tanned during certain seasons. Blood, alder bark and red ochre are traditionally used for dyeing garments and footgear. Most sewers prefer sinew as thread although in some areas sinew cannot be obtained and waxed thread or dental floss is substituted. Skins commonly used for making parkas and mukluks include seal, reindeer, caribou and ground squirrel. Wolf and wolverine are prized for ruffs.

Parka styles, materials and ornamentation (such as pieced calfskin or beadwork trim) vary from village to village, and among Athabascan, Yup'ik, Inupiat and Siberian Yupik sewers. The cut of parkas changes from north to south.

In most regions, mukluk styles and material vary with changes in season and weather conditions. Mukluks advertise the skill of their makers and the villages where they were made.

The manufacture of moccasins and children's toys, primarily clothed dolls and intricately sewn balls, still reflects the traditional ingenuity of skin sewers.

Skookum Skookum means strong or serviceable. The word originated with the Chehalis Indians of western Washington and was incorporated into the Chinook jargon, a trade language dating from the early 1800s.

A skookum chuck is a narrow passage between a saltwater lagoon and the open sea. In many areas of Alaska, because of extreme tides, skookum chucks may resemble fast-flowing river rapids during changes of the tide.

Alaska Sourdough Starter

Sourdough is a subject of much intrigue and debate here in the North. For a true sourdough, you should rely on naturally occurring yeast and lactobacilli in your kitchen. For a quicker version of sourdough, add a packet of active dry yeast to the following recipe, but it won't be a true sourdough.

Ingredients: 2 cups all-purpose flour and 2 cups warm distilled water

Mix the two ingredients in a glass or ceramic bowl or a plastic pitcher. (Never use metal when working with yeast.) Cover with cheesecloth and let the mixture rest in a warm, draft-free place in the kitchen for 48 hours. The mixture should be the consistency of pancake batter, slightly bubbly, and sour smelling. Stir the mixture and store, covered, in the refrigerator. Makes 2 cups.

Care and Feeding of a Sourdough Starter: Once you've made a sourdough starter, you can keep it going indefinitely.

Store your starter in the refrigerator, using any covered glass, ceramic or plastic container. To use the starter, remove as much from the container as you need and let it stand at room temperature until bubbly, about 1 hour. Replenish your starter by adding equal amounts of flour and water.

Feed your starter once every two weeks to a month. Do this by adding 1 cup each of flour and water to the starter. If you need a great deal of starter, increase its volume by adding up to 10 cups of flour per cup of starter and an equal amount of water. Let stand for 48 hours.

If a liquid forms on top of the sourdough, simply stir it back in. If the liquid becomes any color besides straw yellow, discard the sourdough.

Sourdough starter can be frozen for several months. The longer it is frozen, the more likely it is that changes will occur in bacterial cell structure. To use, remove the frozen sourdough from the freezer, thaw, replenish, and keep at room temperature for 24 hours.

—Kirsten Dixon, *The Riversong Lodge Cookbook* ❊

Soapstone This soft, easily worked stone is often carved into art objects by Alaskans. Most of the stone is imported. Alaska soapstone is mined in the Matanuska Valley by blasting, a process that leaves the stone susceptible to fracture when carved.

Sourdough Carried by many early-day pioneers, this versatile, yeasty starter was used to make bread, doughnuts and hotcakes. Sourdough cookery remains popular in Alaska today. Because the sourdough supply is replenished after each use, it can remain active and fresh indefinitely. A popular claim of sourdough cooks is that their batches trace back to pioneers at the turn of the century. The name also came to be applied to any Alaska or Yukon old-timer.

Speed Limits The basic speed law in Alaska states the speed limit is "no speed more than is prudent and reasonable."

The maximum speeds are 15 miles per hour in an alley, 20 miles per hour in a business district or school zone, 25 miles per hour in a residential area and 55 miles per hour on most roadways. The speed limit on portions of the Parks and Glenn Highways is 65 miles per hour.

Locally, municipalities and the state may, and often do, reduce or alter maximums as long as no maximum exceeds 55 miles per hour.

Spruce Bark Beetle

Spruce bark beetles are cold-blooded pests that feed on the trees' phloem, nutrient tissue found under the bark. Adults are blackish brown cylinders, about ¼-inch long, bearing reddish or black wing covers. The range of *Dendroctonus rufipennis Kirby* extends from Alaska across British Columbia to Montana, Idaho and Canada's maritime provinces. The beetle has a one- to three-year life cycle and will infest all spruce species including white, black, Lutz, Sitka and Engelmann.

After the mosquito, the spruce bark beetle is the most notorious insect of the north. Over the past decade the greater Southcentral region has endured a widespread spruce beetle outbreak: Up to 3 million acres of spruce forest show the unsightly results of beetle activity. An estimated 2 billion board feet have been lost in Alaska in the past 25 years.

In the Anchorage Bowl, for example, more than 100,000 acres of forested land have seen up to 90 percent spruce mortality blamed on beetles. On the Kenai Peninsula, 30 million to 50 million trees have been lost annually since 1994. Because warmer, drier springs encourage beetles while simul-taneously placing trees under moisture stress, the meteorological effects of El Niño are considered a contributing factor. In turn, beetle-killed trees create a fire hazard as well as a windstorm hazard.

Squaw Candy

Squaw candy is salmon that has been dried or smoked for a long time until it's very chewy. The food is a staple in winter for rural Alaskans and their dogs. Contemporary terms for this food are "salmon jerky," "strips" or "salmon candy."

State Forests

Created in 1983, the 1.81-million-acre Tanana Valley State Forest is located almost entirely within the Tanana River basin and includes 200 miles of the Tanana River.

Principal tree species are paper birch, quaking aspen, balsam poplar, black spruce, white spruce and tamarack. There are many rivers, streams and lakes with significant fish, wildlife, recreation and water values. Nearly all of the land is open for mineral development. Rivers and trails throughout the river basin provide additional access. The Eagle Trail State Recreation Site is the only developed facility and has 40 camp-sites. Contact the Regional Forester, Northern Region, 3700 Airport Way, Fairbanks 99709; (907) 451-2600.

The Haines State Forst was created in 1982 and contains 270,410 acres including the watersheds of several major rivers. Topography ranges from sea level to more than 7,000 feet. Forest growth is diverse, but is dominated by western hemlock, Sitka spruce, black cottonwood and willow.

About 18 percent of the forest is dedicated to timber harvest with an annual allowable harvest of 6.96 million board feet. All logged areas have been replanted since the 1970s.

The Haines State Forest also offers recreation such as hiking, hunting, fishing, skiing and camping. Contact the Division of Forestry's Haines Area Office, P.O. Box 263, Haines 99827; (907) 766-2120.

State Park System

The Alaska State Park system began in July 1959 with the transfer of federally managed campgrounds and recreation sites from the Bureau of Land Management to the new state. Since October 1970, these sites have been managed by the Division of Parks and Outdoor Recreation.

The Alaska State Park system consists of 119 individual units divided into seven park manage-ment areas. There are

Alaskans are Number 1 in the nation in computer ownership. There is an IRS tax law question hotline on the Internet. Alaskans who logged on were told "The average response time is currently 1,462,670.5 business days." That's 5,827 YEARS!!!

SOUTHEAST AREA

1 Totem Bight SHP
2 Refuge Cove SRS
3 Settlers Cove SRS
4 Pioneer Park SRS
5 Baranof Castle SHS
6 Halibut Point SRS
7 Old Sitka SHP
8 Juneau Trail Sys. ST
9 Johnson Creek SRS
10 Wickersham SHS
11 Point Bridget SP
12 Chilkoot Lake SRS
13 Portage Cove SRS
14 Chilkat SP
15 Chilkat Bald Eagle P
16 Mosquito Lake SRS
17 Gruening SHP
18 Dall Bay SMP

19 Thom's Place SMP
20 Beecher Pass SMP
21 Joe Mace Island SMP
22 Security Bay SMP
23 Taku Harbor SMP
24 Oliver Inlet SMP
25 Funter Bay SMP
26 Shelter Island SMP
27 St. James Bay SMP
28 Sullivan Island SMP
29 Chilkat Islands SMP
30 Magoun Islands SMP
31 Big Bear/Baby Bear SMP
49 Grindall Island SMP
56 Black Sands Beach SMP
62 Eagle Beach SRA

NORTHERN AREA

32 Tok River SRS
33 Eagle Trail SRS
34 Moon Lake SRS
35 Fielding Lake SRS
36 Donnelly Creek SRS
37 Clearwater SRS
38 Delta SRS

39 Big Delta SHP
40 Quartz Lake SRA
41 Birch Lake SRS
42 Harding Lake SRA
43 Salcha River SRS
44 Chena River SRS
45 Chena River SRA
46 Upper Chatanika River SRS
47 Lower Chatanika River SRA

MAT-SU/COPPER BASIN AREA

48 Denali SP
50 Willow Creek SRA
51 Nancy Lake SRA
52 Nancy Lake SRS
53 Rocky Lake SRS
54 Big Lake North SRS
55 Big Lake South SRS
57 Kepler-Bradley Lakes SRA
58 Finger Lake SRS
59 Wolf Lake SRS
60 Independence Mine SHP
61 Summit Lake SRS
63 King Mountain SRS
64 Bonnie Lake SRS
65 Long Lake SRS
66 Matanuska Glacier SRS
67 Little Nelchina SRS
68 Lake Louise SRA
70 Dry Creek SRS
71 Porcupine Creek SRS
72 Liberty Falls SRS
73 Squirrel Creek SRS
74 Little Tonsina SRS

95 Safety Cove SMP
96 Sandspit Point SMP
97 Sunny Cove SMP
98 Thumb Cove SMP
99 Kenai River SMA
100 Caines Head SRA
102 Captain Cook SRA
103 Crooked Creek SRA
104 Kasilof River SRS
105 Johnson Lake SRA
106 Clam Gulch SRA
107 Ninilchik SRA
108 Deep Creek SRA
109 Stariski SRS
110 Anchor River SRA
111 Lowell Point SRS
112 Kachemak Bay SP&WP

KODIAK AREA

113 Fort Abercrombie SHP
114 Buskin River SRS
115 Pasagshak SRS
116 Shuyak Island SP
117 Afognak Island SP
118 Woody Island SRS

UNITED STATES
CANADA

Alaska Highway

Klondike Highway 2

Haines Highway

15 16 Skagway
12
Haines 13 11
14 28 62
29 8, 9, 10, 17
27 26 Juneau
25 23
24
4, 5, 6, 7
31 Sitka
30 20
22 Wrangell
19 1, 2, 3
21
49 Ketchikan
SOUTHEAST 56
18

(Continued from page 209)

Seal. The first governor of Alaska designed a seal for the then-District of Alaska in 1884. In 1910, Gov. Walter E. Clark redesigned the original seal, which became a symbol for the new Territory of Alaska in 1912. The constitution of Alaska adopted the territorial seal as the seal for the state of Alaska in 1959.

Represented in the state seal are icebergs, northern lights, mining, agriculture, fisheries, fur seal rookeries and a railroad. The seal is 2¹/₈ inches in diameter.

Song. *Alaska's Flag*

Eight stars of gold on a field of blue—
   Alaska's flag.
May it mean to you the blue of the sea, the
   evening sky,
The mountain lakes, and the flow'rs nearby;
The gold of the early sourdough's dreams,
The precious gold of the hills and streams;
The brilliant stars in the northern sky,
The "Bear"—the "Dipper"—and, shining
   high,
The great North Star with its steady light,
  Over land and sea a beacon bright.
Alaska's flag—to Alaskans dear,
The simple flag of a last frontier.

© University of Alaska

The lyrics were written by Marie Drake as a poem that first appeared on the cover of the October 1935 *School Bulletin,* a territorial Department of Education publication that she edited while assistant commissioner of education.

The music was written by Elinor Dusenbury, whose husband, Col. Ralph Wayne Dusenbury, was commander of Chilkoot Barracks at Haines from 1933 to 1936. Elinor Dusenbury wrote the music - several years after leaving Alaska because, she later said, "I got so homesick for

Alaska I couldn't stand it." She died Oct. 17, 1980, in Carlsbad, CA.

The Territorial Legislature adopted "Alaska's Flag" as the official song in 1955.

Other State Symbols. Bird—Willow ptarmigan, *Lagopus lagopus,* a small arctic grouse that lives among willows and on open tundra and muskeg. Its plumage changes from brown in summer to white in winter; feathers develop in winter to cover the entire lower leg and foot. Common from southwestern Alaska into the Arctic. Adopted in 1955.

Fish—King salmon (*Oncorhynchus tshawytscha),* an important part of the Native subsistence fisheries and a significant species to the state's commercial salmon fishery. This anadromous fish ranges from beyond the southern extremes of Alaska to as far north as Point Hope. Adopted in 1962.

Flower—Forget-me-not (*Myosotis alpestris).* Adopted in 1949.

Fossil—Woolly mammoth. Adopted in 1986.

Gem—Jade. Adopted in 1968. (*See* Jade)

Insect—Four-spot skimmer dragonfly. Adopted in 1995.

Land Mammal—Moose. Adopted in 1998.

Marine Mammal—Bowhead whale. Adopted in 1983. (*See* Whales and Whaling)

Mineral—Gold. Adopted in 1968. (*See* Gold)

Motto—North to the Future. Adopted in 1967.

Sport—Dog mushing. Adopted in 1972. (*See* Dog Mushing)

Tree—Sitka spruce (*Picea sitchensis),* the largest and one of the most valuable trees in Alaska. Sitka spruce grows to 160 feet in height and 3 feet to 5 feet in diameter. Its long, dark green needles surround twigs that bear cones. It is found

An otter eats 25 percent of its body weight per day. If a 100-pound adult dines on its favorite Dungeness crab at the current market price of $6.95 per pound, it would need an annual income of $63,418.75, without counting melted butter, lemon, or a delicate little Semillon blanc.

Subsistence fishermen often dry fish along a river, then store it for winter. From *The Alaska River Guide* by Karen Jettmar.

throughout Southeast and the Kenai Peninsula, along the Gulf Coast, and along the west coast of Cook Inlet. Adopted in 1962. (*See* Timber)

Subsistence (*See also*

Whales and Whaling) Alaska is unique among states in that it has established the subsistence use of fish and game as the highest-priority consumptive use. Alaska's legislature passed subsistence priority laws in 1978, 1986 and 1992. In addition, Congress passed a priority subsistence law in 1980 for federal lands in Alaska. Studies by the Alaska Department of Fish and Game have shown that many rural communities in Alaska depend upon subsistence hunting and fishing for a large portion of their diets and raw materials.

Subsistence is defined by federal law as "the customary and traditional uses by rural Alaska residents of wild, renewable resources for direct personal or family consumption as food, shelter, fuel, clothing, tools or transportation; for the making and selling of handicraft articles out of nonedible by-products of fish and wildlife resources taken for personal or family

consumption; and for the customary trade, barter or sharing for personal or family consumption."

About 44 million pounds of wild foods are harvested annually by residents of rural areas, and about 10 million pounds by urban residents. The wild food harvest is primarily fish (60 percent by weight), followed by land mammals (20 percent), marine mammals (14 percent), birds, shellfish and plants each account for 2 percent of the annual harvest. On average, rural Alaskans eat about a pound of wild food per person daily.

Rural residents may hunt and fish for subsistence on federal public lands in Alaska under federal regulations. All state residents may hunt and fish for subsistence on state lands under state regulations.

State subsistence fishing regulations are available from the Alaska Department of Fish and Game, P.O. Box 25525, Juneau 99802. State subsistence hunting regulations are included with the annually published state hunting regulations, also available from the Alaska Department of Fish and Game.

Federal subsistence hunting and fishing

regulations are available as a pamphlet from U.S. Fish and Wildlife Service, Office of Subsistence Management, 1011 E. Tudor Road, Anchorage 99503, (800) 478-1456 or (907) 786-3888.

Sundog

Sundogs are "mock suns" (parhelia) usually seen as bright, rainbow-hued spots on opposite sides of the winter sun. This optical phenomenon is created by the refraction of sunlight through tiny ice crystals suspended in the air. The ice crystals are commonly called "diamond dust."

Taiga

(SEE ALSO TUNDRA) Taiga (TIE-guh) is a moist coniferous forest that begins where the tundra ends. Taken from a Russian word that means "land of little sticks," this name is applied to the spindly white spruce and black spruce forests found in much of southcentral and interior Alaska.

Telecommunications

History. Alaska's first telecommunications project, begun in the 1860s, was designed to serve New York, San Francisco and the capitals of Europe, not particularly the residents of Nome or Fairbanks. It was part of Western Union's ambitious plan to link California to Russian America (Alaska) with an intercontinental cable that would continue under the Bering Strait to Siberia and on to Europe. Men and material were brought together on both sides of the Bering Sea, but with the first successful Atlantic cable crossing in 1867, the trans-Siberian intercontinental line was abandoned.

The first operational telegraph link in Alaska was laid in September 1900, when 25 miles of line were stretched from military headquarters in Nome to an outpost at Port Safety. It was part of a $450,000 plan by the Army Signal Corps to connect scattered military posts in the territory with the United States. By the end of 1903, land lines linked western Alaska, Prince William Sound, and interior and southeastern Alaska, where underwater cable was used.

Plagued by ice floes that repeatedly tore loose the underwater cables laid across Norton Sound, the military developed "wireless telegraphy" to span the icy water in 1903. It was the world's first application of radio-telegraph technology and marked the completion of a fragile network connecting all military stations in Alaska with the United States. Sitka, Juneau, Haines and Valdez were connected by a line to Whitehorse, Yukon. Nome, Fort St. Michael, Fort Gibbon (Tanana) and Fort Egbert (Eagle) were linked with Dawson, Yukon. A line from Dawson to Whitehorse continued to Vancouver, British Columbia, and Seattle.

In 1905, the 1,500 miles of land lines, 2,000 miles of submarine cables and the 107-mile wireless link became the Washington–Alaska Military Cable and Telegraph System (WAMCATS). This, in turn, became the Alaska Communications System in 1935, reflecting a shift to greater civilian use and a system relying more heavily on wireless stations than land lines. The Alaska Communications System operated under the Department of Defense until RCA Corp., through its division RCA Alascom, took control in 1971.

AT&T Alascom.

Headquartered in Anchorage, AT&T Alascom is a wholly owned subsidiary of AT&T and employs 448 people.

What is now AT&T Alascom began as the Washington-Alaska Military Cable and Telegraph System, a "talking wire" strung overland in 1900.

On Oct. 27, 1982, Alascom launched its own telecommunications satellite, *Aurora I*, into orbit from Cape Canaveral, FL. It was the first telecommunications satellite dedicated to a single state, and it was the first completely solid-state satellite to be placed in orbit.

On May 29, 1991, Alascom launched a second satellite, *Aurora II*, from Cape Canaveral to replace the original *Aurora*. The newer satellite uses similar design, updated with modern technology, to increase life span. Plans already are under way for the launch of *Aurora III*, scheduled for early 2001.

As a certified long lines carrier for the state of Alaska, AT&T Alascom provides interstate and intrastate long-distance toll telephone service as well as local service in the Anchorage area. The services include AT&T WorldNet service, leased terrestrial and satellite channels and networks, high-speed data services, wide band analog services, fast-packet switching data networks, frame relay, leased transportable earth stations, and live radio and television broadcast transmissions. The company has installed more than 200 satellite earth stations throughout the state.

AT&T Alascom has designed and built the Rapid Deployment Earth Station (RDES), an air-transportable, self-contained mobile earth station. The RDES was used for emergency communications in Puerto Rico in the aftermath of Hurricane Hugo, in Hawaii in the aftermath of Hurricane Inike, for Operation Just Cause in Panama and for operations Desert Shield and Desert Storm in Saudi Arabia and

Kuwait. AT&T Alascom also has several joint-venture partners in the Russia republics.

General Communication Inc.

Founded in 1979, GCI is an Alaska-based company offering voice, video and data communication services to more than 180,000 residential, commercial and government customers statewide.

The company said that in spring 2000, it was Alaska's largest Internet service provider with more than 65,000 dial-up, cable modem and digital subscriber line customers.

In 1999, the company took delivery of its $125 million, 2,331-mile fiber optic cable connecting Anchorage, Fairbanks and Juneau with the Lower 48 and today owns a more than 25 percent local telephone market share in Anchorage.

GCI completed its first long-distance call on Thanksgiving Day 1982; two years later, it filed an antitrust lawsuit against the then-dominant long-distance carrier, Alascom (a precursor to today's AT&T Alascom.) Litigation was settled in 1988; GCI received a payment of $27.5 million and in 1991 purchased capacity on the only fiber optic cable linking Alaska with foreign countries and the contiguous United States. Clients in 1992 included BP Exploration (Alaska) Inc. and National Bank of Alaska.

GCI allied with long-distance carrier MCI Communications in 1993, permitting GCI to access MCI's global network. In 1995, GCI purchased a license for $1.7 million to provide personal communication services statewide. In 1996, competition in the industry was mandated nationwide following passage of the Federal Telecommunications Act.

GCI, a publicly traded company since 1987, completed an $8 million cable capital improvement in 1998 to provide digital cable television to Anchorage and several neighboring communities.

Telephone Numbers in the Bush

Although most Alaska Bush communities now have full

telephone service, a few villages still have only one telephone. For those villages, call the information number, 555-1212. The area code for all of Alaska is 907.

Television Stations

Television in Anchorage and Fairbanks was available years before satellites were sent into orbit. The first satellite broadcast to the state was Neil Armstrong's moon walk in July 1969. Television reached the Bush in the late 1970s with the construction of telephone earth stations that could receive television programming via satellite transmissions. The state funds Alaska Rural Communication Service (ARCS), which broadcasts general and educational programming to over 200 rural communities. For more information about ARCS, contact the Department of Administration, Information Services, 5900 E. Tudor Road, Anchorage 99507; (907) 269-5744.

Regular network programming (ABC, CBS, NBC and PBS) on a time-delayed basis is provided through the RATNet system. Most of the stations listed here carry a mixture of network programming, with local broadcasters specifying programming. Some stations, such as KJNP, carry locally produced programming.

Cable television is available from Ketchikan to Barrow. At least one cable system offers a complete satellite earth station and 24-hour programming. Local television viewing in Bethel, for example, includes Channel 4 (KYUK), which carries programming such as PBS's *NOVA* series, *Sesame Street* and local news; cable Channel 8, which carries regular network programming; and 34 other cable channels carrying specialized programming such as movies, news, weather, sports and specials.

The following list shows the commercial and public television stations in Alaska:

Anchorage. KAKM Channel 7 (public television); 3877 University Drive, 99508.

KCFT (UHF 20/Cable 20); P.O. Box 210830, 99521.

KDMD (Prime Cable 33); 6250 Tuttle Place, Suite 4, 99507.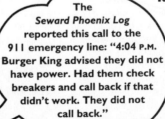

KIMO Channel 13; 2700 E. Tudor Road, 99507.

KTBY Channel 4; 1840 S. Bragaw, Suite 101, 99508.

KTUU Channel 2; 701 E. Tudor Road, Suite 220, 99503.

KTVA Channel 11; 1007 W. 32nd Ave., 99503.

KYES Channel 5; 3700 Woodland Park Drive, Suite 800, 99517.

Bethel. KYUK Channel 4 (public television); Pouch 468, 99559.

Fairbanks. KATN Channel 2; 516 Second Ave., Suite 400, 99701.

KFXF Channel 7; 3650 Braddock St., 99701.

KTVF Channel 11; 3528 International Way, 99701.

KUAC Channel 9 (public television); University of Alaska, P.O. Box 755620, 99775-5620.

KXD Channel 13; 3650 Braddock St., No. 2, 99701.

Juneau. KATH Channel 5; 1107 Eighth St., 99801.

KJUD Channel 8; 175 S. Franklin St., 99801.

KTOO Channel 3 (public television); 360 Egan Drive, 99801.

Ketchikan. KJMW (Cable 3); 501 Dock St., 99901.

Kodiak. KMXT Channel 9 (independent); 620 Egan Way, 99615.

North Pole. KJNP Channel 4; P.O. Box 56359, 99705.

The *Seward Phoenix Log* reported this call to the 911 emergency line: "4:04 P.M. Burger King advised they did not have power. Had them check breakers and call back if that didn't work. They did not call back."

Sitka. KSCT Channel 5; 520 Lake St., 99835.

KTNL Channel 13; 520 Lake St., 99835.

Unalaska. KO8IW Channel 8 (independent); P.O. Box 181, 99685.

Tides (SEE ALSO BORE TIDE)

In southeastern Alaska, Prince William Sound, Cook Inlet and Bristol Bay, salt water undergoes extreme daily fluctuations, creating powerful tidal currents. Some bays may go totally dry at low tide.

The second greatest tide range in North America occurs in upper Cook Inlet near Anchorage, where the maximum diurnal range during spring tides is 38.9 feet. (The greatest tide range in North America is Nova Scotia's Bay of Fundy, with spring tides over 50 feet.)

Here are diurnal ranges for some coastal communities: Bethel, 4 feet; Cold Bay, 7.1 feet; Cordova, 12.4 feet; Haines, 16.8 feet; Herschel Island, 0.7 feet; Ketchikan, 15.4 feet; Kodiak, 8.5 feet; Naknek River entrance, 22.6 feet; Nikiski, 20.7 feet; Nome, 1.6 feet; Nushagak, 19.6 feet; Point Barrow, 0.4 feet; Port Heiden, 12.3 feet; Port Moller, 10.8 feet; Sand Point, 7.3 feet; Sitka, 9.9 feet; Valdez, 12 feet; Whittier, 12.3 feet; Wrangell, 15.7 feet; Yakutat, 10.1 feet.

Timber (SEE ALSO SPRUCE BARK BEETLE)

According to the U.S. Forest Service, Anchorage Forestry Sciences Lab, 127 million acres of Alaska's 365 million acres of land surface are forested, 13 million acres of which are classified as timberland. Timberland is forest land capable of producing in excess of 20 cubic feet of industrial wood an acre a year in natural stands and not withdrawn from timber utilization.

Alaska has two distinct forest ecosystems: the Interior forest and the coastal rain forest. The vast Interior forest covers 114 million acres, extending from the south slope of the Brooks Range to the Kenai Peninsula, and from Canada to Norton Sound. More than 7 million acres of white spruce, paper birch, quaking aspen, black cottonwood and balsam poplar stands are considered timberland, comparing favorably in size and growth with forests of the lake states of Minnesota, Wisconsin and Michigan. There are an additional 2.8 million acres capable of producing as timberland but are unavailable for harvest because they are in parks or wilderness.

The Interior region's remoteness from large markets has limited timber use to approximately 20 sawmills, with most cutting less than 300,000 board feet a year. There are some exports of sawlogs, cants and chips.

The coastal rain forests extend from Cook Inlet to the Alaska–Canada border south of Ketchikan, and they continue to provide the bulk of commercial timber volume in Alaska. Of the 13.9 million acres of forested land, 5 million acres are classified as timberland. Under the Tongass Management Plan only 676,000 acres are available for harvest. An additional 2.6 million acres of timber stands are capable of producing more than 20 cubic feet an acre a year, but are in parks and wilderness.

Western hemlock and Sitka spruce provide most of the timber harvest for domestic and export lumber and pulp markets. Western red cedar and Alaska cedar make up most of the balance, along with mountain hemlock, lodgepole pine and other species.

Lands from which substantial volumes of timber are harvested are divided into two distinct categories: privately owned by Native corporations and villages under the 1971 Native Claims Settlement Act, and publicly owned and managed federal, state

Looking Back

1806

Russian settlers planted the first trees on the Aleutian island of Unalaska. Three of the original spruce still survive—surrounded by countless seedlings.

and borough lands. Timber harvests from publicly owned lands are carried through short-term open sales and Small Business Administration set-aside sales.

The forest products of Alaska are also divided somewhat along the same lines as land ownership. By federal law, timber harvested from federal lands cannot be exported without processing. While processors dependent on federal lands produce primarily rough-sawn lumber, pulpwood, railroad ties and chips, the Native corporations primarily produce round logs, which find more buyers along the Pacific Rim, especially Japan. The Alaska forest products industry is almost entirely dependent on the Japanese market, and the processing requirement has had considerable effect on some sections of the forest industry. Small sawmills are scattered throughout Southeast Alaska. The larger mills in coastal Alaska are located at Hoonah, Klawock, Wrangell, Ketchikan, Ninilchik/Anchor Point and Metlakatla. All of these are currently operating at less than 50 percent of capacity.

In 1999, approximately 21.2 million board feet of timber were harvested and sold, adding $235,000 at 1998–99 prices to state revenues. Forest products exports in 1998 were valued at $171.9 million, a 57 percent decline from the 1997 figure of $403.7 million. The total value of forest products exports for 1999 was $222 million. Additional information on Alaska timber may be obtained from the Department of Natural Resources' Web site: www. dnr.state.ak.us/forestry.

Time Zones (SEE MAP, PAGES
8–9) On Sept. 15, 1983, Transportation Secretary Elizabeth Dole signed a plan to reduce the number of time zones in Alaska from four to two. The plan, which became effective Oct. 30, 1983, when daylight-saving time reverted to standard time, places 90 percent of Alaska residents on Alaska time, one hour behind the West Coast. The far reaches of the Aleutian Islands and St. Lawrence Island observe Hawaii–Aleutian time.

Before the change, Alaska's time zones were Pacific time (southeastern Alaska), Yukon time (Yakutat) and Alaska time (from just east of Cold Bay and west of Yakutat northward, including Nome). Consolidating these time zones aided business and improved communications.

Totems (SEE ALSO NATIVE ARTS
AND CRAFTS AND POTLATCH) In the prehistory of southeastern Alaska and the Pacific Northwest coast, the Native way of life was based on the rich natural resources of the land, respect for living things and on a unique and complex social structure. Totemic art reflects this rich culture.

Carved from the huge cedar trees of the northern coast, totem poles are a traditional art form among the Natives of the Pacific Northwest and southeastern Alaska. Although the best-known type of totem pole is tall and freestanding, totemic art also is applied to house frontal poles, houseposts and mortuary poles. Totem poles are bold statements that make public records of the lives and history of the people who had them carved; they represent pride in clans and ancestors.

Animals of the region are most often represented on the poles. Commonly depicted are eagles, ravens, frogs, bears, beavers, wolves and whales. Also represented are figures from Native mythology: monsters with animal features, humanlike spirits and legendary ancestors. Occasionally included are objects, devices, masks and charms and, more rarely, art illustrating plants and celestial phenomena.

The poles were traditionally painted with natural mineral and vegetable pigments. Salmon eggs were chewed with cedar bark to form the binder for the

Tlingit totem pole, Sitka.
Photo courtesy of Alaska Division of Tourism.

ground pigment. Traditional colors are black, white and red-brown; green, blue-green, blue and yellow are also used, depending on tribal convention. The range of colors broadened when modern paints became available. Totem art grew rapidly in the late 18th century, with the introduction of steel European tools acquired from explorers and through the fur trade. Large totem poles were a thriving cultural feature by the 1830s and signified social standing. For example, wealthy Tlingit often commissioned the Tsimshian to carve totems for them.

Totem pole carving almost died out between the 1880s and 1950s during the enforcement of a law forbidding the "potlatch," the core of Northwest Coast Indian culture. The potlatch ceremony is held to observe events such as marriages; guests are invited from near and far, dancing and feasting take place, property is given away and often poles are raised to commemorate the event. Since the anti-potlatching law was repealed in 1951, a revival of Native culture and the arts has taken place, and many tribes are actively carving and raising poles again. (See Potlatch)

Totem poles were left to stand as long as nature would permit, usually about 50 to 60 years. Once a pole became so rotten that it fell, it was left to decay naturally or used for firewood. Some totem poles still standing in parks today are 40 to 50 years old. Heavy precipitation and acid muskeg soils hasten decomposition even though cedar is resistant to decay.

Collections of fine totem poles may be seen either outdoors or in museums in several Alaska communities including Ketchikan, Wrangell, Hydaburg and Sitka. Carvers practice their art at cultural centers in those towns as well as in Haines and Saxman.

Tourism
Although Alaska has been attracting tourists for more than 100 years, residents sometimes are surprised that the visitor industry has quietly become the state's second-largest primary employer. The visitor industry employs 20,300

Most Visited Tourist Attractions—1999

(Percentage of all state visitors to attractions)

1. Inside Passage	46%
2. Portage Glacier	44%
3. Mendenhall Glacier	40%
3. Ketchikan Totems	40%
4. Denali/McKinley	36%
5. Skagway Gold Rush District	35%
6. Glacier Bay	31%
7. Anchorage Museum	26%
8. Trans-Alaska Pipeline	24%
9. Sitka's Russian Church	22%
Tied:	
10. University of Alaska Museum	20%
10. Sitka National Historical Park	20%
10. Prince William Sound	20%
10. Kenai River	20%

—Ranked by the *Alaska Journal of Commerce*, Jan. 2, 2000 ✣

Alaskans directly during peak seasons and affects another 10,400 Alaskan jobs. More than 2,500 businesses in Alaska derive most of their income from visitor sales. In-state visitor spending reached $949 million in 1998. Tourism is a renewable resource that brings dollars to all regions of Alaska. The visitor industry generates more than $2.6 billion in revenues each year and is expected to continue to grow.

State government has long recognized the value of the visitor industry.

For fiscal 2001, the Division of Tourism's projected budget is $5.6 million for international marketing, rural development and visitor inquiries. The Alaska Travel Industry Association's budget was $4.8 million for domestic marketing. The legislature allocates these monies to promote Alaska as a visitor destination.

Alaska welcomed more than 1.3 million between October 1997 and September 1998. Summer visitor spending for 1998 was $845 million.

The continental United States provided 78 percent of Alaska's visitors in 1998, Canadian visitors accounted for 10 percent, and 7 percent came from overseas. Of these travelers, about half had independent itineraries while the remainder came on package tour programs. The most popular modes of entry for visitors were domestic air (49 percent), cruise ships (36 percent), personal vehicles (10 percent) and the ferry system (2 percent). The remainder arrived by international air (2 percent) and motor coach tours (1 percent).

Alaska's scenic beauty, trophy fish, abundant wildlife and unique history remain its biggest attractions. The adventure travel market is growing in Alaska; an increasing number of visitors participate in river rafting, backcountry trekking and other wilderness experiences.

To access the Division of Tourism Web site, point your browser to www.dced. state.ak.us/tourism

Trees and Shrubs

(SEE ALSO SPRUCE BARK BEETLE) According to the U.S. Department of Agriculture, the number of native tree species in Alaska is less than in any other state. Species of trees and shrubs in Alaska fall under the following families: yew, pine, cypress, willow, bayberry, birch, mistletoe, gooseberry, rose, maple, elaeagnus, ginseng, dogwood, crowberry, pyrola, heath, dispensia, honeysuckle and composite.

Commercial timber species include white spruce, Sitka spruce, western hemlock, mountain hemlock, western red cedar, Alaska cedar, balsam poplar, black cottonwood, quaking aspen and paper birch.

Rare tree species include the Pacific yew, Pacific silver fir, subalpine fir, silver willow and Hooker willow.

Tundra Characteristic of arctic and subarctic regions, tundra is a treeless plain that consists of moisture-retaining soils and permanently frozen subsoil. Tundra climates, marked by frequent winds and low temperatures, are harsh on plants. Soils freeze around root systems and winds wear away portions exposed above rocks and snow. The three distinct types of Alaska tundra—wet, moist and alpine—support low-growing vegetation that includes a variety of delicate flowers, mosses and lichens.

According to *Alaska Science Nuggets*, every acre of arctic tundra contains more than 2 tons of live fungi that survive by feeding on dead organic matter. Since the recession of North Slope ice age glaciers 12,000 years ago, a vegetative residue has accumulated a layer of peat 3 feet to 6 feet thick overlying the tundra.

Ulu A traditional Eskimo woman's knife designed for scraping and chopping, this fan-shaped tool was originally made of stone with a bone handle.

Today, an ulu is often shaped from an old saw blade and a wood handle is attached. The term derives from the Yup'ik word *uluaq* and the Siberian Yup'ik word *ulaaq*.

Umiak (SEE ALSO BAIDARKA) The Eskimo umiak is a traditional skin-covered boat whose design has changed little over the centuries. Although umiaks are mostly powered by outboard motors today, paddles are still used when stalking game and when ice might damage a propeller. Because umiaks must often be pulled long distances over pack ice, the boats are lightweight and easily repaired. The frames are wood, often driftwood found on beaches, and the covering can be sewn if punctured. The bottom is flat and the keel is bone, which prevents the skin from wearing out as it is pulled over the ice.

Female walrus skins are the preferred covering because they are the proper thickness when split (bull hides are too thick and often scarred) and because it takes only two skins to cover a boat. Sometimes female walrus skins are unavailable, so skins of the bearded seal, or *oogruk,* may be used. It may take six or seven skins to cover an umiak.

Umiak is the Inupiat word for skin boat and is commonly used by the coastal Eskimos throughout Alaska. St. Lawrence Islanders speak the Yup'ik dialect and their word for skin boat is *angyaq.*

Unalaska/ Dutch Harbor

(*See also* Military *and* World War II) Located on Unalaska Island, the second-largest island in the Aleutian chain and 800 miles southwest of Anchorage, Ounalashka, or Unalaska, was the Russian-American Company's headquarters for the sea otter fur trade in the 1700s. At the turn of the century, Unalaska was a major stop for ships heading to and from the Nome goldfields.

The international port of Dutch Harbor is located across a bridge from Unalaska on Amaknak Island. The U.S. Army and Navy began building installations there in 1939; in June 1942 the area was bombed by the Japanese and most of the local Aleut people were evacuated.

A memorial to those

killed in the Aleutians in World War II is in Memorial Park near the cemetery.

Unalaska/Dutch Harbor is a significant port and gateway to the Bering Sea region. The climate is referred to as the "Cradle of the Storms." Here the warm Japan Current meets the colder air and water currents of the Bering Sea, creating an annual rainfall of 60.5 inches and colossal winds. Rare plants and birds and the historic Cathedral of the Holy Ascension of Christ draw visitors to the island. The Unalaska/Dutch Harbor area remains ice-free year-round and large canneries form the basis of the local economy, making it one of the most productive seafood processing ports in the United States.

Universities and Colleges

Higher education in Alaska may be achieved through the University of Alaska system and private institutions. The university system includes three regional multicampus universities, one community college and a network of services for rural Alaska. The three regional institutions are the University of Alaska Anchorage (UAA), the University of Alaska Fairbanks (UAF) and the University of Alaska Southeast (UAS). University of Alaska institutions enrolled 30,249 students in 1999.

Campuses of UAS are located in Juneau, Sitka and Ketchikan. The main UAA campus in Anchorage is supplemented by a network of extended schools that includes Kenai Peninsula College, Kodiak College, Matanuska–Susitna College and Prince William Sound Community College, as well as the Chugiak–Eagle River Campus, a branch campus in Kachemak Bay and several military centers.

UAA units include the Center for Alcohol and Addiction Studies; Center for

In preparation for a field trip to the wind-swept and barren Pribilof Islands, a University of Alaska professor told his students that he was trying to get a portable toilet and a large tarp to the site because "ya know, there aren't any bushes for hundreds of miles."

Economic Development; Center for Economic Education; Center for Human Development, University Affiliated Program; Environment and Natural Resources Institute, which includes the Alaska Natural Heritage Program, Alaska State Climate Center and the Arctic Environmental Information and Data Center; Institute for Circumpolar Health Studies; Institute of Social and Economic Research; and the Justice Center.

UAF is a land-, sea- and space-grant university that includes the main campus in Fairbanks; Bristol Bay Campus in Dillingham; Chukchi Campus in Kotzebue; Interior Campus with offices in Fairbanks and centers in Fort Yukon, McGrath, Tok and Unalaska; Kuskokwim Campus in Bethel; Northwest Campus in Nome; and Tanana Valley Campus in downtown Fairbanks.

UAF research facilities include the Alaska Cooperative Fishery and Wildlife Research Unit; Alaska Native Language Center; Alaska Synthetic Aperture Radar Facility; Arctic Region Supercomputing Center; Center for Cross-Cultural Studies; Center for Global Change and Arctic Systems Research; Consortium for Research in Rural Alaska; Environmental Technology Laboratory; Fishery Industrial Technology Center; Forest Products Technology Center; Forest Soils Laboratory; Geophysical Institute; Georgeson Botanical Garden; Institute of Arctic Biology; Institute of Marine Science; Institute of Northern Engineering; Juneau Center for Fisheries and Ocean Sciences; Large Animal Research Station; Mineral Industry Resource Laboratory; Petroleum Development Laboratory; Poker Flat Research Range; Polar Ice Coring Office; Seismology Laboratory; Transportation Research Center; University of

Alaska Museum; Water Research Center; and West Coast National Undersea Research Center.

The Alaska Cooperative Extension and the Alaska Sea Grant College Program interpret and report some of the university's research results to the residents of Alaska.

For more information:

University of Alaska Anchorage, 3211 Providence Drive, Anchorage 99508, www.info.alaska.edu; **Kenai Peninsula College,** 34820 College Drive, Soldotna 99669, www.uaa.alaska.edu/kenai; **Kodiak College,** 117 Benny Benson Drive, Kodiak 99615, www.koc.alaska.edu; **Matanuska–Susitna College,** P.O. Box 2889, Palmer 99645, www.uaa.alaska.edu/matsu; **Prince William Sound Community College,** P.O. Box 97, Valdez 99686, www.uaa.alaska.edu/pwscc.

University of Alaska Fairbanks, Fairbanks 99775, www.uaf.edu; **Bristol Bay Campus,** P.O. Box 1070, Dillingham 99576, www.uaf.edu/bbc; **Chukchi Campus,** P.O. Box 297, Kotzebue 99752, www.beringia.chukchi.alaska.edu; **College of Rural Alaska,** P.O. Box 756500, University of Alaska Fairbanks, Fairbanks 99775, www.uaf.edu/UAF/CRA.html; **Interior Aleutians Campus,** Box 248, Unalaska 99685,www.iac.uaf.edu; **Kuskokwim Campus,** P.O. Box 368, Bethel 99559, www.kuskokwim.bethel.alaska.edu; **Northwest Campus,** Pouch 400, Nome 99762, www.anvil.nome.alaska.edu; **Tanana Valley Campus,** 510 Second Ave., Fairbanks 99701, www.uaf.edu/tvc/index.html.

University of Alaska Southeast, Juneau Campus, 11120 Glacier Highway, Juneau 99801www.uas.alaska.edu; **Ketchikan Campus, 2600** Seventh St., Ketchikan 99901, ketch.

alaska.edu; **Sitka Campus,** 1332 Seward Ave., Sitka 99835, geocities.com/CollegePark/Campus/1909.

For information on private institutions of higher learning:

Alaska Bible College,

This year, Alaska will host over 1.4 million tourists and visitors. Last summer, one of them asked the concierge at the Regal Alaskan Hotel, "What time does the 3 o'clock shuttle leave?"

P.O. Box 289, Glennallen 99588.

Alaska Pacific University, 4101 University Drive, Anchorage 99508.

Sheldon Jackson College, 801 Lincoln St., Sitka 99835.

Many other schools and institutes in Alaska offer religious, vocational and technical study. For a listing of these and other schools, write for the *Directory of Postsecondary Educational Institutions in Alaska,* Alaska Commission on Post-secondary Education, 3030 Vintage Blvd., Juneau 99801-7109.

Veniaminov, Ioann

Father Ioann (Ivan Popov) Veniaminov (1797–1879) often has been called "Paul Bunyan in a cassock." A figure of commanding height and proportions, a linguistic genius who could build furniture and clocks with his own hands, Veniaminov was a central figure in early efforts to convert Alaska's Native population to the Russian way of life through Orthodoxy.

Veniaminov was a Russian Orthodox priest who served as a missionary in the Aleutians and in Southeast Alaska. In each place, he learned the local language and devised a written alphabet for the local Native group, allowing him to translate some books of the Bible. In the Aleutians he traveled thousands of miles by kayak to visit his enormous parish. He rose to become Bishop of Russian America, with his headquarters at Sitka, and eventually was appointed Metropolitan of Moscow. His writings on Aleut language and ethnology are still standard references. A volcano on the Aleutian Peninsula is named after him. As Saint Innocent, Veniaminov is one of the four Orthodox saints of Alaska.

Volcanoes (SEE MAP, PAGES 128–29) Volcanoes on the Aleutian Islands, on the Alaska Peninsula and in the

Looking Back

1917

The University of Alaska system took root in Fairbanks, as the Alaska Agricultural College and School of Mines.

Wrangell Mountains are part of the "Ring of Fire" that surrounds the Pacific Ocean basin. More than 80 potentially active volcanoes dot Alaska, about half of which have had at least one blast since 1760, the date of the earliest written record of eruptions. Pavlof Volcano is one of the most active of Alaska volcanoes, having had more than 40 reported eruptions since 1790. One recent spectacular eruption of Pavlof in April 1986 sent ash 10 miles high, causing black snow to fall on Cold Bay; it remained active through August 1988, producing lava and mud flows. The eruption of Augustine Volcano (4,025 feet) in lower Cook Inlet on March 27, 1986, sent ash 8 miles high and disrupted air traffic in southcentral Alaska for several days.

Southcentral's Mount Redoubt erupted Dec. 14, 1989, its first eruption since 1968. The biggest blasts sent ash throughout most of southcentral Alaska and disrupted air traffic. This eruption continued until April 1990. Mount Spurr erupted in June, August and September 1992. Anchorage received the brunt of ash fallout from the August eruption, which halted air traffic out of the city for several days. Flights were briefly interrupted again during the September eruption.

The most violent Alaska eruption recorded occurred over a 60-hour period in June 1912 from Novarupta Volcano. The eruption darkened the sky over much of the Northern Hemisphere for several days, deposited almost a foot of ash on Kodiak, 100 miles away, and filled the Valley of Ten Thousand Smokes (within Katmai National Park) with more than 2.5 cubic miles of ash during its brief but extremely explosive duration.

More than 10 percent of the world's known volcanoes are in Alaska. A chain of volcanoes arcing along the Aleutians contains at least 60 centers that have

Mount Augustine's 1986 eruption halted air traffic. From *Alaska's Natural Wonders: A Guide to the Phenomena of the Far North* by Robert H. Armstrong and Marge Hermans. Photo by B. Yount, U.S.G.S., courtesy Alaska Volcano Observatory.

erupted in historic times; 40 of these volcanoes have been active since 1700.

ca. 1600 B.C.—Hayes Volcano destroys itself in seven eruptions within 100 years, each eruption producing as much ash as the 1980 eruption of Mount St. Helens.

1779—The Bogoslof group begins to rise from the Bering Sea.

1796—Bogoslof rises again.

1812—Augustine Volcano; Peulik

1883—Fire Island, another member of the Bogoslofs, appears; Augustine Volcano

1908—Augustine Volcano

1909—Bogoslof group

1912—Katmai

1927—Mount Spurr

1929—Chiginagak

1931—The Bogoslof group; Aniakchak Caldera

1935—Augustine Volcano

1953—Mount Spurr

1963–64—Augustine Volcano

1975—Trident

Jan.–Feb. 1976—Augustine Volcano

1977—Ukinrek Maars

1980—Makushin

Mar.–Aug. 1986—Augustine Volcano

1988—Pavlov and Shishaldin

Dec. 1989–April 1990—Mount Redoubt

1990—Kiska

Waves (*SEE ALSO* BORE TIDE; EARTHQUAKES; *AND* TIDES) Alaska's recorded

seismic history is very short yet extremely active. Alaska responds to movement in the Aleutian–Alaska megathrust zone, where the edge of the Pacific plate descends under the North American plate. These vertical movements of the earth's crust result in vertical motion of the sea floor, which can produce great seismic waves known as tsunamis. In fact, these crustal movements in the Alaska Peninsula, Aleutians and Gulf of Alaska can produce Pacific-wide tsunamis.

In southeastern Alaska, the Fairweather Fault lies inland. Though this fault has not triggered tectonic tsunamis as in other Alaska areas, it can unleash nearby underwater landslides, which may cause tsunamis.

According to the Alaska Tsunami Warning Center in Palmer, Alaska has had seven tsunamis that caused fatalities in recorded history. These were of local origin and occurred between 1788 and 1964. Tsunamis originating in Alaska Pacific waters have caused all of the fatalities reported on the West Coast and in Alaska, and most of those in Hawaii. The most recent damaging tsunami was in 1964 following the March 27, Good Friday earthquake. That wave destroyed three Alaska villages before reaching Washington, Oregon and California, and continued to cause damage as far away as Hawaii, Chile and Japan.

Tsunami is taken from the Japanese words *tsu* meaning "harbor" and *nami* meaning "great wave." Often called tidal waves, tsunamis are not caused by tides. Generated by earthquakes occurring on or below the sea floor, tsunamis can race across the Pacific Ocean at speeds of up to 600 miles per hour. Tsunamis rarely cross the Atlantic. Traveling across the open ocean, the waves are only a few feet high and can be up to 100 miles from crest to crest. They cannot be seen from an airplane or felt in a ship at sea. Once they approach shore, however, shallower water causes the waves to grow taller by increasingly restricting their forward motion. Thus, a 2-foot wave traveling 500 miles per hour in deep water becomes a 100-foot killer at 30 miles per hour as it nears the shore. The wave action of a tsunami can repeat every 15 to 30 minutes, and the danger for a given area is generally not considered over until the area has been free from damaging waves for two hours.

Another type of wave action that occurs in Alaska is a seiche. A seiche is a long, rhythmic wave in a closed or partially closed body of water. Caused by earthquakes, winds, tidal currents or atmospheric pressure, the motion of a seiche resembles the back and forth movement of a tipped bowl of water. The water moves only up and down, and can remain active from a few minutes to several hours. The highest recorded wave in Alaska, 1,740 feet, was the result of a seiche that took place in Lituya Bay on July 9, 1958. This unusually high wave was caused by an earthquake-induced landslide that stripped trees from the opposite side of the bay.

For more information about earthquakes and tsunamis, see the WC/ATWC Web page at www.wcat.gov/.

Weather (See Climate)

Whales and Whaling

(See also Baleen) Fifteen species of both toothed and baleen whales are found in Alaska waters. Baleen refers to the hundreds of strips of flexible fingernail-like material that hang from the gum of the upper jaw. The strips are fringed and act as strainers that capture krill—tiny shrimplike organisms—as well as other prey upon which whales feed. Once the baleen fills with prey, whales force water back out

through the sides of their mouth, swallowing the food left behind. Baleen whale females are usually larger than males.

Baleen whales that inhabit Alaska waters include blue, bowhead, northern right, fin or finback, humpback, sei, minke or little piked and gray. Toothed whales include sperm, beluga, orca (or killer whale), pilot, beaked (three species), dolphins (two species) and porpoises (two species). Another toothed whale, the narwhal, a full-time resident of the arctic region, is almost never seen in Alaska waters. St. Lawrence Islanders call narwhals *bousucktugutalik*, or "beluga with tusk," due to a tusk that grows from the left side of the upper jaw on bulls only. Spiraling in a left-hand direction, the tusk can reach lengths up to 8 feet on an adult.

According to the Alaska Department of Fish and Game, gray whales have the distinction of being the most primitive of the living *mysticete* ("moustached") or baleen whales. They can regularly be observed in large numbers from Alaska shores, and are found in the North Pacific Ocean and adjacent waters of the Arctic Ocean. There are two geographically isolated stocks: the Korean or western Pacific stock, and the California or eastern Pacific stock. The California stock migrates between Baja California and the Bering and Chukchi Seas, a round-trip distance of 10,000 miles, and the longest migration of any marine mammal.

Grays are mottled gray in color and covered with scars, abrasions and clusters of parasitic barnacles that are most abundant on their heads and backs, the parts exposed to air when the animals breathe.

The estimated daily consumption of an adult gray whale is about 2,600 pounds. In the approximately five months spent in Alaska waters, one whale eats about 396,000 pounds of food, primarily amphipod crustaceans. Gray whales feed on the bottom by sucking tube-dwelling amphipods out of the sandy sediment and leaving large oval feeding imprints behind. Scientists can study these imprints and gain knowledge about feeding habits. Muddy feeding trails are often seen when gray whales surface after feeding dives. Gray whales were called "devil fish" by early whalers because they were so aggressive and protective of their young when hunted.

Adult grays are about 36 feet to 50 feet long and weigh from 16 tons to 45 tons. Females are larger than males at any given age. They have been known to live up to 70 years, but the average life span is about 50 years.

The beluga, or white whale, belongs to the *odontocetes* ("toothed") group, which includes sperm and killer whales, dolphins

and porpoises. Its closest relative is the narwhal. Belugas range widely in arctic and subarctic waters, and two populations occur in Alaska. The Cook Inlet population can be found in Turnagain Arm and in the Shelikof Straits region, although some belugas have been seen east to Yakutat Bay and west to Kodiak Island. Belugas of the western Arctic population range throughout the Bering, Chukchi and Beaufort Seas. These whales winter in the ice of the Bering Sea, moving in summer over 1,500 miles to concentration areas along the coast from

Bristol Bay to the Mackenzie River delta in northwestern Canada.

In Alaska, large groupings occur in the Bristol Bay area, Norton Sound, Kotzebue Sound and Kasegaluk Lagoon. In Bristol Bay, belugas sometimes swim more than 100 miles a day.

Belugas are very vocal animals, producing a variety of grunts, clicks, chirps and whistles, which are used for navigating, finding prey and communicating. Because of their talkative nature, they are known as "sea canaries." Belugas are also masters of echolocation, using their sophisticated sonar to detect fish and navigate in shallow waters or among gill nets without getting stranded. In some areas, they may dive more than 2,000 feet to feed on the bottom. At birth, belugas are dark blue-gray fading to white by the age of 5 or 6. Adult males are 11 feet to 16 feet long and weigh 1,000 pounds to 2,000 pounds; adult females may reach 12 feet in length. Belugas can live up to 40 years.

Orcas known as killer whales or blackfish, are the largest member of the dolphin family. They range from the Beaufort Sea to Antarctica. In Alaska, two different stocks are designated resident and transient. A third stock offshore is being researched. It is thought that orcas migrate, riding currents south in the winter. The most unusual feature of the orca is the high dorsal fin, which has no muscle but may serve the whale as a keel would a boat. The fin on older males can grow to 6 feet in height.

Orcas are considered very intelligent and to possess all mammalian senses except smell. They take catnaps on the surface of the water and hunt in pods using complex, cooperative patterns of attack. Prey include sea lions, salmon, seals, porpoises, halibut, shark, squid, belugas and other whales. Male killer whales average 23 feet in length; females are smaller. Average life span is 30 to 40 years.

Whaling. Decimated by commercial whaling in the late 1880s, the bowhead whale population today is protected and growing. It is estimated that 199 whales are added to the stock yearly; the 1999 population numbered 8,000–9,000.

Bowhead whales have been protected from commercial whaling for decades by a number of agreements, including the Convention for the Regulation of Whaling (1931), the International Convention for the Regulation of Whaling (1947), and by the Marine Mammal Protection Act (1972) and the Endangered Species Act (1973). Blue, humpback, sei, fin, Northern right, bowhead and sperm whales are on the federal endangered species list.

Gray whales are also protected. Commercial whaling for grays has been banned by the International Convention for the Regulation of Whaling since 1947. Although these conventions and regulations do allow for subsistence harvest by Alaska Natives, the gray whale is not hunted in Alaska.

Since 1978, the International Whaling Commission (IWC) has regulated the taking of both bowheads and grays. The IWC reclassified the eastern stock of gray whales from a protected species to a sustained management stock with an annual catch limit of about 179 whales. The entire catch limit of grays and bowheads is reserved for Natives or by member governments on behalf of Natives.

At a convention in 1994, the IWC revised the bowhead catch limit for Alaska, so that bowheads landed from 1995 to 1998 would not exceed 204. Hunters were forbidden to strike, land or kill calves or any bowhead accompanied by a calf.

Other species of large baleen whales, such as minke and fin whales, are occasion- ally taken by Alaska Eskimos for food. It is not necessary to report minke harvests. The only toothed whale taken by Eskimos is the beluga and its harvest is monitored by the Alaska Beluga Whale Committee.

Beluga Whales Landed 1988–98

Year	Beluga
1988	375–418
1989	247–266
1990	316–338
1991	306–316
1992	163–164
1993	301–321
1994	263–271
1995	163+
1996	298–311
1997	186–198
1998	297*

*Exclusive of Cook Inlet harvests

Wildflowers
Wildflowers in Alaska usually are small, delicate and seldom showy. More than 1,500 plant species occur in the state including trees, shrubs, ferns, grasses and sedges, as well as flowering plants.

Alpine regions are particularly rich in flora and some of these species are rare. Anywhere there is tundra there is apt to be a bountiful population of flowers. The Steese Highway (Eagle Summit), Richardson Highway (Thompson Pass), Denali Highway (Maclaren Summit), Denali National Park and Preserve (Polychrome Pass), Seward Highway (Turnagain Pass), Glenn Highway just north of Anchorage (Eklutna Flats) and a locale near Wasilla (Hatcher Pass) are wonderful wildflower-viewing spots. All are readily accessible by car. Less easily accessible floral Edens are some of the Aleutian Islands, Point Hope, Anvil Mountain and the Nome–Teller Road (both near Nome), Pribilof Islands and other remote areas.

Alaska's official flower, the forget-me-not *(Myosotis alpestris),* is a diminutive beauty found throughout much of the state in alpine meadows and along streams. Growing to 18 inches tall, forget-me-nots are recognized by their bright blue petals surrounding a yellow eye. A northern "cousin," the arctic forget-me-not (*Eritrichium aretioides*), grows in sandy soil on the tundra, or in the mountains, and reaches only 4 inches in height.

Forget-me-not, Alaska's state flower.

Winds

(*SEE ALSO* CLIMATE) Some of Alaska's windiest weather has been recorded on the western islands of the Aleutian chain. Causes are the same as elsewhere—planet rotation and the tendency of the atmosphere to equalize the difference between high and low pressure fronts. A few winds occur often and significantly enough to be given names: chinook, taku and williwaws.

Chinook. Old-timers describe chinook winds as unseasonably warm winds that can cause a thaw in the middle of winter. What they also cause are power failures and property damage, especially in the Anchorage bowl where in recent years hundreds of homes have sprung up on the Chugach Mountains hillsides where chinook winds howl. One such wind occurred on April Fool's Day in 1980, causing $25 million in property damage. Parts of Anchorage were without power for 60 hours.

Until recently, it was not possible to predict chinook wind in Anchorage. Today, however, meteorologists can tell if the winds are gathering, when they will arrive and their relative strength. It was learned that such a warm wind could only originate in Prince William Sound and that its speed had to be at least 55 miles per hour or faster just to cross the 3,500-foot Chugach Mountains. Other factors include a storm near Bethel and relatively stable air over Anchorage. Meteorologists accurately predict chinook winds 55 percent of the time.

Taku. Taku winds are the sudden, fierce gales that sweep down from the ice cap behind Juneau and Douglas. Takus are shivering cold winds capable of reaching 100 miles per hour. They have been known to send a 2x4 timber flying through the wall of a frame house.

Williwaws. Williwaws are sudden gusts of wind that can reach 113 miles per hour after wind "builds up" on one side of a mountain and suddenly spills over into what may appear to be a relatively protected area. Williwaws are a bane of Alaska mariners. The term was originally applied to a strong wind in the Strait of Magellan.

World Eskimo-Indian Olympics

An audience of thousands watches the annual gathering of several hundred Native athletes from Alaska and the circumpolar nations competing in the World Eskimo-Indian Olympics (WEIO) in Fairbanks. Held over four days in July, the games draw participants from all of Alaska's Native populations (Eskimo, Aleut, Athabascan, Tlingit, Haida and Tsimshian). Canadian, Greenlandic and Russian Eskimos are also invited to participate, as well as Native Americans from the contiguous 48 states. Feats may seem exotic—even painful—but they have roots in a hunting, fishing and gathering culture that rewards endurance, observation and cooperation.

Spectators thrill to the knuckle hop and the ear-weight competition. Other traditional Native sports and competitions include the greased pole walk, fish cutting, stick pull, Indian and Eskimo dancing, men's and women's blanket toss, and the spectacular two-foot and one-foot high kicks. Some of the more boisterous games include a lively game of tug-of-war and the muktuk-eating contest.

Each year the judges choose a Native queen to reign over the Olympics. Over the next year she makes several appearances throughout the state, and represents the WEIO at the National Congress of American Indians. There is a baby pageant, and a Native dress pageant displays Native-made and -designed wear.

The games will be held in July 18–21, 2001, at the Big Dipper Recreation Arena in Fairbanks. For exact schedules and advance tickets, contact the World Eskimo-Indian Olympics Committee, P.O. Box 72433, Fairbanks 99707; (907) 452-6646. Web site: www.weio.org.

1999 World Eskimo-Indian Olympic Games, First-Place Winners

Eskimo Fur Parka Contest: Ashlynn Santiago-Brower
Eskimo Cloth Parka Contest: Janie Snyder
Indian Cloth Dress Contest: Charlene Mancuso
Indian Skin Dress Contest: Cecelia Grant
Muktuk-Eating Contest: Charlie Brown
Miss World Eskimo-Indian Olympics: Lily Tuzroyluke
Baby Contest, Eskimo: Everett Edwardsen
Baby Contest, Indian: Calen James Sunnyboy
Dance Team Indian: Fairbanks Native Association—Johnson O'Malley Potlatch Dancers
Dance Team Eskimo: Wainwright Dancers
White Man Versus Native Women Tug 'O War: Native Women
Race of the Torch: *Men,* Stuart Grant; *Women,* Noel Gould
One-Hand Reach: *Men,* Garry Hull; *Women,* Nicola Lincoln
Alaska High Kick: *Men,* George Melton; *Women,* Nicole Johnston
Indian Stick Pull: *Men,* Boogles Johnson; *Women,* Noel Gould
Eskimo Stick Pull: *Men,* Demetrius Van Fleet; *Women* Tselane Angason
Ear Pull: *Men,* Robert Okpeaha, Jr.; *Women,* Noel Gould
Toe Kick: *Men,* Tino Morrow; *Women,* Luanna Treder
Kneel Jump: *Men,* Reggie Joule III; *Women,* Nicole Johnston
Scissors Broad Jump: *Men,* George Melton; *Women,* Emily Frantz
Two Foot High Kick: *Men,* Brian Randazzo; *Women,* Nicole Johnston
Grease Pole Walk: *Men,,* Riley Kaleak, Jr.; *Women,* Gloria Geraldson
Arm Pull: *Men,* Demetrius Van Fleet; *Women,* Tselane Angason
Ear Weight: *Men,* Michael Paulsen; *Women,* Sheila Randazzo
Blanket Toss: *Men,* Tony Bryant; *Women,* Emily Frantz
Drop the Bomb: *Men,* Brad Weyiouanna; *Women,* Lily Tuzroyluke
Four Man Carry: *Men,* Demetrius Van Fleet
Knuckle Hop: *Men,* Brad Weyiouanna; *Women,* Gloria Geraldson

World War II (SEE ALSO MILITARY AND UNALASKA/DUTCH HARBOR)

World War II propelled development of modern Alaska. In 1940 Congress authorized the construction of Fort Richardson outside of Anchorage. After the bombing of Pearl Harbor, Alaska's strategic importance as a staging area for supplying forces in the North Pacific was apparent. The construction of the Alaska Canada Military Highway (the Alcan) began in March 1942, providing an overland route from the Lower 48 into Alaska.

The Japanese bombed a small military base at Dutch Harbor on June 3, 1942, in an attack that was designed to divert American forces north while

A classified ad in the *Anchorage Daily News* offered "Dry mixed split Fire Wood for $125 a quart." For $125, I want at least a *gallon!*

engaging the American fleet in the central Pacific at Midway. The diversion failed and the battle at Midway became a turning point in the Pacific war.

On June 7, 1942, 1,200 Japanese troops landed on the Aleutian islands of Attu and Kiska, where they built an air base, bunkers and anti-aircraft emplacements aimed at preventing the United States from using the Aleutians to launch an attack on Japan. Although the Japanese presence on the islands posed no real threat to the United States, foreign occupation was unthinkable. But the ensuing fight to drive the Japanese from the Aleutians was as much a battle against the bad weather as it was against enemy forces: More American aircraft were lost to the violent 120 mph winds, the dense fog and constant storms than to Japanese fire.

On May 11, 1943, after nearly a year of Japanese occupation, 11,000 American troops landed on Attu and engaged in a bloody battle with 2,600 Japanese troops. At the end of the month, 550 Americans were dead and 1,148 were wounded. Of the Japanese, only 28 prisoners were taken; American soldiers buried 2,351 Japanese troops killed in combat. Hundreds of others were presumed to have died and were buried in the hills or were thought to have committed suicide.

The battle for Kiska was different. On July 28, 1943, the 5,000-man Japanese garrison evacuated the island in dense fog. For three weeks, U.S. forces continued to bomb and shell the island, unaware that the island had been abandoned. In August, 35,000 Allied soldiers arrived on the island, but found only a few stray Japanese dogs.

Yukon Quest International Sled Dog Race (SEE ALSO DOG MUSHING AND IDITAROD TRAIL SLED DOG RACE)

The Sorel Yukon Quest™ International Sled Dog Race was begun by Roger Williams and LeRoy Shank in 1983 to foster a long-distance sled dog race between Fairbanks, and Whitehorse, Yukon. The first race took place in February 1984, when 26 teams competed, and had a purse of $50,000.

Named for the old-time winter "Highway of the North," the Yukon River, the 1,000-mile trek takes between 11 days and 14 days to complete, depending on weather and trail. The Quest is held in February and is known as one of the toughest sled dog races. During their journey between the two cities, teams retrace the footsteps of gold rush trappers, miners, explorers and missionaries (see map, next page). Mushers cross four major summits and diverse, challenging terrain. They travel 250 miles on the frozen Yukon

Winners and Times

Year	Musher	Days	Hrs.	Min.	Prize
1989	Jeff King, Denali	11	20	51	$20,000
1990	Vern Halter, Trapper Creek	11	17	09	20,000
1991	Charlie Boulding, Nenana	10	21	12	25,000
1992	John Schandelmeier, Paxson	11	21	40	29,837
1993	Charlie Boulding, Nenana	10	19	09	25,000
1994	Lavonne Barve	10	22	44	20,000
1995	Frank Turner, Whitehorse, YT.	10	16	20	20,000
1996	John Schandelmeier, Paxson	12	16	47	20,000
1997	Rick Mackey, Nenana	12	05	55	20,000
1998	Bruce Lee, Denali Park	11	11	27	30,000
1999	Ramy Brooks	11	07	59	30,000
2000	Aliy Zirkle, Two River	10*	22	01	30,000

*Due to poor trail conditions, the 2000 race ended at Takhini Hot Springs, near Whitehorse.

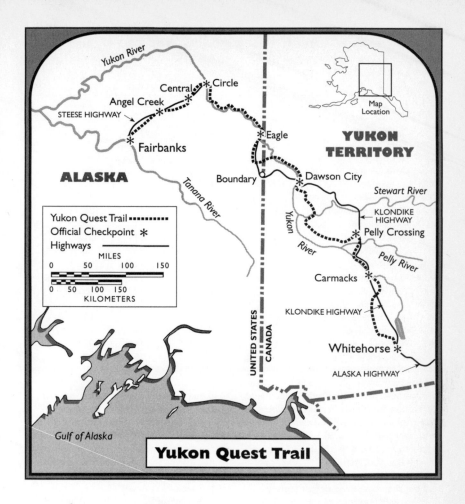

Yukon Quest Trail

River and cross the longest unguarded international border in the world.

The direction of the race alternates each year, and between the start and finish lines, there are six official checkpoints. The longest distance between checkpoints is 290 miles, from Dawson City to Carmacks. The only checkpoint at which a musher may receive help is at Dawson City, where a 36-hour layover is mandatory. Rules allow for eight dogs minimum and 14 dogs maximum at the start. Five dogs are the minimum allowed at the finish, and only four dogs can be dropped during the course of the race. Each musher may use only one sled throughout the race, and mandatory equipment includes a sleeping bag, hand ax, snowshoes, promotional material and eight booties per dog.

In 2000, 21 mushers completed the race; eight racers were scratched. The winner was Aliy Zirkle of Two Rivers, AK. *See* next page for 2000 race results.

For up-to-date information during the race, try Yukon Quest on-line at www. yukonquest.org.

Yukon River (SEE ALSO
RIVERS) The Yukon River is the longest river in Alaska, flowing in a 2,000-mile (1,400 miles in Alaska) arc from its British Columbia headwaters across the Interior's

2000 Sorel Yukon Quest™ Race Results, Top 20 Finishers

(Note: Due to poor trail conditions, the 2000 Sorel Yukon Quest™ ended at Takhini Hot Springs, outside of Whitehorse)

Place	Musher	Days	Hrs.	Min.
1	Aliy Zirkle	10	22	01
2	Thomas Tetz	10	22	31
3	Frank Turner	11	02	31
4	Peter Butteri	11	02	46
5	Jack Berry	11	03	10
6	Dave Olesen	11	08	17
7	Clim Smyth	11	16	45
8	Jim Hendrick	11	18	03
9	Darren Rorabaugh	11	19	22
10	Andrew Lesh	11	20	06
11	Jerry Louden	11	21	10
12	Larry Carroll	11	22	31
13	Hugh Neff	12	00	01
14	Rusty Hagan	12	02	08
15	Tony Blanford	12	08	39
16	Eric Nicolier	13	09	19
17	Peter Ledwidge	13	09	24
18	George Carroll	14	05	55
19	Philippe Russell	14	22	21
20	Bruce Milne	15	00	43

forested hills, narrow mountain valleys and vast tundra flats to the Bering Sea. The fifth-largest river in North America, the third largest in the United States, the Yukon River watershed drains 330,000 square miles—a third of Alaska.

Archaeological evidence indicates that humans may have lived along the river more than 20,000 years ago. Historically, two Native groups occupied the Yukon valley: the Yup'ik Eskimos and the Athabascans. Most Native villages were established on the north bank of the river, apparently the preferred side of the river, to fish for the millions of migrating king, coho and chum salmon that returned to the river system to spawn. These fish return to the Yukon today and fish traps and summer fish camps can still be seen along the river.

With the arrival of European trappers, the Yukon became a well-used supply route for the Interior. Travel was by steamboat or canoe during the summer and by dogsled from October to May, when the river was frozen.

The Yukon has never been dammed and is crossed by only one bridge, the Yukon River Bridge. It is on the Dalton Highway near Stevens Village, just south of the Arctic Circle.

The Yukon River attracts canoeists, kayakers and others for float trips. Many commercial guides offer excursions, and the popular jumping-off point is at Eagle. A

summer float trip downriver through Yukon–Charley Rivers National Preserve to Circle is 154 river miles and averages five to 10 days. Also available are float trips from Dawson City, Yukon, to Circle which make a stop halfway at Eagle.

You can rent canoes in Eagle or choose a trip with a local commercial guide with gear supplied.

For more information on proper clothing, weather conditions and best time to make a float, contact the National Park Service, Box 167, Eagle 99378; (907) 547-2233.

Zip Codes (SEE POPULATIONS AND ZIP CODES)

The Dumbest Criminal Award for 1999 goes to Floyd Brown, who tried to hold up the desk clerk of the downtown Anchorage Holiday Inn during a law enforcement training conference that was advertised on both the marquee out front and banners in the lobby! The ski-mask-wearing robber was attacked by 30 cops, one of whom said, "Money was flying every where, just like in the cartoons."

Yearly Highlights, 1999–2000

Following are brief accounts of Alaska news from mid-1999 to mid-2000. Primary sources are the *Anchorage Daily News;* The Associated Press; *Fairbanks Daily News-Miner; Homer News; Peninsula Clarion;* and *The Voice of the Times.*

Rough going for some cruise ships.

Some 120 people, including at least one passenger who had seen the movie *Titanic,* were safely evacuated when a small cruise ship hit submerged rocks about 60 miles south of Juneau.

The wreck of the 192-foot *Spirit of '98,* en route to Seattle, was the third small cruise ship to go aground in Juneau waters in the 1999 summer season. "This is an anomaly," said Coast Guard Lt. Cmdr. Ray Massey.

Trouble began July 27, 1999, when cruise passengers eating breakfast felt the vessel hit bottom. Passenger Barbara Wilson of Albuquerque, NM, said she heard a "crunching" noise. "It was scary," Wilson told the *Anchorage Daily News.* "I did see *Titanic.*"

Divers surveying the ship later found two 2-inch long holes in the hull as well as damage to the ship's keel cooler. In all, 93 passengers and 18 crewmembers were evacuated by raft to another small vessel and delivered to Juneau. No one was hurt.

A task force was organized to review small cruise vessel safety in Southeast.

The house that women built.

Anchorage's gritty Fairview neighborhood looked on in August as a mostly female crew raised the walls of a new Habitat for Humanity house.

The modest home at 12th Avenue and Karluk Street was a departure since no single entity had sponsored the project; the Women's House instead relied on volunteers united by gender. The house which, eventually would be home to a single mother and her five children.

The women, joined by a few men and children, worked through drizzle, holidays and learning curves. Construction costs of $60,000 were donated largely by the family of Mary Ellen Fogarty, a longtime Habitat donor who died in 1997 in a climbing accident on Ptarmigan Peak near Anchorage.

Railroad tank cars jump tracks, leak fuel.

Cold to −15°F, snowslides and remote terrain hampered cleanup following two Alaska Railroad accidents.

Crews worked through November when a derailed train dumped 8,500 gallons of jet fuel north of Talkeetna; an estimated 100,000 gallons of jet fuel was lost near Gold Creek when a train derailed in December. The two sites are a few miles apart in the Susitna River valley. No injuries were reported.

Some critics, including a state environmental official, said the railroad's response to both derailments was too slow; the railroad said extreme weather and isolated terrain should be taken into account.

The *Anchorage Daily News* reported that by mid-January crews had detected jet fuel pooled atop the underground water table near the Gold Creek accident.

Snow more than 5 feet deep plagued cleanup attempts at Gold Creek and workers used long probes to poke through snow to search out puddles of mixed fuel and snow. Fuel also collected on top of frozen ground to become a slushy mix.

The railroad planned to use a "super-sucker" unit to vacuum the spill. State regulators required an assessment in spring to be sure soil had been treated for contamination and cleaned up.

State files record salmon-waste case.

A Seattle-based fish processor faced criminal charges after the state claimed it illegally dumped more than 3 million pounds of salmon, mostly chum, into Icy Strait in Southeast Alaska.

Authorities said it was the largest salmon-waste case by weight ever pursued by the state. More than 200 million salmon were hauled up statewide during the 1999 fishing season—the second-largest catch on record.

The complaint named Wards Cove Packing Co., among the state's largest cannery operators. Illegal dumping was alleged to have occurred for 19 days ending July 29, 1999. The complaint was filed in Juneau in December.

Alaska law makes it a criminal misdemeanor to waste salmon. Penalties range to $10,000 and six months in jail for each violation.

Chum salmon are least valuable of the five species of Alaska salmon harvested commercially. In times of a fish glut, processors may be given state approval to dump fish that cannot be packed before spoiling.

Seeking God's Will? Try the Gulf of Alaska.
The state's Bristol Bay crab fishery attracts the rugged and ready, but this year even *God's Will* proved no match.

Trouble began for the 85-foot vessel taking part in the October red king crab fishery when a crewman was struck in the chest by a shifting crab pot. The boat headed for False Pass, to seek medical help, when fire broke out and was extinguished by the crew. As *God's Will* neared False Pass, another fire began and the boat eventually was towed in.

Boat owner Matt Shadle says the story doesn't end there: Fire started once more after the boat was tied up at False Pass and, with no firefighting equipment on hand, *God's Will* was towed into the pass and set free, coming to rest on some rocks. The crew reboarded and the boat was towed back for repairs, but Shadle says the crew wanted "no part" of *God's Will*. "I guess they were pretty shaken up by that point."

Shadle, whose wife was about to have a baby, had stayed behind throughout the misadventures, but had hired another man to oversee the crab-fishing operation. Shadle said it was all over when the captain, Rick Edgemond, steered the repaired boat for King Cove—and the vessel began taking on water in 8-foot seas and winds to 40 knots. Edgemond took to a life raft and was rescued by the U.S. Coast Guard. *God's*

Will went down bow first. Shadle later fished the halibut season in his other boat, the *Risky Business.*

Crash claims 88, including Native leader Thompson.
An Alaska Airlines jet en route from Puerto Vallarta, Mexico, to San Francisco plummeted into the Pacific Ocean on Jan. 31, 2000, killing all 88 people aboard.

Five Alaskans died in the accident, including Morris Thompson, a veteran interior Alaska Native leader and president of Doyon Ltd., the Fairbanks-based Native corporation.

The wreck occurred after the pilot reported mechanical problems and Flight 261 had been diverted to Los Angeles for emergency landing. The plane crashed into waters about 40 miles northwest of the Los Angeles airport, authorities said.

In early February, more than 3,000 people streamed into the Carlson Center in Fairbanks to recall Thompson, who with his wife, Thelma, and adult daughter, Sheryl, were killed in the plane crash.

Raised in the Interior village of Tanana where he maintained strong ties, the 60-year-old Thompson was eulogized as a family man, nationally ranked policymaker and a deft executive who, as president of Fairbanks-based Doyon Ltd., helped lift the Native regional corporation from the brink of bankruptcy. Thompson had retired from Doyon in 1999 after 15 years.

Educated at Mount Edgecumbe boarding school in Sitka, Thompson completed electronics training in Los Angeles and eventually returned to Alaska where he became active in the Native land claims effort. He joined the first administration of Gov. Walter J. Hickel and moved to Washington, D.C., when Hickel was appointed Interior Secretary under President Nixon. In 1973, Thompson became the youngest director of the Bureau of Indian Affairs and remained in the post until 1976.

Thompson returned to public service in Alaska and was named to the University of Alaska Board of Regents but it was as Doyon executive that he gained wide recognition. "He brought profitability and stability to Doyon (but) he knew there were other things besides profits," recalled Roy Huhndorf, a friend and former executive of Cook Inlet Region, Inc.

At his memorial service, which included 88 candles to recall each of the passengers aboard Flight 261, business leaders were seated with senators and fishermen, Native officials sat beside cabbies. Thompson was recalled as a "split-screen" man—an Alaska Native equally comfortable in boardrooms or boating the Yukon River on a summer afternoon.

Snow slides punish Girdwood, Cordova.

Avalanches struck just days apart in the Southcentral towns of Girdwood, south of Anchorage, and Cordova on Prince William Sound.

The Cordova slide occurred Jan. 26, when snow raced down a slope above Eyak Lake, leveling five homes, several outbuildings and two warehouses. A 63-year-old woman was killed. Within months Cordova had adopted one of the strictest avalanche zoning laws in the nation: Construction now is banned in highest-risk avalanche areas of the fishing town. Government agencies were cleared to buy land in high-risk zones and move homes still standing to safe ground.

Avalanches and a strong winter storm shut down the Seward Highway between Anchorage and the ski resort town of Girdwood. A slide on Jan. 30 knocked out power and severed the only highway link between the two towns, stranding dozens of people in Girdwood for nearly a week. An Alaska Railroad worker helping clear snow on the Seward Highway was killed on Feb. 1 when a second slide broke free. Avalanche conditions in the region were deemed among the worst in decades.

La Niña nipping at their nose.

Temperatures headed south—and lots of Alaskans wished they could too—in February when cold plunged to -74°F in the Interior.

The big chill was blamed on a weather phenomenon known as La Niña, companion to the unusual warming of eastern Pacific Ocean waters called El Niño. That condition, which disrupted weather worldwide for more than a year, eased in spring 1998, only to be followed in winter by La Niña.

Alaska's cold snap descended when persistent winds funneled cold air from above the Arctic Circle southward to the state. Weather Service experts said the pattern often is seen with La Niña, Spanish for "little girl," and produces colder-than-usual winter readings for Alaska.

Alaskans who indulged wishful thinking and waded into winter without the usual gear—plug-ins to heat car engines before morning starts, for instance—had little excuse this year: Extreme winter cold had been forecast for the state as early as six months before it hit.

If he builds it, some will grumble.

At 76, and after representing Alaska in the U.S. Senate for 32 years, Ted Stevens is pondering his legacy and scouting for a repository for his official papers.

The collection documents key moments in the history of a young state, from national debate over construction of the trans-Alaska oil pipeline to policy decisions that led to the Alaska Native Claims Settlement Act of 1971 and the Alaska National Interest Lands Conservation Act of 1980.

Stevens has begun raising $10 million in private funds to build a new wing to a proposed $30 million library at the University of Alaska Anchorage.

To no one's surprise, the University of Alaska Fairbanks isn't thrilled. Since statehood in 1959, UAF's Rasmuson Library has received papers of every national-level politician from Alaska. "It's kind of incredible that he (Stevens) would break that tradition," UAF history professor Claus-M. Naske said.

If the Stevens wing is built, researchers could find themselves shuttling between Fairbanks and Anchorage to use Alaska archives. The state's two other national lawmakers—U.S. Sen. Frank Murkowski and U.S. Rep. Don Young—have begun sending their collections to UAF or plan to do so.

Count 'em all. To underscore its desire for an accurate head count in 2000, the U.S. Census Bureau sent its director to remote Unalakleet for an early start.

Census counts nationwide began in earnest in April—too late for many rural Alaskans who hunt and fish in spring and aren't at home when census takers knock on the door.

Census Bureau director Kenneth Prewitt flew to Unalakleet in chilly January, donned a borrowed parka and rode into town on a dog sled for an afternoon of Native dancing and a potluck, hosted by the mostly Eskimo village of about 800.

"Welcome to Unalakleet, Census 2000," shouted schoolchildren as Prewitt stepped off the plane in the western Alaska community some 4,500 miles from Washington, D.C.

Officials hoped all the attention would improve Alaskaís census return rate, worst in the nation in 1990. "We want Unalakleet to set a standard for the rest of the country," Prewitt told The Associated Press. "It (the census) doesn't work if somebody is left out."

A done deal. After more than a year of anti-trust investigations by the Federal Trade Commission, a $30 billion deal between BP Amoco and Atlantic Richfield Co. was signed April 18 in London.

BP Amoco's acquisition of Los Angeles-based ARCO "dramatically, suddenly and with a sense of uncertain excitement about the future" had changed Alaska's oil map, *The Voice of the Times* said in an editorial.

The takeover raised fears that consolidated control of Alaska's Prudhoe Bay oil fields, which generate nearly 70 percent of state revenues, would disadvantage the state; oil patch workers fretted about jobs and West Coast motorists wondered if pump prices would jump.

Alaska North Slope oil is a key source of gasoline on the West Coast. Until the April purchase, BP Amoco operated Prudhoe Bay's western half and ARCO operated the eastern.

Under the new ownership agreement approved by the FTC, Exxon Mobil will hold a 36.8 percent stake; Phillips Petroleum will acquire ARCO's Alaska holdings, including a 36.5 percent ownership in Prudhoe; and BP Exploration (Alaska) Inc. will retain a 26.7 percent interest.

"It's a new day in Alaska's oil patch," the *Times* said.

'A strip mall does not a city make.' Alaska's subsistence rights dispute focused on the Kenai Peninsula in May after a federal board declared the entire region, home to some 60,000 people, a rural zone.

The designation clears the way for Native and non-Native residents alike to fish and hunt on federal lands and navigable waters under regulations that give priority to Alaskans who get their food from the land. Opponents of the rural designation worried that increased pressure on fish and game could force managers to curtail other uses, such as sportfishing or guided hunts.

A petition from the region's Kenaitze Indians, who for the past decade have lobbied to place subsistence nets in the Kenai River, prompted the 4-2 ruling by the federal Subsistence Board. Subsistence use on the salmon-rich Kenai adds another constituency to longstanding debate over how Kenai River fish should be portioned out: Until now, that dispute was between commercial fishermen and sport anglers.

The Subsistence Board in 1990 declared most of the Peninsula rural but said densely settled areas, such as the Kenai-Soldotna area, did not qualify for subsistence rights because residents had ready access to grocery stores. Board members in May reversed, saying that despite some retail business, the Peninsula still supported a rural lifestyle. Said Jim Caplan, a Subsistence Board member representing the Forest Service: "A strip mall does not a city make."

Suggested Reading

Other Alaska Books from Alaska Northwest Books and Graphic Arts Center Publishing

Alaska Northwest Books. *Alaska Wild Berry Guide & Cookbook.* Seattle: Alaska Northwest Books, 1982.

———. *Cooking Alaskan.* Seattle: Alaska Northwest Books, 1983.

Armstrong, Robert H. *Alaska's Birds: A Guide to Selected Species.* Seattle: Alaska Northwest Books, 1994.

———. *Alaska's Fish: A Guide to Selected Species.* Seattle: Alaska Northwest Books, 1996.

Armstrong, Robert H. and Marge Hermans. *Alaska's Natural Wonders: A Guide to the Phenomena of the Far North.* Portland, Ore.: Alaska Northwest Books, 2000.

Billburg, Rudy, as told to Jim Rearden. *In the Shadow of Eagles: From Barnstormer to Bush Pilot, A Flyer's Story.* Seattle: Alaska Northwest Books, 1998.

Brown, Tricia (text) and Roy Corral (photographs). *Children of the Midnight Sun: Young Native Voices of Alaska.* Seattle: Alaska Northwest Books, 1998.

———. *Fairbanks: Alaska's Heart of Gold: A Traveler's Guide.* Portland, Ore.: Alaska Northwest Books, 2000.

Bruder, Gerry. *Heroes of the Horizon: Flying Adventures of Alaska's Legendary Bush Pilots.* Seattle: Alaska Northwest Books, 1991.

Chandonnet, Ann. *The Alaska Heritage Seafood Cookbook.* Seattle: Alaska Northwest Books, 1995.

Cole, Dermot. *Frank Barr: Bush Pilot in Alaska and the Yukon.* Seattle: Alaska Northwest Books, 1999.

Corral, Hannah (text), with Kim Corral and Roy Corral (photographs). *My Denali: Exploring Alaska's Favorite National Park.* Seattle: Alaska Northwest Books, 1995.

———. *A Child's Glacier Bay.* Seattle: Alaska Northwest Books, 1998.

Dixon, Kirsten. *The Riversong Lodge Cookbook: World-Class Cooking in the Alaskan Bush.* Seattle: Alaska Northwest Books, 1993.

Dyson, George. *Baidarka: The Kayak.* Seattle: Alaska Northwest Books, 1986.

Eppenbach, Sarah. *Baked Alaska: Recipes for Sweet Comforts from the North Country.* Seattle: Alaska Northwest Books, 1997.

Ewing, Susan. *The Great Alaska Nature Factbook: A Guide to the State's Remarkable Animals, Plants, and Natural Features.* Seattle: Alaska Northwest Books, 1996.

Field, Conrad, and Carmen Field. *Alaska's Seashore Creatures.* Seattle: Alaska Northwest Books, 1999.

Fobes, Natalie. *I Dream Alaska.* Seattle: Alaska Northwest Books, 1998.

Fobes, Natalie (photographs), Tom Jay and Brad Matsen (text). *Reaching Home: Pacific Salmon, Pacific People.* Seattle: Alaska Northwest Books, 1994.

Ford, Corey. *Where the Sea Breaks Its Back: The Epic Story of Early Naturalist Georg Steller and the Russian Exploration of Alaska.* Seattle: Alaska Northwest Books, 1992.

Grescoe, Paul and Audrey. *Alaska: The Cruise-Lover's Guide.* Seattle: Alaska Northwest Books, 1998.

Heacox, Kim. *Alaska's Inside Passage.* Portland, Ore.: Graphic Arts Center Publishing, 1997.

Herben, George. *Picture Journeys in Alaska's Wrangell–St. Elias.* Seattle: Alaska Northwest Books, 1997.

Hirschmann, Fred. *Alaska from the Air.* Portland, Ore.: Graphic Arts Center Publishing, 1999.

Hirschmann, Fred (photographs), and Kim Heacox (text). *Bush Pilots of Alaska.* Portland, Ore.: Graphic Arts Center Publishing, 1989.

Holleman, Marybeth. *Alaska's Prince William Sound: A Traveler's Guide.* Portland, Ore.: Alaska Northwest Books, 2000.

Huntington, Sidney, as told to Jim Rearden. *Shadows on the Koyukuk: An Alaskan Native's Life Along the River.* Seattle: Alaska Northwest Books, 1993.

Jans, Nick. *The Last Light Breaking: Living Among Alaska's Inupiat Eskimos.* Seattle: Alaska Northwest Books, 1993.

——. *A Place Beyond: Finding Home in Arctic Alaska.* Seattle: Alaska Northwest Books, 1996.

Jettmar, Karen. *Alaska's Glacier Bay.* Seattle: Alaska Northwest Books, 1997.

——. *The Alaska River Guide: Canoeing, Kayaking, and Rafting in the Last Frontier.* Seattle: Alaska Northwest Books, Rev. 1998.

Keith, Sam, with Richard Proenneke. *One Man's Wilderness.* Seattle: Alaska Northwest Books, 1999.

Keithahn, Edward L., Illustrated by George Aden Ahgupuk. *Alaskan Igloo Tales.* Seattle: Alaska Northwest Books, 1974.

Kremers, Carolyn. *Place of the Pretend People: Gifts from a Yup'ik Eskimo Village.* Seattle: Alaska Northwest Books, 1996.

Lobb, Allan (text), Art Wolfe (photographs), and Barbara Paxson (illustrations). *Indian Baskets of the Pacific Northwest and Alaska.* Portland, Ore.: Graphic Arts Center Publishing, 1990.

Matsen, Brad. *Fishing Up North.* Seattle: Alaska Northwest Books, 1998.

Mergler, Wayne, ed. *The Last New Land: Stories of Alaska, Past and Present.* Seattle: Alaska Northwest Books, 1996.

Miller, Debbie. *Flight of the Golden Plover.* Seattle: Alaska Northwest Books, 1996.

——. *Midnight Wilderness: Journeys in Alaska's Arctic National Wildlife Refuge.* Portland, Ore.: Alaska Northwest Books, 2000.

Mr. Whitekeys. *Mr. Whitekeys' Alaska Bizarre: Direct from the Whale Fat Follies Revue in Anchorage.* Seattle: Alaska Northwest Books, 1995.

Murie, Margaret. *Two in the Far North.* Seattle: Alaska Northwest Books, 1978. Rev. 1997.

Murphy, Claire Rudolf, and Jane G. Haigh. *Gold Rush Women.* Seattle: Alaska Northwest Books, 1997.

Murphy, Claire Rudolf (text), and Charles Mason (photographs). *A Child's Alaska.* Seattle: Alaska Northwest Books, 1994.

Nelson, Richard. *The Island Within.* San Francisco: North Point Press, 1989.

Nicolai, Margaret (text), and David Rubin (paintings). *Kitaq Goes Ice Fishing.* Seattle: Alaska Northwest Books, 1998.

O'Clair, Rita, Robert Armstrong, and Richard Carstensen. *The Nature of Southeast Alaska.* Seattle: Alaska Northwest Books, 1992. Rev. 1997.

Parker, Harriette. *Alaska's Mushrooms: A Practical Guide.* Seattle: Alaska Northwest Books, 1994.

Paul, Frances Lackey (text), and Rie Muñoz (illustrations). *Kahtahah: A Tlingit Girl.* Seattle: Alaska Northwest Books, 1976, Rev. 1996.

Rich, Kim. *Johnny's Girl.* Seattle: Alaska Northwest Books, 1999.

Ritter, Harry. *Alaska's History: The People, Land, and Events of the North Country.* Seattle: Alaska Northwest Books, 1993.

Schofield, Janice J. *Alaska's Wild Plants: A Guide to Alaska's Edible Harvest.* Seattle: Alaska Northwest Books, 1993.

Sherwonit, Bill. *Alaska's Accessible Wilderness: A Traveler's Guide to Alaska's State Parks.* Seattle: Alaska Northwest Books, 1996.

——. *To the Top of Denali: Climbing Adventures on North America's Highest Peak.* Seattle: Alaska Northwest Books, 1990. Rev. 2000.

Sherwonit, Bill (text), and Tom Walker (photographs). *Alaska's Bears.* Seattle: Alaska Northwest Books, 1998.

Smith, Dave (text), and Tom Walker (photographs). *Alaska's Mammals: A Guide to Selected Species.* Seattle: Alaska Northwest Books, 1995.

Upton, Joe. *Journeys Through the Inside Passage.* Seattle: Alaska Northwest Books, 1998.

Viereck, Eleanor G. *Alaska's Wilderness Medicines: Healthful Plants of the Far North.* Seattle: Alaska Northwest Books, 1987.

Walker, Tom. *Building the Alaska Log Home.* Seattle: Alaska Northwest Books, 1998.

——. *Caribou: Wanderer of the Tundra.* Portland, Ore.: Graphic Arts Center Publishing, 2000.

Whyard, Flo, ed. *Martha Black.* Seattle: Alaska Northwest Books, 1998.

Index

Adak, daylight hours, 55
adaptations to cold: birds, 174; mammals, 116
agriculture, 11–12
air cargo/freight, 14, 60
aircraft, 13
Air Force, U.S., 123–24
airlines, international, 13; interstate, 13
airplanes per capita, 12–13
airports, 13
air taxis, 13
air travel, 12–14; international, 13;
    interstate, 13
akutak (Eskimo ice cream), 65–66
Alascom, 214–15
Alaska Baseball League, 22–23
Alaska–Canada boundary, 14–15, 76, 89
Alaska Highway, 15–16; building of, 15–16;
    length, 15; preparing vehicles for, 16; road
    conditions and services, 16. *See also*
    highways
Alaska National Interest Lands Conservation
    Act (ANILCA), 111–12, 135–36, 142–43,
    149; affect on wilderness acreage, 155–56
Alaska Native Claims Settlement Act
    (ANCSA), 111–12
Alaska Natives, information source, 104. *See
    also* Native peoples
Alaska Peninsula, 196–97
Alaska Public Lands Information Centers,
    41, 90
Alaska state parks. *See* state park system
Alcan Highway. *See* Alaska Highway
alcoholic beverages, 16–17; communities
    banned in, 17; legal age to purchase, 16;
    licenses to sell, 16
Aleut(s), 158, 160–61, 162; arts and crafts, 158;
    basketry, 23, 158; boat, 21; distribution of,
    159; effect of Russians on, 196–97; masks,
    118; traditional lifestyle, 160, 196
Aleutian Islands, 196–97
Alyeska, 17, 205
amphibians, 17. *See also* reptiles
ancestors, gold rush, 82
Anchorage, 17–18; as air cargo hub, 13; air
    service, 13–14; average temperatures and
    precipitation, 46; daylight hours, 17, 55;
    minority population of, 183; naming of,
    17; radio stations, 190–91; skiing, 205;
    television stations, 216; temperatures and
    precipitation, 17

annual events, 35–39. *See also* events and
    festivals
antiquities laws, 18
antlers and horns, 115
archaeology, 18–19, 27
archives, historical, information source, 106
Arctic Circle, 19. *See also* daylight hours
Arctic region, 195–96. *See also* Far North
Arctic Winter Games, 19–20; winners, 19. *See
    also* World Eskimo-Indian Olympics
area: land, 76; per person, 76
Army, U.S., 122–23
arts and crafts, Native, 158–59. *See also*
    baskets; beadwork; Chilkat blankets;
    coppers; ivory; masks; mukluks; skin
    sewing; totem poles
Athabascan Indians, 159, 160, 162; arts and
    crafts, 158–59; basketry, 23, 24; beadwork,
    24; coppers, 50–51; distribution of, 159
AT&T, 215
Audubon Society, 30
auklet, whiskered, 30
aurora borealis, 20–21; photographing, 20–21

baidarka, 21
bald eagle, 28, 29
baleen, 21, 225; baskets, 23. *See also* baleen
    whales; whales
baleen whales, 225, 227. *See also* bowhead
    whales; gray whales; whales
baneberry, 28, 178
barabara, 21–22
Baranov, Alexander, 22. *See also* Sitka
Barrow, 22; average temperatures and
    precipitation, 46; daylight hours, 55; gas
    fields, 154; radio stations, 190, 191
baseball, 22–23, 67
baskets, 23–24; baleen, 23; bark, 23; grass, 23.
    See also Native arts and crafts
bats, 116
beadwork, 24. *See also* Native arts and crafts
bear(s), 24–26; black, 24–25, 113–14; brown,
    25, 114; grizzly, 25, 100,114; largest, 100;
    polar, 25–26, 114; and salmon, 119;
    viewing safely, 24. *See also* hunting;
    mammals; McNeil River State Game
    Sanctuary
beaver, 115
beluga whales, 226; landed annually, 227
Bering, Vitus, 26–27, 90

cost of living, 51–52. *See also* economy; income

court of appeals, Alaska state, 52–53; past and present judges, 54

court system, 52–54

coyote, 115

cranberries: highbush, 27; lowbush, 27

cropland, 11

crops, 11–12; value of, 11, 12

cruises, 54–55. *See also* boating; ferries

cultural centers, 131–39

customs, U.S. and Canadian, information source, 105

dairy products, 11

Dall sheep, 114; largest, 101. *See also* hunting

Dalton Highway, 55. *See also* highways

daylight, hours of, 55

deer, 114. *See also* hunting

Denali (Mount McKinley), 127, 130–31; ascents of, 127, 130–31; height of, 76, 127

Denali National Park and Preserve, campgrounds and shuttle bus reservations, 40

diameter of Alaska, 76

diamond willow, 55

directory assistance, information source, 105

district court, Alaska state, 53

dog mushing, 56–57; information source, 105. *See also* Iditarod Trail Sled Dog Race; Open North American Sled Dog Race; Open World Championship Sled Dog Race; Yukon Quest International Sled Dog Race

Dutch Harbor, 221. *See also* World War II

eagle(s), bald, 28, 29

earthquakes, 57–59; Good Friday, 17, 58–59; per year, 59

easternmost point, 76

economy, 59–61

education, 61–62. *See also* school districts; universities and colleges

elderly, information source, 105

electrical production, 65

elk, Roosevelt, 114

employer and labor organizations, 110

employment, 62–65. *See also* economy; job growth

energy and power, 65

Eskimo(s), 158, 159–60, 162; arts and crafts, 158–59; basketry, 23–24; beadwork, 24;

blanket toss, 30; boat, 220–21; distribution of, 159; effect of Russians on, 196–97; garments, 108, 174–75; ice cream, 65–66; knife, 220; masks, 118; whaling, 227; World Eskimo-Indian Olympics, 228–29. *See also* Inuit Circumpolar Conference

eulachon (hooligan), 95

events and festivals: annual, 35–39; bird-watching, 30; Fairbanks, 67; gold rush, 80; Nome, 169; Sitka, 203–04; Skagway, 204. *See also* Arctic Winter Games; World Eskimo-Indian Olympics

exhibits, 131–39

Extended Railbelt region, energy, 65. *See also* Railbelt region

Exxon Valdez oil spill, 93, 172–74

Fairbanks, 66–67; average temperatures and precipitation, 46; daylight hours, 55; radio stations, 190, 191; skiing, 205–06; television stations, 216

Far North region, historic places, 149. *See also* Arctic region

ferries, 67–69; annual numbers of passengers and vehicles, 69; data on individual, 68–69; information source, 105; nautical miles between ports, 68. *See also* boating; cruises

festivals and events. *See* events and festivals

fires on wild land, 69–70; acres burned annually by, 70; largest in acreage, 70; largest in economic toll, 70

fish, Alaska state, 212; individual state records, 70; production capacity of, 71. *See also* fishing

fishing, 70–75; commercial, 70–73; sport, 73–75; regulations, information source, 106; regulations and licenses, sport, 74–75; value and volume annually, 71. *See also* fish; subsistence lifestyle

fish wheel, 75

flag, Alaska state, 209

float trips, Yukon River, 232–33

flower(s), Alaska state, 212, 227–28; wild, 227–28

flying, 12–14

food, cost of, 51

fossil, Alaska state, 212; fuel, 170

fox, 115

frogs, 17

frostbite, 44

furs and trapping, 75–76; in Russian Alaska, 196–97

jade, 108–09
Japanese occupation, 229–30
job growth, 62–65. *See also* economy; employment
job opportunities, information source, 106; for people with disabilities, 106
jobs: public sector, 60; mining, 64; service, 60, 64. *See also* economy; employment; labor; unions
judges: court of appeals, past and present, 52–53; selection of, 53–54
judicial districts, 53
Juneau, 109; average temperatures and precipitation, 46; daylight hours, 55; radio stations, 191–92; television stations, 216
justices, supreme court: past and present, 54; selection of, 53–54

kayaking, 31, 154; information source, 104; Yukon River, 232–33
Kenai, radio stations, 192
Kenai Peninsula: agriculture in, 11; skiing, 206
Ketchikan, average temperatures and precipitation, 47; daylight hours, 55; radio stations, 190, 192; television stations, 216
King Salmon, average temperatures and precipitation, 47
kittiwake, red-legged, 30
Klondike, 79
Klondike Gold Rush National Park, 43
Knowles, Gov. Tony, 86
Kodiak, 109–10; average temperatures and precipitation, 47; radio stations, 190, 192; television stations, 216
Kodiak Island, 77
kuspuk (parka), 110. *See also* parka

labor: and employer organizations, 110; information source, 106. *See also* jobs; unions
lake(s), 110; largest freshwater, 77
land: acquiring for private use, 112–13; area, 76; area per person, 76; information, 113; owners, 113; public, information source, 106. *See also* land use
landmarks, national historic, 143–49
land use, 110–13
languages, 113
largest city: in area, 77; in population, 77
largest fires, 70
largest freshwater lakes, 77, 110
largest game animals, 100–01

largest glaciers, 79
largest gold nugget, 79–80
largest islands, 77, 107
largest salmon, 74
largest sport fish, 74
legislature, state, 87–88; information source, 106
lemmings, 116–17
length of Alaska–Canada boundary, 14–15, 76
length of Alaska Highway, 15
length of Chilkoot Trail, 43–44
length of coastline, 76
length of Dalton Highway, 55
length of major highways, 90
length of trans-Alaska pipeline, 177
libraries, information source, 106
license(s): hunting and trapping, 99–100; sportfishing, 74–75
lodges, information source, 106
longest glaciers, 79
longest rivers, 77, 197–98
loon, Pacific, 29
lynx, 115

magistrates, selection of, 53–54
mammals, 113–18; adaptations to cold, 116; furbearing, 115–16; large, 113–15; marine, 117; small, 116–17
map(s): Alaska (overall), 8–9; census areas, 188; highways, 89; ice fields, 77; Iditarod Trail Sled Dog Race, 105; mountains, mountain ranges and volcanoes, 128–29; National Interest Lands, 150–51; Native distribution, 159; Native regional corporations, 162; permafrost, 175; state parks, 210–11; topographic, information source, 106; Yukon Quest Trail, 231
Marine Corps, U.S., 124
Marine Highway System, 67–68
marine mammal(s), 117; Alaska state, 212
Marine Mammal Protection Act, 117
marmot, 115
marten, 115
masks, 118; Aleut, 118; Eskimo, 118; Indian, 118
Matanuska Valley: agriculture in, 11–12; New Deal farmer resettlement in, 12
McGrath, average temperatures and precipitation, 47; radio stations, 190, 192
McNeil River State Game Sanctuary, 119
Medal of Heroism, 119–21; recipients, 119–21
metric conversions, 120

information source, 106

Petersburg: average temperatures and precipitation, 47; radio stations, 190, 192

petroleum, information source, 106. *See also* National Petroleum Reserve; oil

pika, 117

pilots, 12–13; per capita, 13

Pioneers' Homes, 176–77

pipeline, trans-Alaska oil, 177–78; construction, 177–78; cost, 177; length, 177; oil pumped through, 177; route, 8–9; trivia, 171

place names, 17, 76, 178, 196

plants, poisonous, 28, 178. *See also* mushrooms

political parties, 179

pollock, 72

population, state, 76; military, 125; boroughs, 189

populations and zip codes of cities, 179–87, 188, 189

porcupine, 117

potlatch, 190. *See also* coppers; totem poles

power and energy, 65

precipitation: average, 46–47; record, 45

Prince William Sound oil spill, 172–74

Prudhoe Bay, 170–72, 177

public sector jobs, 60

puffin(s), horned, 29

qiviut (musk-ox hair), 140

raccoon, 116

radio stations, 190–92

rafting, 31, 197–99; Yukon River, 232–33

Railbelt region, 12. *See also* Extended Railbelt region

railroads, 192–93; shipping via, 202

raptors, 28

rat, 117

recipes: sautéed mushrooms, 140; sourdough starter, 207

regions, geographic, 193–97; Arctic, 195–96; Interior, 194–96; Southcentral/Gulf Coast, 194; Southeast, 193–94; Southwestern/Alaska Peninsula and Aleutians, 196–97; Western/ Bering Sea Coast, 196; map, 8–9

regulations: hunting, 99–100; hunting and fishing, information source, 106; sportfishing, 74–75

reindeer, 114; in agriculture, 11

religion, 197

repositories, 131–39

representatives: state, 86–88; U.S., 87

reptiles, 197. *See also* amphibians

resorts, information source, 106

river(s), 197–99; glacial, 198; longest, 77, 197–98; navigable, 198–99. *See also* National Wild and Scenic Rivers; Yukon River

river running, information source, 106; preparation, 199

roadhouses, 199

rocks and gems, 199–200. *See also* gold; jade; minerals; mining

rose hips, 27–28

Russian Alaska, 26–27, 90–91, 200; fur trading, 196–97; government officials, 84. *See also* Baranov, Alexander; Bering, Vitus; history; Seward, William H.; Sitka; Veniaminov, Ioann

Russian-American Company, officials, 84

Russian Bishop's House, 145

Russian Christmas, 200

salamander, 17

salmon: and bears, 119; commercial harvest, 71; ten largest, 74; value annually, 71; value of commercial harvest by species and region, 72. *See also* squaw candy

school districts, 200–01. *See also* education; universities and colleges

sea ice, 101–02

seal, Alaska state, 212

seals and sea lions. *See* marine mammals

seas, adjacent to Alaska, 76

seiche (splash wave), 225; highest, 58, 225. *See also* tsunamis; waves

senators: state, 86–88; U.S., 87

senior citizen programs, information source, 105

service jobs, 60, 64

Seward, 201; radio stations, 192

Seward, William H., 201–02

sheefish, 214

shellfish: commercial harvest, 71; farming, 11; and fish, value and volume annually, 71, 72

shipping, 202–03; household goods, 203; vehicles, 202–03

shrew, 117

shrubs and trees, 220

Sitka, 203–04; festivals and events, 203–04; radio stations, 190, 192; television stations, 217. *See also* Russian Bishop's House

Sitka slippers, 204. *See also* boots; mukluks

Skagway, 204; radio station, 191; festivals and events, 204. *See also* Chilkoot Trail

skiing, 204–06; Anchorage, 205; Cordova, 205; Fairbanks, 205–06; Kenai Peninsula, 206; Palmer, 206; Southeast region, 206

skin sewing, 206. *See also* beadwork; mukluks; parka

skookum, 206–07

sled dog racing. *See* dog mushing

smelt (hooligan), 95

snowfall, records, 45

soapstone, 207

solstice: at Arctic Circle, 19; hours of daylight at (summer and winter), 55

song, Alaska state, 212

sourdough, 207; starter, 207

Sourdough expedition, 130

Southcentral region, 194; ferry service, 67–68; historic places, 143–45

Southeast region, 193–94; agriculture in, 11; energy, 65; ferry system, 67–68; historic places, 145–46; skiing, 206

southernmost point, 76

Southwest region, 196–97; agriculture in, 11; ferry system, 67–68

Spanish exploration, 27

speed limits, 207–08

sport, Alaska state, 212

sports tournaments and races, annual, 35–39. *See also* Arctic Winter Games; World Eskimo-Indian Olympics

spruce bark beetle, 208

spruce trees, 208, 217–18, 220. *See also* trees and shrubs; timber

squaw candy (salmon jerky), 208

squirrels, 116

state bird, 212

state fish, 212

state flag, 209

state flower, 212, 227–28

state forest (Tanana Valley State Forest), 208, 220

state fossil, 212

state gem, 212

state insect, 212

state marine mammal, 212

state mineral, 212

state motto, 212

state park system, 208–209; cabins, 33–34;

campgrounds, 39–41; map 210–11

state seal, 212

state song, 212

state sport, 212

state symbols, 209, 212–13

state tree, 212–13

Steller, Georg, 29, 90–91

stranded residents, information source, 106

subsistence, 213–14

sundog, 214

superior court, Alaska state, 52–54

supreme court, Alaska state, 52–54

supreme court justices: past and present, 54; selection of, 53–54

taiga, 214

taku (wind), 228

Talkeetna, radio station, 192

tallest mountains, 76; map, 128–29

Tanana Valley, agriculture in, 11–12

Tanana Valley State Forest, 208

taxes, 52

telecommunications, 214–15

telephone numbers in the bush, 215–16

television stations, 216–17

temperatures: average, 46–47; record, 45

tern(s): Aleutian, 29; arctic, 29

tide(s), 217; bore, 32; ranges, 217

timber, 217–18; harvest, 217–18; industry, 217–18

time line, 90–94

time zones, 218; map, 8–9

Tlingit Indians, 159, 160; arts and crafts, 159; basketry, 23; and Chilkat blankets, 43; coppers, 50–51; distribution of, 159; effect of Russians on, 196–97; masks, 118; uses for hooligan, 95

Tongass National Forest, 141–43, 150; cabins, 34; campgrounds, 35, 39; wilderness units in, 142

Tongass Timber Reform Act (TTRA), 143, 156

toothed whales, 225, 226. *See also* beluga whales; narwhal; orca (killer) whales; whales

totem poles, 138, 218–19

tourism, 219–20

tourist attractions, top ten, 219

trans-Alaska oil pipeline. *See* pipeline, trans-Alaska oil

trapping and furs, 75–76

travel and visitor information, information source, 107

tree, Alaska state, 217
trees and shrubs, 220. *See also* spruce trees; timber
tribal governments, 84
Tsimshian Indians, 159, 160; arts and crafts, 159; basketry, 23; and Chilkat blankets, 43; distribution of, 159
tsunamis, 224–25; warning center, 57, 225. *See also* seiche; waves
tundra, 220

U.S. Fish and Wildlife Service: campgrounds, 41; renting cabins from, 34
U.S. Forest Service: campgrounds, 39; renting cabins from, 34
U.S. Public Health Service hospitals, 96
ulu (knife), 220
umiak (boat), 220–21
Unalaska, 221; radio station, 190; television station, 217; trees, 217
unemployment rates, 65. *See also* employment
unions, 110
universities and colleges, 221–23. *See also* education; school districts
Valdez, average temperatures and precipitation, 47; history, 93; radio stations, 192
Vancouver, George, 91
Veniaminov, Ioann, 223; museum, 139; Russian Bishop's House, 145. *See also* Innocent, Bishop
visitor information, 49–50; information source, 107
visitors bureaus, 49–50
volcanoes, 223–24; eruptions, 223–24; map, 128–29
voles, 117

walrus. *See* marine mammals
wagtail, white, 30
warbler(s), arctic, 29
waterways, inland, 198–99
waves, 224–25; highest caused by earthquakes, 59
weasels, 116

weather information, *See* Climate
West Coast/Alaska Tsunami Warning Center, 57, 225
westernmost point, 76
Western region, 196; historic places, 147–48
whales, 225–27; baleen, 225, 227; beluga, 226, 227; bowhead, 227; gray, 225–26, 227; harvested by Native groups, 227; toothed, 225, 227; narwhal, 225; orca (killer), 225, 226. *See also* baleen; muktuk; whaling
whaling, 227; by Alaska Indians, Aleuts and Eskimos, 227. *See also* whales
White Pass & Yukon Route (railway), 193
Wickersham, James, 66, 86, 131; House of, 135
wilderness areas, national, 155–56; permitted uses and activities, 156
wildfires, 69–70
wildflowers, 227–28
wildlife refuges, national, 157–58
williwaws (wind), 228
willow, diamond, 55
wind(s), 228; record, 45
wolf, 114–15
wolverine, 115
woodchuck, 117
wood products industry, 61
woodrat, 117
World Eskimo-Indian Olympics, 228–29. *See also* Arctic Winter Games
World War II, 229–30. *See also* history; Dutch Harbor

Yearly Highlights, 1999–2000, 234–37
Yukon Quest International Sled Dog Race, 56, 57, 230–31; map, 231; 2000 results, 232; winners, times and prizes, 230
Yukon River, 77, 231–32; canoeing, kayaking and float trips, 232–33. *See also* river(s); Yukon Quest International Sled Dog Race
Yupik Eskimo(s), arts and crafts, 158–59; distribution, 159. *See also* Eskimo(s)

zinc mining, 125
zip codes, 179–87